# Daily Light
## on the
# Daily Path

# DAILY LIGHT ON THE DAILY PATH

Morning *and* Evening

DEVOTIONALS *from* *GOD'S WORD*®

BakerBooks
*a division of Baker Publishing Group*
Grand Rapids, Michigan

Published by Baker Books
a division of Baker Publishing Group
P.O. Box 6287, Grand Rapids, MI 49516-6287
www.bakerbooks.com

Printed in the United States of America



Library of Congress Cataloging-in-Publication Data
Bible. English. GWN. Selections. 2010.
Daily light on the daily path : morning and evening devotionals from *God's Word*®.
p. cm.
ISBN 978-0-8010-7280-2 (pbk.)
1. Devotional calendars. I. Title.
BS390.B2 2010
242′.2—dc22 2010016423



10 11 12 13 14 15 16 7 6 5 4 3 2 1

# Introduction

"From your guiding principles I gain understanding," said the psalmist, adding, "your word is a lamp for my feet and a light for my path" (Ps. 119:104–5).

If the lamp seems dimmed, it may be because people do not immerse daily life in the guiding principles of God's Word. Perhaps in part they fall out of the habit of Bible reading and devotions because of the difficulty of connecting themes from one passage of the Bible to another and applying biblical principles to daily life.

Nineteenth-century London bookseller Samuel Bagster daily gathered his large family to read the Bible. He tested their knowledge by connecting the day's verses to other passages. They were taught to think through how texts from all over the Bible can come together to make clearer meaning and application.

Many years later Samuel's children and grandchildren compiled *Daily Light on the Daily Path* to share with others the instruction they had received around his table. Each Scripture was chosen with care to give spiritual insight and inspire devotion to God. The order in which the passages are presented was designed to develop the theme of the reading.

*Daily Light on the Daily Path* became one of the most widely read collections of daily readings from the Bible ever published. It set the pattern for modern books of devotional readings for every day of the year, but it remains distinctive. Each reading is built on nothing but Bible passages. A Scripture text at the top of the reading presents a theme that other texts examine. Readings collect verses from Genesis through Revelation.

Now compiled with passages from *God's Word* Translation, which accurately translates the meaning of the original biblical texts into clear, everyday language, this *Daily Light* will illuminate your path through each day.

## MORNING READING

This is what I do: I don't look back. . . . I run straight toward the goal to win the prize that God's heavenly call offers in Christ Jesus.

"Father, I want those you have given to me to be with me, to be where I am. I want them to see my glory, which you gave me." ✦ I know whom I trust. I'm convinced that he is able to protect what he had entrusted to me until that day. ✦ God, who began this good work in you, will carry it through to completion on the day of Christ Jesus. ✦ Don't you realize that everyone who runs in a race runs to win, but only one runner gets the prize? Run like them, so that you can win. Everyone who enters an athletic contest goes into strict training. They do it to win a temporary crown, but we do it to win one that will be permanent. ✦ Since we are surrounded by so many examples of faith, we must get rid of everything that slows us down, especially sin that distracts us. We must run the race that lies ahead of us and never give up. We must focus on Jesus.

*Philippians 3:13–14; John 17:24; 2 Timothy 1:12; Philippians 1:6; 1 Corinthians 9:24–25; Hebrews 12:1–2*

## EVENING READING

"The LORD is the one who is going ahead of you. He will be with you. He won't abandon you or leave you."

"If your presence is not going with us, don't make us leave this place." ✦ O LORD, I know that the way humans act is not under their control. Humans do not direct their steps as they walk. ✦ A person's steps are directed by the LORD, and the LORD delights in his way. When he falls, he will not be thrown down headfirst because the LORD holds on to his hand. ✦ I am always with you. You hold on to my right hand. With your advice you guide me, and in the end you will take me to glory. ✦ I am convinced that nothing can ever separate us from God's love which Christ Jesus our Lord shows us. We can't be separated by death or life, by angels or rulers, by anything in the present or anything in the future, by forces or powers in the world above or in the world below, or by anything else in creation.

*Deuteronomy 31:8; Exodus 33:15; Jeremiah 10:23; Psalm 37:23–24; Psalm 73:23–24; Romans 8:38–39*

## MORNING READING

Sing a new song to the LORD.

Sing joyfully to God, our strength. Shout happily to the God of Jacob. Begin a psalm, and strike a tambourine. Play lyres and harps with their pleasant music. ✦ He placed a new song in my mouth, a song of praise to our God. Many will see this and worship. They will trust the LORD. ✦ "Be strong and courageous! Don't tremble or be terrified, because the LORD your God is with you wherever you go." ✦ Paul . . . thanked God and felt encouraged. ✦ You know the times in which we are living. It's time for you to wake up. Our salvation is nearer now than when we first became believers. The night is almost over, and the day is near. So we should get rid of the things that belong to the dark and take up the weapons that belong to the light. We should live decently, as people who live in the light of day. Wild parties, drunkenness, sexual immorality, promiscuity, rivalry, and jealousy cannot be part of our lives. Instead, live like the Lord Jesus Christ did, and forget about satisfying the desires of your sinful nature.

*Isaiah 42:10; Psalm 81:1–2; Psalm 40:3; Joshua 1:9; Nehemiah 8:10; Acts 28:15; Romans 13:11–14*

## EVENING READING

Let my prayer be accepted as
sweet-smelling incense in your presence.
Let the lifting up of my hands in prayer
be accepted as an evening sacrifice.

"Build an altar out of acacia wood for burning incense. . . . Put the altar in front of the canopy which hangs over the ark containing the words of my promise. I will meet with you there in front of the throne of mercy that is on the ark. Aaron must burn sweet-smelling incense on this altar every morning. . . . Also, when Aaron lights the lamps at dusk, he must burn incense. For generations to come an incense offering must burn constantly in the LORD's presence." ✦ [Jesus] is always able to save those who come to God through him. He can do this because he always lives and intercedes for them. ✦ The smoke from the incense went up from the angel's hand to God along with the prayers of God's people. ✦ You come to him as living stones, a spiritual house that is being built into a holy priesthood. So offer spiritual sacrifices that God accepts through Jesus Christ. ✦ Never stop praying.

*Psalm 141:2; Exodus 30:1, 6–8; Hebrews 7:25; Revelation 8:4; 1 Peter 2:5; 1 Thessalonians 5:17*

## MORNING READING

He led them on a road that went straight.

He found his people in a desert land, in a barren place where animals howl. He guarded them, took care of them, and protected them because they were helpless. Like an eagle that stirs up its nest, hovers over its young, spreads its wings to catch them, and carries them on its feathers, so the LORD alone led his people. ✦ Even when you're old, I'll take care of you. Even when your hair turns gray, I'll support you. I made you and will continue to care for you. I'll support you and save you. ✦ He renews my soul. He guides me along the paths of righteousness for the sake of his name. Even though I walk through the dark valley of death, because you are with me, I fear no harm. Your rod and your staff give me courage. ✦ The LORD will continually guide you and satisfy you even in sun-baked places. He will strengthen your bones. You will become like a watered garden and like a spring whose water does not stop flowing. ✦ "This God is our God forever and ever. He will lead us beyond death." ✦ "Is there any teacher like him?"

*Psalm 107:7; Deuteronomy 32:10–12; Isaiah 46:4; Psalm 23:3–4; Isaiah 58:11; Psalm 48:14; Job 36:22*

## EVENING READING

Jesus asked him, "What do you want me to do for you?" The blind man said, "Lord, I want to see again."

Uncover my eyes so that I may see the miraculous things in your teachings. ✦ Then he opened their minds to understand the Scriptures. ✦ "The helper, the Holy Spirit, whom the Father will send in my name, will teach you everything." ✦ Every good present and every perfect gift comes from above, from the Father who made the sun, moon, and stars. ✦ [May] the glorious Father, the God of our Lord Jesus Christ . . . give you a spirit of wisdom and revelation as you come to know Christ better. Then you will have deeper insight. You will know the confidence that he calls you to have and the glorious wealth that God's people will inherit. You will also know the unlimited greatness of his power as it works with might and strength for us, the believers.

*Luke 18:41; Psalm 119:18; Luke 24:45; John 14:26; James 1:17; Ephesians 1:17–19*

## MORNING READING

Up until now you haven't come to your place of rest,
the property the LORD your God is giving you.

This is not a place to rest! ✦ Therefore, a time of rest and worship exists for God's people. ✦ We have this confidence as a sure and strong anchor for our lives. This confidence goes into the holy place behind the curtain where Jesus went before us on our behalf. ✦ "My Father's house has many rooms. If that were not true, would I have told you that I'm going to prepare a place for you? If I go to prepare a place for you, I will come again. Then I will bring you into my presence so that you will be where I am." ✦ With Christ. That's by far the better choice. ✦ "He will wipe every tear from their eyes. There won't be any more death. There won't be any grief, crying, or pain, because the first things have disappeared." ✦ There the wicked stop their raging. There the weary are able to rest. ✦ "Store up treasures for yourselves in heaven. . . . Your heart will be where your treasure is." ✦ Keep your mind on things above, not on worldly things.

*Deuteronomy 12:9; Micah 2:10; Hebrews 4:9; Hebrews 6:19–20; John 14:2–3; Philippians 1:23; Revelation 21:4; Job 3:17; Matthew 6:20–21; Colossians 3:2*

## EVENING READING

"Death, where is your victory?
Death, where is your sting?"

Sin gives death its sting. ✦ But now, at the end of the ages, he has appeared once to remove sin by his sacrifice. People die once, and after that they are judged. Likewise, Christ was sacrificed once to take away the sins of humanity, and after that he will appear a second time. This time he will not deal with sin, but he will save those who eagerly wait for him. ✦ Since all of these sons and daughters have flesh and blood, Jesus took on flesh and blood to be like them. He did this so that by dying he would destroy the one who had power over death (that is, the devil). In this way he would free those who were slaves all their lives because they were afraid of dying. ✦ My life is coming to an end, and it is now time for me to be poured out as a sacrifice to God. I have fought the good fight. I have completed the race. I have kept the faith. The prize that shows I have God's approval is now waiting for me.

*1 Corinthians 15:55; 1 Corinthians 15:56; Hebrews 9:26–28; Hebrews 2:14–15; 2 Timothy 4:6–8*

## MORNING READING

We who believe are entering that place of rest.

They wear themselves out doing wrong. ✦ I see a different standard at work throughout my body. It is at war with the standards my mind sets and tries to take me captive to sin's standards which still exist throughout my body. What a miserable person I am! Who will rescue me from my dying body? ✦ "Come to me, all who are tired from carrying heavy loads, and I will give you rest." ✦ Now that we have God's approval by faith, we have peace with God because of what our Lord Jesus Christ has done. Through Christ we can approach God and stand in his favor. So we brag because of our confidence that we will receive glory from God. ✦ Those who entered his place of rest also rested from their work. ✦ I didn't receive God's approval by obeying his laws. The opposite is true! I have God's approval through faith in Christ. ✦ "This is a place for comfort. This is a place of rest for those who are tired. This is a place for them to rest."

*Hebrews 4:3; Jeremiah 9:5; Romans 7:23–24; Matthew 11:28; Romans 5:1–2; Hebrews 4:10; Philippians 3:9; Isaiah 28:12*

## EVENING READING

O LORD, set a guard at my mouth.
Keep watch over the door of my lips.

O LORD, who would be able to stand if you kept a record of sins? ✦ They made him [Moses] bitter so that he spoke recklessly. ✦ "What goes into a person's mouth doesn't make him unclean. It's what comes out of the mouth that makes a person unclean." ✦ A gossip separates the closest of friends. ✦ Careless words stab like a sword, but the words of wise people bring healing. The word of truth lasts forever, but lies last only a moment. ✦ No one can tame the tongue. It is an uncontrollable evil filled with deadly poison. ✦ Praise and curses come from the same mouth. My brothers and sisters, this should not happen! ✦ Also get rid of your anger, hot tempers, hatred, cursing, obscene language, and all similar sins. Don't lie to each other. You've gotten rid of the person you used to be and the life you used to live. ✦ It is God's will that you keep away from sexual sin. ✦ They've never told a lie.

*Psalm 141:3; Psalm 130:3; Psalm 106:33; Matthew 15:11; Proverbs 16:28; Proverbs 12:18–19; James 3:8; James 3:10; Colossians 3:8–9; 1 Thessalonians 4:3; Revelation 14:5*

## MORNING READING

Let the kindness of the Lord our God be with us.
Make us successful in everything we do.

You became famous in every nation because of your beauty. Your beauty was perfect because I gave you my glory, declares the Almighty LORD. ✦ As all of us reflect the Lord's glory with faces that are not covered with veils, we are being changed into his image with ever-increasing glory. This comes from the Lord, who is the Spirit. ✦ The Spirit of glory—the Spirit of God—is resting on you. ✦ Blessed are all who fear the LORD and live his way. You will certainly eat what your own hands have provided. Blessings to you! ✦ Entrust your efforts to the LORD, and your plans will succeed. ✦ Work out your salvation with fear and trembling. It is God who produces in you the desires and actions that please him. ✦ God our Father loved us and by his kindness gave us everlasting encouragement and good hope. Together with our Lord Jesus Christ, may he encourage and strengthen you to do and say everything that is good.

*Psalm 90:17; Ezekiel 16:14; 2 Corinthians 3:18; 1 Peter 4:14; Psalm 128:1–2; Proverbs 16:3; Philippians 2:12–13; 2 Thessalonians 2:16–17*

## EVENING READING

The apostles gathered around Jesus.
They reported to him everything they had done and taught.

A loving friend can stick closer than family. ✦ The LORD would speak to Moses personally, as a man speaks to his friend. ✦ "You are my friends if you obey my commandments. I don't call you servants anymore, because a servant doesn't know what his master is doing. But I've called you friends because I've made known to you everything that I've heard from my Father." ✦ "When you've done everything you're ordered to do, say, 'We're worthless servants. We've only done our duty.' " ✦ You haven't received the spirit of slaves that leads you into fear again. Instead, you have received the spirit of God's adopted children by which we call out, "Abba! Father!" ✦ Let God know what you need in prayers and requests while giving thanks. ✦ The prayers of decent people please [God].

*Mark 6:30; Proverbs 18:24; Exodus 33:11; John 15:14–15; Luke 17:10; Romans 8:15; Philippians 4:6; Proverbs 15:8*

## MORNING READING

"Remember me, my God."

"This is what the LORD says: I remember the unfailing loyalty of your youth, the love you had for me as a bride. I remember how you followed me into the desert." ✦ I will remember the promise that I made with you when you were young, and I will make it a promise that will last forever. ✦ I will keep my promise to you. . . . I know the plans that I have for you, declares the LORD. They are plans for peace and not disaster, plans to give you a future filled with hope. ✦ "Just as the heavens are higher than the earth, so my ways are higher than your ways, and my thoughts are higher than your thoughts." ✦ "But I would seek God's help and present my case to him. He does great things that we cannot understand and miracles that we cannot count." ✦ You have done many miraculous things, O LORD my God. You have made many wonderful plans for us. No one compares to you! I will tell others about your miracles, which are more than I can count.

*Nehemiah 5:19; Jeremiah 2:2; Ezekiel 16:60; Jeremiah 29:10–11; Isaiah 55:9; Job 5:8–9; Psalm 40:5*

## EVENING READING

"I will never neglect you or abandon you."

Every single good promise that the LORD had given the nation of Israel came true. ✦ "God is not like people. He tells no lies. He is not like humans. He doesn't change his mind. When he says something, he does it. When he makes a promise, he keeps it." ✦ The LORD your God is the only God. He is a faithful God, who keeps his promise and is merciful to thousands of generations of those who love him and obey his commands. ✦ He always remembers his promise. ✦ Can a woman forget her nursing child? Will she have no compassion on the child from her womb? Although mothers may forget, I will not forget you. I have engraved you on the palms of my hands. Your walls are always in my presence. ✦ The LORD your God is with you. He is a hero who saves you. He happily rejoices over you, renews you with his love, and celebrates over you with shouts of joy.

*Joshua 1:5; Joshua 21:45; Numbers 23:19; Deuteronomy 7:9; Psalm 111:5; Isaiah 49:15–16; Zephaniah 3:17*

## MORNING READING

Those who know your name trust you,
O LORD, because you have never deserted those who seek your help.

The name of the LORD is a strong tower. A righteous person runs to it and is safe.✦ "I am confident and unafraid, because the LORD is my strength and my song. He is my Savior." ✦ I have never seen a righteous person abandoned or his descendants begging for food. . . . The LORD loves justice, and he will not abandon his godly ones. They will be kept safe forever, but the descendants of wicked people will be cut off. ✦ For the sake of his great name, the LORD will not abandon his people, because the LORD wants to make you his people. ✦ He has rescued us from a terrible death, and he will rescue us in the future. We are confident that he will continue to rescue us. ✦ Be happy with what you have because God has said, "I will never abandon you or leave you." So we can confidently say, "The Lord is my helper. I will not be afraid. What can mortals do to me?"

*Psalm 9:10; Proverbs 18:10; Isaiah 12:2; Psalm 37:25, 28;*
*1 Samuel 12:22; 2 Corinthians 1:10; Hebrews 13:5–6*

## EVENING READING

They are blameless.

"People will look for Israel's crimes, but they will find none. They will look for Judah's sins, but none will be found. I will forgive the faithful few whom I have spared."✦ Who is a God like you? You forgive sin and overlook the rebellion of your faithful people. You will not be angry forever, because you would rather show mercy. You will again have compassion on us. You will overcome our wrongdoing. You will throw all our sins into the deep sea. ✦ So that the kindness he had given us in his dear Son would be praised and given glory. ✦ So that you could come into God's presence without sin, fault, or blame. ✦ God can guard you so that you don't fall and so that you can be full of joy as you stand in his glorious presence without fault. Before time began, now, and for eternity glory, majesty, power, and authority belong to the only God, our Savior, through Jesus Christ our Lord. Amen.

*Revelation 14:5; Jeremiah 50:20; Micah 7:18–19;*
*Ephesians 1:6; Colossians 1:22; Jude 24–25*

## MORNING READING

Yet, you have raised a flag for those who fear you
so that they can rally to it.

The LORD Is My Banner. ✦ The people of the west will fear the name of the LORD. Those in the east will fear his glory. He will come like a rushing stream. The wind of the LORD pushes him. ✦ We will joyfully sing about your victory. We will wave our flags in the name of our God. ✦ The LORD has brought about our victory. Let's announce in Zion what the LORD our God has done. ✦ The one who loves us gives us an overwhelming victory in all these difficulties. ✦ Thank God that he gives us the victory through our Lord Jesus Christ. ✦ The source of their salvation. ✦ Receive your power from the Lord and from his mighty strength. ✦ "Not for truth are they strong in the land." ✦ "Fight the LORD's battles." ✦ "Everyone in the land, be strong," declares the LORD. "Work. . . . Don't be afraid." ✦ "Look and see that the fields are ready to be harvested." ✦ "Yet, the one who is coming will come soon. He will not delay."

*Psalm 60:4; Exodus 17:15; Isaiah 59:19; Psalm 20:5; Jeremiah 51:10; Romans 8:37; 1 Corinthians 15:57; Hebrews 2:10; Ephesians 6:10; Jeremiah 9:3; 1 Samuel 18:17; Haggai 2:4–5; John 4:35; Hebrews 10:37*

## EVENING READING

"There's only one thing you need."

Many are saying, "Who can show us anything good?" Let the light of your presence shine on us, O LORD. You put more joy in my heart than when their grain and new wine increase.✦ As a deer longs for flowing streams, so my soul longs for you, O God. My soul thirsts for God, for the living God. ✦ O God, you are my God. At dawn I search for you. My soul thirsts for you. My body longs for you in a dry, parched land where there is no water. ✦ "I am the bread of life. Whoever comes to me will never become hungry, and whoever believes in me will never become thirsty." ✦ "Sir, give us this bread all the time." ✦ Mary sat at the Lord's feet and listened to him talk. ✦ I have asked one thing from the LORD. This I will seek: to remain in the LORD's house all the days of my life in order to gaze at the LORD's beauty and to search for an answer in his temple.

*Luke 10:42; Psalm 4:6–7; Psalm 42:1–2; Psalm 63:1; John 6:35; John 6:34; Luke 10:39; Psalm 27:4*

## MORNING READING

May he keep your whole being—spirit, soul, and body—
blameless when our Lord Jesus Christ comes.

Christ loved the church and gave his life for it. . . . Then he could present it to himself as a glorious church, without any kind of stain or wrinkle—holy and without faults. ✦ We spread the message about Christ as we instruct and teach everyone with all the wisdom there is. We want to present everyone as mature Christian people. ✦ God's peace . . . goes beyond anything we can imagine. ✦ Let Christ's peace control you. God has called you into this peace by bringing you into one body. ✦ God our Father loved us and by his kindness gave us everlasting encouragement and good hope. . . . May he encourage and strengthen you to do and say everything that is good. ✦ He will continue to give you strength until the end so that no one can accuse you of anything on the day of our Lord Jesus Christ.

*1 Thessalonians 5:23; Ephesians 5:25, 27; Colossians. 1:28; Philippians 4:7; Colossians 3:15; 2 Thessalonians 2:16–17; 1 Corinthians 1:8*

## EVENING READING

"Does God really live on earth with people?"

Then have them make a holy place for me, and I will live among them. ✦ I will also meet with the Israelites there, and my glory will make this place holy. . . . Then I will live among the Israelites and be their God. ✦ You went to the highest place. You took prisoners captive. You received gifts from people, even from rebellious people, so that the LORD God may live there. ✦ We are the temple of the living God. As God said, "I will live and walk among them. I will be their God, and they will be my people." ✦ Your body is a temple that belongs to the Holy Spirit? The Holy Spirit, whom you received from God, lives in you. ✦ You . . . are being built in the Spirit together with others into a place where God lives. ✦ "Then the nations will know that I, the LORD, have set Israel apart as holy, because my holy place will be among them permanently."

*2 Chronicles 6:18; Exodus 25:8; Exodus 29:43, 45; Psalm 68:18; 2 Corinthians 6:16; 1 Corinthians 6:19; Ephesians 2:22; Ezekiel 37:28*

## MORNING READING

You are praised with silence in Zion, O God.

For us, "There is only one God, the Father. Everything came from him, and we live for him. There is only one Lord, Jesus Christ. Everything came into being through him, and we live because of him." ✦ "Everyone will honor the Son as they honor the Father. Whoever doesn't honor the Son doesn't honor the Father who sent him." ✦ Through Jesus we should always bring God a sacrifice of praise, that is, words that acknowledge him. ✦ Whoever offers thanks as a sacrifice honors me. I will let everyone who continues in my way see the salvation that comes from God. ✦ I saw a large crowd from every nation, tribe, people, and language. No one was able to count how many people there were. They were standing in front of the throne and the lamb. They were wearing white robes, holding palm branches in their hands, and crying out in a loud voice, "Salvation belongs to our God, who sits on the throne, and to the lamb!" ✦ "Amen! Praise, glory, wisdom, thanks, honor, power, and strength be to our God forever and ever! Amen!"

*Psalm 65:1; 1 Corinthians 8:6; John 5:23; Hebrews 13:15; Psalm 50:23; Revelation 7:9–10; Revelation 7:12*

## EVENING READING

Who rescues your life from the pit.

Their defender is strong. His name is the LORD of Armies. ✦ "I want to free them from the power of the grave. I want to reclaim them from death. Death, I want to be a plague to you. Grave, I want to destroy you." ✦ Since all of these sons and daughters have flesh and blood, Jesus took on flesh and blood to be like them. He did this so that by dying he would destroy the one who had power over death (that is, the devil). In this way he would free those who were slaves all their lives because they were afraid of dying. ✦ "Whoever believes in the Son has eternal life, but whoever rejects the Son will not see life. Instead, he will see God's constant anger." ✦ You have died, and your life is hidden with Christ in God. When Christ is your life. When he appears, then you, too, will appear with him in glory. ✦ When he comes to be honored among all his holy people and admired by all who have believed in him. This includes you because you believed the testimony we gave you.

*Psalm 103:4; Jeremiah 50:34; Hosea 13:14; Hebrews 2:14–15; John 3:36; Colossians 3:3–4; 2 Thessalonians 1:10*

## Morning Reading

To the only God, our Savior.

You are partners with Christ Jesus because of God. Jesus has become our wisdom sent from God, our righteousness, our holiness, and our ransom from sin. ✦ "Can you discover God's hidden secrets, or are you able to find the Almighty's limits? God's wisdom is higher than heaven. What can you do? It is deeper than the depths of hell. What can you know?" ✦ We speak about the mystery of God's wisdom. It is a wisdom that has been hidden, which God had planned for our glory before the world began. ✦ God, who created all things, kept it hidden in the past. He did this so that now, through the church, he could let the rulers and authorities in heaven know his infinite wisdom. ✦ If any of you needs wisdom to know what you should do, you should ask God, and he will give it to you. ✦ The wisdom that comes from above is first of all pure. Then it is peaceful, gentle, obedient, filled with mercy and good deeds, impartial, and sincere.

*Jude 25; 1 Corinthians 1:30; Job 11:7–8;*
*1 Corinthians 2:7; Ephesians 3:9–10; James 1:5; James 3:17*

## Evening Reading

"When will I get up?" But the evening is long.

Someone is calling, . . . "Watchman, how much of the night is left?" The watchman answers, "Morning is coming." ✦ He is like the morning light as the sun rises, like a morning without clouds. ✦ "I'm going to prepare a place for you? If I go to prepare a place for you, I will come again. Then I will bring you into my presence so that you will be where I am. . . . So don't be troubled or cowardly. You heard me tell you, 'I'm going away, but I'm coming back to you.' " ✦ May all your enemies die like that, O Lord. But may those who love the Lord be like the sun when it rises in all its brightness. ✦ You belong to the day and the light not to the night and the dark. ✦ Its gates will be open all day. They will never close because there won't be any night there.

*Job 7:4; Isaiah 21:11–12; 2 Samuel 23:4; John 14:2–3, 27–28;*
*Judges 5:31; 1 Thessalonians 5:5; Revelation 21:25*

## MORNING READING

With perfect peace you will protect those whose minds cannot be changed, because they trust you.

Turn your burdens over to the LORD, and he will take care of you. He will never let the righteous person stumble. ✦ "I am confident and unafraid, because the LORD is my strength and my song. He is my Savior." ✦ "Why do you cowards have so little faith?" ✦ Never worry about anything. But in every situation let God know what you need in prayers and requests while giving thanks. Then God's peace, which goes beyond anything we can imagine, will guard your thoughts and emotions through Christ Jesus. ✦ You can be strong by being quiet and by trusting me. ✦ Then an act of righteousness will bring about peace, calm, and safety forever. ✦ "I'm leaving you peace. I'm giving you my peace. I don't give you the kind of peace that the world gives. So don't be troubled or cowardly." ✦ Peace to you from the one who is, the one who was, and the one who is coming.

*Isaiah 26:3; Psalm 55:22; Isaiah 12:2; Matthew 8:26; Philippians 4:6–7; Isaiah 30:15; Isaiah 32:17; John 14:27; Revelation 1:4*

## EVENING READING

Don't go to bed angry.

"If a believer does something wrong, go, confront him when the two of you are alone. If he listens to you, you have won back that believer." ✦ Peter came to Jesus and asked him, "Lord, how often do I have to forgive a believer who wrongs me? Seven times?" Jesus answered him, "I tell you, not just seven times, but seventy times seven." ✦ "Whenever you pray, forgive anything you have against anyone. Then your Father in heaven will forgive your failures." ✦ As holy people whom God has chosen and loved, be sympathetic, kind, humble, gentle, and patient. Put up with each other, and forgive each other if anyone has a complaint. Forgive as the Lord forgave you. ✦ Be kind to each other, sympathetic, forgiving each other as God has forgiven you through Christ. ✦ Then the apostles said to the Lord, "Give us more faith."

*Ephesians 4:26; Matthew 18:15; Matthew 18:21–22; Mark 11:25; Colossians 3:12–13; Ephesians 4:32; Luke 17:5*

# January 14

## MORNING READING

"The Father is greater than I am."

"When you pray, say this: Father." ✦ "My Father and your Father . . . my God and your God." ✦ "I am doing exactly what the Father has commanded me to do." ✦ "What I'm telling you doesn't come from me. The Father, who lives in me, does what he wants." ✦ "The Father loves his Son and has put everything in his power." ✦ "You've given him authority over all humanity so that he can give eternal life to all those you gave to him." ✦ Philip said to Jesus, "Lord, show us the Father, and that will satisfy us." Jesus replied, "I have been with all of you for a long time. Don't you know me yet, Philip? The person who has seen me has seen the Father. So how can you say, 'Show us the Father'? Don't you believe that I am in the Father and the Father is in me?" ✦ "The Father and I are one." ✦ "I have loved you the same way the Father has loved me. So live in my love. If you obey my commandments, you will live in my love. I have obeyed my Father's commandments, and in that way I live in his love."

*John 14:28; Luke 11:2; John 20:17; John 14:31; John 14:10; John 3:35; John 17:2; John 14:8–10; John 10:30; John 15:9–10*

## EVENING READING

"He will crush your head, and you will bruise his heel."

His appearance will be so disfigured that he won't look like any other man. His looks will be so disfigured that he will hardly look like a human. ✦ He was wounded for our rebellious acts. He was crushed for our sins. He was punished so that we could have peace, and we received healing from his wounds. ✦ [Jesus said to the Jewish leaders,] "This is your time, when darkness rules." ✦ Jesus answered Pilate, "You wouldn't have any authority over me if it hadn't been given to you from above." ✦ The reason that the Son of God appeared was to destroy what the devil does. ✦ He . . . forced many demons out of people. However, he would not allow the demons to speak. After all, they knew who he was. ✦ "All authority in heaven and on earth has been given to me." ✦ "They will use the power and authority of my name to force demons out of people." ✦ The God of peace will quickly crush Satan under your feet.

*Genesis 3:15; Isaiah 52:14; Isaiah 53:5; Luke 22:53; John 19:11; 1 John 3:8; Mark 1:34; Matthew 28:18; Mark 16:17; Romans 16:20*

## MORNING READING

I am close to death. Give me a new life as you promised.

Since you were brought back to life with Christ, focus on the things that are above—where Christ holds the highest position. Keep your mind on things above, not on worldly things. You have died, and your life is hidden with Christ in God. ✦ We, however, are citizens of heaven. We look forward to the Lord Jesus Christ coming from heaven as our Savior. Through his power to bring everything under his authority, he will change our humble bodies and make them like his glorified body. ✦ What your corrupt nature wants is contrary to what your spiritual nature wants, and what your spiritual nature wants is contrary to what your corrupt nature wants. They are opposed to each other. As a result, you don't always do what you intend to do. ✦ So, brothers and sisters, we have no obligation to live the way our corrupt nature wants us to live. If you live by your corrupt nature, you are going to die. But if you use your spiritual nature to put to death the evil activities of the body, you will live. ✦ Dear friends, since you are foreigners and temporary residents in the world, I'm encouraging you to keep away from the desires of your corrupt nature. These desires constantly attack you.

*Psalm 119:25; Colossians 3:1–3; Philippians 3:20–21; Galatians 5:17; Romans 8:12–13; 1 Peter 2:11*

## EVENING READING

What God has given each of you as believers.

Welcome people who are weak in faith. ✦ Giving honor to God for the promise, [Abraham] became strong because of faith. ✦ "You have so little faith! Why did you doubt?" ✦ "You have strong faith! What you wanted will be done for you." ✦ Jesus . . . said to [the blind men], "Do you believe that I can do this?" "Yes, Lord," they answered. He touched their eyes and said, "What you have believed will be done for you!" ✦ "Give us more faith." ✦ Use your most holy faith to grow. ✦ Sink your roots in him and build on him. Be strengthened by the faith that you were taught. ✦ God establishes us, together with you, in a relationship with Christ. ✦ God, who shows you his kindness and who has called you through Christ Jesus to his eternal glory, will restore you, strengthen you, make you strong, and support you as you suffer for a little while. ✦ So those of us who have a strong faith must be patient with the weaknesses of those whose faith is not so strong. We must not think only of ourselves. ✦ Let's stop criticizing each other. Instead, you should decide never to do anything that would make other Christians have doubts or lose their faith.

*Romans 12:3; Romans 14:1; Romans 4:20; Matthew 14:31; Matthew 15:28; Matthew 9:28–29; Luke 17:5; Jude 20; Colossians 2:7; 2 Corinthians 1:21; 1 Peter 5:10; Romans 15:1; Romans 14:13*

## MORNING READING

God was pleased to have all of himself live in Christ.

"The Father loves his Son and has put everything in his power." ✦ God has given him an exceptional honor—the name honored above all other names—so that at the name of Jesus everyone in heaven, on earth, and in the world below will kneel and confess that Jesus Christ is Lord to the glory of God the Father. ✦ He is far above all rulers, authorities, powers, lords, and all other names that can be named, not only in this present world but also in the world to come. ✦ He created all things in heaven and on earth, visible and invisible. Whether they are kings or lords, rulers or powers—everything has been created through him and for him. ✦ Christ died and came back to life so that he would be the Lord of both the living and the dead. ✦ God has made you complete in Christ. Christ is in charge of every ruler and authority. ✦ Each of us has received one gift after another because of all that the Word is.

*Colossians 1:19; John 3:35; Philippians 2:9–11; Ephesians 1:21; Colossians 1:16; Romans 14:9; Colossians 2:10; John 1:16*

## EVENING READING

Write down what you have seen, what is, and what is going to happen after these things.

✦ [Prophecy] was given by the Holy Spirit as humans spoke under God's direction. ✦ This is the life we have seen and heard. We are reporting about it to you also so that you, too, can have a relationship with us. Our relationship is with the Father and with his Son Jesus Christ. ✦ [Jesus said to his disciples,] "Look at my hands and feet, and see that it's really me. Touch me, and see for yourselves. Ghosts don't have flesh and bones, but you can see that I do." As he said this, he showed them his hands and feet. ✦ The one who saw this is an eyewitness. What he says is true, and he knows that he is telling the truth so that you, too, will believe. ✦ When we apostles told you about the powerful coming of our Lord Jesus Christ, we didn't base our message on clever myths that we made up. Rather, we witnessed his majesty with our own eyes. ✦ That your faith would not be based on human wisdom but on God's power.

*Revelation 1:19; 2 Peter 1:21; 1 John 1:3; Luke 24:39–40; John 19:35; 2 Peter 1:16; 1 Corinthians 2:5*

## MORNING READING

You have saved me and kept me from the rotting pit.

God has shown us his love by sending his only Son into the world so that we could have life through him. This is love: not that we have loved God, but that he loved us and sent his Son to be the payment for our sins. ✦ Who is a God like you? You forgive sin and overlook the rebellion of your faithful people. You will not be angry forever, because you would rather show mercy. You will again have compassion on us. You will overcome our wrongdoing. You will throw all our sins into the deep sea. ✦ O LORD my God, I cried out to you for help, and you healed me. O LORD, you brought me up from the grave. You called me back to life from among those who had gone into the pit. ✦ "As my life was slipping away, I remembered the LORD. My prayer came to you in your holy temple." ✦ I waited patiently for the LORD. He turned to me and heard my cry for help. He pulled me out of a horrible pit, out of the mud and clay. He set my feet on a rock and made my steps secure.

*Isaiah 38:17; 1 John 4:9–10; Micah 7:18–19;*
*Psalm 30:2–3; Jonah 2:7; Psalm 40:1–2*

## EVENING READING

What is.

Now we see a blurred image in a mirror. ✦ At the present time we still don't see everything under his Son's control. ✦ So we regard the words of the prophets as confirmed beyond all doubt. You're doing well by paying attention to their words. Continue to pay attention as you would to a light that shines in a dark place as you wait for day to come and the morning star to rise in your hearts. ✦ Your word is a lamp for my feet and a light for my path. ✦ Dear friends, remember what the apostles of our Lord Jesus Christ told you to expect: "In the last times people who ridicule God will appear. They will follow their own ungodly desires." These are the people who cause divisions. They are concerned about physical things, not spiritual things. ✦ The Spirit says clearly that in later times some believers will desert the Christian faith. They will follow spirits that deceive, and they will believe the teachings of demons. ✦ Children, it's the end of time. ✦ The night is almost over, and the day is near. So we should get rid of the things that belong to the dark and take up the weapons that belong to the light.

*Revelation 1:19; 1 Corinthians 13:12; Hebrews 2:8; 2 Peter 1:19;*
*Psalm 119:105; Jude 17–18; 1 Timothy 4:1; 1 John 2:18; Romans 13:12*

## MORNING READING

The one who would come.

Jesus was made a little lower than the angels, but we see him crowned with glory and honor because he suffered death. . . . He died on behalf of everyone. ✦ One man has died for all people. ✦ Through one person's disobedience humanity became sinful, and through one person's obedience humanity will receive God's approval. ✦ This is what Scripture says: "The first man, Adam, became a living being." The last Adam became a life-giving spirit. ✦ God said, "Let us make humans in our image, in our likeness." . . . So God created humans in his image. In the image of God he created them. ✦ In these last days [God] has spoken to us through his Son. . . . His Son is the reflection of God's glory and the exact likeness of God's being. ✦ "You've given him authority over all humanity." ✦ The first man was made from the dust of the earth. He came from the earth. The second man came from heaven. The people on earth are like the man who was made from the dust of the earth. The people in heaven are like the man who came from heaven.

*Romans 5:14; Hebrews 2:9; 2 Corinthians 5:14; Romans 5:19; 1 Corinthians 15:45; Genesis 1:26–27; Hebrews 1:1–3; John 17:2; 1 Corinthians 15:47–48*

## EVENING READING

What is going to happen after these things.

As Scripture says: "No eye has seen, no ear has heard, and no mind has imagined the things that God has prepared for those who love him." God has revealed those things to us by his Spirit.✦ "When the Spirit of Truth comes, he will . . . tell you about things to come." ✦ Look! He is coming in the clouds. Every eye will see him, even those who pierced him. Every tribe on earth will mourn because of him. This is true. Amen. ✦ Brothers and sisters, we don't want you to be ignorant about those who have died. We don't want you to grieve like other people who have no hope. We believe that Jesus died and came back to life. We also believe that, through Jesus, God will bring back those who have died. . . . The Lord will come from heaven with a command, with the voice of the archangel, and with the trumpet call of God. First, the dead who believed in Christ will come back to life. Then, together with them, we who are still alive will be taken in the clouds to meet the Lord in the air. In this way we will always be with the Lord.

*Revelation 1:19; 1 Corinthians 2:9–10; John 16:13; Revelation 1:7; 1 Thessalonians 4:13–14, 16–17*

## MORNING READING

I humbly served the Lord.

"Whoever wants to become great among you will be your servant. Whoever wants to be most important among you will be your slave. It's the same way with the Son of Man. He didn't come so that others could serve him. He came to serve and to give his life as a ransom for many people."✦ If any one of you thinks you're important when you're really not, you're only fooling yourself. ✦ Because of the kindness that God has shown me, I ask you not to think of yourselves more highly than you should. Instead, your thoughts should lead you to use good judgment based on what God has given each of you as believers. ✦ "When you've done everything you're ordered to do, say, 'We're worthless servants. We've only done our duty.' " ✦ We are proud that our conscience is clear. We are proud of the way that we have lived in this world. We have lived with a God-given holiness. ✦ Our bodies are made of clay, yet we have the treasure of the Good News in them. This shows that the superior power of this treasure belongs to God and doesn't come from us.

*Acts 20:19; Matthew 20:26–28; Galatians 6:3; Romans 12:3; Luke 17:10; 2 Corinthians 1:12; 2 Corinthians 4:7*

## EVENING READING

Each one of us has turned to go his own way.

Noah, a farmer, was the first person to plant a vineyard. He drank some wine [and] got drunk. ✦ Abram said to his wife Sarai, ". . . Please say that you're my sister. Then everything will be alright for me, and because of you I will live." ✦ "Are you really my son Esau?" [Isaac] asked [Jacob]. "I am," Jacob answered." ✦ [Moses] spoke recklessly. ✦ The men believed the evidence they were shown, but they did not ask the LORD about it. So Joshua made peace with them. ✦ The LORD did this because David did what the LORD considered right: David never failed to do anything the LORD commanded him to do his entire life (except in the matter concerning Uriah the Hittite). ✦ All these people were known for their faith. ✦ They receive God's approval freely by an act of his kindness through the price Christ Jesus paid to set us free from sin. ✦ The LORD has laid all our sins on him. ✦ I'm not doing this for your sake, declares the Almighty LORD. Be ashamed and disgraced because of your ways.

*Isaiah 53:6; Genesis 9:20–21; Genesis 12:11, 13; Genesis 27:24; Psalm 106:33; Joshua 9:14–15; 1 Kings 15:5; Hebrews 11:39; Romans 3:24; Isaiah 53:6; Ezekiel 36:32*

## MORNING READING

He will be named: Wonderful Counselor.

The Word became human and lived among us. We saw his glory. It was the glory that the Father shares with his only Son, a glory full of kindness and truth. ✦ You have made your name and your promise greater than everything. ✦ "They will name him Immanuel," which means "God is with us." ✦ "You will name him Jesus [He Saves], because he will save his people from their sins." ✦ "Everyone will honor the Son as they honor the Father." ✦ God has given him an exceptional honor—the name honored above all other names. ✦ He is far above all rulers, authorities, powers, lords, and all other names that can be named, not only in this present world but also in the world to come. God has put everything under the control of Christ. ✦ He has a name written on him, but only he knows what it is. ✦ King of kings and Lord of lords. ✦ The Almighty . . . we can't reach. ✦ What is his name or the name of his son? Certainly, you must know!

*Isaiah 9:6; John 1:14; Psalm 138:2; Matthew 1:23; Matthew 1:21; John 5:23; Philippians 2:9; Ephesians 1:21–22; Revelation 19:12; Revelation 19:16; Job 37:23; Proverbs 30:4*

## EVENING READING

But the LORD's people were his property.

You belong to Christ, and Christ belongs to God. ✦ I am my beloved's, and he longs for me. ✦ I am his. ✦ God's Son . . . loved me and took the punishment for my sins. ✦ You don't belong to yourselves. You were bought for a price. So bring glory to God in the way you use your body. ✦ You are the people the LORD brought out of Egypt, the iron smelter, in order to make you his own people as you still are today. ✦ You are God's field. You are God's building. ✦ Christ is a faithful son in charge of God's household. We are his household if we continue to have courage and to be proud of the confidence we have. ✦ A spiritual house that is being built into a holy priesthood. ✦ "They will be mine," says the LORD of Armies. "On that day I will make them my special possession." ✦ Everything I have is yours, and everything you have is mine. I have been given glory by the people you have given me. ✦ The glorious wealth that God's people will inherit.

*Deuteronomy 32:9; 1 Corinthians 3:23; Song of Songs 7:10; Song of Songs 2:16; Galatians 2:20; 1 Corinthians 6:19–20; Deuteronomy 4:20; 1 Corinthians 3:9; Hebrews 3:6; 1 Peter 2:5; Malachi 3:17; John 17:10; Ephesians 1:18*

## MORNING READING

"He . . . prunes every branch that does produce fruit
to make it produce more fruit."

He is like a purifying fire and like a cleansing soap. He will act like a refiner and a purifier of silver. He will purify Levi's sons and refine them like gold and silver. Then they will bring acceptable offerings to the LORD. ✦ We also brag when we are suffering. We know that suffering creates endurance, endurance creates character, and character creates confidence. We're not ashamed to have this confidence, because God's love has been poured into our hearts by the Holy Spirit, who has been given to us. ✦ Endure your discipline. God corrects you as a father corrects his children. All children are disciplined by their fathers. If you aren't disciplined like the other children, you aren't part of the family. We don't enjoy being disciplined. It always seems to cause more pain than joy. But later on, those who learn from that discipline have peace that comes from doing what is right. Strengthen your tired arms and weak knees.

*John 15:2; Malachi 3:2–3; Romans 5:3–5; Hebrews 12:7–8, 11–12*

## EVENING READING

So now we call arrogant people blessed.

The High and Lofty One lives forever, and his name is holy. This is what he says: I live in a high and holy place. But I am with those who are crushed and humble. I will renew the spirit of those who are humble and the courage of those who are crushed. ✦ Better to be humble with lowly people than to share stolen goods with arrogant people. ✦ "Blessed are those who recognize they are spiritually helpless. The kingdom of heaven belongs to them." ✦ There are six things that the LORD hates, even seven that are disgusting to him: arrogant eyes. . . . ✦ Everyone with a conceited heart is disgusting to the LORD. ✦ Examine me, O God, and know my mind. Test me, and know my thoughts. See whether I am on an evil path. Then lead me on the everlasting path. ✦ Good will and peace from God our Father and the Lord Jesus Christ are yours! I thank my God for all the memories I have of you. ✦ "Blessed are those who are gentle. They will inherit the earth."

*Malachi 3:15; Isaiah 57:15; Proverbs 16:19; Matthew 5:3; Proverbs 6:16–17; Proverbs 16:5; Psalm 139:23–24; Philippians 1:2–3; Matthew 5:5*

## Morning Reading

This God is our God forever and ever.
He will lead us beyond death.

O Lord, you are my God. I will highly honor you; I will praise your name. You have done miraculous things. You have been completely reliable in carrying out your plans from long ago. ✦ The Lord is my inheritance and my cup. ✦ He guides me along the paths of righteousness for the sake of his name. Even though I walk through the dark valley of death, because you are with me, I fear no harm. Your rod and your staff give me courage. ✦ You hold on to my right hand. With your advice you guide me, and in the end you will take me to glory. As long as I have you, I don't need anyone else in heaven or on earth. My body and mind may waste away, but God remains the foundation of my life and my inheritance forever. ✦ In him our hearts find joy. In his holy name we trust. ✦ The Lord will do everything for me. O Lord, your mercy endures forever. Do not let go of what your hands have made.

*Psalm 48:14; Isaiah 25:1; Psalm 16:5; Psalm 23:3–4; Psalm 73:23–26; Psalm 33:21; Psalm 138:8*

## Evening Reading

When I worried about many things,
your assuring words soothed my soul.

When I begin to lose heart. Lead me to the rock that is high above me. ✦ I've suffered miserably, O Lord! Please help me! ✦ Turn your burdens over to the Lord, and he will take care of you. ✦ "Lord my God, . . . I'm young and inexperienced." ✦ If any of you needs wisdom to know what you should do, you should ask God, and he will give it to you. ✦ Who is qualified to tell about Christ? ✦ I know that nothing good lives in me; that is, nothing good lives in my corrupt nature. ✦ "My kindness is all you need. My power is strongest when you are weak." ✦ "Cheer up, friend! Your sins are forgiven." ✦ "Cheer up, daughter! Your faith has made you well." ✦ You satisfy my soul with the richest foods. . . . As I lie on my bed, I remember you. Through the long hours of the night, I think about you.

*Psalm 94:19; Psalm 61:2; Isaiah 38:14; Psalm 55:22; 1 Kings 3:7; James 1:5; 2 Corinthians 2:16; Romans 7:18; 2 Corinthians 12:9; Matthew 9:2; Matthew 9:22; Psalm 63:5–6*

## Morning Reading

We're not ashamed to have this confidence.

I am the Lord. Those who wait with hope for me will not be put to shame. ✦ Blessed is the person who trusts the Lord. The Lord will be his confidence. ✦ With perfect peace you will protect those whose minds cannot be changed, because they trust you. Trust the Lord always, because the Lord, the Lord alone, is an everlasting rock. ✦ Wait calmly for God alone, my soul, because my hope comes from him. He alone is my rock and my savior—my stronghold. I cannot be shaken. ✦ I'm not ashamed. I know whom I trust. ✦ God wouldn't change his plan. He wanted to make this perfectly clear to those who would receive his promise, so he took an oath. God did this so that we would be encouraged. God cannot lie when he takes an oath or makes a promise. These two things can never be changed. Those of us who have taken refuge in him hold on to the confidence we have been given. We have this confidence as a sure and strong anchor for our lives. This confidence goes into the holy place behind the curtain where Jesus went before us on our behalf.

*Romans 5:5; Isaiah 49:23; Jeremiah 17:7; Isaiah 26:3–4; Psalm 62:5–6; 2 Timothy 1:12; Hebrews 6:17–20*

## Evening Reading

"We must suffer a lot to enter the kingdom of God."

"Those who want to come with me must say no to the things they want, pick up their crosses, and follow me." ✦ Don't you know that love for this evil world is hatred toward God? Whoever wants to be a friend of this world is an enemy of God. ✦ If I am still preaching that circumcision is necessary, why am I still being persecuted? In that case the cross wouldn't be offensive anymore. ✦ "Whoever believes in him will not be ashamed." ✦ To those who don't believe: "The stone that the builders rejected has become the cornerstone, a stone that people trip over, a large rock that people find offensive." ✦ It's unthinkable that I could ever brag about anything except the cross of our Lord Jesus Christ. By his cross my relationship to the world and its relationship to me have been crucified. ✦ I have been crucified with Christ. ✦ Those who belong to Christ Jesus have crucified their corrupt nature along with its passions and desires. ✦ If we endure, we will rule with him. If we disown him, he will disown us.

*Acts 14:22; Matthew 16:24; James 4:4; Galatians 5:11; Romans 9:33; 1 Peter 2:7–8; Galatians 6:14; Galatians 2:19; Galatians 5:24; 2 Timothy 2:12*

## Morning Reading

The Lord is near.

The Lord will come from heaven with a command, with the voice of the archangel, and with the trumpet call of God. First, the dead who believed in Christ will come back to life. Then, together with them, we who are still alive will be taken in the clouds to meet the Lord in the air. In this way we will always be with the Lord. So then, comfort each other with these words! ✦ The one who is testifying to these things says, "Yes, I'm coming soon!" Amen! Come, Lord Jesus! ✦ Therefore, dear friends, with this to look forward to, make every effort to have him find you at peace, without spiritual stains or blemishes. ✦ Keep away from every kind of evil. May the God who gives peace make you holy in every way. May he keep your whole being—spirit, soul, and body—blameless when our Lord Jesus Christ comes. The one who calls you is faithful, and he will do this. ✦ You, too, must be patient. Don't give up hope. The Lord will soon be here.

*Philippians 4:5; 1 Thessalonians 4:16–18; Revelation 22:20; 2 Peter 3:14; 1 Thessalonians 5:22–24; James 5:8*

## Evening Reading

The best vine.

My beloved had a vineyard on a fertile hill. He dug it up, removed its stones, planted it with the choicest vines. . . . Then he waited for it to produce good grapes, but it produced only sour, wild grapes. ✦ I planted you like a choice grapevine from the very best seed. Now you have turned against me and have become a wild vine. ✦ Now, the effects of the corrupt nature are obvious: illicit sex, perversion, promiscuity . . . envy, drunkenness, wild partying, and similar things. But the spiritual nature produces love, joy, peace, patience, kindness, goodness, faithfulness, gentleness, and self-control. ✦ "I am the true vine, and my Father takes care of the vineyard. He removes every one of my branches that doesn't produce fruit. He also prunes every branch that does produce fruit to make it produce more fruit." ✦ "Live in me, and I will live in you. . . . You give glory to my Father when you produce a lot of fruit and therefore show that you are my disciples."

*Genesis 49:11; Isaiah 5:1–2; Jeremiah 2:21; Galatians 5:19, 21–23; John 15:1–2; John 15:4, 8*

## MORNING READING

Everyone who believes has God's approval through faith in Jesus Christ.

God had Christ, who was sinless, take our sin so that we might receive God's approval through him. ✦ Christ paid the price to free us from the curse that God's laws bring by becoming cursed instead of us. ✦ You are partners with Christ Jesus because of God. Jesus has become our wisdom sent from God, our righteousness, our holiness, and our ransom from sin. ✦ He saved us, but not because of anything we had done to gain his approval. Instead, because of his mercy he saved us through the washing in which the Holy Spirit gives us new birth and renewal. God poured a generous amount of the Spirit on us through Jesus Christ our Savior. ✦ I consider everything else worthless because I'm much better off knowing Christ Jesus my Lord. It's because of him that I think of everything as worthless. I threw it all away in order to gain Christ and to have a relationship with him. This means that I didn't receive God's approval by obeying his laws. The opposite is true! I have God's approval through faith in Christ. This is the approval that comes from God and is based on faith.

*Romans 3:22; 2 Corinthians 5:21; Galatians 3:13; 1 Corinthians 1:30; Titus 3:5–6; Philippians 3:8–9*

## EVENING READING

The spirit of God's adopted children by which we call out, "Abba! Father!"

Jesus looked up to heaven and said, "Father . . . Holy Father . . . Righteous Father. . . ." ✦ He said, "Abba! Father!" ✦ Because you are God's children, God has sent the Spirit of his Son into us to call out, "Abba! Father!" ✦ So Jewish and non-Jewish people can go to the Father in one Spirit. That is why you are no longer foreigners and outsiders but citizens together with God's people and members of God's family. ✦ You are our Father. . . . O LORD, you are our Father. Your name is our Defender From Everlasting. ✦ [The prodigal son said,] "I'll go at once to my father, and I'll say to him, 'Father, I've sinned against heaven and you. I don't deserve to be called your son anymore. Make me one of your hired men.' So he went at once to his father. While he was still at a distance, his father saw him and felt sorry for him. He ran to his son, put his arms around him, and kissed him." ✦ Imitate God, since you are the children he loves.

*Romans 8:15; John 17:1, 11, 25; Mark 14:36; Galatians 4:6; Ephesians 2:18–19; Isaiah 63:16; Luke 15:18–20; Ephesians 5:1*

## MORNING READING

So we must go to him outside the camp
and endure the insults he endured.
We don't have a permanent city here on earth,
but we are looking for the city that we will have in the future.

Dear friends, don't be surprised by the fiery troubles that are coming in order to test you. Don't feel as though something strange is happening to you, but be happy as you share Christ's sufferings. Then you will also be full of joy when he appears again in his glory. ✦ As you share our sufferings, you also share our comfort. ✦ If you are insulted because of the name of Christ, you are blessed because the Spirit of glory—the Spirit of God—is resting on you. ✦ The apostles left the council room. They were happy to have been considered worthy to suffer dishonor for speaking about Jesus. ✦ He chose to suffer with God's people rather than to enjoy the pleasures of sin for a little while. He thought that being insulted for Christ would be better than having the treasures of Egypt. He was looking ahead to his reward.

*Hebrews 13:13–14; 1 Peter 4:12–13; 2 Corinthians 1:7;
1 Peter 4:14; Acts 5:41; Hebrews 11:25–26*

## EVENING READING

The Lord Jesus Christ . . . will change our humble bodies
and make them like his glorified body.

On the throne was a figure that looked like a human. Then I saw what he looked like from the waist up. He looked like glowing bronze with fire all around it. From the waist down, he looked like fire. A bright light surrounded him. The brightness all around him looked like a rainbow in the clouds. It was like the LORD's glory. ✦ As all of us reflect the Lord's glory with faces that are not covered with veils, we are being changed into his image with ever-increasing glory. This comes from the Lord, who is the Spirit. ✦ What we will be isn't completely clear yet. We do know that when Christ appears we will be like him because we will see him as he is. ✦ They will never be hungry or thirsty again. ✦ They were . . . singing the song of God's servant Moses and the song of the lamb.

*Philippians 3:20–21; Ezekiel 1:26–28; 2 Corinthians 3:18;
1 John 3:2; Revelation 7:16; Revelation 15:2–3*

## MORNING READING

You know that Christ appeared in order
to take away our sins. He isn't sinful.

In these last days [God] has spoken to us through his Son. God made his Son responsible for everything. His Son is the one through whom God made the universe. His Son is the reflection of God's glory and the exact likeness of God's being. He holds everything together through his powerful words. After he had cleansed people from their sins, he received the highest position, the one next to the Father in heaven. ✦ God had Christ, who was sinless, take our sin so that we might receive God's approval through him. ✦ Live your time as temporary residents on earth in fear. . . . Realize that you weren't set free from the worthless life handed down to you from your ancestors by a payment of silver or gold which can be destroyed. Rather, the payment that freed you was the precious blood of Christ, the lamb with no defects or imperfections. He is the lamb who was known long ago before the world existed, but for your good he became publicly known in the last period of time. ✦ Christ's love guides us. We are convinced of the fact that one man has died for all people. Therefore, all people have died. He died for all people so that those who live should no longer live for themselves but for the man who died and was brought back to life for them.

*1 John 3:5; Hebrews 1:1–3; 2 Corinthians 5:21;
1 Peter 1:17–20; 2 Corinthians 5:14–15*

## EVENING READING

I have offered you life or death, blessings or curses. Choose life.

"I don't want anyone to die," declares the Almighty LORD. "Change the way you think and act!" ✦ "If I hadn't come and spoken to them, they wouldn't have any sin. But now they have no excuse for their sin." ✦ "The servant who knew what his master wanted but didn't get ready to do it will receive a hard beating." ✦ The payment for sin is death, but the gift that God freely gives is everlasting life found in Christ Jesus our Lord. ✦ "Whoever believes in the Son has eternal life, but whoever rejects the Son will not see life. Instead, he will see God's constant anger." ✦ Don't you know that if you offer to be someone's slave, you must obey that master? Either your master is sin, or your master is obedience. Letting sin be your master leads to death. Letting obedience be your master leads to God's approval. ✦ Those who serve me must follow me. My servants will be with me wherever I will be. If people serve me, the Father will honor them.

*Deuteronomy 30:19; Ezekiel 18:32; John 15:22; Luke 12:47;
Romans 6:23; John 3:36; Romans 6:16; John 12:26*

## MORNING READING

May your strength last as long as you live.

"When they take you away to hand you over to the authorities, don't worry ahead of time about what you will say. Instead, say whatever is given to you to say when the time comes. Indeed, you are not the one who will be speaking, but the Holy Spirit will." ✦ "So don't ever worry about tomorrow. After all, tomorrow will worry about itself. Each day has enough trouble of its own." ✦ God, the God of Israel, is awe-inspiring in his holy place. He gives strength and power to his people. Thanks be to God! ✦ He gives strength to those who grow tired and increases the strength of those who are weak. ✦ But [the Lord Jesus] told me: "My kindness is all you need. My power is strongest when you are weak." So I will brag even more about my weaknesses in order that Christ's power will live in me. Therefore, I accept weakness, mistreatment, hardship, persecution, and difficulties suffered for Christ. It's clear that when I'm weak, I'm strong. ✦ I can do everything through Christ who strengthens me. ✦ I must march on with strength.

*Deuteronomy 33:25; Mark 13:11; Matthew 6:34; Psalm 68:35; Isaiah 40:29; 2 Corinthians 12:9–10; Philippians 4:13; Judges 5:21*

## EVENING READING

Awake, north wind! . . .
Blow on my garden!
Let its spices flow from it.

We don't enjoy being disciplined. It always seems to cause more pain than joy. But later on, those who learn from that discipline have peace that comes from doing what is right. ✦ The spiritual nature. ✦ He removed it with a fierce blast from the east winds. ✦ As a father has compassion for his children, so the LORD has compassion for those who fear him. ✦ Though outwardly we are wearing out, inwardly we are renewed day by day. Our suffering is light and temporary and is producing for us an eternal glory that is greater than anything we can imagine. We don't look for things that can be seen but for things that can't be seen. Things that can be seen are only temporary. But things that can't be seen last forever. ✦ Although Jesus was the Son of God, he learned to be obedient through his sufferings. ✦ He was tempted in every way that we are, but he didn't sin.

*Song of Songs 4:16; Hebrews 12:11; Galatians 5:22; Isaiah 27:8; Psalm 103:13; 2 Corinthians 4:16–18; Hebrews 5:8; Hebrews 4:15*

## MORNING READING

"You Are the God Who Watches Over Me."

O LORD, you have examined me, and you know me. You alone know when I sit down and when I get up. You read my thoughts from far away. You watch me when I travel and when I rest. You are familiar with all my ways. Even before there is a single word on my tongue, you know all about it, LORD. . . . Such knowledge is beyond my grasp. It is so high I cannot reach it. ✦ The eyes of the LORD are everywhere. They watch evil people and good people. ✦ Each person's ways are clearly seen by the LORD, and he surveys all his actions. ✦ "You try to justify your actions in front of people. But God knows what's in your hearts. What is important to humans is disgusting to God." ✦ "The LORD's eyes scan the whole world to find those whose hearts are committed to him and to strengthen them." ✦ Jesus . . . understood people and didn't need anyone to tell him about human nature. He knew what people were really like. ✦ "Lord, you know everything. You know that I love you."

*Genesis 16:13; Psalm 139:1–4, 6; Proverbs 15:3; Proverbs 5:21; Luke 16:15; 2 Chronicles 16:9; John 2:24–25; John 21:17*

## EVENING READING

I will give thanks to you with all my heart,
O Lord my God. I will honor you forever.

Whoever offers thanks as a sacrifice honors me. ✦ It is good to give thanks to the LORD, to make music to praise your name, O Most High. It is good to announce your mercy in the morning and your faithfulness in the evening. ✦ Let everything that breathes praise the LORD! ✦ Brothers and sisters, in view of all we have just shared about God's compassion, I encourage you to offer your bodies as living sacrifices, dedicated to God and pleasing to him. ✦ That is why Jesus suffered outside the gates of Jerusalem. He suffered to make the people holy with his own blood. . . . Through Jesus we should always bring God a sacrifice of praise, that is, words that acknowledge him. ✦ Always thank God the Father for everything in the name of our Lord Jesus Christ. ✦ "The lamb who was slain deserves to receive power, wealth, wisdom, strength, honor, glory, and praise."

*Psalm 86:12; Psalm 50:23; Psalm 92:1–2; Psalm 150:6; Romans 12:1; Hebrews 13:12, 15; Ephesians 5:20; Revelation 5:12*

## MORNING READING

We must run the race that lies ahead of us and never give up.
We must focus on Jesus, the source and goal of our faith.

He said to all of them, "Those who want to come with me must say no to the things they want, pick up their crosses every day, and follow me." ✦ "In the same way, none of you can be my disciples unless you give up everything." ✦ We should get rid of the things that belong to the dark. ✦ Everyone who enters an athletic contest goes into strict training. They do it to win a temporary crown, but we do it to win one that will be permanent. So I run—but not without a clear goal ahead of me. So I box—but not as if I were just shadow boxing. Rather, I toughen my body with punches and make it my slave so that I will not be disqualified after I have spread the Good News to others. ✦ Brothers and sisters, I can't consider myself a winner yet. This is what I do: I don't look back, I lengthen my stride, and run straight toward the goal to win the prize that God's heavenly call offers in Christ Jesus. ✦ Let's learn about the LORD. Let's get to know the LORD.

*Hebrews12:1–2; Luke 9:23; Luke 14:33; Romans 13:12; 1 Corinthians 9:25–27; Philippians 3:13–14; Hosea 6:3*

## EVENING READING

It is good for people to endure burdens when they're young.

Train a child in the way he should go, and even when he is old he will not turn away from it. ✦ On earth we have fathers who disciplined us, and we respect them. Shouldn't we place ourselves under the authority of God, the father of spirits, so that we will live? For a short time our fathers disciplined us as they thought best. Yet, God disciplines us for our own good so that we can become holy like him. ✦ It was good that I had to suffer in order to learn your laws. ✦ I know the plans that I have for you, declares the LORD. They are plans for peace and not disaster, plans to give you a future filled with hope. ✦ Be humbled by God's power so that when the right time comes he will honor you.

*Lamentations 3:27; Proverbs 22:6; Hebrews 12:9–10; Psalm 119:67; Psalm 119:71; Jeremiah 29:11; 1 Peter 5:6*

## MORNING READING

But if you do not force out those who live in the land,
they will be like splinters in your eyes and thorns in your sides.
They will constantly fight with you over the land you live in.

Fight the good fight for the Christian faith. ✦ The weapons we use in our fight are not made by humans. Rather, they are powerful weapons from God. With them we destroy people's defenses, that is, their arguments and . . . we take every thought captive so that it is obedient to Christ. ✦ So, brothers and sisters, we have no obligation to live the way our corrupt nature wants us to live. If you live by your corrupt nature, you are going to die. But if you use your spiritual nature to put to death the evil activities of the body, you will live. ✦ What your corrupt nature wants is contrary to what your spiritual nature wants, and what your spiritual nature wants is contrary to what your corrupt nature wants. They are opposed to each other. As a result, you don't always do what you intend to do. ✦ However, I see a different standard at work throughout my body. It is at war with the standards my mind sets and tries to take me captive to sin's standards which still exist throughout my body. ✦ The one who loves us gives us an overwhelming victory in all these difficulties.

*Numbers 33:55; 1 Timothy 6:12; 2 Corinthians 10:4–5; Romans 8:12–13; Galatians 5:17; Romans 7:23; Romans 8:37*

## EVENING READING

When a person sins against the LORD, who will pray for him?

If anyone does sin, we have Jesus Christ, who has God's full approval. He speaks on our behalf when we come into the presence of the Father. He is the payment for our sins, and not only for our sins, but also for the sins of the whole world. ✦ God showed that Christ is the throne of mercy where God's approval is given through faith in Christ's blood. In his patience God waited to deal with sins committed in the past. He waited so that he could display his approval at the present time. This shows that he is a God of justice, a God who approves of people who believe in Jesus. ✦ Then he will have pity on [people] and say, "Free them from going into the pit. I have found a ransom." ✦ What can we say about all of this? If God is for us, who can be against us? . . . Who will accuse those whom God has chosen? God has approved of them. Who will condemn them? Christ has died, and more importantly, he was brought back to life. Christ has the highest position in heaven. Christ also intercedes for us.

*1 Samuel 2:25; 1 John 2:1–2; Romans 3:25–26; Job 33:24; Romans 8:31, 33–34*

## Morning Reading

Although you have never seen Christ, you love him.

Our lives are guided by faith, not by sight. ✦ We love because God loved us first. ✦ We have known and believed that God loves us. God is love. Those who live in God's love live in God, and God lives in them. ✦ You heard and believed the message of truth, the Good News that he has saved you. In him you were sealed with the Holy Spirit whom he promised. ✦ God wanted his people throughout the world to know the glorious riches of this mystery—which is Christ living in you, giving you the hope of glory. ✦ Whoever says, "I love God," but hates another believer is a liar. People who don't love other believers, whom they have seen, can't love God, whom they have not seen. ✦ Jesus said to Thomas, "You believe because you've seen me. Blessed are those who haven't seen me but believe." ✦ Blessed is everyone who takes refuge in him.

*1 Peter 1:8; 2 Corinthians 5:7; 1 John 4:19; 1 John 4:16; Ephesians 1:13; Colossians 1:27; 1 John 4:20; John 20:29; Psalm 2:12*

## Evening Reading

The Lord Our Righteousness.

We've all become unclean, and all our righteous acts are like permanently stained rags. ✦ I will come with the mighty deeds of the Almighty Lord. I will praise your righteousness, yours alone. ✦ I will find joy in the Lord. I will delight in my God. He has dressed me in the clothes of salvation. He has wrapped me in the robe of righteousness like a bridegroom with a priest's turban, like a bride with her jewels. ✦ "Bring out the best robe, and put it on him." ✦ "She has been given the privilege of wearing dazzling, pure linen." This fine linen represents the things that God's holy people do that have his approval. ✦ I consider everything else worthless because I'm much better off knowing Christ Jesus my Lord . . . in order to gain Christ and to have a relationship with him. This means that I didn't receive God's approval by obeying his laws. The opposite is true! I have God's approval through faith in Christ. This is the approval that comes from God and is based on faith.

*Jeremiah 23:6; Isaiah 64:6; Psalm 71:16; Isaiah 61:10; Luke 15:22; Revelation 19:8; Philippians 3:8–9*

## MORNING READING

May your power be with me and free me from evil.

"Why are you sleeping? Get up, and pray that you won't be tempted." ✦ "You want to do what's right, but you're weak." ✦ "I've asked you for two things. Don't keep them from me before I die: Keep vanity and lies far away from me. Don't give me either poverty or riches. Feed me only the food I need, or I may feel satisfied and deny you and say, 'Who is the LORD?' or I may become poor and steal and give the name of my God a bad reputation." ✦ The LORD guards you from every evil. He guards your life. ✦ I will rescue you from the power of wicked people and free you from the power of tyrants. ✦ We know that those who have been born from God don't go on sinning. Rather, the Son of God protects them, and the evil one can't harm them. ✦ Because you have obeyed my command to endure, I will keep you safe during the time of testing which is coming to the whole world to test those living on earth. ✦ [The Lord] knows how to rescue godly people when they are tested.

*1 Chronicles 4:10; Luke 22:46; Matthew 26:41; Proverbs 30:7–9; Psalm 121:7; Jeremiah 15:21; 1 John 5:18; Revelation 3:10; 2 Peter 2:9*

## EVENING READING

Even one star differs in splendor from another star.

On the road they had argued about who was the greatest. He sat down and called the twelve apostles. He told them, "Whoever wants to be the most important person must take the last place and be a servant to everyone else." ✦ All of you must serve each other with humility, because God opposes the arrogant but favors the humble. Be humbled by God's power so that when the right time comes he will honor you. ✦ Have the same attitude that Christ Jesus had. Although he was in the form of God and equal with God, he did not take advantage of this equality. Instead, he emptied himself by taking on the form of a servant, by becoming like other humans, by having a human appearance. . . . This is why God has given him an exceptional honor—the name honored above all other names—so that at the name of Jesus everyone in heaven, on earth, and in the world below will kneel. ✦ Those who are wise will shine like the brightness on the horizon. Those who lead many people to righteousness will shine like the stars forever and ever.

*1 Corinthians 15:41; Mark 9:34–35; 1 Peter 5:5–6; Philippians 2:5–7, 9–10; Daniel 12:3*

# February 3

## MORNING READING

"Be strong. . . . Work, because I am with you,"
declares the LORD of Armies.

"I am the vine. You are the branches. Those who live in me while I live in them will produce a lot of fruit. But you can't produce anything without me." ✦ I can do everything through Christ who strengthens me. ✦ Receive your power from the Lord and from his mighty strength. ✦ "The joy you have in the LORD is your strength." ✦ This is what the LORD of Armies says: Be strong so that the temple might be rebuilt, you people who are presently listening to the words from the mouths of the prophets. ✦ Strengthen limp hands. Steady weak knees. Tell those who are terrified, "Be brave; don't be afraid." ✦ The LORD turned to him and said, "You will rescue Israel . . . with the strength you have." ✦ If God is for us, who can be against us? ✦ We don't become discouraged, since God has given us this ministry through his mercy. ✦ Certainly, each of us will receive everlasting life at the proper time, if we don't give up. ✦ Thank God that he gives us the victory through our Lord Jesus Christ.

*Haggai 2:4; John 15:5; Philippians 4:13; Ephesians 6:10; Nehemiah 8:10; Zechariah 8:9; Isaiah 35:3–4; Judges 6:14; Romans 8:31; 2 Corinthians 4:1; Galatians 6:9; 1 Corinthians 15:57*

## EVENING READING

Even the darkness is not too dark for you.

God's eyes are on a person's ways. He sees all his steps. There's no darkness or deep shadow where troublemakers can hide. ✦ "No one can hide so that I can't see him. . . . I fill heaven and earth!" declares the LORD. ✦ You do not need to fear terrors of the night . . . plagues that roam the dark. . . . You have made the Most High your home. No harm will come to you. No sickness will come near your house. ✦ Your guardian will not fall asleep. . . . The LORD is your guardian. The LORD is the shade over your right hand. The sun will not beat down on you during the day, nor will the moon at night. The LORD guards you from every evil. ✦ Even though I walk through the dark valley of death, because you are with me, I fear no harm.

*Psalm 139:12; Job 34:21–22; Jeremiah 23:24; Psalm 91:5–6, 9–10; Psalm 121:3, 5–7; Psalm 23:4*

## MORNING READING

"You will never go back there again."

If they had been thinking about the country that they had left, they could have found a way to go back. Instead, these men were longing for a better country—a heavenly country. That is why God is not ashamed to be called their God. He has prepared a city for them. ✦ He chose to suffer with God's people rather than to enjoy the pleasures of sin for a little while. He thought that being insulted for Christ would be better than having the treasures of Egypt. He was looking ahead to his reward. ✦ [The Lord said,] "The person who has God's approval will live by faith. But if he turns back, I will not be pleased with him." We don't belong with those who turn back and are destroyed. Instead, we belong with those who have faith and are saved. ✦ "Whoever starts to plow and looks back is not fit for the kingdom of God." ✦ But it's unthinkable that I could ever brag about anything except the cross of our Lord Jesus Christ. By his cross my relationship to the world and its relationship to me have been crucified. ✦ "Get away from unbelievers. Separate yourselves from them. Have nothing to do with anything unclean. Then I will welcome you." ✦ I'm convinced that God, who began this good work in you, will carry it through to completion on the day of Christ Jesus.

*Deuteronomy 17:16; Hebrews 11:15–16; Hebrews 11:25–26; Hebrews 10:38–39; Luke 9:62; Galatians 6:14; 2 Corinthians 6:17; Philippians 1:6*

## EVENING READING

They talk about the pain of those you have wounded.

[The Lord said,] I was only a little angry, but they made things worse. ✦ Brothers and sisters, if a person gets trapped by wrongdoing, those of you who are spiritual should help that person turn away from doing wrong. Do it in a gentle way. At the same time watch yourself so that you also are not tempted. ✦ Realize that whoever brings a sinner back from the error of his ways will save him from death, and many sins will be forgiven. ✦ Cheer up those who are discouraged, help the weak, and be patient with everyone. ✦ So let's stop criticizing each other. Instead, you should decide never to do anything that would make other Christians have doubts or lose their faith. ✦ So those of us who have a strong faith must be patient with the weaknesses of those whose faith is not so strong. We must not think only of ourselves. ✦ Love . . . isn't happy when injustice is done, but it is happy with the truth. ✦ So, people who think they are standing firmly should be careful that they don't fall.

*Psalm 69:26; Zechariah 1:15; Galatians 6:1; James 5:20; 1 Thessalonians 5:14; Romans 14:13; Romans 15:1; 1 Corinthians 13:4, 6; 1 Corinthians 10:12*

## MORNING READING

"I came so that my sheep will have life and so that they will have everything they need."

[God said] "You must never eat from the tree of the knowledge of good and evil because when you eat from it, you will certainly die." ✦ [Eve] took some of the fruit and ate it. She also gave some to her husband, who was with her, and he ate it. ✦ The payment for sin is death, but the gift that God freely gives is everlasting life found in Christ Jesus our Lord. ✦ It is certain that death ruled because of one person's failure. It's even more certain that those who receive God's overflowing kindness and the gift of his approval will rule in life because of one person, Jesus Christ. ✦ Since a man brought death, a man also brought life back from death. As everyone dies because of Adam, so also everyone will be made alive because of Christ. ✦ Christ has destroyed death, and through the Good News he has brought eternal life into full view. ✦ God has given us eternal life, and this life is found in his Son. The person who has the Son has this life. The person who doesn't have the Son of God doesn't have this life. ✦ God sent his Son into the world, not to condemn the world, but to save the world.

*John 10:10; Genesis 2:17; Genesis 3:6; Romans 6:23; Romans 5:17; 1 Corinthians 15:21–22; 2 Timothy 1:10; 1 John 5:11–12; John 3:17*

## EVENING READING

Christ's judgment seat.

We know that God's judgment is right when he condemns people for doing these things. ✦ "When the Son of Man comes in his glory and all his angels are with him, he will sit on his glorious throne. The people of every nation will be gathered in front of him. He will separate them as a shepherd separates the sheep from the goats." ✦ "Then the people who have God's approval will shine like the sun in their Father's kingdom." ✦ Who will accuse those whom God has chosen? God has approved of them. Who will condemn them? Christ has died, and more importantly, he was brought back to life. Christ has the highest position in heaven. Christ also intercedes for us. ✦ So those who are believers in Christ Jesus can no longer be condemned. ✦ But when the Lord judges us, he disciplines us so that we won't be condemned along with the rest of the world.

*2 Corinthians 5:10; Romans 2:2; Matthew 25:31–32; Matthew 13:43; Romans 8:33–34; Romans 8:1; 1 Corinthians 11:32*

## MORNING READING

Our Lord was very kind to me.
Through his kindness he brought me to faith and
gave me the love that Christ Jesus shows people.

You know about the kindness of our Lord Jesus Christ. He was rich, yet for your sake he became poor in order to make you rich through his poverty. ✦ Where sin increased, God's kindness increased even more. ✦ He did this through Christ Jesus out of his generosity to us in order to show his extremely rich kindness in the world to come. God saved you through faith as an act of kindness. You had nothing to do with it. Being saved is a gift from God. It's not the result of anything you've done, so no one can brag about it. ✦ We know that people don't receive God's approval because of their own efforts to live according to a set of standards, but only by believing in Jesus Christ. So we also believed in Jesus Christ in order to receive God's approval by faith in Christ and not because of our own efforts. People won't receive God's approval because of their own efforts to live according to a set of standards. ✦ He saved us, but not because of anything we had done to gain his approval. Instead, because of his mercy he saved us through the washing in which the Holy Spirit gives us new birth and renewal. God poured a generous amount of the Spirit on us through Jesus Christ our Savior.

*1 Timothy 1:14; 2 Corinthians 8:9; Romans 5:20; Ephesians 2:7–9; Galatians 2:16; Titus 3:5–6*

## EVENING READING

"I am the bright morning star."

A star will come from Jacob. ✦ The night is almost over, and the day is near. So we should get rid of the things that belong to the dark and take up the weapons that belong to the light. ✦ When the day brings a cooling breeze and the shadows flee, turn around, my beloved. Run like a gazelle or a young stag on the mountains that separate us! ✦ Someone is calling. . . . "Watchman, how much of the night is left? Watchman, how much of the night is left?" The watchman answers, "Morning is coming, and night will come again. If you need to ask, come back and ask." ✦ "I am the light of the world." ✦ I will also give them the morning star. ✦ Be careful! Watch! You don't know the exact time. It is like a man who went on a trip. As he left home, he put his servants in charge. He assigned work to each one and ordered the guard to be alert. Therefore, be alert. . . . Make sure he doesn't come suddenly and find you asleep. I'm telling everyone what I'm telling you: 'Be alert!' "

*Revelation 22:16; Numbers 24:17; Romans 13:12; Song of Songs 2:17; Isaiah 21:11–12; John 8:12; Revelation 2:28; Mark 13:33–37*

## MORNING READING

When you have eaten all you want,
thank the LORD your God for the good land he has given you.

Be careful that you don't forget the LORD your God. ✦ When one of them saw that he was healed, he turned back and praised God in a loud voice. He quickly bowed at Jesus' feet and thanked him. (The man was a Samaritan.) Jesus asked, "Weren't ten men made clean? Where are the other nine? Only this foreigner came back to praise God." ✦ Everything God created is good. Nothing should be rejected if it is received with prayers of thanks. The word of God and prayer set it apart as holy. ✦ When people eat all kinds of foods, they honor the Lord as they eat, since they give thanks to God. ✦ It is the LORD's blessing that makes a person rich, and hard work adds nothing to it. ✦ Praise the LORD, my soul! Praise his holy name, all that is within me. Praise the LORD, my soul. . . . He is the one who forgives all your sins . . . the one who crowns you with mercy and compassion.

*Deuteronomy 8:10; Deuteronomy 8:11; Luke 17:15–18;*
*1 Timothy 4:4–5; Proverbs 10:22; Psalm 103:1–4*

## EVENING READING

[Jesus] felt sorry for them.

Jesus Christ is the same yesterday, today, and forever. ✦ We have a chief priest who is able to sympathize with our weaknesses. He was tempted in every way that we are, but he didn't sin. ✦ The chief priest can be gentle with people who are ignorant and easily deceived. ✦ He went back and found them asleep. He said to Peter, "Simon, are you sleeping? Couldn't you stay awake for one hour? Stay awake, and pray that you won't be tempted. You want to do what's right, but you're weak." ✦ As a father has compassion for his children, so the LORD has compassion for those who fear him. He certainly knows what we are made of. He bears in mind that we are dust. ✦ You, O Lord, are a compassionate and merciful God. You are patient, always faithful and ready to forgive. Turn toward me, and have pity on me. Give me your strength because I am your servant. Save me because I am the son of your female servant.

*Matthew 14:14; Hebrews 13:8; Hebrews 4:15; Hebrews 5:2;*
*Mark 14:37–38; Psalm 103:13–14; Psalm 86:15–16*

## Morning Reading

"I don't call you servants anymore,
because a servant doesn't know what his master is doing.
But I've called you friends."

The Lord said, "I shouldn't hide what I am going to do from Abraham." ✦ "Knowledge about the mysteries of the kingdom of heaven has been given to you." ✦ God has revealed those things to us by his Spirit. The Spirit searches everything, especially the deep things of God. ✦ We speak about the mystery of God's wisdom. It is a wisdom that has been hidden, which God had planned for our glory before the world began. ✦ Blessed is the person you choose and invite to live with you in your courtyards. We will be filled with good food from your house, from your holy temple. ✦ The Lord advises those who fear him. He reveals to them the intent of his promise. ✦ "I gave them the message that you gave me. They have accepted this message, and they know for sure that I came from you. They have believed that you sent me." ✦ "You are my friends if you obey my commandments."

*John 15:15; Genesis 18:17; Matthew 13:11; 1 Corinthians 2:10; 1 Corinthians 2:7; Psalm 65:4; Psalm 25:14; John 17:8; John 15:14*

## Evening Reading

You will call your walls Salvation and your gates Praise.

The wall of the city had 12 foundations. The 12 names of the 12 apostles of the lamb were written on them. ✦ That is why you are no longer foreigners and outsiders but citizens together with God's people and members of God's family. You are built on the foundation of the apostles and prophets. Christ Jesus himself is the cornerstone. In him all the parts of the building fit together and grow into a holy temple in the Lord. Through him you, also, are being built in the Spirit together with others into a place where God lives. ✦ Certainly you have tasted that the Lord is good! You are coming to Christ, the living stone who was rejected by humans but was chosen as precious by God. You come to him as living stones, a spiritual house that is being built into a holy priesthood. So offer spiritual sacrifices that God accepts through Jesus Christ. ✦ You are praised with silence in Zion, O God.

*Isaiah 60:18; Revelation 21:14; Ephesians 2:19–22; 1 Peter 2:3–5; Psalm 65:1*

## MORNING READING

"Now he has peace."

Your sun will no longer go down, nor will your moon disappear. The LORD will be your everlasting light, and your days of sadness will be over. ✦ He will swallow up death forever. The Almighty LORD will wipe away tears from every face, and he will remove the disgrace of his people from the whole earth. ✦ "These are the people who are coming out of the terrible suffering. They have washed their robes and made them white in the blood of the lamb. That is why they are in front of the throne of God. They serve him day and night in his temple. The one who sits on the throne will spread his tent over them. They will never be hungry or thirsty again. Neither the sun nor any burning heat will ever overcome them. The lamb in the center near the throne will be their shepherd. He will lead them to springs filled with the water of life." ✦ "He will wipe every tear from their eyes. There won't be any more death. There won't be any grief, crying, or pain, because the first things have disappeared."

*Luke 16:25; Isaiah 60:20; Isaiah 25:8; Revelation 7:14–17; Revelation 21:4*

## EVENING READING

"The night when no one can do anything is coming."

"From now on those who die believing in the Lord are blessed." "Yes," says the Spirit. "Let them rest from their hard work. What they have done goes with them." ✦ There the wicked stop their raging. There the weary are able to rest. ✦ Samuel asked Saul, "Why did you disturb me by conjuring me up?" ✦ Whatever presents itself for you to do, do it with all your might, because there is no work, planning, knowledge, or skill in the grave where you're going. ✦ Those who are dead do not praise the LORD, nor do those who go into the silence of the grave. ✦ My life is coming to an end, and it is now time for me to be poured out as a sacrifice to God. I have fought the good fight. I have completed the race. I have kept the faith. The prize that shows I have God's approval is now waiting for me. The Lord, who is a fair judge, will give me that prize on that day. ✦ Therefore, a time of rest and worship exists for God's people. Those who entered his place of rest also rested from their work as God did from his.

*John 9:4; Revelation 14:13; Job 3:17; 1 Samuel 28:15; Ecclesiastes 9:10; Psalm 115:17; 2 Timothy 4:6–8; Hebrews 4:9–10*

## MORNING READING

"Your eye is the lamp of your body.
When your eye is unclouded, your whole body is full of light."

A person who isn't spiritual doesn't accept the teachings of God's Spirit. He thinks they're nonsense. He can't understand them because a person must be spiritual to evaluate them. ✦ Uncover my eyes so that I may see the miraculous things in your teachings. ✦ "I am the light of the world. Whoever follows me will have a life filled with light and will never live in the dark." ✦ As all of us reflect the Lord's glory with faces that are not covered with veils, we are being changed into his image with ever-increasing glory. This comes from the Lord, who is the Spirit. ✦ God who said that light should shine out of darkness has given us light. For that reason we bring to light the knowledge about God's glory which shines from Christ's face. ✦ I pray that the glorious Father . . . would give you a spirit of wisdom and revelation as you come to know Christ better. . . . You will know the confidence that he calls you to have and the glorious wealth that God's people will inherit.

*Luke 11:34; 1 Corinthians 2:14; Psalm 119:18; John 8:12; 2 Corinthians 3:18; 2 Corinthians 4:6; Ephesians 1:17–18*

## EVENING READING

"He did strike a rock,
and water did gush out,
and the streams did overflow."

All our ancestors who left Egypt were under the cloud, and they all went through the sea. They were all united with Moses by baptism in the cloud and in the sea. All of them ate the same spiritual food, and all of them drank the same spiritual drink. They drank from the spiritual rock that went with them, and that rock was Christ. ✦ One of the soldiers stabbed Jesus' side with his spear, and blood and water immediately came out. ✦ He was wounded for our rebellious acts. He was crushed for our sins. He was punished so that we could have peace, and we received healing from his wounds. ✦ "You don't want to come to me to get eternal life." ✦ "My people have done two things wrong. They have abandoned me, the fountain of life-giving water. They have also dug their own cisterns, broken cisterns that can't hold water." ✦ [Jesus] said loudly, "Whoever is thirsty must come to me to drink." ✦ Let those who are thirsty come! Let those who want the water of life take it as a gift.

*Psalm 78:20; 1 Corinthians 10:1–4; John 19:34; Isaiah 53:5; John 5:40; Jeremiah 2:13; John 7:37; Revelation 22:17*

## MORNING READING

Then those who feared the LORD spoke to one another,
and the LORD paid attention and listened.
A book was written in his presence to be a reminder
to those who feared the LORD and respected his name.

While they were talking, Jesus approached them and began walking with them. ✦ "Where two or three have come together in my name, I am there among them." ✦ My coworkers, whose names are in the Book of Life. ✦ Let Christ's word with all its wisdom and richness live in you. Use psalms, hymns, and spiritual songs to teach and instruct yourselves about God's kindness. Sing to God in your hearts. ✦ Encourage each other every day while you have the opportunity. If you do this, none of you will be deceived by sin and become stubborn. ✦ "I can guarantee that on judgment day people will have to give an account of every careless word they say. By your words you will be declared innocent, or by your words you will be declared guilty." ✦ "Look! It is written in front of me. I will not be silent, but I will repay. I will repay you in full."

*Malachi 3:16; Luke 24:15; Matthew 18:20; Philippians 4:3; Colossians 3:16; Hebrews 3:13; Matthew 12:36–37; Isaiah 65:6*

## EVENING READING

The LORD's trees . . . drink their fill.

I will be like dew to the people of Israel. They will blossom like flowers. They will be firmly rooted like cedars from Lebanon. They will be like growing branches. They will be beautiful like olive trees. They will be fragrant like cedars from Lebanon. ✦ Blessed is the person who trusts the LORD. The LORD will be his confidence. He will be like a tree that is planted by water. It will send its roots down to a stream. It will not be afraid in the heat of summer. Its leaves will turn green. It will not be anxious during droughts. It will not stop producing fruit. ✦ "I cut down tall trees, and I make small trees grow tall. I dry up green trees, and I make dry trees grow. I, the LORD, have spoken, and I will do it." ✦ Righteous people flourish like palm trees and grow tall like the cedars in Lebanon. They are planted in the LORD's house. They blossom in our God's courtyards. Even when they are old, they still bear fruit. They are always healthy and fresh.

*Psalm 104:16; Hosea 14:5–6; Jeremiah 17:7–8; Ezekiel 17:24; Psalm 92:12–14*

## MORNING READING

"They will be mine," says the Lord of Armies.
"On that day I will make them my special possession."

"I made your name known to the people you gave me. They are from this world. They belonged to you, and you gave them to me. They did what you told them. . . . I pray for them. I'm not praying for the world but for those you gave me, because they are yours. Everything I have is yours, and everything you have is mine. I have been given glory by the people you have given me. . . . Father, I want those you have given to me to be with me, to be where I am. I want them to see my glory, which you gave me because you loved me before the world was made." ✦ "I will come again. . . . Then I will bring you into my presence." ✦ When he comes to be honored among all his holy people and admired by all who have believed in him. ✦ We who are still alive will be taken in the clouds to meet the Lord in the air. In this way we will always be with the Lord. ✦ Then you will be a beautiful crown in the hand of the Lord, a royal crown in the hand of your God.

*Malachi 3:17; John 17:6, 9–10, 24; John 14:3;
2 Thessalonians 1:10; 1 Thessalonians 4:17; Isaiah 62:3*

## EVENING READING

"Please let me see your glory."

The same God who said that light should shine out of darkness has given us light. For that reason we bring to light the knowledge about God's glory which shines from Christ's face. ✦ The Word became human and lived among us. We saw his glory. It was the glory that the Father shares with his only Son, a glory full of kindness and truth. ✦ No one has ever seen God. God's only Son, the one who is closest to the Father's heart, has made him known. ✦ My soul thirsts for God, for the living God. When may I come to see God's face? ✦ When you said, "Seek my face," my heart said to you, "O Lord, I will seek your face." ✦ As all of us reflect the Lord's glory with faces that are not covered with veils, we are being changed into his image with ever-increasing glory. This comes from the Lord, who is the Spirit. ✦ "Father, I want those you have given to me to be with me, to be where I am. I want them to see my glory, which you gave me because you loved me before the world was made."

*Exodus 33:18; 2 Corinthians 4:6; John 1:14; John 1:18;
Psalm 42:2; Psalm 27:8; 2 Corinthians 3:18; John 17:24*

## Morning Reading

Something . . . looked like a throne made of sapphire.
On the throne was a figure that looked like a human.

A human, Christ Jesus. ✦ Becoming like other humans, by having a human appearance. ✦ Since all of these sons and daughters have flesh and blood, Jesus took on flesh and blood to be like them. He did this so that by dying he would destroy the one who had power over death (that is, the devil). ✦ "I am the first and the last, the living one. I was dead, but now I am alive forever." ✦ We know that Christ, who was brought back to life, will never die again. Death no longer has any power over him. When he died, he died once and for all to sin's power. But now he lives, and he lives for God. ✦ What if you see the Son of Man go where he was before? ✦ He worked with that same power in Christ when he brought him back to life and gave him the highest position in heaven. ✦ All of God lives in Christ's body. ✦ He was weak when he was crucified, but by God's power he lives. We are weak with him, but by God's power we will live for you with his help.

*Ezekiel 1:26; 1 Timothy 2:5; Philippians 2:7; Hebrews 2:14; Revelation 1:18; Romans 6:9–10; John 6:62; Ephesians 1:20; Colossians 2:9; 2 Corinthians 13:4*

## Evening Reading

Your promise gave me a new life.

This is what Scripture says: "The first man, Adam, became a living being." The last Adam became a life-giving spirit. ✦ The Father is the source of life, and he has enabled the Son to be the source of life too. ✦ Jesus said to her, "I am the one who brings people back to life, and I am life itself. Those who believe in me will live even if they die. Everyone who lives and believes in me will never die." ✦ He was the source of life, and that life was the light for humanity. ✦ However, he gave the right to become God's children to everyone who believed in him. These people didn't become God's children in a physical way—from a human impulse or from a husband's desire to have a child. They were born from God. ✦ Life is spiritual. Your physical existence doesn't contribute to that life. The words that I have spoken to you are spiritual. They are life. ✦ God's word is living and active. It is sharper than any two-edged sword and cuts as deep as the place where soul and spirit meet, the place where joints and marrow meet. God's word judges a person's thoughts and intentions.

*Psalm 119:50; 1 Corinthians 15:45; John 5:26; John 11:25–26; John 1:4; John 1:12–13; John 6:63; Hebrews 4:12*

## MORNING READING

"This is the way it has to be now.
This is the proper way to do everything that God requires of us."

"I am happy to do your will, O my God." Your teachings are deep within me. ✦ "Don't ever think that I came to set aside Moses' Teachings or the Prophets. I didn't come to set them aside but to make them come true. I can guarantee this truth: Until the earth and the heavens disappear, neither a period nor a comma will disappear from Moses' Teachings before everything has come true." ✦ The LORD is pleased because he does what is right. He praises the greatness of his teachings and makes them glorious. ✦ "Unless you live a life that has God's approval and do it more faithfully than the scribes and Pharisees, you will never enter the kingdom of heaven." ✦ It is impossible to do what God's standards demand because of the weakness our human nature has. But God sent his Son to have a human nature as sinners have and to pay for sin. That way God condemned sin in our corrupt nature. Therefore, we, who do not live by our corrupt nature but by our spiritual nature, are able to meet God's standards. ✦ Christ is the fulfillment of Moses' Teachings so that everyone who has faith may receive God's approval.

*Matthew 3:15; Psalm 40:8; Matthew 5:17–18; Isaiah 42:21; Matthew 5:20; Romans 8:3–4; Romans 10:4*

## EVENING READING

I am your possession and your property.

As long as I have you, I don't need anyone else in heaven or on earth. My body and mind may waste away, but God remains the foundation of my life and my inheritance forever. ✦ The LORD is my inheritance and my cup. You are the one who determines my destiny. Your boundary lines mark out pleasant places for me. Indeed, my inheritance is something beautiful. ✦ My soul can say, "The LORD is my lot in life. That is why I find hope in him." ✦ Your written instructions are mine forever. They are the joy of my heart. ✦ O God, you are my God. At dawn I search for you. My soul thirsts for you. My body longs for you in a dry, parched land where there is no water. ✦ You have been my help. In the shadow of your wings, I sing joyfully. ✦ My beloved is mine, and I am his.

*Numbers 18:20; Psalm 73:25–26; Psalm 16:5–6; Lamentations 3:24; Psalm 119:111; Psalm 63:1; Psalm 63:7; Song of Songs 2:16*

## MORNING READING

Who can say,
"I've made my heart pure."

The Lord looks down from heaven on Adam's descendants to see if there is anyone who acts wisely, if there is anyone who seeks help from God. Everyone has turned away. Together they have become rotten to the core. No one, not even one person, does good things. ✦ Those who are under the control of the corrupt nature can't please God. ✦ Although I have the desire to do what is right, I don't do it. I don't do the good I want to do. Instead, I do the evil that I don't want to do. ✦ We've all become unclean, and all our righteous acts are like permanently stained rags. All of us shrivel like leaves, and our sins carry us away like the wind. ✦ Scripture states that the whole world is controlled by the power of sin. Therefore, a promise based on faith in Jesus Christ could be given to those who believe. ✦ God was using Christ to restore his relationship with humanity. He didn't hold people's faults against them. ✦ If we say, "We aren't sinful" we are deceiving ourselves, and the truth is not in us. God is faithful and reliable. If we confess our sins, he forgives them and cleanses us from everything we've done wrong.

*Proverbs 20:9; Psalm 14:2–3; Romans 8:8; Romans 7:18–19; Isaiah 64:6; Galatians 3:22; 2 Corinthians 5:19; 1 John 1:8–9*

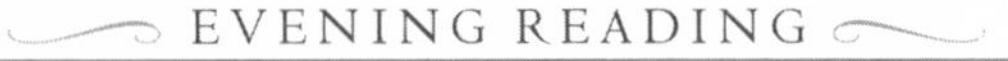

## EVENING READING

The ocean rises with its pounding waves.

The Lord above is mighty—mightier than the sound of raging water, mightier than the foaming waves of the sea. ✦ O Lord God of Armies, who is like you? Mighty Lord, even your faithfulness surrounds you. You rule the raging sea. When its waves rise, you quiet them. ✦ Don't you fear me?" asks the Lord. "Don't you tremble in my presence? I made the sand a boundary for the sea, a permanent barrier that it cannot cross. ✦ When you go through the sea, I am with you. When you go through rivers, they will not sweep you away. ✦ Peter got out of the boat and walked on the water toward Jesus. But when he noticed how strong the wind was, he became afraid and started to sink. He shouted, "Lord, save me!" Immediately, Jesus reached out, caught hold of him, and said, "You have so little faith! Why did you doubt? ✦ Even when I am afraid, I still trust you.

*Psalm 93:3; Psalm 93:4; Psalm 89:8–9; Jeremiah 5:22; Isaiah 43:2; Matthew 14:29–31; Psalm 56:3*

## MORNING READING

Your expressions of love are better than wine,
better than the fragrance of cologne.

Christ also loved us. He gave his life for us as an offering and sacrifice, a soothing aroma to God. ✦ "I am laying a chosen and precious cornerstone in Zion." ✦ This is why God has given him an exceptional honor—the name honored above all other names—so that at the name of Jesus everyone in heaven, on earth, and in the world below will kneel. ✦ All of God lives in Christ's body. ✦ "If you love me, you will obey my commandments." ✦ God's love has been poured into our hearts by the Holy Spirit, who has been given to us. ✦ The fragrance of the perfume filled the house. ✦ They realized that these men had been with Jesus. ✦ O LORD, our Lord, how majestic is your name throughout the earth! Your glory is sung above the heavens. ✦ "Immanuel" . . . "God is with us." ✦ He will be named: Wonderful Counselor, Mighty God, Everlasting Father, Prince of Peace. ✦ The name of the LORD is a strong tower. A righteous person runs to it and is safe.

*Song of Songs 1:2–3; Ephesians 5:2; 1 Peter 2:6; Philippians 2:9–10; Colossians 2:9; John 14:15; Romans 5:5; John 12:3; Acts 4:13; Psalm 8:1; Matthew 1:23; Isaiah 9:6; Proverbs 18:10*

## EVENING READING

While we are in this tent, we sigh.

You know all my desires, O Lord, and my groaning has not been hidden from you. ✦ My guilt has overwhelmed me. Like a heavy load, it is more than I can bear. ✦ What a miserable person I am! Who will rescue me from my dying body? ✦ We know that all creation has been groaning with the pains of childbirth up to the present time. However, not only creation groans. We, who have the Spirit as the first of God's gifts, also groan inwardly. We groan as we eagerly wait for our adoption, the freeing of our bodies from sin. ✦ You have to suffer different kinds of trouble for a little while now. ✦ I know that I will die soon. ✦ This body that decays must be changed into a body that cannot decay. This mortal body must be changed into a body that will live forever. When this body that decays is changed into a body that cannot decay, and this mortal body is changed into a body that will live forever, then the teaching of Scripture will come true: "Death is turned into victory!"

*2 Corinthians 5:4; Psalm 38:9; Psalm 38:4; Romans 7:24; Romans 8:22–23; 1 Peter 1:6; 2 Peter 1:14; 1 Corinthians 15:53–54*

## MORNING READING

He will take the entire bull . . .
to a clean place outside the camp
where the ashes are dumped.
He will burn it there on a wood fire.

So the soldiers took Jesus. He carried his own cross and went out of the city to a location called The Skull. (In Hebrew this place is called *Golgotha.*) The soldiers crucified Jesus. ✦ The bodies of those animals were burned outside the Israelite camp. That is why Jesus suffered outside the gates of Jerusalem. He suffered to make the people holy with his own blood. So we must go to him outside the camp and endure the insults he endured. ✦ Faith knows . . . what it means to share his suffering. ✦ Be happy as you share Christ's sufferings. Then you will also be full of joy when he appears again in his glory. ✦ Our suffering is light and temporary and is producing for us an eternal glory that is greater than anything we can imagine.

*Leviticus 4:11–12; John 19:16–18; Hebrews 13:11–13;*
*Philippians 3:10; 1 Peter 4:13; 2 Corinthians 4:17*

## EVENING READING

God created humans in his image.

If we are God's children, we shouldn't think that the divine being is like an image made from gold, silver, or stone, an image that is the product of human imagination and skill. ✦ God is rich in mercy because of his great love for us. We were dead because of our failures, but he made us alive together with Christ. ✦ God has made us what we are. He has created us in Christ Jesus to live lives filled with good works that he has prepared for us to do. ✦ This is true because he already knew his people and had already appointed them to have the same form as the image of his Son. Therefore, his Son is the firstborn among many children. ✦ We do know that when Christ appears we will be like him because we will see him as he is. ✦ When I wake up, I will be satisfied with seeing you. ✦ Everyone who wins the victory will inherit these things. I will be their God, and they will be my children. ✦ If we are his children, we are also God's heirs. If we share in Christ's suffering in order to share his glory, we are heirs together with him.

*Genesis 1:27; Acts 17:29; Ephesians 2:4–5; Ephesians 2:10;*
*Romans 8:29; 1 John 3:2; Psalm 17:15; Revelation 21:7; Romans 8:17*

## MORNING READING

You are my refuge on the day of disaster.

Many are saying, "Who can show us anything good?" Let the light of your presence shine on us, O LORD. ✦ I will sing about your strength. In the morning I will joyfully sing about your mercy. You have been my stronghold and a place of safety in times of trouble. ✦ When all was well with me, I said, "I will never be shaken." . . . I will cry out to you, O LORD. I will plead to the Lord for mercy: "How will you profit if my blood is shed, if I go into the pit? Will the dust of my body give thanks to you? Will it tell about your truth?" Hear, O LORD, and have pity on me! O LORD, be my helper! ✦ "I abandoned you for one brief moment, but I will bring you back with unlimited compassion. I hid my face from you for a moment in a burst of anger, but I will have compassion on you with everlasting kindness," says the LORD your defender. ✦ "Your pain will turn to happiness." ✦ Weeping may last for the night, but there is a song of joy in the morning.

*Jeremiah 17:17; Psalm 4:6; Psalm 59:16; Psalm 30:6, 8–10; Isaiah 54:7–8; John 16:20; Psalm 30:5*

## EVENING READING

Adam . . . became the father of a son in his own likeness.

"If only an unclean person could become clean!" ✦ Indeed, I was born guilty. I was a sinner when my mother conceived me. ✦ You were once dead because of your failures and sins. . . . Because of our nature, we deserved God's anger just like everyone else. ✦ I know that God's standards are spiritual, but I have a corrupt nature, sold as a slave to sin. I don't realize what I'm doing. I don't do what I want to do. Instead, I do what I hate. ✦ I know that nothing good lives in me. ✦ Sin came into the world through one person. . . . Through one person's disobedience humanity became sinful. ✦ If humanity died as the result of one person's failure, it is certainly true that God's kindness and the gift given through the kindness of one person, Jesus Christ, have been showered on humanity. ✦ The standards of the Spirit, who gives life through Christ Jesus, have set you free from the standards of sin and death. ✦ Thank God that he gives us the victory through our Lord Jesus Christ.

*Genesis 5:3; Job 14:4; Psalm 51:5; Ephesians 2:1, 3; Romans 7:14–15; Romans 7:18; Romans 5:12, 19; Romans 5:15; Romans 8:2; 1 Corinthians 15:57*

## MORNING READING

The LORD gives wisdom.
From his mouth come knowledge and understanding.

Trust the LORD with all your heart, and do not rely on your own understanding. ✦ If any of you needs wisdom to know what you should do, you should ask God, and he will give it to you. ✦ God's nonsense is wiser than human wisdom, and God's weakness is stronger than human strength. . . . God chose what the world considers nonsense to put wise people to shame. . . . As a result, no one can brag in God's presence. ✦ Your word is a doorway that lets in light, and it helps gullible people understand. ✦ I have treasured your promise in my heart so that I may not sin against you. ✦ All the people spoke well of him. They were amazed to hear the gracious words flowing from his lips. ✦ The temple guards answered, "No human has ever spoken like this man." ✦ You are partners with Christ Jesus because of God. Jesus has become our wisdom sent from God, our righteousness, our holiness, and our ransom from sin.

*Proverbs 2:6; Proverbs 3:5; James 1:5; 1 Corinthians 1:25, 27, 29; Psalm 119:130; Psalm 119:11; Luke 4:22; John 7:46; 1 Corinthians 1:30*

## EVENING READING

The year for my reclaiming you has come.

"Set apart the fiftieth year as holy, and proclaim liberty to everyone living in the land. This is your jubilee year. Every slave will be freed in order to return to his property and to his family." ✦ Your dead will live. Their corpses will rise. Those who lie dead in the dust will wake up and shout for joy, because your dew is a refreshing dew, and the earth will revive the spirits of the dead. ✦ The Lord will come from heaven with a command, with the voice of the archangel, and with the trumpet call of God. First, the dead who believed in Christ will come back to life. Then, together with them, we who are still alive will be taken in the clouds to meet the Lord in the air. In this way we will always be with the Lord. ✦ "I want to free them from the power of the grave. I want to reclaim them from death. Death, I want to be a plague to you. Grave, I want to destroy you." ✦ Their defender is strong. His name is the LORD of Armies.

*Isaiah 63:4; Leviticus 25:10; Isaiah 26:19; 1 Thessalonians 4:16–17; Hosea 13:14; Jeremiah 50:34*

## MORNING READING

He will see and be satisfied because of his suffering.

[Jesus] said, "It is finished!" Then he bowed his head and died. ✦ God had Christ, who was sinless, take our sin so that we might receive God's approval through him. ✦ I have formed these people for myself. They will praise me. ✦ He did this so that now, through the church, he could let the rulers and authorities in heaven know his infinite wisdom. This was God's plan for all of history which he carried out through Christ Jesus our Lord. ✦ He did this through Christ Jesus out of his generosity to us in order to show his extremely rich kindness in the world to come. ✦ You heard and believed the message of truth, the Good News that he has saved you. In him you were sealed with the Holy Spirit whom he promised. This Holy Spirit is the guarantee that we will receive our inheritance. We have this guarantee until we are set free to belong to him. God receives praise and glory for this. ✦ You are chosen people, a royal priesthood, a holy nation, people who belong to God. You were chosen to tell about the excellent qualities of God, who called you out of darkness into his marvelous light.

*Isaiah 53:11; John 19:30; 2 Corinthians 5:21; Isaiah 43:21;*
*Ephesians 3:10–11; Ephesians 2:7; Ephesians 1:13–14; 1 Peter 2:9*

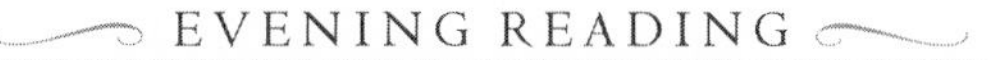

## EVENING READING

[They] tested me in the desert.

When someone is tempted, he shouldn't say that God is tempting him. God can't be tempted by evil, and God doesn't tempt anyone. Everyone is tempted by his own desires as they lure him away and trap him. Then desire becomes pregnant and gives birth to sin. When sin grows up, it gives birth to death. ✦ [The children of Israel] had an unreasonable desire for food in the wilderness. In the desert they tested God. ✦ The Spirit led him while he was in the desert, where he was tempted by the devil for 40 days. During those days Jesus ate nothing, so when they were over, he was hungry. The devil said to him, "If you are the Son of God, tell this stone to become a loaf of bread." ✦ Because Jesus experienced temptation when he suffered, he is able to help others when they are tempted. ✦ Then the Lord said, "Simon, Simon, listen! Satan has demanded to have you apostles for himself. He wants to separate you from me as a farmer separates wheat from husks. But I have prayed for you, Simon, that your faith will not fail."

*Hebrews 3:8; James 1:13–15; Psalm 106:14;*
*Luke 4:1–3; Hebrews 2:18; Luke 22:31–32*

## Morning Reading

I am the Lord who sets you apart as holy.

I am the Lord your God who separated you from other people. . . . Be my holy people because I, the Lord, am holy. I have separated you from other people to be my very own. ✦ Loved by God the Father. ✦ "Use the truth to make them holy. Your words are truth." ✦ May the God who gives peace make you holy in every way. May he keep your whole being—spirit, soul, and body—blameless when our Lord Jesus Christ comes. ✦ That is why Jesus suffered outside the gates of Jerusalem. He suffered to make the people holy with his own blood. ✦ At the same time we can expect what we hope for—the appearance of the glory of our great God and Savior, Jesus Christ. He gave himself for us to set us free from every sin and to cleanse us so that we can be his special people who are enthusiastic about doing good things. ✦ Jesus, who makes people holy, and all those who are made holy have the same Father. That is why Jesus isn't ashamed to call them brothers and sisters. ✦ "I'm dedicating myself to this holy work I'm doing for them so that they, too, will use the truth to be holy." ✦ To live holy lives with the Spirit's help so that you are obedient to Jesus Christ and are sprinkled with his blood.

*Leviticus 20:8; Leviticus 20:24, 26; Jude 1; John 17:17; 1 Thessalonians 5:23; Hebrews 13:12; Titus 2:13–14; Hebrews 2:11; John 17:19; 1 Peter 1:2*

## Evening Reading

Light dawns for righteous people
and joy for those whose motives are decent.

Those who cry while they plant will joyfully sing while they harvest. The person who goes out weeping, carrying his bag of seed, will come home singing, carrying his bundles of grain. ✦ What you plant, whether it's wheat or something else, is only a seed. It doesn't have the form that the plant will have. ✦ Praise the God and Father of our Lord Jesus Christ! God has given us a new birth because of his great mercy. We have been born into a new life that has a confidence which is alive because Jesus Christ has come back to life. . . . You are extremely happy about these things, even though you have to suffer different kinds of trouble for a little while now. The purpose of these troubles is to test your faith as fire tests how genuine gold is. Your faith is more precious than gold, and by passing the test, it gives praise, glory, and honor to God. This will happen when Jesus Christ appears again.

*Psalm 97:11; Psalm 126:5–6; 1 Corinthians 15:37; 1 Peter 1:3, 6–7*

## MORNING READING

Who, then, is this person that fears the LORD?
He is the one whom the LORD will teach which path to choose.

"The eye is the lamp of the body. So if your eye is unclouded, your whole body will be full of light." ✦ Your word is a lamp for my feet and a light for my path. ✦ You will hear a voice behind you saying, "This is the way. Follow it, whether it turns to the right or to the left." ✦ "I will instruct you. I will teach you the way that you should go. I will advise you as my eyes watch over you. Don't be stubborn like a horse or mule. They need a bit and bridle in their mouth to restrain them, or they will not come near you." Many heartaches await wicked people, but mercy surrounds those who trust the LORD. Be glad and find joy in the LORD, you righteous people. Sing with joy, all whose motives are decent. ✦ O LORD, I know that the way humans act is not under their control. Humans do not direct their steps as they walk.

*Psalm 25:12; Matthew 6:22; Psalm 119:105; Isaiah 30:21; Psalm 32:8–11; Jeremiah 10:23*

## EVENING READING

When you lie down, you will not be afraid.
As you lie there, your sleep will be sweet.

A violent windstorm came up. The waves were breaking into the boat so that it was quickly filling up. But he was sleeping on a cushion in the back of the boat. ✦ Never worry about anything. But in every situation let God know what you need in prayers and requests while giving thanks. Then God's peace, which goes beyond anything we can imagine, will guard your thoughts and emotions through Christ Jesus. ✦ I fall asleep in peace the moment I lie down because you alone, O LORD, enable me to live securely. ✦ The LORD gives food to those he loves while they sleep. ✦ While council members were executing Stephen, he called out, "Lord Jesus, welcome my spirit." Then he knelt down and shouted, "Lord, don't hold this sin against them." After he had said this, he died. ✦ We are confident and prefer to live away from this body and to live with the Lord.

*Proverbs 3:24; Mark 4:37–38; Philippians 4:6–7; Psalm 4:8; Psalm 127:2; Acts 7:59–60; 2 Corinthians 5:8*

# February 23

## MORNING READING

The sprinkled blood that speaks a better message than Abel's.

"Look! This is the Lamb of God who takes away the sin of the world." ✦ The lamb who was slaughtered before the creation of the world. ✦ (The blood of bulls and goats cannot take away sins.) For this reason, when Christ came into the world, he said, "You did not want sacrifices and offerings, but you prepared a body for me." ✦ We have been set apart as holy because Jesus Christ did what God wanted him to do by sacrificing his body once and for all. ✦ Abel also brought some choice parts of the firstborn animals from his flock. The Lord approved of Abel and his offering. ✦ Christ . . . loved us. He gave his life for us as an offering and sacrifice, a soothing aroma to God. ✦ We have been sprinkled with his blood to free us from a guilty conscience, and our bodies have been washed with clean water. So we must continue to come to him with a sincere heart and strong faith. ✦ Because of the blood of Jesus we can now confidently go into the holy place.

*Hebrews 12:24; John 1:29; Revelation 13:8; Hebrews 10:4–5; Hebrews 10:10; Genesis 4:4; Ephesians 5:2; Hebrews 10:22; Hebrews 10:19*

## EVENING READING

Who fully understands the power of your anger?

At noon darkness came over the whole land until three in the afternoon. About three o'clock Jesus cried out in a loud voice, "Eli, Eli, lema sabachthani?" which means, "My God, my God, why have you abandoned me?" ✦ The Lord has laid all our sins on him. ✦ So those who are believers in Christ Jesus can no longer be condemned. ✦ Now that we have God's approval by faith, we have peace with God because of what our Lord Jesus Christ has done. ✦ Christ paid the price to free us from the curse that God's laws bring by becoming cursed instead of us. ✦ God has shown us his love by sending his only Son into the world so that we could have life through him. This is love: not that we have loved God, but that he loved us and sent his Son to be the payment for our sins. ✦ That he is a God of justice, a God who approves of people who believe in Jesus.

*Psalm 90:11; Matthew 27:45–46; Isaiah 53:6; Romans 8:1; Romans 5:1; Galatians 3:13; 1 John 4:9–10; Romans 3:26*

## Morning Reading

"This is what the Almighty Lord says:
I will also let the people of Israel ask me
to make them as numerous as sheep."

You don't have the things you want, because you don't pray for them. ✦ "Ask, and you will receive. Search, and you will find. Knock, and the door will be opened for you. Everyone who asks will receive. The one who searches will find, and for the one who knocks, the door will be opened." ✦ We are confident that God listens to us if we ask for anything that has his approval. We know that he listens to our requests. So we know that we already have what we ask him for. ✦ If any of you needs wisdom to know what you should do, you should ask God, and he will give it to you. God is generous to everyone and doesn't find fault with them. ✦ "I am the Lord your God, the one who brought you out of Egypt. Open your mouth wide, and I will fill it." ✦ They need to pray all the time and never give up. ✦ The Lord's eyes are on righteous people. His ears hear their cry for help. . . . Righteous people cry out. The Lord hears and rescues them from all their troubles. ✦ "You will ask for what you want in my name. I'm telling you that I won't have to ask the Father for you. The Father loves you because you have loved me and have believed that I came from God." ✦ "Ask and you will receive so that you can be completely happy."

*Ezekiel 36:37; James 4:2; Matthew 7:7–8; 1 John 5:14–15; James 1:5; Psalm 81:10; Luke 18:1; Psalm 34:15, 17; John 16:26–27; John 16:24*

## Evening Reading

"We accept the good that God gives us.
Shouldn't we also accept the bad?"

I know that your regulations are fair, O Lord, and that you were right to make me suffer. ✦ But now, Lord, you are our Father. We are the clay, and you are our potter. We are the work of your hands. ✦ "He is the Lord. May he do what he thinks is right." ✦ O Lord, even if I would argue my case with you, you would always be right. Yet, I want to talk to you about your justice. ✦ He will act like a refiner and a purifier of silver. ✦ "The Lord disciplines everyone he loves. He severely disciplines everyone he accepts as his child." ✦ Although Jesus was the Son of God, he learned to be obedient through his sufferings. ✦ But be happy as you share Christ's sufferings. Then you will also be full of joy when he appears again in his glory. ✦ "These are the people who are coming out of the terrible suffering. They have washed their robes and made them white in the blood of the lamb."

*Job 2:10; Psalm 119:75; Isaiah 64:8; 1 Samuel 3:18; Jeremiah 12:1; Malachi 3:3; Hebrews 12:6; Hebrews 5:8; 1 Peter 4:13; Revelation 7:14*

# February 25

## MORNING READING

Resist the devil, and he will run away from you.

He will come like a rushing stream. The wind of the LORD pushes him. ✦ Jesus said to him, "Go away, Satan! Scripture says, 'Worship the Lord your God and serve only him.'" Then the devil left him, and angels came to take care of him. ✦ Receive your power from the Lord and from his mighty strength. Put on all the armor that God supplies. In this way you can take a stand against the devil's strategies. ✦ Have nothing to do with the useless works that darkness produces. Instead, expose them for what they are. ✦ I don't want Satan to outwit us. After all, we are not ignorant about Satan's scheming. ✦ Keep your mind clear, and be alert. Your opponent the devil is prowling around like a roaring lion as he looks for someone to devour. Be firm in the faith and resist him, knowing that other believers throughout the world are going through the same kind of suffering. ✦ Our faith is what wins the victory over the world. ✦ Who will accuse those whom God has chosen? God has approved of them.

*James 4:7; Isaiah 59:19; Matthew 4:10–11; Ephesians 6:10–11; Ephesians 5:11; 2 Corinthians 2:11; 1 Peter 5:8–9; 1 John 5:4; Romans 8:33*

## EVENING READING

"If only I knew where I could find God!"

Who among you fears the LORD and obeys his servant? Let those who walk in darkness and have no light trust the name of the LORD and depend upon their God. ✦ When you look for me, you will find me. When you wholeheartedly seek me. ✦ "Search, and you will find. Knock, and the door will be opened for you. Everyone who asks will receive. The one who searches will find, and for the person who knocks, the door will be opened." ✦ Our relationship is with the Father and with his Son Jesus Christ. ✦ But now through Christ Jesus you, who were once far away, have been brought near by the blood of Christ. . . . So Jewish and non-Jewish people can go to the Father in one Spirit. ✦ If we say, "We have a relationship with God" and yet live in the dark, we're lying. We aren't being truthful. ✦ "And remember that I am always with you until the end of time." ✦ "I will never abandon you or leave you." ✦ "[The helper] lives with you and will be in you."

*Job 23:3; Isaiah 50:10; Jeremiah 29:13; Luke 11:9–10; 1 John 1:3; Ephesians 2:13, 18; 1 John 1:6; Matthew 28:20; Hebrews 13:5; John 14:17*

## MORNING READING

Let us look closely at our ways and examine them
and then return to the LORD.

Examine me, O LORD, and test me. Look closely into my heart and mind. ✦ Yet, you desire truth and sincerity. Deep down inside me you teach me wisdom. ✦ I have thought about my life, and I have directed my feet back to your written instructions. Without any hesitation I hurry to obey your commandments. ✦ With this in mind, individuals must determine whether what they are doing is proper when they eat the bread and drink from the cup. ✦ God is faithful and reliable. If we confess our sins, he forgives them and cleanses us from everything we've done wrong. ✦ We have Jesus Christ, who has God's full approval. He speaks on our behalf when we come into the presence of the Father. ✦ Brothers and sisters, because of the blood of Jesus we can now confidently go into the holy place. Jesus has opened a new and living way for us to go through the curtain. (The curtain is his own body.) We have a superior priest in charge of God's house. We have been sprinkled with his blood to free us from a guilty conscience, and our bodies have been washed with clean water. So we must continue to come to him with a sincere heart and strong faith.

*Lamentations 3:40; Psalm 26:2; Psalm 51:6; Psalm 119:59–60;
1 Corinthians 11:28; 1 John 1:9; 1 John 2:1; Hebrews 10:19–22*

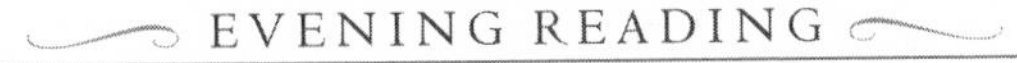

## EVENING READING

There was a rainbow around the throne
which looked like an emerald.

God said, "This is the sign of the promise I am giving to you and every living being that is with you for generations to come. I will put my rainbow in the clouds to be a sign of my promise to the earth. . . . Whenever the rainbow appears in the clouds, I will see it and remember my everlasting promise to every living animal on earth." ✦ A lasting promise to me, with every detail arranged and assured. ✦ God cannot lie when he takes an oath or makes a promise. These two things can never be changed. Those of us who have taken refuge in him hold on to the confidence we have been given. ✦ We are telling you the Good News: What God promised our ancestors has happened. God has fulfilled the promise for us, their descendants, by bringing Jesus back to life. ✦ Jesus Christ is the same yesterday, today, and forever.

*Revelation 4:3; Genesis 9:12–13, 16; 2 Samuel 23:5;
Hebrews 6:18; Acts 13:32–33; Hebrews 13:8*

## Morning Reading

Consider yourselves dead to sin's power but
living for God in the power Christ Jesus gives you.

"Those who listen to what I say and believe in the one who sent me will have eternal life. They won't be judged because they have already passed from death to life." ✦ When I tried to obey the law's standards, those laws killed me. As a result, I live in a relationship with God. I have been crucified with Christ. I no longer live, but Christ lives in me. The life I now live I live by believing in God's Son, who loved me and took the punishment for my sins. ✦ "You will live because I live." ✦ "I give them eternal life. They will never be lost, and no one will tear them away from me. My Father, who gave them to me, is greater than everyone else, and no one can tear them away from my Father. The Father and I are one." ✦ Since you were brought back to life with Christ, focus on the things that are above—where Christ holds the highest position. . . . You have died, and your life is hidden with Christ in God.

*Romans 6:11; John 5:24; Galatians 2:19–20;
John 14:19; John 10:28–30; Colossians 3:1, 3*

## Evening Reading

God is generous to everyone and doesn't find fault with them.

Jesus . . . asked her, "Where did they go? Has anyone condemned you?" The woman answered, "No one, sir." Jesus said, "I don't condemn you either. Go! From now on don't sin." ✦ It is certainly true that God's kindness and the gift given through the kindness of one person, Jesus Christ, have been showered on humanity. . . . The gift brought God's approval. ✦ God is rich in mercy because of his great love for us. We were dead because of our failures, but he made us alive together with Christ. (It is God's kindness that saved you.) God has brought us back to life together with Christ Jesus and has given us a position in heaven with him. He did this through Christ Jesus out of his generosity to us in order to show his extremely rich kindness in the world to come. ✦ God didn't spare his own Son but handed him over to death for all of us. So he will also give us everything along with him.

*James 1:5; John 8:10–11; Romans 5:15–16; Ephesians 2:4–7; Romans 8:32*

## MORNING READING

God loved the world this way:
He gave his only Son so that everyone who
believes in him will not die but will have eternal life.

God . . . has restored our relationship with him through Christ, and has given us this ministry of restoring relationships. In other words, God was using Christ to restore his relationship with humanity. He didn't hold people's faults against them, and he has given us this message of restored relationships to tell others. Therefore, we are Christ's representatives, and through us God is calling you. We beg you on behalf of Christ to become reunited with God. God had Christ, who was sinless, take our sin so that we might receive God's approval through him. ✦ God is love. God has shown us his love by sending his only Son into the world so that we could have life through him. This is love: not that we have loved God, but that he loved us and sent his Son to be the payment for our sins. Dear friends, if this is the way God loved us, we must also love each other.

*John 3:16; 2 Corinthians 5:18–21; 1 John 4:8–11*

## EVENING READING

A person's soul is the LORD's lamp.

When they persisted in asking him questions, he straightened up and said, "The person who is sinless should be the first to throw a stone at her." . . . One by one, beginning with the older men, the scribes and Pharisees left. ✦ God asked, "Who told you that you were naked? Did you eat fruit from the tree I commanded you not to eat from?" ✦ Whoever knows what is right but doesn't do it is sinning. ✦ Whenever our conscience condemns us, we will be reassured that God is greater than our conscience and knows everything. Dear friends, if our conscience doesn't condemn us, we can boldly look to God. ✦ Don't ruin God's work because of what you eat. All food is acceptable, but it's wrong for a person to eat something if it causes someone else to have doubts. . . . The person who does what he knows is right shouldn't feel guilty. He is blessed. ✦ Examine me, O God, and know my mind. Test me, and know my thoughts. See whether I am on an evil path. Then lead me on the everlasting path.

*Proverbs 20:27; John 8:7, 9; Genesis 3:11; James 4:17;*
*1 John 3:20–21; Romans 14:20, 22; Psalm 139:23–24*

## MORNING READING

Do not brag about tomorrow,
because you do not know what another day may bring.

Now is God's acceptable time! Now is the day of salvation! ✦ "The light will still be with you for a little while. Walk while you have light so that darkness won't defeat you. Those who walk in the dark don't know where they're going. While you have the light, believe in the light so that you will become people whose lives show the light." ✦ Whatever presents itself for you to do, do it with all your might, because there is no work, planning, knowledge, or skill in the grave where you're going. ✦ "Then I'll say to myself, 'You've stored up a lot of good things for years to come. Take life easy, eat, drink, and enjoy yourself.' But God said to him, 'You fool! I will demand your life from you tonight! Now who will get what you've accumulated?' That's how it is when a person has material riches but is not rich in his relationship with God." ✦ What is life? You are a mist that is seen for a moment and then disappears. ✦ The world and its evil desires are passing away. But the person who does what God wants lives forever.

*Proverbs 27:1; 2 Corinthians 6:2; John 12:35–36; Ecclesiastes 9:10; Luke 12:19–21; James 4:14; 1 John 2:17*

## EVENING READING

You remain the same, and your life will never end.

Before the mountains were born, before you gave birth to the earth and the world, you were God. You are God from everlasting to everlasting. ✦ "I, the LORD, never change. That is why you descendants of Jacob haven't been destroyed yet." ✦ The same yesterday, today, and forever. ✦ Every good present and every perfect gift comes from above, from the Father who made the sun, moon, and stars. The Father doesn't change like the shifting shadows produced by the sun and the moon. ✦ God never changes his mind when he gives gifts or when he calls someone. ✦ God is not like people. He tells no lies. He is not like humans. He doesn't change his mind. ✦ We were not completely wiped out. His compassion is never limited. ✦ But Jesus lives forever, so he serves as a priest forever. That is why he is always able to save those who come to God through him. He can do this because he always lives and intercedes for them. ✦ "Don't be afraid! I am the first and the last."

*Psalm 102:27; Psalm 90:2; Malachi 3:6; Hebrews 13:8; James 1:17; Romans 11:29; Numbers 23:19; Lamentations 3:22; Hebrews 7:24–25; Revelation 1:17*

## MORNING READING

The spiritual nature produces love.

God is love. Those who live in God's love live in God, and God lives in them. ✦ God's love has been poured into our hearts by the Holy Spirit, who has been given to us. ✦ This honor belongs to those who believe. ✦ We love because God loved us first. ✦ Christ's love guides us. We are convinced of the fact that one man has died for all people. Therefore, all people have died. He died for all people so that those who live should no longer live for themselves but for the man who died and was brought back to life for them. ✦ God has taught you to love each other. ✦ "Love each other as I have loved you. This is what I'm commanding you to do." ✦ Above all, love each other warmly, because love covers many sins. ✦ Live in love as Christ also loved us. He gave his life for us as an offering and sacrifice, a soothing aroma to God.

*Galatians 5:22; 1 John 4:16; Romans 5:5; 1 Peter 2:7; 1 John 4:19; 2 Corinthians 5:14–15; 1 Thessalonians 4:9; John 15:12; 1 Peter 4:8; Ephesians 5:2*

## EVENING READING

The Lord Is My Banner.

If God is for us, who can be against us? ✦ The Lord is on my side. I am not afraid. What can mortals do to me? ✦ You have raised a flag for those who fear you. ✦ The Lord is my light and my salvation. Who is there to fear? The Lord is my life's fortress. Who is there to be afraid of? . . . Even though an army sets up camp against me, my heart will not be afraid. Even though a war breaks out against me, I will still have confidence in the Lord. ✦ "God is with us as our leader." ✦ The Lord of Armies is with us. The God of Jacob is our stronghold. ✦ They will go to war against the lamb. The lamb will conquer them. ✦ Why do the nations gather together? Why do their people devise useless plots? . . . The one enthroned in heaven laughs. The Lord makes fun of them. ✦ Make plans for battle, but they will never succeed. Give orders, but they won't be carried out, because God is with us!

*Exodus 17:15; Romans 8:31; Psalm 118:6; Psalm 60:4; Psalm 27:1, 3; 2 Chronicles 13:12; Psalm 46:7; Revelation 17:14; Psalm 2:1, 4; Isaiah 8:10*

## Morning Reading

God gave him children in the land where he had suffered.

Praise the God and Father of our Lord Jesus Christ! He is the Father who is compassionate and the God who gives comfort. He comforts us whenever we suffer. That is why whenever other people suffer, we are able to comfort them by using the same comfort we have received from God. Because Christ suffered so much for us, we can receive so much comfort from him. ✦ You have to suffer different kinds of trouble for a little while now. The purpose of these troubles is to test your faith as fire tests how genuine gold is. Your faith is more precious than gold, and by passing the test, it gives praise, glory, and honor to God. This will happen when Jesus Christ appears again. ✦ The Lord stood by me and gave me strength so that I could finish spreading the Good News for all the nations to hear. I was snatched out of a lion's mouth. ✦ Those who suffer because that is God's will for them must entrust themselves to a faithful creator and continue to do what is good.

*Genesis 41:52; 2 Corinthians 1:3–5; 1 Peter 1:6–7; 2 Timothy 4:17; 1 Peter 4:19*

## Evening Reading

A time of rest and worship exists for God's people.

There the wicked stop their raging. There the weary are able to rest. There the captives have no troubles at all. There they do not hear the shouting of the slave driver. ✦ "From now on those who die believing in the Lord are blessed." . . . "Let them rest from their hard work. What they have done goes with them." ✦ [Jesus] told his disciples, "Our friend Lazarus is sleeping. . . ." Jesus meant that Lazarus was dead, but the disciples thought Jesus meant that Lazarus was only sleeping. ✦ While we are in this tent, we sigh. ✦ We, who have the Spirit as the first of God's gifts, also groan inwardly. We groan as we eagerly wait for our adoption, the freeing of our bodies from sin. We were saved with this hope in mind. If we hope for something we already see, it's not really hope. Who hopes for what can be seen? But if we hope for what we don't see, we eagerly wait for it with perseverance.

*Hebrews 4:9; Job 3:17–18; Revelation 14:13; John 11:11, 13;*
*2 Corinthians 5:4; Romans 8:23–25*

## MORNING READING

Trust the Lord with all your heart,
and do not rely on your own understanding.
In all your ways acknowledge him,
and he will make your paths smooth.

Trust him at all times, you people. Pour out your hearts in his presence. God is our refuge. ✦ "I will instruct you. I will teach you the way that you should go. I will advise you as my eyes watch over you. Don't be stubborn like a horse or mule. They need a bit and bridle in their mouth to restrain them, or they will not come near you." Many heartaches await wicked people, but mercy surrounds those who trust the Lord. ✦ You will hear a voice behind you saying, "This is the way. Follow it, whether it turns to the right or to the left." ✦ Then Moses said to him, "If your presence is not going with us, don't make us leave this place. How will anyone ever know you're pleased with your people and me unless you go with us? Then we will be different from all other people on the face of the earth."

*Proverbs 3:5–6; Psalm 62:8; Psalm 32:8–10; Isaiah 30:21; Exodus 33:15–16*

## EVENING READING

I run straight toward the goal to win the prize that
God's heavenly call offers in Christ Jesus.

"You will have treasure in heaven. Then follow me!" ✦ "I am your shield. Your reward will be very great." ✦ "Good job! You're a good and faithful servant! You proved that you could be trusted with a small amount. I will put you in charge of a large amount. Come and share your master's happiness." ✦ They will rule as kings forever and ever. ✦ You will receive the crown of glory that will never fade away. ✦ The crown of life. ✦ The prize that shows I have God's approval. ✦ A crown . . . that will be permanent. ✦ "Father, I want those you have given to me to be with me, to be where I am. I want them to see my glory, which you gave me." ✦ In this way we will always be with the Lord. ✦ I consider our present sufferings insignificant compared to the glory that will soon be revealed to us.

*Philippians 3:14; Matthew 19:21; Genesis 15:1; Matthew 25:21;
Revelation 22:5; 1 Peter 5:4; James 1:12; 2 Timothy 4:8;
1 Corinthians 9:25; John 17:24; 1 Thessalonians 4:17; Romans 8:18*

## MORNING READING

Keep your mind on things above, not on worldly things.

Don't love the world and what it offers. Those who love the world don't have the Father's love in them. ✦ "Stop storing up treasures for yourselves on earth, where moths and rust destroy and thieves break in and steal. Instead, store up treasures for yourselves in heaven, where moths and rust don't destroy and thieves don't break in and steal. Your heart will be where your treasure is." ✦ Indeed, our lives are guided by faith, not by sight. ✦ We are not discouraged. Though outwardly we are wearing out, inwardly we are renewed day by day. Our suffering is light and temporary and is producing for us an eternal glory that is greater than anything we can imagine. We don't look for things that can be seen but for things that can't be seen. Things that can be seen are only temporary. But things that can't be seen last forever. ✦ An inheritance that can't be destroyed or corrupted and can't fade away. That inheritance is kept in heaven for you.

*Colossians 3:2; 1 John 2:15; Matthew 6:19–21; 2 Corinthians 5:7; 2 Corinthians 4:16–18; 1 Peter 1:4*

## EVENING READING

He will bend his back to the burden.

Brothers and sisters, follow the example of the prophets who spoke in the name of the Lord. They were patient when they suffered unjustly. ✦ These things happened to make them an example for others. These things were written down as a warning for us who are living in the closing days of history. ✦ "We accept the good that God gives us. Shouldn't we also accept the bad?" ✦ Aaron was speechless. ✦ "He is the Lord. May he do what he thinks is right." ✦ Turn your burdens over to the Lord, and he will take care of you. ✦ He certainly has taken upon himself our suffering and carried our sorrows. ✦ "Come to me, all who are tired from carrying heavy loads, and I will give you rest. Place my yoke over your shoulders, and learn from me, because I am gentle and humble. Then you will find rest for yourselves because my yoke is easy and my burden is light."

*Genesis 49:15; James 5:10; 1 Corinthians 10:11; Job 2:10; Leviticus 10:3; 1 Samuel 3:18; Psalm 55:22; Isaiah 53:4; Matthew 11:28–30*

## MORNING READING

I've suffered miserably, O Lord!
Please help me!

I look up to you, to the one who sits enthroned in heaven. As servants depend on their masters, as a maid depends on her mistress, so we depend on the LORD our God. ✦ Listen to my cry for help, O God. Pay attention to my prayer. From the ends of the earth, I call to you when I begin to lose heart. Lead me to the rock that is high above me. You have been my refuge, a tower of strength against the enemy. I would like to be a guest in your tent forever and to take refuge under the protection of your wings. ✦ You have been a refuge for the poor, a refuge for the needy in their distress, a shelter from the rain. ✦ God called you to endure suffering because Christ suffered for you. He left you an example so that you could follow in his footsteps. Christ never committed any sin. He never spoke deceitfully. Christ never verbally abused those who verbally abused him. When he suffered, he didn't make any threats but left everything to the one who judges fairly.

*Isaiah 38:14; Psalm 123:1–2; Psalm 61:1–4; Isaiah 25:4; 1 Peter 2:21–23*

## EVENING READING

Fight the good fight for the Christian faith.

We suffer in a number of ways. Outwardly we have conflicts, and inwardly we have fears. ✦ "Don't be afraid. We have more forces on our side than they have on theirs." ✦ Finally, receive your power from the Lord and from his mighty strength. ✦ David told the Philistine, "You come to me with sword and spear and javelin, but I come to you in the name of the LORD of Armies, the God of the army of Israel, whom you have insulted." ✦ God arms me with strength. . . . He trains my hands for battle so that my arms can bend an archer's bow of bronze. ✦ God makes us qualified. ✦ The Messenger of the LORD camps around those who fear him, and he rescues them. ✦ The mountain around Elisha was full of fiery horses and chariots. ✦ I don't have enough time to tell you about Gideon, Barak, Samson, Jephthah, David, Samuel, and the prophets. Through faith they conquered kingdoms, did what God approved, and received what God had promised. They shut the mouths of lions, put out raging fires, and escaped death. They found strength when they were weak. They were powerful in battle and defeated other armies.

*1 Timothy 6:12; 2 Corinthians 7:5; 2 Kings 6:16; Ephesians 6:10; 1 Samuel 17:45; 2 Samuel 22:33, 35; 2 Corinthians 3:5; Psalm 34:7; 2 Kings 6:17; Hebrews 11:32–34*

## MORNING READING

He is a shield . . . to watch over the way of his godly ones.

The LORD your God . . . went ahead of you to find places for you to camp. He appeared in a column of fire at night and in a column of smoke during the day to show you which route to take. ✦ Like an eagle that stirs up its nest, hovers over its young, spreads its wings to catch them, and carries them on its feathers, so the LORD alone led his people. No foreign god was with him. ✦ A person's steps are directed by the LORD, and the LORD delights in his way. When he falls, he will not be thrown down headfirst because the LORD holds on to his hand ✦ The righteous person has many troubles, but the LORD rescues him from all of them. ✦ The LORD knows the way of righteous people, but the way of wicked people will end. ✦ We know that all things work together for the good of those who love God—those whom he has called according to his plan. ✦ The king of Assyria has human power on his side, but the LORD our God is on our side to help us and fight our battles." ✦ The LORD your God is with you. He is a hero who saves you. He happily rejoices over you.

*Proverbs 2:8; Deuteronomy 1:32–33; Deuteronomy 32:11–12; Psalm 37:23–24; Psalm 34:19; Psalm 1:6; Romans 8:28; 2 Chronicles 32:8; Zephaniah 3:17*

## EVENING READING

"My God, my God, why have you abandoned me?"

He was wounded for our rebellious acts. He was crushed for our sins. He was punished so that we could have peace . . . and the LORD has laid all our sins on him. ✦ He was killed because of my people's rebellion. . . . Yet, it was the LORD's will to crush him with suffering. ✦ Jesus, our Lord, was handed over to death because of our failures. ✦ Christ suffered for our sins once. He was an innocent person, but he suffered for guilty people so that he could bring you to God. ✦ Christ carried our sins in his body on the cross so that freed from our sins, we could live a life that has God's approval. His wounds have healed you. ✦ God had Christ, who was sinless, take our sin so that we might receive God's approval through him. ✦ Christ paid the price to free us from the curse that God's laws bring by becoming cursed.

*Matthew 27:46; Isaiah 53:5–6; Isaiah 53:8, 10; Romans 4:24–25; 1 Peter 3:18; 1 Peter 2:24; 2 Corinthians 5:21; Galatians 3:13*

## MORNING READING

Your husband is your maker.
His name is the LORD of Armies.

This is a great mystery. (I'm talking about Christ's relationship to the church.) ✦ You will no longer be called Deserted. . . . But you will be named My Delight, and your land will be named Married. The LORD is delighted with you, and your land will be married. . . . As a bridegroom rejoices over his bride, so your God will rejoice over you. ✦ The LORD has anointed me . . . to heal those who are brokenhearted, to announce that captives will be set free. . . . to provide for all those who grieve in Zion, to give them crowns instead of ashes, the oil of joy instead of tears of grief, and clothes of praise instead of a spirit of weakness. ✦ I will find joy in the LORD. I will delight in my God. He has dressed me in the clothes of salvation. He has wrapped me in the robe of righteousness like a bridegroom with a priest's turban, like a bride with her jewels. ✦ "Israel, I will make you my wife forever. I will be honest and faithful to you. I will show you my love and compassion." ✦ What will separate us from the love Christ has for us?

*Isaiah 54:5; Ephesians 5:32; Isaiah 62:4–5; Isaiah 61:1–3; Isaiah 61:10; Hosea 2:19; Romans 8:35*

## EVENING READING

My future is in your hands.

All your holy ones are in your hands. ✦ Then the LORD spoke his word to Elijah: "Leave here, turn east, and hide beside the Cherith River, which is east of the Jordan River. You can drink from the stream, and I've commanded ravens to feed you there." . . . Then the LORD spoke his word to Elijah: "Get up, go to Zarephath (which belongs to Sidon), and stay there. I've commanded a widow there to feed you." ✦ "So I tell you to stop worrying about what you will eat, drink, or wear. Isn't life more than food and the body more than clothes? . . . Your heavenly Father certainly knows you need all of them." ✦ Trust the LORD with all your heart, and do not rely on your own understanding. In all your ways acknowledge him, and he will make your paths smooth. ✦ Turn all your anxiety over to God because he cares for you.

*Psalm 31:15; Deuteronomy 33:3; 1 Kings 17:2–4, 8–9; Matthew 6:25, 32; Proverbs 3:5–6; 1 Peter 5:7*

## MORNING READING

You have thrown all my sins behind you.

Who is a God like you? You forgive sin and overlook the rebellion of your faithful people. You will not be angry forever, because you would rather show mercy. You will again have compassion on us. You will overcome our wrongdoing. You will throw all our sins into the deep sea. ✦ "I abandoned you for one brief moment, but I will bring you back with unlimited compassion. I hid my face from you for a moment in a burst of anger, but I will have compassion on you with everlasting kindness," says the LORD your defender. ✦ "I will forgive their wickedness and I will no longer hold their sins against them." ✦ Blessed is the person whose disobedience is forgiven and whose sin is pardoned. Blessed is the person whom the LORD no longer accuses of sin and who has no deceitful thoughts. ✦ But if we live in the light in the same way that God is in the light, we have a relationship with each other. And the blood of his Son Jesus cleanses us from every sin.

*Isaiah 38:17; Micah 7:18–19; Isaiah 54:7–8;*
*Jeremiah 31:34; Psalm 32:1–2; 1 John 1:7*

## EVENING READING

I know whom I trust. I'm convinced that
he is able to protect what he had entrusted to me until that day.

By this power he can do infinitely more than we can ask or imagine. ✦ God will give you his constantly overflowing kindness. Then, when you always have everything you need, you can do more and more good things. ✦ He is able to help others when they are tempted. ✦ He is always able to save those who come to God through him. He can do this because he always lives and intercedes for them. ✦ God can guard you so that you don't fall and so that you can be full of joy as you stand in his glorious presence without fault. ✦ He is able to protect what he had entrusted to me until that day. ✦ Through [Christ's] power to bring everything under his authority, he will change our humble bodies and make them like his glorified body. ✦ Jesus said to [the blind men], "Do you believe that I can do this? . . . What you have believed will be done for you!"

*2 Timothy 1:12; Ephesians 3:20; 2 Corinthians 9:8; Hebrews 2:18;*
*Hebrews 7:25; Jude 24; 2 Timothy 1:12; Philippians 3:21; Matthew 9:28–29*

## Morning Reading

Place . . . confidence in God who
richly provides us with everything to enjoy.

Be careful that you don't forget the Lord your God. Don't fail to obey his commands, rules, and laws that I'm giving you today. You will eat all you want. You will build nice houses and live in them. . . . Be careful that you don't become arrogant and forget the Lord your God. . . . But remember the Lord your God is the one who makes you wealthy. ✦ If the Lord does not build the house, it is useless for the builders to work on it. If the Lord does not protect a city, it is useless for the guard to stay alert. It is useless to work hard for the food you eat by getting up early and going to bed late. The Lord gives food to those he loves while they sleep. ✦ It was not with their swords that they took possession of the land. They did not gain victory with their own strength. It was your right hand, your arm, and the light of your presence that did it, because you were pleased with them. ✦ Many are saying, "Who can show us anything good?" Let the light of your presence shine on us, O Lord.

*1 Timothy 6:17; Deuteronomy 8:11–12, 14, 18;*
*Psalm 127:1–2; Psalm 44:3; Psalm 4:6*

## Evening Reading

They were singing a new song.

A new and living way for us to go through the curtain. ✦ He saved us, but not because of anything we had done to gain his approval. Instead, because of his mercy he saved us through the washing in which the Holy Spirit gives us new birth and renewal. God poured a generous amount of the Spirit on us through Jesus Christ our Savior. ✦ God saved you through faith as an act of kindness. You had nothing to do with it. Being saved is a gift from God. It's not the result of anything you've done, so no one can brag about it. ✦ Don't give glory to us, O Lord. Don't give glory to us. Instead, give glory to your name. ✦ To the one who loves us and has freed us from our sins by his blood and has made us a kingdom, priests for God his Father. Amen. ✦ They sang a new song, ". . . You were slaughtered. You bought people with your blood to be God's own. They are from every tribe, language, people, and nation." ✦ I saw a large crowd from every nation, tribe, people, and language. No one was able to count how many people there were. . . . They were . . . crying out in a loud voice, "Salvation belongs to our God, who sits on the throne, and to the lamb!"

*Revelation 14:3; Hebrews 10:20; Titus 3:5–6; Ephesians 2:8–9;*
*Psalm 115:1; Revelation 1:5–6; Revelation 5:9; Revelation 7:9–10*

## MORNING READING

The LORD Will Provide.

"God will provide a lamb for the burnt offering." ✦ The LORD is not too weak to save or his ear too deaf to hear. ✦ "The Savior will come from Zion. He will remove godlessness from Jacob." ✦ Blessed are those who receive help from the God of Jacob. Their hope rests on the LORD their God. ✦ The LORD's eyes are on those who fear him, on those who wait with hope for his mercy to rescue their souls from death and keep them alive during a famine. ✦ My God will richly fill your every need in a glorious way through Christ Jesus. ✦ God has said, "I will never abandon you or leave you." So we can confidently say, "The Lord is my helper. I will not be afraid. What can mortals do to me?" ✦ The LORD is my strength and my shield. My heart trusted him, so I received help. My heart is triumphant; I give thanks to him with my song.

*Genesis 22:14; Genesis 22:8; Isaiah 59:1; Romans 11:26; Psalm 146:5; Psalm 33:18–19; Philippians 4:19; Hebrews 13:5–6; Psalm 28:7*

## EVENING READING

He is the one who grazes his flock among the lilies.

"Where two or three have come together in my name, I am there among them." ✦ "Those who love me will do what I say. My Father will love them, and we will go to them and make our home with them." ✦ "If you obey my commandments, you will live in my love. I have obeyed my Father's commandments, and in that way I live in his love." ✦ Let my beloved come to his garden, and let him eat his own precious fruit. ✦ My bride, my sister, I will come to my garden. I will gather my myrrh with my spice. I will eat my honeycomb with my honey. ✦ But the spiritual nature produces love, joy, peace, patience, kindness, goodness, faithfulness, gentleness, and self-control. ✦ "You give glory to my Father when you produce a lot of fruit and therefore show that you are my disciples." ✦ "He removes every one of my branches that doesn't produce fruit. He also prunes every branch that does produce fruit to make it produce more fruit." ✦ Jesus Christ will fill your lives with everything that God's approval produces. Your lives will then bring glory and praise to God.

*Song of Songs 2:16; Matthew 18:20; John 14:23; John 15:10; Song of Songs 4:16; Song of Songs 5:1; Galatians 5:22–23; John 15:8; John 15:2; Philippians 1:11*

## MORNING READING

The LORD will bless you and watch over you.

It is the LORD's blessing that makes a person rich, and hard work adds nothing to it. ✦ You bless righteous people, O LORD. Like a large shield, you surround them with your favor. ✦ He will not let you fall. Your guardian will not fall asleep. Indeed, the Guardian of Israel never rests or sleeps. The LORD is your guardian. The LORD is the shade over your right hand. . . . The LORD guards you from every evil. He guards your life. The LORD guards you as you come and go, now and forever. ✦ I, the LORD, watch over it. I water it continually. I watch over it day and night so that no one will harm it. ✦ Holy Father, keep them safe by the power of your name, the name that you gave me, so that their unity may be like ours. While I was with them, I kept them safe by the power of your name, the name that you gave me. ✦ The Lord will rescue me from all harm and will take me safely to his heavenly kingdom. Glory belongs to him forever! Amen.

*Numbers 6:24; Proverbs 10:22; Psalm 5:12;*
*Psalm 121:3–5, 7–8; Isaiah 27:3; John 17:11–12; 2 Timothy 4:18*

## EVENING READING

Jesus cried.

He was a man of sorrows, familiar with suffering. ✦ We have a chief priest who is able to sympathize with our weaknesses. ✦ God is the one for whom and through whom everything exists. Therefore, while God was bringing many sons and daughters to glory, it was the right time to bring Jesus, the source of their salvation, to the end of his work through suffering. ✦ Although Jesus was the Son of God, he learned to be obedient through his sufferings. ✦ I will not rebel, nor will I turn away from him. I will offer my back to those who whip me and my cheeks to those who pluck hairs out of my beard. I will not turn my face away from those who humiliate me and spit on me. ✦ "See how much Jesus loved him." ✦ So Jesus helps Abraham's descendants rather than helping angels. Therefore, he had to become like his brothers and sisters so that he could be merciful. He became like them so that he could serve as a faithful chief priest in God's presence and make peace with God for their sins.

*John 11:35; Isaiah 53:3; Hebrews 4:15; Hebrews 2:10;*
*Hebrews 5:8; Isaiah 50:5–6; John 11:36; Hebrews 2:16–17*

## Morning Reading

"The Lord will smile on you and be kind to you.
The Lord will look on you with favor and give you peace."

No one has ever seen God. God's only Son, the one who is closest to the Father's heart, has made him known. ✦ The reflection of God's glory and the exact likeness of God's being. ✦ The god of this world has blinded the minds of those who don't believe. As a result, they don't see the light of the Good News about Christ's glory. It is Christ who is God's image. ✦ Smile on me. Save me with your mercy. O Lord, I have called on you, so do not let me be put to shame. ✦ O Lord, by your favor you have made my mountain stand firm. When you hid your face, I was terrified. ✦ Blessed are the people who know how to praise you. They walk in the light of your presence, O Lord. ✦ The Lord will give power to his people. The Lord will bless his people with peace. ✦ Immediately, Jesus said, "Calm down! It's me. Don't be afraid!"

*Numbers 6:25–26; John 1:18; Hebrews 1:3; 2 Corinthians 4:4; Psalm 31:16–17; Psalm 30:7; Psalm 89:15; Psalm 29:11; Matthew 14:27*

## Evening Reading

What pleases him.

No one can please God without faith. ✦ Those who are under the control of the corrupt nature can't please God. ✦ The Lord takes pleasure in his people. ✦ God is pleased if a person is aware of him while enduring the pains of unjust suffering. . . . If you endure suffering for doing something good, God is pleased with you. ✦ Beauty is something internal that can't be destroyed. Beauty expresses itself in a gentle and quiet attitude which God considers precious. ✦ "Whoever offers thanks as a sacrifice honors me. I will let everyone who continues in my way see the salvation that comes from God." ✦ I want to praise the name of God with a song. I want to praise its greatness with a song of thanksgiving. This will please the Lord more than sacrificing an ox or a bull with horns and hoofs. ✦ Brothers and sisters, in view of all we have just shared about God's compassion, I encourage you to offer your bodies as living sacrifices, dedicated to God and pleasing to him. This kind of worship is appropriate for you.

*1 John 3:22; Hebrews 11:6; Romans 8:8; Psalm 149:4; 1 Peter 2:19–20; 1 Peter 3:4; Psalm 50:23; Psalm 69:30–31; Romans 12:1*

## Morning Reading

There is one God.
There is also one mediator between God and humans—
a human, Christ Jesus.

Since all of these sons and daughters have flesh and blood, Jesus took on flesh and blood to be like them. ✦ Turn to me and be saved, all who live at the ends of the earth, because I am God, and there is no other. ✦ We have Jesus Christ, who has God's full approval. He speaks on our behalf when we come into the presence of the Father. ✦ Through Christ Jesus you, who were once far away, have been brought near by the blood of Christ. So he is our peace. ✦ He used his own blood. . . . He went into the most holy place and offered this sacrifice once and for all to free us forever. ✦ Because Christ offered himself to God, he is able to bring a new promise from God. Through his death he paid the price to set people free from the sins they committed under the first promise. He did this so that those who are called can be guaranteed an inheritance that will last forever. ✦ That is why he is always able to save those who come to God through him. He can do this because he always lives and intercedes for them.

*1 Timothy 2:5; Hebrews 2:14; Isaiah 45:22; 1 John 2:1; Ephesians 2:13–14; Hebrews 9:12; Hebrews 9:15; Hebrews 7:25*

## Evening Reading

My soul is discouraged.

With perfect peace you will protect those whose minds cannot be changed, because they trust you. Trust the Lord always, because the Lord, the Lord alone, is an everlasting rock. ✦ Turn your burdens over to the Lord, and he will take care of you. ✦ The Lord has not despised or been disgusted with the plight of the oppressed one. He has not hidden his face from that person. The Lord heard when that oppressed person cried out to him for help. ✦ If any of you are having trouble, pray. ✦ "Don't be troubled or cowardly." ✦ "So I tell you to stop worrying about what you will eat, drink, or wear. Isn't life more than food and the body more than clothes? Look at the birds. They don't plant, harvest, or gather the harvest into barns. Yet, your heavenly Father feeds them. Aren't you worth more than they?" ✦ "Stop doubting, and believe." ✦ "Remember that I am always with you."

*Psalm 42:6; Isaiah 26:3–4; Psalm 55:22; Psalm 22:24; James 5:13; John 14:27; Matthew 6:25–26; John 20:27; Matthew 28:20*

## Morning Reading

Show the beauty of the teachings about God our Savior in everything.

Live as citizens who reflect the Good News about Christ. ✦ Keep away from every kind of evil. ✦ If you are insulted because of the name of Christ, you are blessed. . . . If you suffer, you shouldn't suffer for being a murderer, thief, criminal, or troublemaker. ✦ Then you will be blameless and innocent. You will be God's children without any faults among people who are crooked and corrupt. You will shine like stars among them in the world. ✦ "In the same way let your light shine in front of people. Then they will see the good that you do and praise your Father in heaven." ✦ Do not let mercy and truth leave you. Fasten them around your neck. Write them on the tablet of your heart. Then you will find favor and much success in the sight of God and humanity. ✦ Finally, brothers and sisters, keep your thoughts on whatever is right or deserves praise: things that are true, honorable, fair, pure, acceptable, or commendable.

*Titus 2:10; Philippians 1:27; 1 Thessalonians 5:22; 1 Peter 4:14–15; Philippians 2:15; Matthew 5:16; Proverbs 3:3–4; Philippians 4:8*

## Evening Reading

"The words that I have spoken to you are spiritual. They are life."

God decided to give us life through the word of truth. ✦ What was written brings death, but the Spirit brings life. ✦ Christ loved the church and gave his life for it. He did this to make the church holy by cleansing it, washing it using water along with spoken words. Then he could present it to himself as a glorious church, without any kind of stain or wrinkle—holy and without faults. ✦ How can a young person keep his life pure? He can do it by holding on to your word. ✦ Your promise gave me a new life. ✦ I have treasured your promise in my heart so that I may not sin against you. ✦ I never forget your word. ✦ I trust your word. ✦ The teachings that come from your mouth are worth more to me than thousands in gold or silver. ✦ I will never forget your guiding principles, because you gave me a new life through them. ✦ How sweet the taste of your promise is! It tastes sweeter than honey. From your guiding principles I gain understanding. That is why I hate every path that leads to lying.

*John 6:63; James 1:18; 2 Corinthians 3:6; Ephesians 5:25–27; Psalm 119:9; Psalm 119:50; Psalm 119:11; Psalm 119:16; Psalm 119:42; Psalm 119:72; Psalm 119:93; Psalm 119:103–4*

## MORNING READING

Jesus, the source of their salvation,
to the end of his work through suffering.

Then [Jesus] said to them, "My anguish is so great that I feel as if I'm dying. Wait here, and stay awake with me." After walking a little farther, he quickly bowed with his face to the ground and prayed, "Father, if it's possible, let this cup of suffering be taken away from me. But let your will be done rather than mine." ✦ So he prayed very hard in anguish. His sweat became like drops of blood falling to the ground. ✦ The ropes of death became tangled around me. The horrors of the grave took hold of me. I experienced pain and agony. ✦ Insults have broken my heart, and I am sick. I looked for sympathy, but there was none. I looked for people to comfort me, but I found no one. ✦ Look to my right and see that no one notices me. Escape is impossible for me. No one cares about me. ✦ He was despised and rejected by people. He was a man of sorrows, familiar with suffering. He was despised like one from whom people turn their faces, and we didn't consider him to be worth anything.

*Hebrews 2:10; Matthew 26:38–39; Luke 22:44;*
*Psalm 116:3; Psalm 69:20; Psalm 142:4; Isaiah 53:3*

## EVENING READING

The Lord made heaven, earth, and the sea,
along with everything in them.

The heavens declare the glory of God, and the sky displays what his hands have made. ✦ The heavens were made by the word of the Lord and all the stars by the breath of his mouth. . . . He spoke, and it came into being. He gave the order, and there it stood. ✦ The nations are like a drop in a bucket and are considered to be like dust on a scale. The weight of the islands is like fine dust. ✦ Faith convinces us that God created the world through his word. This means what can be seen was made by something that could not be seen. ✦ When I look at your heavens, the creation of your fingers, the moon and the stars that you have set in place—what is a mortal that you remember him or the Son of Man that you take care of him?

*Exodus 20:11; Psalm 19:1; Psalm 33:6, 9; Isaiah 40:15; Hebrews 11:3; Psalm 8:3–4*

## MORNING READING

What is life? You are a mist that is
seen for a moment and then disappears.

"My days go by more quickly than a runner. They sprint away. They don't see anything good. They pass by quickly like boats made from reeds, like an eagle swooping down on its prey." ✦ You sweep mortals away. They are a dream. They sprout again in the morning like cut grass. In the morning they blossom and sprout. In the evening they wither and dry up. ✦ "A person who is born of a woman is short-lived and is full of trouble. He comes up like a flower; then he withers." ✦ The world and its evil desires are passing away. But the person who does what God wants lives forever. ✦ [The earth and the heavens] will come to an end, but you will still go on. They will all wear out like clothing. You will change them like clothes, and they will be thrown away. But you remain the same, and your life will never end. ✦ Jesus Christ is the same yesterday, today, and forever.

*James 4:14; Job 9:25–26; Psalm 90:5–6; Job 14:1–2;
1 John 2:17; Psalm 102:26–27; Hebrews 13:8*

## EVENING READING

I will sing psalms with my spirit,
and I will sing psalms with my mind.

Be filled with the Spirit by reciting psalms, hymns, and spiritual songs for your own good. Sing and make music to the Lord with your hearts. ✦ Let Christ's word with all its wisdom and richness live in you. Use psalms, hymns, and spiritual songs to teach and instruct yourselves about God's kindness. Sing to God in your hearts. ✦ My mouth will speak the praise of the Lord, and all living creatures will praise his holy name forever and ever. ✦ Hallelujah! It is good to sing psalms to our God. It is pleasant to sing his praise beautifully. ✦ Sing to the Lord a song of thanksgiving. Make music to our God with a lyre. ✦ I heard a sound from heaven like the noise of raging water and the noise of loud thunder. The sound I heard was like the music played by harpists.

*1 Corinthians 14:15; Ephesians 5:18–19; Colossians 3:16;
Psalm 145:21; Psalm 147:1; Psalm 147:7; Revelation 14:2*

## MORNING READING

Place your hand on the animal's head.
The burnt offering will be accepted to make peace with the LORD.

Realize that you weren't set free from the worthless life handed down to you from your ancestors by a payment of silver or gold which can be destroyed. Rather, the payment that freed you was the precious blood of Christ, the lamb with no defects or imperfections. ✦ Christ carried our sins in his body on the cross. ✦ The kindness he had given us in his dear Son. ✦ As living stones, a spiritual house that is being built into a holy priesthood. So offer spiritual sacrifices that God accepts through Jesus Christ. ✦ Brothers and sisters, in view of all we have just shared about God's compassion, I encourage you to offer your bodies as living sacrifices, dedicated to God and pleasing to him. This kind of worship is appropriate for you. ✦ God can guard you so that you don't fall and so that you can be full of joy as you stand in his glorious presence without fault. Before time began, now, and for eternity glory, majesty, power, and authority belong to the only God, our Savior, through Jesus Christ our Lord.

*Leviticus 1:4; 1 Peter 1:18–19; 1 Peter 2:24;*
*Ephesians 1:6; 1 Peter 2:5; Romans 12:1; Jude 24–25*

## EVENING READING

He was tempted in every way that we are, but he didn't sin.

Not everything that the world offers—physical gratification, greed, and extravagant lifestyles—comes from the Father. It comes from the world. ✦ The woman saw that the tree had fruit that was good to eat [physical gratification], nice to look at [greed], and desirable for making someone wise [extravagant lifestyle]. So she took some of the fruit and ate it. She also gave some to her husband, who was with her, and he ate it. ✦ The tempter came to him and said, "If you are the Son of God, tell these stones to become loaves of bread [physical gratification]." Jesus answered, "Scripture says, 'A person cannot live on bread alone but on every word that God speaks.' " . . . Once more the devil took him to a very high mountain and showed him all the kingdoms in the world and their glory [greed and extravagant lifestyle]. . . . Jesus said to him, "Go away, Satan!" ✦ Because Jesus experienced temptation when he suffered, he is able to help others when they are tempted. ✦ Blessed are those who endure when they are tested.

*Hebrews 4:15; 1 John 2:16; Genesis 3:6;*
*Matthew 4:3–4, 8, 10; Hebrews 2:18; James 1:12*

## MORNING READING

My eyes were tired from looking up to heaven.

Have pity on me, O Lord, because I am weak. Heal me, O Lord, because my bones shake with terror. My soul has been deeply shaken with terror. But you, O Lord, how long . . . ? Come back, O Lord. Rescue me. Save me because of your mercy! ✦ My heart is in turmoil. The terrors of death have seized me. Fear and trembling have overcome me. Horror has overwhelmed me. I said, "If only I had wings like a dove—I would fly away and find rest. ✦ You need endurance. ✦ They were staring into the sky as he departed. Suddenly, two men in white clothes stood near them. They asked, "Why are you men from Galilee standing here looking at the sky? Jesus, who was taken from you to heaven, will come back in the same way that you saw him go to heaven." ✦ We, however, are citizens of heaven. We look forward to the Lord Jesus Christ coming from heaven as our Savior. ✦ We can expect what we hope for—the appearance of the glory of our great God and Savior, Jesus Christ.

*Isaiah 38:14; Psalm 6:2–4; Psalm 55:4–6; Hebrews 10:36; Acts 1:10–11; Philippians 3:20; Titus 2:13*

## EVENING READING

His servants will worship him and see his face.
His name will be on their foreheads.

"I am the good shepherd. I know my sheep." ✦ God's people have a solid foundation. These words are engraved on it: "The Lord knows those who belong to him," and "Whoever worships the Lord must give up doing wrong." ✦ The Lord is good. He is a fortress in the day of trouble. He knows those who seek shelter in him. ✦ "Don't harm the land, the sea, or the trees until we have put the seal on the foreheads of the servants of our God." ✦ In him you were sealed with the Holy Spirit whom he promised. This Holy Spirit is the guarantee that we will receive our inheritance. ✦ God establishes us, together with you, in a relationship with Christ. He has also anointed us. In addition, he has put his seal of ownership on us and has given us the Spirit as his guarantee. ✦ I will write on them the name of my God, the name of the city of my God (the New Jerusalem coming down out of heaven from my God), and my new name. ✦ Jerusalem will be called The Lord Our Righteousness.

*Revelation 22:3–4; John 10:14; 2 Timothy 2:19; Nahum 1:7; Revelation 7:3; Ephesians 1:13–14; 2 Corinthians 1:21–22; Revelation 3:12; Jeremiah 33:16*

## MORNING READING

"God has brought his servant back to life and has sent him to you first. God did this to bless you by turning every one of you from your evil ways."

Praise the God and Father of our Lord Jesus Christ! God has given us a new birth because of his great mercy. We have been born into a new life that has a confidence which is alive because Jesus Christ has come back to life. ✦ The life of his Son will save us. ✦ Our great God and Savior, Jesus Christ . . . gave himself for us to set us free from every sin and to cleanse us so that we can be his special people who are enthusiastic about doing good things. ✦ Because the God who called you is holy you must be holy in every aspect of your life. Scripture says, "Be holy, because I am holy." ✦ Through Christ, God has blessed us with every spiritual blessing that heaven has to offer. ✦ All of God lives in Christ's body, and God has made you complete in Christ. ✦ Each of us has received one gift after another because of all that the Word is. ✦ God didn't spare his own Son but handed him over to death for all of us. So he will also give us everything along with him.

*Acts 3:26; 1 Peter 1:3; Romans 5:10; Titus 2:13–14; 1 Peter 1:15–16; Ephesians 1:3; Colossians 2:9–10; John 1:16; Romans 8:32*

## EVENING READING

Strengthen me as you promised.

Remember the word you gave me. Through it you gave me hope. ✦ I've suffered miserably, O Lord! Please help me! ✦ "The earth and the heavens will disappear, but my words will never disappear." ✦ You know with all your heart and soul that not one single promise which the Lord your God has given you has ever failed to come true. Every single word has come true. ✦ He said, "Don't be afraid. You are highly respected. Everything is alright! Be strong! Be strong!" As he talked to me, I became stronger. I said, "Sir, tell me what you came to say. You have strengthened me." ✦ "Be strong," declares the Lord. "Work, because I am with you," declares the Lord of Armies. ✦ You won't succeed by might or by power, but by my Spirit, says the Lord of Armies. ✦ Receive your power from the Lord and from his mighty strength.

*Psalm 119:28; Psalm 119:49; Isaiah 38:14; Luke 21:33; Joshua 23:14; Daniel 10:19; Haggai 2:4; Zechariah 4:6; Ephesians 6:10*

## Morning Reading

Your word is a doorway that lets in light.

This is the message we heard from Christ and are reporting to you: God is light, and there isn't any darkness in him. ✦ The same God who said that light should shine out of darkness has given us light. For that reason we bring to light the knowledge about God's glory which shines from Christ's face. ✦ The Word was God. ✦ He was the source of life, and that life was the light for humanity. ✦ If we live in the light in the same way that God is in the light, we have a relationship with each other. And the blood of his Son Jesus cleanses us from every sin. ✦ I have treasured your promise in my heart so that I may not sin against you. ✦ "You are already clean because of what I have told you." ✦ Once you lived in the dark, but now the Lord has filled you with light. Live as children who have light. ✦ You are chosen people, a royal priesthood, a holy nation, people who belong to God. You were chosen to tell about the excellent qualities of God, who called you out of darkness into his marvelous light.

*Psalm 119:130; 1 John 1:5; 2 Corinthians 4:6; John 1:1; John 1:4; 1 John 1:7; Psalm 119:11; John 15:3; Ephesians 5:8; 1 Peter 2:9*

## Evening Reading

Noah . . . was a man of integrity.

"The person who has God's approval will live by faith." ✦ Noah built an altar to the Lord. On it he made a burnt offering of each type of clean animal and clean bird. The Lord smelled the soothing aroma. ✦ The lamb who was slaughtered before the creation of the world. ✦ Now that we have God's approval by faith, we have peace with God because of what our Lord Jesus Christ has done. ✦ Not one person can have God's approval by following Moses' Teachings. Moses' Teachings show what sin is. Now, the way to receive God's approval has been made plain in a way other than Moses' Teachings. Moses' Teachings and the Prophets tell us this. Everyone who believes has God's approval through faith in Jesus Christ. ✦ Our Lord Jesus Christ lets us continue to brag about God. After all, it is through Christ that we now have this restored relationship with God. ✦ God has approved of them. ✦ He also called those whom he had already appointed. He approved of those whom he had called, and he gave glory to those whom he had approved of.

*Genesis 6:9; Galatians 3:11; Genesis 8:20–21; Revelation 13:8; Romans 5:1; Romans 3:20–22; Romans 5:11; Romans 8:33; Romans 8:30*

## MORNING READING

Be alert, and strengthen the things
that are left which are about to die.

The end of everything is near. Therefore, practice self-control, and keep your minds clear so that you can pray. ✦ Keep your mind clear, and be alert. Your opponent the devil is prowling around like a roaring lion as he looks for someone to devour. ✦ However, be careful, and watch yourselves closely so that you don't forget the things which you have seen with your own eyes. Don't let them fade from your memory as long as you live. ✦ [The Lord said,] "The person who has God's approval will live by faith. But if he turns back, I will not be pleased with him." We don't belong with those who turn back and are destroyed. Instead, we belong with those who have faith and are saved. ✦ "I'm telling everyone what I'm telling you: 'Be alert!' " ✦ Don't be afraid, because I am with you. Don't be intimidated; I am your God. I will strengthen you. I will help you. I will support you with my victorious right hand. . . . I, the LORD your God, hold your right hand.

*Revelation 3:2; 1 Peter 4:7; 1 Peter 5:8; Deuteronomy 4:9;
Hebrews 10:38–39; Mark 13:37; Isaiah 41:10, 13*

## EVENING READING

Has his mercy come to an end forever?

His mercy endures forever. ✦ The LORD . . . patient, forever loving. ✦ Who is a God like you? You forgive sin. . . .You will not be angry forever, because you would rather show mercy. You will again have compassion on us. You will overcome our wrongdoing. You will throw all our sins into the deep sea. ✦ He saved us, but not because of anything we had done to gain his approval. Instead, because of his mercy he saved us. ✦ Praise the God and Father of our Lord Jesus Christ! He is the Father who is compassionate and the God who gives comfort. He comforts us whenever we suffer. That is why whenever other people suffer, we are able to comfort them by using the same comfort we have received from God. ✦ He had to become like his brothers and sisters so that he could be merciful. He became like them so that he could serve as a faithful chief priest in God's presence and make peace with God for their sins. Because Jesus experienced temptation when he suffered, he is able to help others when they are tempted.

*Psalm 77:8; Psalm 136:23; Numbers 14:18; Micah 7:18–19;
Titus 3:5; 2 Corinthians 1:3–4; Hebrews 2:17–18*

## MORNING READING

Lot looked in the direction of Zoar as far as he could see.
He saw that the whole Jordan Plain was well-watered like the
Lord's garden or like Egypt. (This was before the Lord
destroyed Sodom and Gomorrah.)
Lot chose the whole Jordan Plain for himself.

God rescued Lot, a man who had his approval. ✦ Make no mistake about this: You can never make a fool out of God. Whatever you plant is what you'll harvest. ✦ "Remember Lot's wife!" ✦ Stop forming inappropriate relationships with unbelievers. Can right and wrong be partners? Can light have anything in common with darkness? ✦ The Lord says, "Get away from unbelievers. Separate yourselves from them. Have nothing to do with anything unclean." ✦ Don't be partners with them. Once you lived in the dark, but now the Lord has filled you with light. Live as children who have light. Determine which things please the Lord. Have nothing to do with the useless works that darkness produces. Instead, expose them for what they are.

*Genesis 13:10–11; 2 Peter 2:7–8; Galatians 6:7; Luke 17:32;
2 Corinthians 6:14; 2 Corinthians 6:17; Ephesians 5:7–8, 10–11*

## EVENING READING

"If the Lord is with me, I can force them out, as he promised."

God has said, "I will never abandon you or leave you." So we can confidently say, "The Lord is my helper. I will not be afraid. What can mortals do to me?" ✦ I will come with the mighty deeds of the Almighty Lord. I will praise your righteousness, yours alone. ✦ Then an act of righteousness will bring about peace, calm, and safety forever. ✦ So then, take your stand! Fasten truth around your waist like a belt. Put on God's approval as your breastplate. ✦ This is not a wrestling match against a human opponent. We are wrestling with rulers, authorities, the powers who govern this world of darkness, and spiritual forces that control evil in the heavenly world. For this reason, take up all the armor that God supplies. Then you will be able to take a stand during these evil days. Once you have overcome all obstacles, you will be able to stand your ground. ✦ The Messenger of the Lord appeared to Gideon and said, "The Lord is with you, brave man." . . . The Lord turned to him and said, "You will rescue Israel from Midian with the strength you have. I am sending you."

*Joshua 14:12; Hebrews 13:5–6; Psalm 71:16; Isaiah 32:17;
Ephesians 6:14; Ephesians 6:12–13; Judges 6:12, 14*

## MORNING READING

Holy, holy, holy is the Lord God Almighty.

Yet, you are holy, enthroned on the praises of Israel. ✦ God said, "Don't come any closer! Take off your sandals because this place where you are standing is holy ground. I am the God of your ancestors, the God of Abraham, Isaac, and Jacob." Moses hid his face because he was afraid to look at God. ✦ "To whom, then, can you compare me? Who is my equal?" asks the Holy One. ✦ I am the LORD your God, the Holy One of Israel, your Savior. . . . I alone am the LORD, and there is no savior except me. ✦ But because the God who called you is holy you must be holy in every aspect of your life. Scripture says, "Be holy, because I am holy." ✦ Don't you know that your body is a temple that belongs to the Holy Spirit? The Holy Spirit, whom you received from God, lives in you. You don't belong to yourselves. ✦ As God said, "I will live and walk among them. I will be their God, and they will be my people." ✦ Do two people ever walk together without meeting first?

*Revelation 4:8; Psalm 22:3; Exodus 3:5–6; Isaiah 40:25; Isaiah 43:3, 11; 1 Peter 1:15–16; 1 Corinthians 6:19; 2 Corinthians 6:16; Amos 3:3*

## EVENING READING

They urged him, "Stay with us!"

"Look, I'm standing at the door and knocking. If anyone listens to my voice and opens the door, I'll come in and we'll eat together." ✦ Please tell me, you whom I love, where do you graze your flock? Where does your flock lie down at noon? Tell me, or I will be considered a prostitute wandering among the flocks of your companions. ✦ I found the one I love. I held on to him and would not let him go ✦ Let my beloved come to his garden, and let him eat his own precious fruit. ✦ I will come to my garden. ✦ I didn't say to Jacob's descendants, "Search for me in vain!" ✦ "And remember that I am always with you until the end of time." ✦ "I will never abandon you or leave you." ✦ "Where two or three have come together in my name, I am there among them." ✦ "In a little while the world will no longer see me, but you will see me."

*Luke 24:29; Revelation 3:20; Song of Songs 1:7; Song of Songs 3:4; Song of Songs 4:16; Song of Songs 5:1; Isaiah 45:19; Matthew 28:20; Hebrews 13:5; Matthew 18:20; John 14:19*

# March 24

## MORNING READING

Then Abram believed the Lord, and the Lord regarded that faith to be his approval of Abram.

He didn't doubt God's promise out of a lack of faith. Instead, giving honor to God for the promise, he became strong because of faith and was absolutely confident that God would do what he promised. That is why his faith was regarded as God's approval of him. But the words "his faith was regarded as God's approval of him" were written not only for him but also for us. Our faith will be regarded as God's approval of us who believe in the one who brought Jesus, our Lord, back to life. ✦ So it was not by obeying Moses' Teachings that Abraham or his descendants received the promise that he would inherit the world. Rather, it was through God's approval of his faith. ✦ The person who has God's approval will live by faith. ✦ We must continue to hold firmly to our declaration of faith. The one who made the promise is faithful. ✦ Our God is in heaven. He does whatever he wants. ✦ "But nothing is impossible for God." ✦ "You are blessed for believing that the Lord would keep his promise to you."

*Genesis 15:6; Romans 4:20–24; Romans 4:13; Romans 1:17; Hebrews 10:23; Psalm 115:3; Luke 1:37; Luke 1:45*

## EVENING READING

God . . . calls you into his kingdom and glory.

Jesus answered, "My kingdom doesn't belong to this world. If my kingdom belonged to this world, my followers would fight. . . . My kingdom doesn't have its origin on earth." ✦ He has been waiting for his enemies to be made his footstool. ✦ "The kingdom of the world has become the kingdom of our Lord and of his Messiah, and he will rule as king forever and ever." ✦ "You made them a kingdom and priests for our God. They will rule as kings on the earth." ✦ I saw thrones, and those who sat on them were allowed to judge. . . . They lived and ruled with Christ for 1,000 years. ✦ "Then the people who have God's approval will shine like the sun in their Father's kingdom." ✦ Don't be afraid, little flock. Your Father is pleased to give you the kingdom. ✦ "So as my Father has given me a kingdom, I'm giving it to you. You will eat and drink at my table in my kingdom. You will also sit on thrones and judge the twelve tribes of Israel." ✦ "Let your kingdom come."

*1 Thessalonians 2:12; John 18:36; Hebrews 10:13; Revelation 11:15; Revelation 5:10; Revelation 20:4; Matthew 13:43; Luke 12:32; Luke 22:29–30; Matthew 6:10*

## MORNING READING

"I will never abandon you or leave you."

So we can confidently say, "The Lord is my helper. I will not be afraid. What can mortals do to me?" ✦ "Remember, I am with you and will watch over you wherever you go. I will also bring you back to this land because I will not leave you until I do what I've promised you." ✦ Be strong and courageous. Don't tremble! Don't be afraid of them! The LORD your God is the one who is going with you. He won't abandon you or leave you." ✦ Demas has abandoned me. He fell in love with this present world. ✦ At my first hearing no one stood up in my defense. Everyone abandoned me. I pray that it won't be held against them. However, the Lord stood by me and gave me strength. ✦ Even if my father and mother abandon me, the LORD will take care of me. ✦ "Remember that I am always with you until the end of time." ✦ "The living one. I was dead, but now I am alive forever." ✦ "I will not leave you all alone. I will come back to you." ✦ "I'm giving you my peace."

*Hebrews 13:5; Hebrews 13:6; Genesis 28:15; Deuteronomy 31:6; 2 Timothy 4:10; 2 Timothy 4:16–17; Psalm 27:10; Matthew 28:20; Revelation 1:18; John 14:18; John 14:27*

## EVENING READING

"Teacher, we worked hard all night and caught nothing. But if you say so, I'll lower the nets."

"All authority in heaven and on earth has been given to me. So wherever you go, make disciples of all nations: Baptize them in the name of the Father, and of the Son, and of the Holy Spirit. . . . And remember that I am always with you until the end of time." ✦ "The kingdom of heaven is like a net that was thrown into the sea. It gathered all kinds of fish." ✦ If I spread the Good News, I have nothing to brag about because I have an obligation to do this. How horrible it will be for me if I don't spread the Good News! ✦ I have become everything to everyone in order to save at least some of them. ✦ We can't allow ourselves to get tired of living the right way. Certainly, each of us will receive everlasting life at the proper time, if we don't give up. ✦ "My word . . . will not come back to me without results. It will accomplish whatever I want." ✦ So neither the one who plants nor the one who waters is important because only God makes it grow.

*Luke 5:5; Matthew 28:18–20; Matthew 13:47; 1 Corinthians 9:16; 1 Corinthians 9:22; Galatians 6:9; Isaiah 55:11; 1 Corinthians 3:7*

## Morning Reading

"The kingdom of heaven is like a man going on a trip.
He called his servants and entrusted some money to them.
Each was given money based on his ability."

Don't you know that if you offer to be someone's slave, you must obey that master? ✦ There is only one Spirit who does all these things by giving what God wants to give to each person. ✦ The evidence of the Spirit's presence is given to each person for the common good of everyone. ✦ Managers are required to be trustworthy. ✦ Each of you as a good manager must use the gift that God has given you to serve others. ✦ A lot will be expected from everyone who has been given a lot. More will be demanded from everyone who has been entrusted with a lot. ✦ Who is qualified to tell about Christ? ✦ I can do everything through Christ who strengthens me.

*Matthew 25:14–15; Romans 6:16; 1 Corinthians 12:11; 1 Corinthians 12:7; 1 Corinthians 4:2; 1 Peter 4:10; Luke 12:48; 2 Corinthians 2:16; Philippians 4:13*

## Evening Reading

Share what you have with God's people who are in need.

David asked, "Is there anyone left in Saul's family to whom I can show kindness for Jonathan's sake?" ✦ "Come, my Father has blessed you! Inherit the kingdom prepared for you from the creation of the world. I was hungry, and you gave me something to eat. I was thirsty, and you gave me something to drink. I was a stranger, and you took me into your home. I needed clothes, and you gave me something to wear. I was sick, and you took care of me. I was in prison, and you visited me." . . . "Whatever you did for one of my brothers or sisters, no matter how unimportant they seemed, you did for me." ✦ Whoever gives any of my humble followers a cup of cold water because that person is my disciple will certainly never lose his reward. ✦ Don't forget to do good things for others and to share what you have with them. These are the kinds of sacrifices that please God. ✦ God is fair. He won't forget what you've done or the love you've shown for him. You helped his holy people, and you continue to help them.

*Romans 12:13; 2 Samuel 9:1; Matthew 25:34–36, 40; Matthew 10:42; Hebrews 13:16; Hebrews 6:10*

## MORNING READING

Whoever spreads righteousness earns honest pay.

"After a long time the master of those servants returned and settled accounts with them. The one who received ten thousand dollars brought the additional ten thousand. He said, 'Sir, you gave me ten thousand dollars. I've doubled the amount.' "His master replied, 'Good job! You're a good and faithful servant! You proved that you could be trusted with a small amount. I will put you in charge of a large amount. Come and share your master's happiness.' " ✦ All of us must appear in front of Christ's judgment seat. Then all people will receive what they deserve for the good or evil they have done while living in their bodies. ✦ I have fought the good fight. I have completed the race. I have kept the faith. The prize that shows I have God's approval is now waiting for me. The Lord, who is a fair judge, will give me that prize on that day. He will give it not only to me but also to everyone who is eagerly waiting for him to come again. ✦ "I am coming soon! Hold on to what you have so that no one takes your crown."

*Proverbs 11:18; Matthew 25:19–21; 2 Corinthians 5:10; 2 Timothy 4:7–9; Revelation 3:11*

## EVENING READING

God, who faithfully keeps his promises.

God is not like people. He tells no lies. He is not like humans. He doesn't change his mind. When he says something, he does it. When he makes a promise, he keeps it. ✦ "The Lord has taken an oath and will not change his mind." ✦ God wouldn't change his plan. He wanted to make this perfectly clear to those who would receive his promise, so he took an oath. God did this so that we would be encouraged. God cannot lie when he takes an oath or makes a promise. These two things can never be changed. Those of us who have taken refuge in him hold on to the confidence we have been given. ✦ Those who suffer because that is God's will for them must entrust themselves to a faithful creator and continue to do what is good. ✦ For this reason I suffer as I do. However, I'm not ashamed. I know whom I trust. I'm convinced that he is able to protect what he had entrusted to me until that day. ✦ The one who calls you is faithful, and he will do this. ✦ Certainly, Christ made God's many promises come true. For that reason, because of our message, people also honor God by saying, "Amen!"

*1 Corinthians 10:13; Numbers 23:19; Hebrews 7:21; Hebrews 6:17–18; 1 Peter 4:19; 2 Timothy 1:12; 1 Thessalonians 5:24; 2 Corinthians 1:20*

# March 28

## MORNING READING

Be strong and courageous!

The Lord is my light and my salvation. Who is there to fear? The Lord is my life's fortress. Who is there to be afraid of? ✦ He gives strength to those who grow tired and increases the strength of those who are weak. Even young people grow tired and become weary, and young men will stumble and fall. Yet, the strength of those who wait with hope in the Lord will be renewed. They will soar on wings like eagles. They will run and won't become weary. They will walk and won't grow tired. ✦ My body and mind may waste away, but God remains the foundation of my life and my inheritance forever. ✦ If God is for us, who can be against us? ✦ The Lord is on my side. I am not afraid. What can mortals do to me? ✦ With you we can walk over our enemies. With your name we can trample those who attack us. ✦ The one who loves us gives us an overwhelming victory in all these difficulties. ✦ Get to work! May the Lord be with you.

*Joshua 1:18; Psalm 27:1; Isaiah 40:29–31; Psalm 73:26; Romans 8:31; Psalm 118:6; Psalm 44:5; Romans 8:37; 1 Chronicles 22:16*

## EVENING READING

"Our friend . . . is sleeping."

Brothers and sisters, we don't want you to be ignorant about those who have died. We don't want you to grieve like other people who have no hope. We believe that Jesus died and came back to life. We also believe that, through Jesus, God will bring back those who have died. ✦ Certainly, if the dead don't come back to life, then Christ hasn't come back to life either. If Christ hasn't come back to life, your faith is worthless and sin still has you in its power. Then those who have died as believers in Christ no longer exist. . . . But now Christ has come back from the dead. He is the very first person of those who have died to come back to life ✦ The whole nation finished crossing the Jordan River. The Lord had told Joshua, "Order them to pick up 12 stones from the middle of the Jordan, where the priests' feet stood firmly. . . . These stones are a permanent reminder for the people of Israel." ✦ "God brought this man Jesus back to life. We are all witnesses to that." ✦ He showed Jesus to witnesses, apostles he had already chosen . . . who ate and drank with Jesus after he came back to life.

*John 11:11; 1 Thessalonians 4:13–14; 1 Corinthians 15:16–18, 20; Joshua 4:1, 3, 7; Acts 2:32; Acts 10:41*

## MORNING READING

"Come, my Father has blessed you!
Inherit the kingdom prepared for you from the creation of the world."

"Don't be afraid, little flock. Your Father is pleased to give you the kingdom." ✦ Didn't God choose poor people in the world to become rich in faith and to receive the kingdom that he promised to those who love him? ✦ If we are his children, we are also God's heirs. If we share in Christ's suffering in order to share his glory, we are heirs together with him. ✦ "The Father loves you because you have loved me and have believed that I came from God." ✦ God is not ashamed to be called their God. He has prepared a city for them. ✦ Everyone who wins the victory will inherit these things. I will be their God, and they will be my children. ✦ The prize that shows I have God's approval is now waiting for me. The Lord, who is a fair judge, will give me that prize on that day. He will give it not only to me but also to everyone who is eagerly waiting for him to come again. ✦ I'm convinced that God, who began this good work in you, will carry it through to completion on the day of Christ Jesus.

*Matthew 25:34; Luke 12:32; James 2:5; Romans 8:17; John 16:27; Hebrews 11:16; Revelation 21:7; 2 Timothy 4:8; Philippians 1:6*

## EVENING READING

Wealth is not forever.
Nor does a crown last from one generation to the next.

Each person who walks around is like a shadow. They are busy for no reason. They accumulate riches without knowing who will get them. ✦ Keep your mind on things above, not on worldly things. ✦ "Stop storing up treasures for yourselves on earth, where moths and rust destroy and thieves break in and steal. Instead, store up treasures for yourselves in heaven, where moths and rust don't destroy and thieves don't break in and steal. Your heart will be where your treasure is." ✦ They do it to win a temporary crown, but we do it to win one that will be permanent. ✦ We don't look for things that can be seen but for things that can't be seen. ✦ A wicked person earns dishonest wages, but whoever spreads righteousness earns honest pay. ✦ The prize that shows I have God's approval is now waiting for me. The Lord, who is a fair judge, will give me that prize on that day. He will give it not only to me but also to everyone who is eagerly waiting for him to come again. ✦ The crown of glory that will never fade away.

*Proverbs 27:24; Psalm 39:6; Colossians 3:2; Matthew 6:19–21; 1 Corinthians 9:25; 2 Corinthians 4:18; Proverbs 11:18; 2 Timothy 4:8; 1 Peter 5:4*

## Morning Reading

Toward evening Isaac went out into the field to meditate.

May the words from my mouth and the thoughts from my heart be acceptable to you, O Lord, my rock and my defender. ✦ When I look at your heavens, the creation of your fingers, the moon and the stars that you have set in place—what is a mortal that you remember him or the Son of Man that you take care of him? ✦ The Lord's deeds are spectacular. They should be studied by all who enjoy them. ✦ Blessed is the person who does not follow the advice of wicked people, take the path of sinners, or join the company of mockers. Rather, he delights in the teachings of the Lord and reflects on his teachings day and night. ✦ Never stop reciting these teachings. You must think about them night and day so that you will faithfully do everything written in them. ✦ You satisfy my soul with the richest foods. My mouth will sing your praise with joyful lips. As I lie on my bed, I remember you.

*Genesis 24:63; Psalm 19:14; Psalm 8:3–4; Psalm 111:2; Psalm 1:1–2; Joshua 1:8; Psalm 63:5–6*

## Evening Reading

How long, O Lord? Will you forget me forever?
How long will you hide your face from me?

Every good present and every perfect gift comes from above, from the Father who made the sun, moon, and stars. The Father doesn't change like the shifting shadows produced by the sun and the moon. ✦ Zion said, "The Lord has abandoned me. My Lord has forgotten me." Can a woman forget her nursing child? Will she have no compassion on the child from her womb? Although mothers may forget, I will not forget you. ✦ I will not forget you. I made your rebellious acts disappear like a thick cloud and your sins like the morning mist. ✦ Jesus loved Martha, her sister, and Lazarus. Yet, when Jesus heard that Lazarus was sick, he stayed where he was for two more days. ✦ A [woman] began to shout, "Have mercy on me, Lord, Son of David! My daughter is tormented by a demon." But he did not answer her at all. ✦ Your faith is more precious than gold.

*Psalm 13:1; James 1:17; Isaiah 49:14–15; Isaiah 44:21–22; John 11:5–6; Matthew 15:22–23; 1 Peter 1:7*

## MORNING READING

My God will richly fill your every need in
a glorious way through Christ Jesus.

"But first, be concerned about his kingdom and what has his approval. Then all these things will be provided for you." ✦ God didn't spare his own Son but handed him over to death for all of us. So he will also give us everything along with him. ✦ Everything belongs to you. Whether it is Paul, Apollos, Cephas, the world, life or death, present or future things, everything belongs to you. You belong to Christ, and Christ belongs to God. ✦ We have nothing although we possess everything. ✦ The LORD is my shepherd. I am never in need. ✦ The LORD God is a sun and shield. The LORD grants favor and honor. He does not hold back any blessing from those who live innocently. ✦ They should place their confidence in God who richly provides us with everything to enjoy. ✦ God will give you his constantly overflowing kindness. Then, when you always have everything you need, you can do more and more good things.

*Philippians 4:19; Matthew 6:33; Romans 8:32; 1 Corinthians 3:21–23; 2 Corinthians 6:10; Psalm 23:1; Psalm 84:11; 1 Timothy 6:17; 2 Corinthians 9:8*

## EVENING READING

Can right and wrong be partners?

People loved the dark rather than the light because their actions were evil. ✦ You belong to the day and the light. ✦ They can't see in the dark. ✦ Your word is a lamp for my feet and a light for my path. ✦ Every dark corner of the land is filled with violence. ✦ Love comes from God. Everyone who loves has been born from God and knows God. The person who doesn't love doesn't know God, because God is love. ✦ The way of wicked people is like deep darkness. They do not know what makes them stumble. ✦ But the path of righteous people is like the light of dawn that becomes brighter and brighter until it reaches midday. ✦ I am the light that has come into the world so that everyone who believes in me will not live in the dark. ✦ Once you lived in the dark, but now the Lord has filled you with light. Live as children who have light.

*2 Corinthians 6:14; John 3:19; 1 Thessalonians 5:5; 1 John 2:11; Psalm 119:105; Psalm 74:20; 1 John 4:7–8; Proverbs 4:19; Proverbs 4:18; John 12:46; Ephesians 5:8*

## MORNING READING

But the spiritual nature produces . . . joy.

Joy that the Holy Spirit gives. ✦ You are extremely happy with joy and praise. ✦ People think we are sad although we're always glad. ✦ Even as we suffer, I'm encouraged and feel very happy. ✦ We also brag when we are suffering. ✦ We must focus on Jesus, the source and goal of our faith. He saw the joy ahead of him, so he endured death on the cross and ignored the disgrace it brought him. ✦ I have told you this so that you will be as joyful as I am, and your joy will be complete. ✦ Because Christ suffered so much for us, we can receive so much comfort from him. ✦ Always be joyful in the Lord! I'll say it again: Be joyful! ✦ The joy you have in the Lord is your strength. ✦ Complete joy is in your presence. Pleasures are by your side forever. ✦ The lamb in the center near the throne will be their shepherd. He will lead them to springs filled with the water of life, and God will wipe every tear from their eyes.

*Galatians 5:22; Romans 14:17; 1 Peter 1:8; 2 Corinthians 6:10; 2 Corinthians 7:4; Romans 5:3; Hebrews 12:2; John 15:11; 2 Corinthians 1:5; Philippians 4:4; Nehemiah 8:10; Psalm 16:11; Revelation 7:17*

## EVENING READING

The Lord Calms.

You will have a son who will be a peaceful man. I will give him peace from all the enemies around him. His name will be Solomon [Peace], and in his time I will give Israel peace and quiet. ✦ Someone greater than Solomon is here! ✦ A child will be born for us. A son will be given to us. The government will rest on his shoulders. He will be named: Wonderful Counselor, Mighty God, Everlasting Father, Prince of Peace. ✦ My people will live in a peaceful place, in safe homes and quiet places of rest. The forest will be flattened because of hail, and the city will be completely leveled. ✦ So he is our peace. ✦ This man will be their peace. When the Assyrians invade our land. ✦ They will go to war against the lamb. The lamb will conquer them because he is Lord of lords and King of kings. ✦ "I'm leaving you peace. I'm giving you my peace."

*Judges 6:24; 1 Chronicles 22:9; Matthew 12:42; Isaiah 9:6; Isaiah 32:18–19; Ephesians 2:14; Micah 5:5; Revelation 17:14; John 14:27*

## Morning Reading

"If you are returning to the Lord wholeheartedly,
get rid of the foreign gods you have, including
the statues of the goddess Astarte.
Make a commitment to the Lord, and serve only him."

Dear children, guard yourselves from false gods. ✦ The Lord says, "Get away from unbelievers. Separate yourselves from them. Have nothing to do with anything unclean. Then I will welcome you." The Lord Almighty says, "I will be your Father, and you will be my sons and daughters." ✦ "You cannot serve God and wealth." ✦ Never worship any other god, because the Lord is a God who does not tolerate rivals. ✦ Serve the Lord wholeheartedly and willingly because he searches every heart and understands every thought we have. ✦ Yet, you desire truth and sincerity. Deep down inside me you teach me wisdom. ✦ "Humans look at outward appearances, but the Lord looks into the heart." ✦ Dear friends, if our conscience doesn't condemn us, we can boldly look to God.

*1 Samuel 7:3; 1 John 5:21; 2 Corinthians 6:17–18; Matthew 6:24; Exodus 34:14; 1 Chronicles 28:9; Psalm 51:6; 1 Samuel 16:7; 1 John 3:21*

## Evening Reading

When the Son of Man comes, will he find faith on earth?

He went to his own people, and his own people didn't accept him. ✦ The Spirit says clearly that in later times some believers will desert the Christian faith. ✦ Be ready to spread the word whether or not the time is right. Point out errors, warn people, and encourage them. Be very patient when you teach. A time will come when people will not listen to accurate teachings. Instead, they will follow their own desires and surround themselves with teachers who tell them what they want to hear. People will refuse to listen to the truth and turn to myths. ✦ "No one knows when that day or hour will come. Even the angels in heaven and the Son don't know. Only the Father knows. Be careful! Watch! You don't know the exact time." ✦ "Blessed are those servants whom the master finds awake when he comes." ✦ At the same time we can expect what we hope for—the appearance of the glory of our great God and Savior, Jesus Christ.

*Luke 18:8; John 1:11; 1 Timothy 4:1; 2 Timothy 4:2–4; Mark 13:32–33; Luke 12:37; Titus 2:13*

## MORNING READING

Dear friends, don't ignore this fact:
One day with the Lord is like a thousand years,
and a thousand years are like one day.
The Lord isn't slow to do what he promised, as some people think.

"My thoughts are not your thoughts, and my ways are not your ways," declares the LORD. "Just as the heavens are higher than the earth, so my ways are higher than your ways, and my thoughts are higher than your thoughts. Rain and snow come down from the sky. They do not go back again until they water the earth. . . . My word, which comes from my mouth, is like the rain and snow. It will not come back to me without results. It will accomplish whatever I want and achieve whatever I send it to do." ✦ God has placed all people into the prison of their own disobedience so that he could be merciful to all people. God's riches, wisdom, and knowledge are so deep that it is impossible to explain his decisions or to understand his ways.

*2 Peter 3:8–9; Isaiah 55:8–11; Romans 11:32–33*

## EVENING READING

You were like a burning log snatched from a fire.

The sinners in Zion are terrified. Trembling seizes the ungodly. Can any of us live through a fire that destroys? Can any of us live through a fire that burns forever? ✦ In fact, we still feel as if we're under a death sentence. But we suffered so that we would stop trusting ourselves and learn to trust God, who brings the dead back to life. He has rescued us from a terrible death, and he will rescue us in the future. We are confident that he will continue to rescue us. ✦ The payment for sin is death, but the gift that God freely gives is everlasting life found in Christ Jesus our Lord. ✦ Falling into the hands of the living God is a terrifying thing. ✦ As people who know what it means to fear the Lord, we try to persuade others. ✦ Be ready to spread the word whether or not the time is right. ✦ Save others by snatching them from the fire of hell. ✦ You won't succeed by might or by power, but by my Spirit, says the LORD of Armies. ✦ He wants all people to be saved and to learn the truth.

*Amos 4:11; Isaiah 33:14; 2 Corinthians 1:9–10; Romans 6:23; Hebrews 10:31; 2 Corinthians 5:11; 2 Timothy 4:2; Jude 23; Zechariah 4:6; 1 Timothy 2:4*

## MORNING READING

I am the first and the last.

You have not come to something that you can feel, to a blazing fire, to darkness, to gloom, to a storm. . . . Instead, you have come to Mount Zion. . . . You have come to a judge (the God of all people) and to the spirits of people who have God's approval and have gained eternal life. You have come to Jesus, who brings the new promise. ✦ We must focus on Jesus, the source and goal of our faith. ✦ We have a chief priest who is able to sympathize with our weaknesses. He was tempted in every way that we are, but he didn't sin. So we can go confidently to the throne of God's kindness to receive mercy and find kindness, which will help us at the right time. ✦ The LORD is Israel's king and defender. He is the LORD of Armies. This is what the LORD says: I am the first and the last, and there is no God except me. ✦ Mighty God, Everlasting Father, Prince of Peace. ✦ Didn't you exist before time began, O LORD, my God, my Holy One? ✦ Who is God but the LORD? Who is a rock other than our God?

*Revelation 1:17; Hebrews 12:18, 22–24; Hebrews 12:2; Hebrews 4:15–16; Isaiah 44:6; Isaiah 9:6; Habakkuk 1:12; 2 Samuel 22:32*

## EVENING READING

Lead me to the rock that is high above me.

Never worry about anything. But in every situation let God know what you need in prayers and requests while giving thanks. Then God's peace, which goes beyond anything we can imagine, will guard your thoughts and emotions through Christ Jesus. ✦ When I begin to lose hope, you already know what I am experiencing. ✦ I can't find him because he knows the road I take. When he tests me, I'll come out as pure as gold. ✦ O Lord, you have been our refuge throughout every generation. ✦ You have been a refuge for the poor, a refuge for the needy in their distress, a shelter from the rain, and shade from the heat. ✦ Who is a rock except our God? ✦ "I give them eternal life. They will never be lost, and no one will tear them away from me." ✦ Help me God, as you promised, so that I may live. Do not turn my hope into disappointment. ✦ We have this confidence as a sure and strong anchor for our lives. This confidence goes into the holy place behind the curtain.

*Psalm 61:2; Philippians 4:6–7; Psalm 142:3; Job 23:10; Psalm 90:1; Isaiah 25:4; Psalm 18:31; John 10:28; Psalm 119:116; Hebrews 6:19*

## April 5

### MORNING READING

I won't let you go until you bless me.

Let them come to me for protection. Let them make peace with me. Yes, let them make peace with me ✦ "Woman, you have strong faith! What you wanted will be done for you." ✦ "What you have believed will be done for you!" ✦When you ask for something, don't have any doubts. A person who has doubts is like a wave that is blown by the wind and tossed by the sea. A person who has doubts shouldn't expect to receive anything from the Lord. ✦ When they came near the village where they were going, Jesus acted as if he were going farther. They urged him, "Stay with us!" . . . Then their eyes were opened, and they recognized him. But he vanished from their sight. They said to each other, "Weren't we excited when he talked with us on the road and opened up the meaning of the Scriptures for us?" ✦ [Moses said,] "If you really are pleased with me, show me your ways so that I can know you and so that you will continue to be pleased with me." The LORD answered, "My presence will go with you, and I will give you peace."

*Genesis 32:26; Isaiah 27:5; Matthew 15:28; Matthew 9:29; James 1:6–7; Luke 24:28–29, 31–32; Exodus 33:13–14*

### EVENING READING

Jesus, the source and goal of our faith.

"I am the A and the Z," says the Lord God, the one who is, the one who was, and the one who is coming, the Almighty. ✦ Who has accomplished this? "Who has determined the course of history from the beginning? I, the LORD, was there first, and I will be there to the end. I am the one!" ✦ To those who have been called, who are loved by God the Father, and who are kept safe for Jesus Christ. ✦ May the God who gives peace make you holy in every way. May he keep your whole being—spirit, soul, and body—blameless when our Lord Jesus Christ comes. The one who calls you is faithful, and he will do this. ✦ I'm convinced that God, who began this good work in you, will carry it through to completion on the day of Christ Jesus. ✦ Are you that stupid? Did you begin in a spiritual way only to end up doing things in a human way? ✦ The LORD will do everything for me. ✦ It is God who produces in you the desires and actions that please him.

*Hebrews 12:2; Revelation 1:8; Isaiah 41:4; Jude 1; 1 Thessalonians 5:23–24; Philippians 1:6; Galatians 3:3; Psalm 138:8; Philippians 2:13*

## MORNING READING

He always lives and intercedes.

Who will condemn them? Christ has died. . . . Christ also intercedes for us. ✦ Christ didn't go into a holy place made by human hands. He didn't go into a model of the real thing. Instead, he went into heaven to appear in God's presence on our behalf. ✦ If anyone does sin, we have Jesus Christ, who has God's full approval. ✦ There is one God. There is also one mediator between God and humans—a human, Christ Jesus. ✦ We need to hold on to our declaration of faith: We have a superior chief priest who has gone through the heavens. That person is Jesus, the Son of God. We have a chief priest who is able to sympathize with our weaknesses. He was tempted in every way that we are, but he didn't sin. So we can go confidently to the throne of God's kindness to receive mercy and find kindness, which will help us at the right time. ✦ So Jewish and non-Jewish people can go to the Father in one Spirit.

*Hebrews 7:25; Romans 8:34; Hebrews 9:24; 1 John 2:1;*
*1 Timothy 2:5; Hebrews 4:14–16; Ephesians 2:18*

## EVENING READING

Those who know your name trust you.

This is the name that he will be given: The LORD Our Righteousness. ✦ I will come with the mighty deeds of the Almighty LORD. I will praise your righteousness, yours alone. ✦ He will be named: Wonderful Counselor. ✦ O LORD, I know that the way humans act is not under their control. Humans do not direct their steps as they walk. ✦ Mighty God, Everlasting Father. ✦ I know whom I trust. I'm convinced that he is able to protect what he had entrusted to me until that day. ✦ Prince of Peace. ✦ He is our peace. ✦ Now that we have God's approval by faith, we have peace with God because of what our Lord Jesus Christ has done. ✦ The name of the LORD is a strong tower. A righteous person runs to it and is safe. ✦ How horrible it will be for those who go to Egypt for help. ✦ The LORD of Armies will defend Jerusalem like a hovering bird. He will defend it and rescue it. He will pass over it and protect it.

*Psalm 9:10; Jeremiah 23:6; Psalm 71:16; Isaiah 9:6; Jeremiah 10:23;*
*Isaiah 9:6; 2 Timothy 1:12; Isaiah 9:6; Ephesians 2:14;*
*Romans 5:1; Proverbs 18:10; Isaiah 31:1; Isaiah 31:5*

## Morning Reading

People think we are sad although we're always glad,
that we're beggars although we make many people spiritually rich,
that we have nothing although we possess everything.

We brag because of our confidence that we will receive glory from God. But that's not all. We also brag when we are suffering. ✦ Even as we suffer, I'm encouraged and feel very happy. ✦ You are extremely happy with joy and praise that can hardly be expressed in words. ✦ Their overflowing joy, along with their extreme poverty, has made them even more generous. ✦ I am the least of all God's people. Yet, God showed me his kindness by allowing me to spread the Good News of the immeasurable wealth of Christ to people who are not Jewish. He allowed me to explain the way this mystery works. God, who created all things, kept it hidden in the past. ✦ Didn't God choose poor people in the world to become rich in faith and to receive the kingdom that he promised to those who love him? ✦ Besides, God will give you his constantly overflowing kindness. Then, when you always have everything you need, you can do more and more good things.

*2 Corinthians 6:10; Romans 5:2–3; 2 Corinthians 7:4; 1 Peter 1:8; 2 Corinthians 8:2; Ephesians 3:8–9; James 2:5; 2 Corinthians 9:8*

## Evening Reading

The Lord will support him on his sickbed.
You will restore this person to health when he is ill.

In all their troubles he was troubled, and he was the Messenger who saved them. In his love and compassion he reclaimed them. He always held them and carried them in the past. ✦ "Lord, your close friend is sick." ✦ "My kindness is all you need. My power is strongest when you are weak." ✦ I will brag even more about my weaknesses in order that Christ's power will live in me. ✦ I can do everything through Christ who strengthens me. ✦ That is why we are not discouraged. Though outwardly we are wearing out, inwardly we are renewed day by day. ✦ Certainly, we live, move, and exist because of him. ✦ He gives strength to those who grow tired and increases the strength of those who are weak. Even young people grow tired and become weary, and young men will stumble and fall. Yet, the strength of those who wait with hope in the Lord will be renewed. ✦ The eternal God is your shelter, and his everlasting arms support you.

*Psalm 41:3; Isaiah 63:9; John 11:3; 2 Corinthians 12:9; 2 Corinthians 12:9; Philippians 4:13; 2 Corinthians 4:16; Acts 17:28; Isaiah 40:29–31; Deuteronomy 33:27*

## Morning Reading

Through Christ Jesus you have become rich in every way.

At the right time, while we were still helpless, Christ died for ungodly people. ✦ God didn't spare his own Son but handed him over to death for all of us. So he will also give us everything along with him. ✦ All of God lives in Christ's body, and God has made you complete in Christ. Christ is in charge of every ruler and authority. ✦ "Live in me, and I will live in you. A branch cannot produce any fruit by itself. It has to stay attached to the vine. In the same way, you cannot produce fruit unless you live in me. I am the vine. You are the branches. Those who live in me while I live in them will produce a lot of fruit. But you can't produce anything without me." ✦ Although I have the desire to do what is right, I don't do it. ✦ God's favor has been given to each of us. It was measured out to us by Christ who gave it. ✦ "If you live in me and what I say lives in you, then ask for anything you want, and it will be yours." ✦ Let Christ's word with all its wisdom and richness live in you.

*1 Corinthians 1:5; Romans 5:6; Romans 8:32; Colossians 2:9–10; John 15:4–5; Romans 7:18; Ephesians 4:7; John 15:7; Colossians 3:16*

## Evening Reading

They will see his face.

Then Moses said, "Please let me see your glory." . . . [God said,] "But you can't see my face, because no one may see me and live." ✦ No one has ever seen God. God's only Son, the one who is closest to the Father's heart, has made him known. ✦ Every eye will see him, even those who pierced him. Every tribe on earth will mourn because of him. ✦ I see someone who is not here now. I look at someone who is not nearby. ✦ But I know that my defender lives, and afterwards, he will rise on the earth. Even after my skin has been stripped off my body, I will see God in my own flesh. ✦ I will see your face when I am declared innocent. When I wake up, I will be satisfied with seeing you. ✦ We will be like him because we will see him as he is. ✦ The Lord will come from heaven. . . . First, the dead who believed in Christ will come back to life. Then, together with them, we who are still alive will be taken in the clouds to meet the Lord in the air. In this way we will always be with the Lord.

*Revelation 22:4; Exodus 33:18, 20; John 1:18; Revelation 1:7; Numbers 24:17; Job 19:25–26; Psalm 17:15; 1 John 3:2; 1 Thessalonians 4:16–17*

## MORNING READING

Do not be afraid, because I have reclaimed you.

Don't be afraid, because you won't be put to shame. Don't be discouraged, because you won't be disgraced. You'll forget the shame you've had since you were young. You won't remember the disgrace of your husband's death anymore. Your husband is your maker. His name is the Lord of Armies. Your defender is the Holy One of Israel. ✦ I made your rebellious acts disappear like a thick cloud and your sins like the morning mist. Come back to me, because I have reclaimed you. ✦ The precious blood of Christ, the lamb with no defects or imperfections. ✦ Their defender is strong. His name is the Lord of Armies. He will certainly take up their cause. ✦ "My Father, who gave them to me, is greater than everyone else, and no one can tear them away from my Father." ✦ Good will and peace are yours from God the Father and our Lord Jesus Christ! In order to free us from this present evil world, Christ took the punishment for our sins, because that was what our God and Father wanted. Glory belongs to our God and Father forever! Amen.

*Isaiah 43:1; Isaiah 54:4–5; Isaiah 44:22; 1 Peter 1:19; Jeremiah 50:34; John 10:29; Galatians 1:3–5*

## EVENING READING

I will acknowledge the Lord's acts of mercy,
and sing the praises of the Lord,
because of everything that the Lord has done for us.

He pulled me out of a horrible pit, out of the mud and clay. He set my feet on a rock and made my steps secure. ✦ The life I now live I live by believing in God's Son, who loved me and took the punishment for my sins. ✦ God didn't spare his own Son but handed him over to death for all of us. So he will also give us everything along with him. ✦ Christ died for us while we were still sinners. This demonstrates God's love for us. ✦ He has put his seal of ownership on us and has given us the Spirit as his guarantee. ✦ This Holy Spirit is the guarantee that we will receive our inheritance. We have this guarantee until we are set free to belong to him. God receives praise and glory for this. ✦ God is rich in mercy because of his great love for us. We were dead because of our failures, but he made us alive together with Christ. (It is God's kindness that saved you.) God has brought us back to life together with Christ Jesus and has given us a position in heaven with him.

*Isaiah 63:7; Psalm 40:2; Galatians 2:20; Romans 8:32; Romans 5:8; 2 Corinthians 1:22; Ephesians 1:14; Ephesians 2:4–6*

## MORNING READING

I am dark and lovely.

Indeed, I was born guilty. I was a sinner when my mother conceived me. ✦ You became famous in every nation because of your beauty. Your beauty was perfect because I gave you my glory, declares the Almighty LORD. ✦ "Lord! I'm a sinful person!" ✦ Look at you! You are beautiful, my true love. ✦ I sit in dust and ashes to show that I am sorry. ✦ You are beautiful in every way, my true love. There is no blemish on you. ✦ Evil is present with me even when I want to do what God's standards say is good. ✦ "Cheer up, friend! Your sins are forgiven." ✦ I know that nothing good lives in me. ✦ God has made you complete in Christ. ✦ We want to present everyone as mature Christian people. ✦ You have been washed and made holy, and you have received God's approval in the name of the Lord Jesus Christ and in the Spirit of our God. ✦ You were chosen to tell about the excellent qualities of God, who called you out of darkness into his marvelous light.

*Song of Songs 1:5; Psalm 51:5; Ezekiel 16:14; Luke 5:8; Song of Songs 4:1; Job 42:6; Song of Songs 4:7; Romans 7:21; Matthew 9:2; Romans 7:18; Colossians 2:10; Colossians 1:28; 1 Corinthians 6:11; 1 Peter 2:9*

## EVENING READING

Those who try to live a godly life because they believe in Christ Jesus will be persecuted.

"I came to turn a man against his father, a daughter against her mother, a daughter-in-law against her mother-in-law. A person's enemies will be the members of his own family." ✦ Whoever wants to be a friend of this world is an enemy of God. ✦ Don't love the world and what it offers. Those who love the world don't have the Father's love in them. Not everything that the world offers—physical gratification, greed, and extravagant lifestyles—comes from the Father. It comes from the world. ✦ "If the world hates you, realize that it hated me before it hated you. If you had anything in common with the world, the world would love you as one of its own. But you don't have anything in common with the world. I chose you from the world, and that's why the world hates you. Remember what I told you: 'A servant isn't greater than his master.'" ✦ "I have given them your message. But the world has hated them because they don't belong to the world any more than I belong to the world."

*2 Timothy 3:12; Matthew 10:35–36; James 4:4; 1 John 2:15–16; John 15:18–20; John 17:14*

## MORNING READING

Sin is unavoidable when there is much talk,
but whoever seals his lips is wise.

Remember this, my dear brothers and sisters: Everyone should be quick to listen, slow to speak, and should not get angry easily. ✦ Better to get angry slowly than to be a hero. Better to be even-tempered than to capture a city. ✦ All of us make a lot of mistakes. If someone doesn't make any mistakes when he speaks, he would be perfect. He would be able to control everything he does. ✦ "By your words you will be declared innocent, or by your words you will be declared guilty." ✦ O Lord, set a guard at my mouth. Keep watch over the door of my lips. ✦ God called you to endure suffering because Christ suffered for you. He left you an example so that you could follow in his footsteps. Christ never committed any sin. He never spoke deceitfully. Christ never verbally abused those who verbally abused him. When he suffered, he didn't make any threats but left everything to the one who judges fairly. ✦ Think about Jesus, who endured opposition from sinners, so that you don't become tired and give up. ✦ They've never told a lie. They are blameless.

*Proverbs 10:19; James 1:19; Proverbs 16:32; James 3:2; Matthew 12:37; Psalm 141:3; 1 Peter 2:21–23; Hebrews 12:3; Revelation 14:5*

## EVENING READING

Teach me your way, O Lord.

"I will instruct you. I will teach you the way that you should go. I will advise you as my eyes watch over you." ✦ The Lord is good and decent. That is why he teaches sinners the way they should live. He leads humble people to do what is right, and he teaches them his way. ✦ "I am the gate. Those who enter the sheep pen through me will be saved. They will go in and out of the sheep pen and find food." ✦ Jesus answered him, "I am the way, the truth, and the life. No one goes to the Father except through me." ✦ Brothers and sisters, because of the blood of Jesus we can now confidently go into the holy place. Jesus has opened a new and living way for us to go through the curtain. (The curtain is his own body.) We have a superior priest in charge of God's house. We have been sprinkled with his blood to free us from a guilty conscience, and our bodies have been washed with clean water. So we must continue to come to him with a sincere heart and strong faith. ✦ Let's learn about the Lord. Let's get to know the Lord. ✦ Every path of the Lord is one of mercy and truth for those who cling to his promise and written instructions.

*Psalm 27:11; Psalm 32:8; Psalm 25:8–9; John 10:9; John 14:6; Hebrews 10:19–22; Hosea 6:3; Psalm 25:10*

## MORNING READING

It is impossible to do what God's standards demand
because of the weakness our human nature has.
But God sent his Son to have a human nature as sinners have
and to pay for sin. That way God condemned sin in our corrupt nature.

Moses' Teachings . . . are only a shadow of the good things in the future. They aren't an exact likeness of those things. They can never make those who worship perfect. If these sacrifices could have made the worshipers perfect, the sacrifices would have stopped long ago. ✦ However, everyone who believes in Jesus receives God's approval. ✦ Since all of these sons and daughters have flesh and blood, Jesus took on flesh and blood to be like them. He did this so that by dying he would destroy the one who had power over death (that is, the devil). In this way he would free those who were slaves all their lives because they were afraid of dying. So Jesus helps Abraham's descendants rather than helping angels. Therefore, he had to become like his brothers and sisters so that he could be merciful. He became like them.

*Romans 8:3; Hebrews 10:1–2; Acts 13:39; Hebrews 2:14–17*

## EVENING READING

All people have sinned, they have fallen short of God's glory.

Not one person has God's approval. Everyone has turned away. . . . No one does anything good, not even one person. ✦ Certainly, there is no one so righteous on earth that he always does what is good and never sins. ✦ How can anyone born of a woman be pure? ✦ God's promise that we may enter his place of rest still stands. We are afraid that some of you think you won't enter his place of rest. ✦ I admit that I am rebellious. My sin is always in front of me. . . . Indeed, I was born guilty. I was a sinner when my mother conceived me. ✦ The Lord has taken away your sin; you will not die. ✦ He approved of those whom he had called, and he gave glory to those whom he had approved of. ✦ As all of us reflect the Lord's glory with faces that are not covered with veils, we are being changed into his image with ever-increasing glory. This comes from the Lord, who is the Spirit. ✦ This is on the condition that you continue in faith without being moved from the solid foundation of the hope that the Good News contains. ✦ You should live in a way that proves you belong to the God who calls you into his kingdom and glory.

*Romans 3:23; Romans 3:10, 12; Ecclesiastes 7:20; Job 25:4;
Hebrews 4:1; Psalm 51:3, 5; 2 Samuel 12:13; Romans 8:30;
2 Corinthians 3:18; Colossians 1:23; 1 Thessalonians 2:12*

## Morning Reading

Honor the Lord with your wealth and
with the first and best part of all your income.

Remember this: The farmer who plants a few seeds will have a very small harvest. But the farmer who plants because he has received God's blessings will receive a harvest of God's blessings in return. ✦ Every Sunday each of you should set aside some of your money and save it. ✦ God is fair. He won't forget what you've done or the love you've shown for him. You helped his holy people, and you continue to help them. ✦ Brothers and sisters, in view of all we have just shared about God's compassion, I encourage you to offer your bodies as living sacrifices, dedicated to God and pleasing to him. This kind of worship is appropriate for you. ✦ Christ's love guides us. We are convinced of the fact that one man has died for all people. Therefore, all people have died. He died for all people so that those who live should no longer live for themselves but for the man who died and was brought back to life for them. ✦ So, whether you eat or drink, or whatever you do, do everything to the glory of God.

*Proverbs 3:9; 2 Corinthians 9:6; 1 Corinthians 16:2; Hebrews 6:10; Romans 12:1; 2 Corinthians 5:14–15; 1 Corinthians 10:31*

## Evening Reading

There won't be any night there.

But the Lord will be your everlasting light. Your God will be your glory. ✦ The city doesn't need any sun or moon to give it light because the glory of God gave it light. The lamb was its lamp. ✦ There will be no more night, and they will not need any light from lamps or the sun because the Lord God will shine on them. ✦ You are chosen people, a royal priesthood, a holy nation, people who belong to God. You were chosen to tell about the excellent qualities of God, who called you out of darkness into his marvelous light. ✦ You will also thank the Father, who has made you able to share the light, which is what God's people inherit. God has rescued us from the power of darkness and has brought us into the kingdom of his Son, whom he loves. ✦ Once you lived in the dark, but now the Lord has filled you with light. Live as children who have light. ✦ You belong to the day and the light not to the night and the dark. ✦ But the path of righteous people is like the light of dawn that becomes brighter and brighter until it reaches midday.

*Revelation 21:25; Isaiah 60:19; Revelation 21:23; Revelation 22:5; 1 Peter 2:9; Colossians 1:12–13; Ephesians 5:8; 1 Thessalonians 5:5; Proverbs 4:18*

## Morning Reading

You satisfy my soul with the richest foods.
My mouth will sing your praise with joyful lips.
As I lie on my bed, I remember you.
Through the long hours of the night, I think about you.

How precious are your thoughts concerning me, O God! How vast in number they are! ✦ How sweet the taste of your promise is! It tastes sweeter than honey. ✦ Let him kiss me with the kisses of his mouth. Your expressions of love are better than wine. ✦ As long as I have you, I don't need anyone else in heaven or on earth. ✦ You are the most handsome of Adam's descendants. ✦ Like an apple tree among the trees in the forest, so is my beloved among the young men. I want to sit in his shadow. His fruit tastes sweet to me. He leads me into a banquet room and looks at me with love. ✦ His form is like Lebanon, choice as the cedars. His mouth is sweet in every way. Everything about him is desirable! This is my beloved, and this is my friend.

*Psalm 63:5–6; Psalm 139:17; Psalm 119:103; Song of Songs 1:2; Psalm 73:25; Psalm 45:2; Song of Songs 2:3–4; Song of Songs 5:15–16*

## Evening Reading

Restore the joy of your salvation to me.

I've seen their sinful ways, but I'll heal them. I'll guide them and give them rest. I'll comfort them and their mourners. ✦ "Come on now, let's discuss this!" says the Lord. "Though your sins are bright red, they will become as white as snow. Though they are dark red, they will become as white as wool." ✦ "Come back, you rebellious people, and I will forgive you for being unfaithful." Here we are! We have come to you because you are the Lord our God. ✦ I want to hear what God the Lord says, because he promises peace to his people, to his godly ones. But they must not go back to their stupidity. ✦ Praise the Lord, my soul, and never forget all the good he has done: He is the one who forgives all your sins, the one who heals all your diseases. ✦ He renews my soul. ✦ I will praise you, O Lord. Although you had been angry with me, you turned your anger away from me, and you comforted me. ✦ Hold me, and I will be safe. ✦ I alone am the one who is going to wipe away your rebellious actions for my own sake. I will not remember your sins anymore.

*Psalm 51:12; Isaiah 57:18; Isaiah 1:18; Jeremiah 3:22; Psalm 85:8; Psalm 103:2–3; Psalm 23:3; Isaiah 12:1; Psalm 119:117; Isaiah 43:25*

## MORNING READING

Their defender is strong.

I know that your crimes are numerous and your sins are many. ✦ I have raised up one chosen from the people. ✦ Then all humanity will know that I am the Lord, who saves you, the Mighty One of Jacob, who reclaims you. ✦ I am powerful enough to save you. ✦ God can guard you so that you don't fall. ✦ Laws were added to increase the failure. But where sin increased, God's kindness increased even more. ✦ Those who believe in him won't be condemned. But those who don't believe are already condemned because they don't believe in God's only Son. ✦ That is why he is always able to save those who come to God through him. He can do this because he always lives and intercedes for them. ✦ Am I too weak to reclaim you? ✦ What will separate us from the love Christ has for us? . . . I am convinced that nothing can ever separate us from God's love which Christ Jesus our Lord shows us. We can't be separated by death or life, by angels or rulers, by anything in the present or anything in the future, by forces or powers in the world above or in the world below, or by anything else in creation.

*Jeremiah 50:34; Amos 5:12; Psalm 89:19; Isaiah 49:26; Isaiah 63:1; Jude 24; Romans 5:20; John 3:18; Hebrews 7:25; Isaiah 50:2; Romans 8:35, 38–39*

## EVENING READING

Are you looking for great things for yourself? Don't look for them.

Place my yoke over your shoulders, and learn from me, because I am gentle and humble. Then you will find rest for yourselves. ✦ Have the same attitude that Christ Jesus had. Although he was in the form of God and equal with God, he did not take advantage of this equality. Instead, he emptied himself by taking on the form of a servant, by becoming like other humans, by having a human appearance. He humbled himself by becoming obedient to the point of death, death on a cross.✦ Whoever doesn't take up his cross and follow me doesn't deserve to be my disciple. ✦ God called you to endure suffering because Christ suffered for you. He left you an example so that you could follow in his footsteps. ✦ A godly life brings huge profits to people who are content with what they have. We didn't bring anything into the world, and we can't take anything out of it. As long as we have food and clothes, we should be satisfied. ✦ I've learned to be content in whatever situation I'm in.

*Jeremiah 45:5; Matthew 11:29; Philippians 2:5–8; Matthew 10:38; 1 Peter 2:21; 1 Timothy 6:6–8; Philippians 4:11*

## MORNING READING

When I was panic-stricken, I said,
"I have been cut off from your sight."
But you heard my pleas for mercy
when I cried out to you for help.

I am sinking in deep mud. There is nothing to stand on. I am in deep water. A flood is sweeping me away. ✦ Water flowed over my head. I thought I was finished. "I call your name from the deepest pit, O Lord. Listen to my cry for help. Don't close your ears when I cry out for relief. Be close at hand when I call to you. You told me not to be afraid. ✦ Will the Lord reject me for all time? Will he ever accept me? Has his mercy come to an end forever? Has his promise been canceled throughout every generation? Has God forgotten to be merciful? . . . Then I said, "It makes me feel sick that the power of the Most High is no longer the same." I will remember the deeds of the Lord. I will remember your ancient miracles. ✦ I believe that I will see the goodness of the Lord in this world of the living.

*Psalm 31:22; Psalm 69:2; Lamentations 3:54–57; Psalm 77:7–11; Psalm 27:13*

## EVENING READING

When you call to me, I will answer you.
I will be with you when you are in trouble.

Jabez prayed to the God of Israel, "Please bless me and give me more territory. May your power be with me and free me from evil so that I will not be in pain." God gave him what he prayed for. ✦ That night God appeared to Solomon. He said, "What can I give you?" Solomon responded to God. . . . "Give me wisdom and knowledge so that I may lead these people. After all, who can judge this great people of yours?" ✦ God gave Solomon wisdom—keen insight and a mind as limitless as the sand on the seashore. ✦ Asa called on the Lord his God. He said, "Lord, there is no one except you who can help those who are not strong so that they can fight against a large army. . . . You are the Lord our God. Don't let anyone successfully oppose you." The Lord attacked the Sudanese army in front of Asa and Judah. ✦ You are the one who hears prayers. Everyone will come to you.

*Psalm 91:15; 1 Chronicles 4:10; 2 Chronicles 1:7–8, 10;*
*1 Kings 4:29; 2 Chronicles 14:11–12; Psalm 65:2*

## MORNING READING

Whoever offers thanks as a sacrifice honors me.

Let Christ's word with all its wisdom and richness live in you. Use psalms, hymns, and spiritual songs to teach and instruct yourselves about God's kindness. Sing to God in your hearts. Everything you say or do should be done in the name of the Lord Jesus, giving thanks to God the Father through him. ✦ You were bought for a price. So bring glory to God in the way you use your body. ✦ You are chosen people, a royal priesthood, a holy nation, people who belong to God. ✦ You come to him as living stones, a spiritual house that is being built into a holy priesthood. So offer spiritual sacrifices that God accepts through Jesus Christ. ✦ Through Jesus we should always bring God a sacrifice of praise, that is, words that acknowledge him. ✦ My soul will boast about the Lord. Those who are oppressed will hear it and rejoice. Praise the Lord's greatness with me. Let us highly honor his name together.

*Psalm 50:23; Colossians 3:16–17; 1 Corinthians 6:20; 1 Peter 2:9; 1 Peter 2:5; Hebrews 13:15; Psalm 34:2–3*

## EVENING READING

Take me with you. Let's run away.

"I love you with an everlasting love. So I will continue to show you my kindness." ✦ "I led them with cords of human kindness, with ropes of love." ✦ "When I have been lifted up from the earth, I will draw all people toward me" ✦ "Look! This is the Lamb of God." ✦ "As Moses lifted up the snake on a pole in the desert, so the Son of Man must be lifted up. Then everyone who believes in him will have eternal life." ✦ As long as I have you, I don't need anyone else in heaven or on earth. ✦ We love because God loved us first. ✦ My beloved said to me, "Get up, my true love, my beautiful one, and come with me. Look! The winter is past. The rain is over and gone. Blossoms appear in the land. The time of the songbird has arrived. The cooing of the mourning dove is heard in our land. The green figs ripen. The grapevines bloom and give off a fragrance. Get up, my true love, my beautiful one, and come with me."

*Song of Songs 1:4; Jeremiah 31:3; Hosea 11:4; John 12:32; John 1:36; John 3:14–15; Psalm 73:25; 1 John 4:19; Song of Songs 2:10–13*

## MORNING READING

I will send them a prophet, an Israelite like you.

I [Moses] stood between the Lord and you to tell you the word of the Lord, because you were afraid. ✦ There is one God. There is also one mediator between God and humans—a human, Christ Jesus. ✦ Moses was a very humble man, more humble than anyone else on earth. ✦ "Place my yoke over your shoulders, and learn from me, because I am gentle and humble. Then you will find rest for yourselves." ✦ Have the same attitude that Christ Jesus had. Although he was in the form of God and equal with God, he did not take advantage of this equality. Instead, he emptied himself by taking on the form of a servant, by becoming like other humans, by having a human appearance. ✦ Moses was a faithful servant in God's household. He told the people what God would say in the future. But Christ is a faithful son in charge of God's household. We are his household if we continue to have courage and to be proud of the confidence we have.

*Deuteronomy 18:18; Deuteronomy 5:5; 1 Timothy 2:5; Numbers 12:3; Matthew 11:29; Philippians 2:5–7; Hebrews 3:5–6*

## EVENING READING

Everlasting encouragement and good hope.

"I will remember the promise that I made with you when you were young, and I will make it a promise that will last forever." ✦ With one sacrifice he accomplished the work of setting them apart for God forever. ✦ That is why he is always able to save those who come to God through him. He can do this because he always lives and intercedes for them. ✦ I know whom I trust. I'm convinced that he is able to protect what he had entrusted to me until that day. ✦ God never changes his mind when he gives gifts or when he calls someone. ✦ What will separate us from the love Christ has for us? ✦ "The lamb in the center near the throne will be their shepherd. He will lead them to springs filled with the water of life, and God will wipe every tear from their eyes." ✦ In this way we will always be with the Lord. So then, comfort each other with these words! ✦ This is not a place to rest! ✦ We don't have a permanent city here on earth, but we are looking for the city that we will have in the future.

*2 Thessalonians 2:16; Ezekiel 16:60; Hebrews 10:14; Hebrews 7:25; 2 Timothy 1:12; Romans 11:29; Romans 8:35; Revelation 7:17; 1 Thessalonians 4:17–18; Micah 2:10; Hebrews 13:14*

## MORNING READING

"I can guarantee this truth: I am the gate for the sheep."

Suddenly, the curtain in the temple was split in two from top to bottom. ✦ Christ suffered for our sins once. He was an innocent person, but he suffered for guilty people so that he could bring you to God. ✦ The way into the most holy place was not open while the tent was still in use. ✦ "I am the gate. Those who enter the sheep pen through me will be saved. They will go in and out of the sheep pen and find food." ✦ "No one goes to the Father except through me." ✦ So Jewish and non-Jewish people can go to the Father in one Spirit. That is why you are no longer foreigners and outsiders but citizens together with God's people and members of God's family. ✦ Brothers and sisters, because of the blood of Jesus we can now confidently go into the holy place. Jesus has opened a new and living way for us to go through the curtain. (The curtain is his own body.) ✦ We have peace with God because of what our Lord Jesus Christ has done. Through Christ we can approach God and stand in his favor. So we brag because of our confidence that we will receive glory from God.

*John 10:7; Matthew 27:51; 1 Peter 3:18; Hebrews 9:8; John 10:9; John 14:6; Ephesians 2:18–19; Hebrews 10:19–20; Romans 5:1–2*

## EVENING READING

His word is inside me like a burning fire shut up in my bones.
I wear myself out holding it in, but I can't do it any longer.

If I spread the Good News, I have nothing to brag about because I have an obligation to do this. How horrible it will be for me if I don't spread the Good News! . . . So what is my reward? It is to spread the Good News free of charge. In that way I won't use the rights that belong to those who spread the Good News. ✦ They called Peter and John and ordered them never to teach about Jesus or even mention his name. Peter and John answered them, ". . . We cannot stop talking about what we've seen and heard." ✦ Christ's love guides us. ✦ " 'I was afraid. So I hid your two thousand dollars in the ground.' . . . His master responded, 'You evil and lazy servant! . . . You should have invested my money with the bankers. When I returned, I would have received my money back with interest.' " ✦ "Go home to your family, and tell them how much the Lord has done for you."

*Jeremiah 20:9; 1 Corinthians 9:16, 18; Acts 4:18–20; 2 Corinthians 5:14; Matthew 25:25–27; Mark 5:19*

## MORNING READING

Don't ever take any of the things claimed for destruction.

The Lord says, "Get away from unbelievers. Separate yourselves from them. Have nothing to do with anything unclean." ✦ Dear friends, since you are foreigners and temporary residents in the world, I'm encouraging you to keep away from the desires of your corrupt nature. ✦ Show mercy to others, even though you are afraid that you might be stained by their sinful lives. ✦ Dear friends, now we are God's children. What we will be isn't completely clear yet. We do know that when Christ appears we will be like him because we will see him as he is. So all people who have this confidence in Christ keep themselves pure, as Christ is pure. ✦ God's saving kindness has appeared for the benefit of all people. It trains us to avoid ungodly lives filled with worldly desires so that we can live self-controlled, moral, and godly lives in this present world. At the same time we can expect what we hope for—the appearance of the glory of our great God and Savior, Jesus Christ. He gave himself for us to set us free from every sin and to cleanse us so that we can be his special people who are enthusiastic about doing good things.

*Deuteronomy 13:17; 2 Corinthians 6:17; 1 Peter 2:11; Jude 23; 1 John 3:2–3; Titus 2:11–14*

## EVENING READING

I [Paul] asked, "Who are you, sir?"
The Lord answered, "I am Jesus."

Jesus said, "Calm down! It's me. Don't be afraid!" ✦ When you go through the sea, I am with you. When you go through rivers, they will not sweep you away. When you walk through fire, you will not be burned, and the flames will not harm you. I am the Lord your God, the Holy One of Israel, your Savior. ✦ Even though I walk through the dark valley of death, because you are with me, I fear no harm. Your rod and your staff give me courage. ✦ "Immanuel," . . . "God is with us." ✦ "You will name him Jesus [He Saves], because he will save his people from their sins." ✦ If anyone does sin, we have Jesus Christ, who has God's full approval. He speaks on our behalf when we come into the presence of the Father. ✦ Who will condemn them? Christ has died, and more importantly, he was brought back to life. Christ has the highest position in heaven. Christ also intercedes for us. What will separate us from the love Christ has for us? Can trouble, distress, persecution, hunger, nakedness, danger, or violent death separate us from his love?

*Act 26:15; Matthew 14:27; Isaiah 43:2–3; Psalm 23:4; Matthew 1:23; Matthew 1:21; 1 John 2:1; Romans 8:34–35*

## MORNING READING

Keep your relationship with the Lord firm!

I have followed his footsteps closely. I have stayed on his path and did not turn from it. ✦ The LORD loves justice, and he will not abandon his godly ones. They will be kept safe forever. ✦ The LORD guards you from every evil. He guards your life. ✦ "The person who has God's approval will live by faith. But if he turns back, I will not be pleased with him." We don't belong with those who turn back and are destroyed. Instead, we belong with those who have faith and are saved. ✦ They left us. However, they were never really part of us. If they had been, they would have stayed with us. But by leaving they made it clear that none of them were part of us. ✦ "If you live by what I say, you are truly my disciples." ✦ "But the person who endures to the end will be saved." ✦ Be alert. Be firm in the Christian faith. Be courageous and strong. ✦ Hold on to what you have so that no one takes your crown. ✦ Everyone who wins the victory this way will wear white clothes. I will never erase their names from the Book of Life.

*Philippians 4:1; Job 23:11; Psalm 37:28; Psalm 121:7; Hebrews 10:38–39; 1 John 2:19; John 8:31; Matthew 24:13; 1 Corinthians 16:13; Revelation 3:11; Revelation 3:5*

## EVENING READING

Enoch walked with God.

Do two people ever walk together without meeting first? ✦ God was also pleased to bring everything on earth and in heaven back to himself through Christ. He did this by making peace through Christ's blood sacrificed on the cross. Once you were separated from God. The evil things you did showed your hostile attitude. But now Christ has brought you back to God by dying in his physical body. He did this so that you could come into God's presence without sin, fault, or blame. ✦ Through Christ Jesus you, who were once far away, have been brought near by the blood of Christ. ✦ If the death of his Son restored our relationship with God while we were still his enemies, we are even more certain that, because of this restored relationship, the life of his Son will save us. In addition, our Lord Jesus Christ lets us continue to brag about God. ✦ Our relationship is with the Father and with his Son Jesus Christ. ✦ May the Lord Jesus Christ's good will, God's love, and the Holy Spirit's presence be with all of you!

*Genesis 5:22; Amos 3:3; Colossians 1:20–22; Ephesians 2:13; Romans 5:10–11; 1 John 1:3; 2 Corinthians 13:13*

## Morning Reading

If you bring a burnt offering from your cattle,
you must offer a male that has no defects.
Offer it at the entrance to the tent of meeting so that
the Lord will accept you. Place your hand on the animal's head.
The burnt offering will be accepted to make peace with the Lord.

"God will provide a lamb for the burnt offering." ✦ "Look! This is the Lamb of God who takes away the sin of the world." ✦ We have been set apart as holy because Jesus Christ did what God wanted him to do by sacrificing his body once and for all. ✦ "A ransom for many people." ✦ No one takes my life from me. I give my life of my own free will. I have the authority to give my life, and I have the authority to take my life back again. ✦ I will love them freely. ✦ God's Son, who loved me and took the punishment for my sins. ✦ God had Christ, who was sinless, take our sin so that we might receive God's approval through him. ✦ So that the kindness he had given us in his dear Son would be praised and given glory.

*Leviticus 1:3–4; Genesis 22:8; John 1:29; Hebrews 10:10; Matthew 20:28; John 10:18; Hosea 14:4; Galatians 2:20; 2 Corinthians 5:21; Ephesians 1:6*

## Evening Reading

Because your mercy toward me is great.
You have rescued me from the depths of hell.

"Fear the one who can destroy both body and soul in hell." ✦ Do not be afraid, because I have reclaimed you. I have called you by name; you are mine. ✦ I alone am the Lord, and there is no savior except me. ✦ I alone am the one who is going to wipe away your rebellious actions for my own sake. I will not remember your sins anymore. ✦ They trust their riches and brag about their abundant wealth. No one can ever buy back another person or pay God a ransom for his life. The price to be paid for his soul is too costly. ✦ I have found a ransom. ✦ But God is rich in mercy because of his great love for us. We were dead because of our failures, but he made us alive together with Christ. ✦ No one else can save us. Indeed, we can be saved only by the power of the one named Jesus and not by any other person.

*Psalm 86:13; Matthew 10:28; Isaiah 43:1; Isaiah 43:11; Isaiah 43:25; Psalm 49:6–8; Job 33:24; Ephesians 2:4–5; Acts 4:12*

## MORNING READING

The Lord came to my defense.

Truly, the noise from the hills, from the mountains, is the noise of false worship. Truly, the Lord our God will rescue us. ✦ The Lord is my rock and my fortress and my Savior, my God, my rock in whom I take refuge, my shield, and the strength of my salvation, my stronghold. ✦ Shout loudly, and sing with joy, people of Zion! The Holy One of Israel is great. He is among you. ✦ The Messenger of the Lord camps around those who fear him, and he rescues them. ✦ Righteous people cry out. The Lord hears and rescues them from all their troubles. ✦ The eternal God is your shelter, and his everlasting arms support you. ✦ So we can confidently say, "The Lord is my helper. I will not be afraid. What can mortals do to me?" ✦ Who is God but the Lord? God arms me with strength and makes my way perfect. ✦ But God's kindness made me what I am.

*Psalm 18:18; Jeremiah 3:23; Psalm 18:2; Isaiah 12:6; Psalm 34:7; Psalm 34:17; Deuteronomy 33:27; Hebrews 13:6; Psalm 18:31–32; 1 Corinthians 15:10*

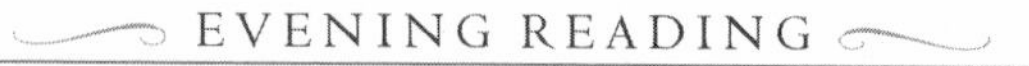

## EVENING READING

We have all strayed like sheep.

If we say, "We aren't sinful" we are deceiving ourselves, and the truth is not in us. ✦ Not one person has God's approval. No one understands. No one searches for God. Everyone has turned away. Together they have become rotten to the core. ✦ You were like lost sheep. Now you have come back to the shepherd and bishop of your lives. ✦ I have wandered away like a lost lamb. Search for me, because I have never forgotten your commandments. ✦ He renews my soul. He guides me along the paths of righteousness for the sake of his name. ✦ "My sheep respond to my voice, and I know who they are. They follow me, and I give them eternal life. They will never be lost, and no one will tear them away from me." ✦ "Suppose a man has 100 sheep and loses one of them. Doesn't he leave the 99 sheep grazing in the pasture and look for the lost sheep until he finds it?"

*Isaiah 53:6; 1 John 1:8; Romans 3:10–12; 1 Peter 2:25; Psalm 119:176; Psalm 23:3; John 10:27–28; Luke 15:4*

## MORNING READING

The Lord came to help Sarah
and did for her what he had promised.

Trust him at all times, you people. Pour out your hearts in his presence. God is our refuge. ✦ David found strength in the Lord his God. ✦ "God will definitely take care of you and take you out of this land to the land he swore with an oath to give to Abraham, Isaac, and Jacob." ✦ The Lord told Moses, ". . . I've seen how my people are mistreated in Egypt. I've heard their groaning and have come to rescue them." . . . This is the man who led our ancestors out of Egypt. He is the person who did amazing things and worked miracles in Egypt, at the Red Sea, and in the desert for 40 years. ✦ Every single good promise that the Lord had given the nation of Israel came true. ✦ The one who made the promise is faithful. ✦ God is not like people. He tells no lies. He is not like humans. He doesn't change his mind. When he says something, he does it. ✦ "The earth and the heavens will disappear, but my words will never disappear." ✦ Grass dries up, and flowers wither, but the word of our God will last forever.

*Genesis 21:1; Psalm 62:8; 1 Samuel 30:6; Genesis 50:24; Acts 7:33–34, 36; Joshua 21:45; Hebrews 10:23; Numbers 23:19; Matthew 24:35; Isaiah 40:8*

## EVENING READING

The eyes of all creatures look to you.

He gives everyone life, breath, and everything they have. ✦ The Lord is good to everyone and has compassion for everything that he has made. ✦ "Look at the birds. They don't plant, harvest, or gather the harvest into barns. Yet, your heavenly Father feeds them." ✦ They all have the same Lord, who gives his riches to everyone who calls on him. ✦ I look up toward the mountains. Where can I find help? ✦ As servants depend on their masters, as a maid depends on her mistress, so we depend on the Lord our God until he has pity on us. ✦ The Lord is a God of justice. ✦ On that day his people will say, "This is our God; we have waited for him, and now he will save us. This is the Lord; we have waited for him. Let us rejoice and be glad because he will save us." ✦ But if we hope for what we don't see, we eagerly wait for it with perseverance.

*Psalm 145:15; Acts 17:25; Psalm 145:9; Matthew 6:26; Romans 10:12; Psalm 121:1; Psalm 123:2; Isaiah 30:18; Isaiah 25:9; Romans 8:25*

## MORNING READING

"You will name him Jesus [He Saves],
because he will save his people from their sins."

You know that Christ appeared in order to take away our sins. ✦ Freed from our sins, we could live a life that has God's approval. His wounds have healed you. ✦ He is always able to save those who come to God through him. ✦ He was wounded for our rebellious acts. He was crushed for our sins. He was punished so that we could have peace, and we received healing from his wounds. . . . The Lord has laid all our sins on him. ✦ "Scripture says that the Messiah would suffer . . . that by the authority of Jesus people would be told to turn to God and change the way they think and act so that their sins will be forgiven. This would be told to people from all nations." ✦ He has appeared once to remove sin by his sacrifice. ✦ God used his power to give Jesus the highest position as leader and savior . . . to forgive their sins. ✦ Through Jesus your sins can be forgiven. Sins kept you from receiving God's approval through Moses' Teachings. However, everyone who believes in Jesus receives God's approval.✦ Your sins are forgiven through Christ.

*Matthew 1:21; 1 John 3:5; 1 Peter 2:24; Hebrews 7:25; Isaiah 53:5–6; Luke 24:46–47; Hebrews 9:26; Acts 5:31; Acts 13:38–39; 1 John 2:12*

## EVENING READING

Our Lord Jesus Christ. He was rich, yet . . .
he became poor in order to make you rich through his poverty.

God was pleased to have all of himself live in Christ. ✦ His Son is the reflection of God's glory and the exact likeness of God's being. He holds everything together through his powerful words. After he had cleansed people from their sins, he received the highest position, the one next to the Father in heaven. The Son has become greater than the angels since he has been given a name that is superior to theirs. ✦ Although he was in the form of God and equal with God, he did not take advantage of this equality. Instead, he emptied himself. ✦ "Foxes have holes, and birds have nests, but the Son of Man has nowhere to sleep." ✦ Everything belongs to you. Whether it is Paul, Apollos, Cephas, the world, life or death, present or future things, everything belongs to you. You belong to Christ, and Christ belongs to God.

*2 Corinthians 8:9; Colossians 1:19; Hebrews 1:3–4; Philippians 2:6–7; Matthew 8:20; 1 Corinthians 3:21–23*

## MORNING READING

His left hand is under my head.
His right hand caresses me.

His everlasting arms support you. ✦ But when he noticed how strong the wind was, [Peter] became afraid and started to sink. He shouted, "Lord, save me!" Immediately, Jesus reached out, caught hold of him, and said, "You have so little faith! Why did you doubt?" ✦ A person's steps are directed by the Lord, and the Lord delights in his way. When he falls, he will not be thrown down headfirst because the Lord holds on to his hand. ✦ The Lord's beloved people will live securely with him. The Lord will shelter them all day long, since he, too, lives on the mountain slopes. ✦ Turn all your anxiety over to God because he cares for you. ✦ Whoever touches you touches the apple of his eye. ✦ They will never be lost, and no one will tear them away from me. My Father, who gave them to me, is greater than everyone else.

*Song of Songs 2:6; Deuteronomy 33:27; Matthew 14:30–31; Psalm 37:23–24; Deuteronomy 33:12; 1 Peter 5:7; Zechariah 2:8; John 10:28–29*

## EVENING READING

Who is this young woman? She looks like the dawn.
She is beautiful like the moon, pure like the sun,
awe-inspiring like those heavenly bodies.

God's church which he acquired with his own blood. ✦ Christ loved the church and gave his life for it. He did this to make the church holy by cleansing it, washing it using water along with spoken words. Then he could present it to himself as a glorious church, without any kind of stain or wrinkle—holy and without faults. ✦ A spectacular sign appeared in the sky: There was a woman who was dressed in the sun. ✦ [A great crowd said,] "Let us rejoice, be happy, and give him glory because it's time for the marriage of the lamb. His bride has made herself ready. She has been given the privilege of wearing dazzling, pure linen. This fine linen represents the things that God's holy people do that have his approval." ✦ Everyone who believes has God's approval through faith in Jesus Christ. ✦ "I have given them the glory that you gave me."

*Song of Songs 6:10; Acts 20:28; Ephesians 5:25–27; Revelation 12:1; Revelation 19:7–8; Romans 3:22; John 17:22*

## Morning Reading

Brothers and sisters: The time has been shortened.

A person who is born of a woman is short-lived and is full of trouble. He comes up like a flower; then he withers. He is like a fleeting shadow; he doesn't stay long. ✦ The world and its evil desires are passing away. But the person who does what God wants lives forever. ✦ As everyone dies because of Adam, so also everyone will be made alive because of Christ. ✦ "Death is turned into victory!" ✦ If we live, we honor the Lord, and if we die, we honor the Lord. So whether we live or die, we belong to the Lord. ✦ Christ means everything to me in this life, and when I die I'll have even more. ✦ So don't lose your confidence. It will bring you a great reward. You need endurance so that after you have done what God wants you to do, you can receive what he has promised. Yet, the one who is coming will come soon. He will not delay. ✦ The night is almost over, and the day is near. So we should get rid of the things that belong to the dark and take up the weapons that belong to the light. ✦ The end of everything is near. Therefore, practice self-control, and keep your minds clear so that you can pray.

*1 Corinthians 7:29; Job 14:1–2; 1 John 2:17; 1 Corinthians 15:22; 1 Corinthians 15:54; Romans 14:8; Philippians 1:21; Hebrews 10:35–37; Romans 13:12; 1 Peter 4:7*

## Evening Reading

A new name.

The disciples were called Christians for the first time in the city of Antioch. ✦ Whoever worships the Lord must give up doing wrong. ✦ Those who belong to Christ Jesus have crucified their corrupt nature along with its passions and desires. ✦ You were bought for a price. So bring glory to God in the way you use your body. ✦ But it's unthinkable that I could ever brag about anything except the cross of our Lord Jesus Christ. By his cross my relationship to the world and its relationship to me have been crucified. Certainly, it doesn't matter whether a person is circumcised or not. Rather, what matters is being a new creation. ✦ Imitate God, since you are the children he loves. Live in love as Christ also loved us. He gave his life for us as an offering and sacrifice, a soothing aroma to God. Don't let sexual sin, perversion of any kind, or greed even be mentioned among you. This is not appropriate behavior for God's holy people. . . . Now the Lord has filled you with light. Live as children who have light.

*Revelation 2:17; Acts 11:26; 2 Timothy 2:19; Galatians 5:24; 1 Corinthians 6:20; Galatians 6:14–15; Ephesians 5:1–3, 8*

## MORNING READING

"Look! This is the Lamb of God!"

(The blood of bulls and goats cannot take away sins.) For this reason, when Christ came into the world, he said, " 'You did not want sacrifices and offerings, but you prepared a body for me. You did not approve of burnt offerings and sacrifices for sin.' Then I said, 'I have come! (It is written about me in the scroll of the book.) I have come to do what you want, my God.' " ✦ He was abused and punished, but he didn't open his mouth. He was led like a lamb to the slaughter. He was like a sheep that is silent when its wool is cut off. He didn't open his mouth. ✦ Realize that you weren't set free from the worthless life handed down to you from your ancestors by a payment of silver or gold. . . . Rather, the payment that freed you was the precious blood of Christ, the lamb with no defects or imperfections. . . . became publicly known in the last period of time. Through him you believe in God. . . . So your faith and confidence are in God. ✦ "The lamb who was slain deserves to receive power, wealth, wisdom, strength, honor, glory, and praise."

*John 1:29; Hebrews 10:4–7; Isaiah 53:7; 1 Peter 1:18–21; Revelation 5:12*

## EVENING READING

But I will always have hope.
I will praise you more and more.

It's not that I've already reached the goal or have already completed the course. ✦ We should stop going over the elementary truths about Christ and move on to topics for more mature people. We shouldn't repeat the basics about turning away from the useless things we did and the basics about faith in God. ✦ But the path of righteous people is like the light of dawn that becomes brighter and brighter until it reaches midday. ✦ I love the Lord because he hears my voice, my pleas for mercy. I will call on him as long as I live because he turns his ear toward me. ✦ I will thank the Lord at all times. My mouth will always praise him. ✦ You are praised with silence in Zion, O God. ✦ Without stopping day or night [the four living creatures] were singing, "Holy, holy, holy is the Lord God Almighty." ✦ Whoever offers thanks as a sacrifice honors me. ✦ Always be joyful. Never stop praying. Whatever happens, give thanks, because it is God's will in Christ Jesus that you do this. ✦ Always be joyful in the Lord! I'll say it again: Be joyful!

*Psalm 71:14; Philippians 3:12; Hebrews 6:1; Proverbs 4:18; Psalm 116:1–2; Psalm 34:1; Psalm 65:1; Revelation 4:8; Psalm 50:23; 1 Thessalonians 5:16–18; Philippians 4:4*

## Morning Reading

Consider the great things he did for you.

Remember that for 40 years the Lord your God led you on your journey in the desert. He did this in order to humble you and test you. He wanted to know whether or not you would wholeheartedly obey his commands. ✦ Learn this lesson by heart: The Lord your God was disciplining you as parents discipline their children. ✦ I know that your regulations are fair, O Lord, and that you were right to make me suffer. ✦ It was good that I had to suffer in order to learn your laws. ✦ Before you made me suffer, I used to wander off, but now I hold on to your word. ✦ The Lord disciplined me severely, but he did not allow me to be killed. ✦ He has not treated us as we deserve for our sins or paid us back for our wrongs. As high as the heavens are above the earth—that is how vast his mercy is toward those who fear him. . . . He certainly knows what we are made of. He bears in mind that we are dust.

*1 Samuel 12:24; Deuteronomy 8:2; Deuteronomy 8:5; Psalm 119:75; Psalm 119:71; Psalm 119:67; Psalm 118:18; Psalm 103:10–11, 14*

## Evening Reading

We can expect what we hope for—
the appearance of the glory of our great
God and Savior, Jesus Christ.

We have this confidence as a sure and strong anchor for our lives. This confidence goes into the holy place behind the curtain where Jesus went before us on our behalf. ✦ Heaven must receive Jesus until the time when everything will be restored. ✦ On that day when he comes to be honored among all his holy people and admired by all who have believed in him. ✦ All creation has been groaning with the pains of childbirth up to the present time. However, not only creation groans. We, who have the Spirit as the first of God's gifts, also groan inwardly. We groan as we eagerly wait for our adoption, the freeing of our bodies from sin. ✦ Dear friends, now we are God's children. What we will be isn't completely clear yet. We do know that when Christ appears we will be like him because we will see him as he is. ✦ Christ is your life. When he appears, then you, too, will appear with him in glory. ✦ The one who is testifying to these things says, "Yes, I'm coming soon!" Amen! Come, Lord Jesus!

*Titus 2:13; Hebrews 6:19–20; Acts 3:21; 2 Thessalonians 1:10; Romans 8:22–23; 1 John 3:2; Colossians 3:4; Revelation 22:20*

## MORNING READING

But whoever obeys what Christ says is
the kind of person in whom God's love is perfected.
That's how we know we are in Christ.

The God of peace brought the great shepherd of the sheep, our Lord Jesus, back to life through the blood of an eternal promise. May this God of peace prepare you to do every good thing he wants. May he work in us through Jesus Christ to do what is pleasing to him. Glory belongs to Jesus Christ forever. Amen. ✦ We are sure that we know Christ if we obey his commandments. ✦ "Those who love me will do what I say. My Father will love them, and we will go to them and make our home with them." ✦ Those who live in Christ don't go on sinning. Those who go on sinning haven't seen or known Christ. Dear children, don't let anyone deceive you. Whoever does what God approves of has God's approval as Christ has God's approval. ✦ God's love has reached its goal in us. So we look ahead with confidence to the day of judgment. While we are in this world, we are exactly like him with regard to love.

*1 John 2:5; Hebrews 13:20–21; 1 John 2:3; John 14:23; 1 John 3:6–7; 1 John 4:17*

## EVENING READING

A person of great understanding is patient.

Then he passed in front of Moses, calling out, "The Lord, the Lord, a compassionate and merciful God, patient, always faithful and ready to forgive." ✦ The Lord isn't slow to do what he promised, as some people think. Rather, he is patient for your sake. He doesn't want to destroy anyone but wants all people to have an opportunity to turn to him and change the way they think and act. ✦ Imitate God, since you are the children he loves. Live in love. ✦ But the spiritual nature produces love, joy, peace, patience, kindness, goodness, faithfulness, gentleness, and self-control. There are no laws against things like that. ✦ God is pleased if a person is aware of him while enduring the pains of unjust suffering. What credit do you deserve if you endure a beating for doing something wrong? But if you endure suffering for doing something good, God is pleased with you. God called you to endure suffering because Christ suffered for you. He left you an example so that you could follow in his footsteps. . . . Christ never verbally abused those who verbally abused him. When he suffered, he didn't make any threats but left everything to the one who judges fairly. ✦ Be angry without sinning.

*Proverbs 14:29; Exodus 34:6; 2 Peter 3:9; Ephesians 5:1–2;*
*Galatians 5:22–23; 1 Peter 2:19–21, 23; Ephesians 4:26*

## MORNING READING

The spiritual nature produces . . . peace.

The spiritual nature's attitude leads to life and peace. ✦ God has called you to live in peace. ✦ "I'm leaving you peace. I'm giving you my peace. I don't give you the kind of peace that the world gives. So don't be troubled or cowardly." ✦ May God, the source of hope, fill you with joy and peace through your faith in him. Then you will overflow with hope by the power of the Holy Spirit. ✦ For this reason I suffer as I do. However, I'm not ashamed. I know whom I trust. I'm convinced that he is able to protect what he had entrusted to me until that day. ✦ With perfect peace you will protect those whose minds cannot be changed, because they trust you. ✦ Then an act of righteousness will bring about peace, calm, and safety forever. My people will live in a peaceful place, in safe homes and quiet places of rest. ✦ But whoever listens to me will live without worry and will be free from the dread of disaster. ✦ There is lasting peace for those who love your teachings.

*Galatians 5:22; Romans 8:6; 1 Corinthians 7:15; John 14:27; Romans 15:13; 2 Timothy 1:12; Isaiah 26:3; Isaiah 32:17–18; Proverbs 1:33; Psalm 119:165*

## EVENING READING

The Lord Is There.

"God lives with humans! God will make his home with them, and they will be his people. God himself will be with them and be their God." ✦ I did not see any temple in it, because the Lord God Almighty and the lamb are its temple. The city doesn't need any sun or moon to give it light because the glory of God gave it light. The lamb was its lamp. ✦ When I wake up, I will be satisfied with seeing you. ✦ As long as I have you, I don't need anyone else in heaven or on earth. ✦ "People will always live in Judah. People will live in Jerusalem from now on. I will punish those who murder." The Lord lives in Zion! ✦ Sing for joy and rejoice, people of Zion. I'm going to come and live among you, declares the Lord. ✦ There will no longer be any curse. The throne of God and the lamb will be in the city. His servants will worship him.

*Ezekiel 48:35; Revelation 21:3; Revelation 21:22–23; Psalm 17:15; Psalm 73:25; Joel 3:20–21; Zechariah 2:10; Revelation 22:3*

## MORNING READING

"Certainly, the LORD is in this place, and I didn't know it!"

"Where two or three have come together in my name, I am there among them." ✦ "And remember that I am always with you until the end of time." ✦ "My presence will go with you, and I will give you peace." ✦ Where can I go to get away from your Spirit? Where can I run to get away from you? If I go up to heaven, you are there. If I make my bed in hell, you are there. ✦ "I am a God who is near. I am also a God who is far away," declares the LORD. "No one can hide so that I can't see him," declares the LORD. "I fill heaven and earth!" declares the LORD. ✦ If heaven itself, the highest heaven, cannot hold you, then how can this temple that I have built? ✦ The High and Lofty One lives forever, and his name is holy. This is what he says: I live in a high and holy place. But I am with those who are crushed and humble. I will renew the spirit of those who are humble and the courage of those who are crushed. ✦ We are the temple of the living God. As God said, "I will live and walk among them. I will be their God, and they will be my people."

*Genesis 28:16; Matthew 18:20; Matthew 28:20; Exodus 33:14; Psalm 139:7–8; Jeremiah 23:23–24; 1 Kings 8:27; Isaiah 57:15; 2 Corinthians 6:16*

## EVENING READING

Guard yourselves from false gods.

My son, give me your heart. ✦ Keep your mind on things above, not on worldly things. ✦ "Son of man, these people are devoted to their idols, and they are allowing themselves to fall into sin. Should they be allowed to ask me for help?" ✦ Therefore, put to death whatever is worldly in you: your sexual sin, perversion, passion, lust, and greed (which is the same thing as worshiping wealth). ✦ But people who want to get rich keep falling into temptation. They are trapped by many stupid and harmful desires which drown them in destruction and ruin. Certainly, the love of money is the root of all kinds of evil. Some people who have set their hearts on getting rich have wandered away from the Christian faith and have caused themselves a lot of grief. But you, man of God, must avoid these things. ✦ When riches increase, do not depend on them. ✦ What I produce is better than gold, pure gold. What I yield is better than fine silver. ✦ "Your heart will be where your treasure is." ✦ "The LORD looks into the heart."

*1 John 5:21; Proverbs 23:26; Colossians 3:2; Ezekiel 14:3; Colossians 3:5; 1 Timothy 6:9–11; Psalm 62:10; Proverbs 8:19; Matthew 6:21; 1 Samuel 16:7*

## MORNING READING

"You must be perfect as your Father in heaven is perfect."

"I am God Almighty. Live in my presence with integrity." ✦ "Be my holy people because I, the Lord, am holy. I have separated you from other people to be my very own." ✦ You were bought for a price. So bring glory to God in the way you use your body. ✦ God has made you complete in Christ. Christ is in charge of every ruler and authority. ✦ He gave himself for us to set us free from every sin. ✦ Make every effort to have him find you at peace, without spiritual stains or blemishes. ✦ Blessed are those whose lives have integrity, those who follow the teachings of the Lord. ✦ The person who continues to study God's perfect teachings that make people free and who remains committed to them will be blessed. People like that don't merely listen and forget; they actually do what God's teachings say. ✦ Examine me, O God, and know my mind. Test me, and know my thoughts. See whether I am on an evil path. Then lead me on the everlasting path.

*Matthew 5:48; Genesis 17:1; Leviticus 20:26; 1 Corinthians 6:20; Colossians 2:10; Titus 2:14; 2 Peter 3:14; Psalm 119:1; James 1:25; Psalm 139:23–24*

## EVENING READING

Live a holy life in the fear of God.

We need to cleanse ourselves from everything that contaminates body and spirit. ✦ You desire truth and sincerity. Deep down inside me you teach me wisdom. ✦ It trains us to avoid ungodly lives filled with worldly desires so that we can live self-controlled, moral, and godly lives in this present world. ✦ "Let your light shine in front of people. Then they will see the good that you do and praise your Father in heaven." ✦ It's not that I've already reached the goal or have already completed the course. ✦ All people who have this confidence in Christ keep themselves pure, as Christ is pure. ✦ God has prepared us for this and has given us his Spirit to guarantee it. ✦ To serve and to build up the body of Christ. This is to continue until all of us are united in our faith and in our knowledge about God's Son, until we become mature, until we measure up to Christ, who is the standard.

*2 Corinthians 7:1; 2 Corinthians 7:1; Psalm 51:6; Titus 2:12; Matthew 5:16; Philippians 3:12; 1 John 3:3; 2 Corinthians 5:5; Ephesians 4:12–13*

## MORNING READING

The Lord is not too weak to save or his ear too deaf to hear.

When I called, you answered me. You made me bold by strengthening my soul. ✦ While I [Daniel] was praying, the man Gabriel, whom I had seen in the first vision, came to me about the time of the evening sacrifice. ✦ Do not hide your face from me. Do not angrily turn me away. You have been my help. Do not leave me! Do not abandon me, O God, my savior! ✦ Do not be so far away, O Lord. Come quickly to help me, O my strength. ✦ Almighty Lord, you made heaven and earth by your great strength and powerful arm. Nothing is too hard for you. ✦ He has rescued us from a terrible death, and he will rescue us in the future. We are confident that he will continue to rescue us. ✦ Won't God give his chosen people justice when they cry out to him for help day and night? Is he slow to help them? I can guarantee that he will give them justice quickly.

*Isaiah 59:1; Psalm 138:3; Daniel 9:21; Psalm 27:9; Psalm 22:19; Jeremiah 32:17; 2 Corinthians 1:10; Luke 18:7–8*

## EVENING READING

On earth I have given you glory.

"My food is to do what the one who sent me wants me to do and to finish the work he has given me." ✦ "We must do what the one who sent me wants us to do while it is day. The night when no one can do anything is coming." ✦ Jesus said to them, ". . . Didn't you realize that I had to be in my Father's house?" But they didn't understand what he meant. ✦ "His sickness won't result in death. Instead, this sickness will bring glory to God so that the Son of God will receive glory through it." ✦ "Didn't I tell you that if you believe, you would see God's glory?" ✦ Jesus grew in wisdom and maturity. He gained favor from God and people. ✦ "You are my Son, whom I love. I am pleased with you." ✦ All the people spoke well of him. They were amazed to hear the gracious words flowing from his lips. ✦ "You deserve to take the scroll and open the seals on it, because you were slaughtered. You bought people with your blood to be God's own. They are from every tribe, language, people, and nation. You made them a kingdom and priests for our God. They will rule as kings on the earth."

*John 17:4; John 4:34; John 9:4; Luke 2:49–50; John 11:4; John 11:40; Luke 2:52; Luke 3:22; Luke 4:22; Revelation 5:9–10*

## MORNING READING

"Don't ever worry and say, 'What are we going to eat?' or 'What are we going to drink?' or 'What are we going to wear?' Everyone is concerned about these things, and your heavenly Father certainly knows you need all of them."

Fear the Lord, you holy people who belong to him. Those who fear him are never in need. Young lions go hungry and may starve, but those who seek the Lord's help have all the good things they need. ✦ He does not hold back any blessing from those who live innocently. O Lord of Armies, blessed is the person who trusts you. ✦ I don't want you to have any concerns. ✦ Never worry about anything. But in every situation let God know what you need in prayers and requests while giving thanks. ✦ "Aren't two sparrows sold for a penny? Not one of them will fall to the ground without your Father's permission. Every hair on your head has been counted. Don't be afraid! You are worth more than many sparrows." ✦ "Why are you such cowards? Don't you have any faith yet?" ✦ "Have faith in God!"

*Matthew 6:31–32; Psalm 34:9–10; Psalm 84:11–12; 1 Corinthians 7:32; Philippians 4:6; Matthew 10:29–31; Mark 4:40; Mark 11:22*

## EVENING READING

He spread out a cloud as a protective covering and a fire to light up the night.

As a father has compassion for his children, so the Lord has compassion for those who fear him. He certainly knows what we are made of. He bears in mind that we are dust. ✦ The sun will not beat down on you during the day, nor will the moon at night. ✦ It will be a shelter from the heat during the day as well as a refuge and hiding place from storms and rain. ✦ The Lord is your guardian. The Lord is the shade over your right hand. . . . The Lord guards you as you come and go, now and forever. ✦ By day the Lord went ahead of them in a column of smoke to lead them on their way. By night he went ahead of them in a column of fire to give them light so that they could travel by day or by night. The column of smoke was always in front of the people during the day. The column of fire was always there at night. ✦ Jesus Christ is the same yesterday, today, and forever.

*Psalm 105:39; Psalm 103:13–14; Psalm 121:6; Isaiah 4:6; Psalm 121:5, 8; Exodus 13:21–22; Hebrews 13:8*

## MORNING READING

Mercy and truth have met.
Righteousness and peace have kissed.

There is no other righteous God and Savior. ✦ The LORD is pleased because he does what is right. He praises the greatness of his teachings and makes them glorious. ✦ God was using Christ to restore his relationship with humanity. He didn't hold people's faults against them. ✦ God showed that Christ is the throne of mercy where God's approval is given through faith in Christ's blood. In his patience God waited to deal with sins committed in the past. He waited so that he could display his approval at the present time. This shows that he is a God of justice, a God who approves of people who believe in Jesus. ✦ He was wounded for our rebellious acts. He was crushed for our sins. He was punished so that we could have peace, and we received healing from his wounds. ✦ Who will accuse those whom God has chosen? God has approved of them. ✦ When people don't work but believe God, the one who approves ungodly people, their faith is regarded as God's approval.

*Psalm 85:10; Isaiah 45:21; Isaiah 42:21; 2 Corinthians 5:19; Romans 3:25–26; Isaiah 53:5; Romans 8:33; Romans 4:5*

## EVENING READING

"How do the dead come back to life?
With what kind of body will they come back?"

Dear friends, now we are God's children. What we will be isn't completely clear yet. We do know that when Christ appears we will be like him because we will see him as he is. ✦ As we have worn the likeness of the man who was made from the dust of the earth, we will also wear the likeness of the man who came from heaven. ✦ Through his power to bring everything under his authority, [Jesus] will change our humble bodies and make them like his glorified body. ✦ Jesus stood among them. He said to them, "Peace be with you!" They were terrified, and thought they were seeing a ghost. ✦ He appeared to Cephas. Next he appeared to the twelve apostles. Then he appeared to more than 500 believers at one time. ✦ Does the Spirit of the one who brought Jesus back to life live in you? Then the one who brought Christ back to life will also make your mortal bodies alive by his Spirit who lives in you.

*1 Corinthians 15:35; 1 John 3:2; 1 Corinthians 15:49; Philippians 3:20–21; Luke 24:36–37; 1 Corinthians 15:5–6; Romans 8:11*

## MORNING READING

"You will hear of wars and rumors of wars. Don't be alarmed!"

God is our refuge and strength, an ever-present help in times of trouble. That is why we are not afraid even when the earth quakes or the mountains topple into the depths of the sea. Water roars and foams, and mountains shake at the surging waves. ✦ My people, go to your rooms, and shut the doors behind you. Hide for a little while until his fury has ended. The Lord is going to come out from his dwelling place to punish those who live on earth for their sins. ✦ I will take refuge in the shadow of your wings until destructive storms pass by. ✦ You have died, and your life is hidden with Christ in God. ✦ He is not afraid of bad news. His heart remains secure, full of confidence in the Lord. ✦ "I've told you this so that my peace will be with you. In the world you'll have trouble. But cheer up! I have overcome the world."

*Matthew 24:6; Psalm 46:1–3; Isaiah 26:20–21; Psalm 57:1; Colossians 3:3; Psalm 112:7; John 16:33*

## EVENING READING

They persecute the one you have struck.

"Situations that cause people to lose their faith are certain to arise. But how horrible it will be for the person who causes someone to lose his faith!" ✦ By using men who don't acknowledge Moses' Teachings, you crucified Jesus, who was given over to death by a plan that God had determined in advance. ✦ Then they spit in his face, hit him with their fists, and some of them slapped him. They said, "You Christ, if you're a prophet, tell us who hit you." ✦ The chief priests together with the scribes and the leaders made fun of him in the same way. They said, "He saved others, but he can't save himself. So he's Israel's king! Let him come down from the cross now, and we'll believe him." ✦ "In this city Herod and Pontius Pilate made plans together with non-Jewish people and the people of Israel. They made their plans against your holy servant Jesus, whom you anointed. Through your will and power, they did everything that you had already decided should be done." ✦ He certainly has taken upon himself our suffering and carried our sorrows, but we thought that God had wounded him, beat him, and punished him.

*Psalm 69:26; Luke 17:1; Acts 2:23; Matthew 26:67–68; Matthew 27:41–42; Acts 4:27–28; Isaiah 53:4*

## MORNING READING

It was the Lord's will to crush him with suffering.

[Jesus said] "I am too deeply troubled now to know how to express my feelings. Should I say, 'Father, save me from this time of suffering'? No! I came for this time of suffering. Father, give glory to your name." A voice from heaven said, "I have given it glory, and I will give it glory again." ✦ [Jesus prayed] "Father, if it is your will, take this cup of suffering away from me. However, your will must be done, not mine." Then an angel from heaven appeared to him and gave him strength. ✦ He humbled himself by becoming obedient to the point of death, death on a cross. ✦ The Father loves me because I give my life in order to take it back again. ✦ "I haven't come from heaven to do what I want to do. I've come to do what the one who sent me wants me to do." ✦ "Shouldn't I drink the cup of suffering that my Father has given me?" ✦ "The one who sent me is with me. He hasn't left me by myself. I always do what pleases him." ✦ Then a voice from heaven said, "This is my Son, whom I love—my Son with whom I am pleased." ✦ Here is my chosen one, with whom I am pleased.

*Isaiah 53:10; John 12:27–28; Luke 22:42–43; Philippians 2:8; John 10:17; John 6:38; John 18:11; John 8:29; Matthew 3:17; Isaiah 42:1*

## EVENING READING

Whoever calls on the Lord, do not give yourselves any rest.

[Jesus has] made them a kingdom and priests for our God. ✦ The sons of Aaron, the priests, will blow the trumpets. This will be a permanent law for you and your descendants. "When you go to war in your own country against an enemy who is oppressing you, the trumpets will sound a fanfare. Then the Lord your God will remember you and rescue you from your enemies." ✦ I didn't say to Jacob's descendants, "Search for me in vain!" ✦ Their voices were heard, and their prayers went to God's holy place in heaven. ✦ The Lord's eyes are on righteous people. His ears hear their cry for help. ✦ Pray for each other so that you will be healed. Prayers offered by those who have God's approval are effective. ✦ Come, Lord Jesus! ✦ O my God, do not delay! ✦ You look forward to the day of God and eagerly wait for [the day of the Lord] to come.

*Isaiah 62:6; Revelation 5:10; Numbers 10:8–9; Isaiah 45:19; 2 Chronicles 30:27; Psalm 34:15; James 5:16; Revelation 22:20; Psalm 40:17; 2 Peter 3:12*

## MORNING READING

Faith assures us of things we expect and
convinces us of the existence of things we cannot see.

If Christ is our hope in this life only, we deserve more pity than any other people. ✦ "No eye has seen, no ear has heard, and no mind has imagined the things that God has prepared for those who love him." ✦ You heard and believed the message of truth, the Good News that he has saved you. In him you were sealed with the Holy Spirit whom he promised. This Holy Spirit is the guarantee that we will receive our inheritance. We have this guarantee until we are set free to belong to him. God receives praise and glory for this. ✦ Jesus said to Thomas, "You believe because you've seen me. Blessed are those who haven't seen me but believe." ✦ Although you have never seen Christ, you love him. You don't see him now, but you believe in him. You are extremely happy with joy and praise that can hardly be expressed in words as you obtain the salvation that is the goal of your faith. ✦ Our lives are guided by faith, not by sight. ✦ So don't lose your confidence. It will bring you a great reward.

*Hebrews 11:1; 1 Corinthians 15:19; 1 Corinthians 2:9; Ephesians 1:13–14; John 20:29; 1 Peter 1:8–9; 2 Corinthians 5:7; Hebrews 10:35*

## EVENING READING

"It's me. Don't be afraid!"

When I saw him, I fell down at his feet like a dead man. Then he laid his right hand on me and said, "Don't be afraid! I am the first and the last, the living one. I was dead, but now I am alive forever. I have the keys of death and hell." ✦ I alone am the one who is going to wipe away your rebellious actions for my own sake. ✦ I [Isaiah] said, "Oh, no! I'm doomed. . . . I have seen the king, the Lord of Armies!" Then one of the angels flew to me. In his hand was a burning coal that he had taken from the altar with tongs. He touched my mouth with it and said, "This has touched your lips. Your guilt has been taken away, and your sin has been forgiven." ✦ I made your rebellious acts disappear like a thick cloud and your sins like the morning mist. Come back to me, because I have reclaimed you. ✦ If anyone does sin, we have Jesus Christ, who has God's full approval.

*John 6:20; Revelation 1:17–18; Isaiah 43:25; Isaiah 6:5–7; Isaiah 44:22; 1 John 2:1*

## Morning Reading

The reason that the Son of God appeared was to destroy what the devil does.

This is not a wrestling match against a human opponent. We are wrestling with rulers, authorities, the powers who govern this world of darkness, and spiritual forces that control evil in the heavenly world. ✦ Since all of these sons and daughters have flesh and blood, Jesus took on flesh and blood to be like them. He did this so that by dying he would destroy the one who had power over death (that is, the devil). ✦ He stripped the rulers and authorities of their power and made a public spectacle of them as he celebrated his victory in Christ. ✦ Then I heard a loud voice in heaven, saying, "Now the salvation, power, kingdom of our God, and the authority of his Messiah have come. The one accusing our brothers and sisters, the one accusing them day and night in the presence of our God, has been thrown out. They won the victory over him because of the blood of the lamb and the word of their testimony. They didn't love their life so much that they refused to give it up. ✦ Thank God that he gives us the victory through our Lord Jesus Christ.

*1 John 3:8; Ephesians 6:12; Hebrews 2:14; Colossians 2:15; Revelation 12:10–11; 1 Corinthians 15:57*

## Evening Reading

"Absolutely pointless! Everything is pointless."

We live out our years like one long sigh. Each of us lives for 70 years—or even 80 if we are in good health. But the best of them bring trouble and misery. Indeed, they are soon gone, and we fly away. ✦ If Christ is our hope in this life only, we deserve more pity than any other people. ✦ We don't have a permanent city here on earth, but we are looking for the city that we will have in the future. ✦ "I, the Lord, never change. That is why you descendants of Jacob haven't been destroyed yet." ✦ We, however, are citizens of heaven. We look forward to the Lord Jesus Christ coming from heaven as our Savior. Through his power to bring everything under his authority, he will change our humble bodies and make them like his glorified body. ✦ Creation was subjected to frustration but not by its own choice. The one who subjected it to frustration did so in the hope that it would also be set free. ✦ Jesus Christ is the same yesterday, today, and forever. ✦ "Holy, holy, holy is the Lord God Almighty, who was, who is, and who is coming."

*Ecclesiastes 1:2; Psalm 90:9–10; 1 Corinthians 15:19; Hebrews 13:14; Malachi 3:6; Philippians 3:20–21; Romans 8:20–21; Hebrews 13:8; Revelation 4:8*

## MORNING READING

Come back to the right point of view, and stop sinning.

You belong to the day and the light not to the night and the dark. Therefore, we must not fall asleep like other people, but we must stay awake and be sober. ✦ It's time for you to wake up. Our salvation is nearer now than when we first became believers. The night is almost over, and the day is near. So we should get rid of the things that belong to the dark and take up the weapons that belong to the light. ✦ For this reason, take up all the armor that God supplies. Then you will be able to take a stand during these evil days. Once you have overcome all obstacles, you will be able to stand your ground. ✦ Stop all the rebellious things that you are doing. Get yourselves new hearts and new spirits. ✦ So get rid of all immoral behavior and all the wicked things you do. Humbly accept the word that God has placed in you. This word can save you. ✦ Now, dear children, live in Christ. Then, when he appears we will have confidence, and when he comes we won't turn from him in shame. If you know that Christ has God's approval, you also know that everyone who does what God approves of has been born from God.

*1 Corinthians 15:34; 1 Thessalonians 5:5–6; Romans 13:11–12; Ephesians 6:13; Ezekiel 18:31; James 1:21; 1 John 2:28–29*

## EVENING READING

"My sheep respond to my voice."

Look, I'm standing at the door and knocking. If anyone listens to my voice and opens the door, I'll come in and we'll eat together. ✦ I sleep, but my mind is awake. Listen! My beloved is knocking. Open to me, my true love, my sister, my dove, my perfect one. My head is wet with dew, my hair with the dewdrops of night. I have taken off my clothes! Why should I put them on again? I have washed my feet! Why should I get them dirty again? My beloved put his hand through the keyhole. . . . I opened for my beloved, but my beloved had turned away. He was gone! I almost died when he left. I looked for him, but I did not find him. I called for him, but he did not answer me. ✦ "Speak. I'm listening." ✦ When Jesus came to the tree, he looked up and said, "Zacchaeus, come down! I must stay at your house today." Zacchaeus came down and was glad to welcome Jesus into his home. ✦ I want to hear what God the Lord says, because he promises peace to his people, to his godly ones. But they must not go back to their stupidity.

*John 10:27; Revelation 3:20; Song of Songs 5:2–4, 6; 1 Samuel 3:10; Luke 19:5–6; Psalm 85:8*

## MORNING READING

Dear friends, we must love each other because love comes from God. Everyone who loves has been born from God and knows God.

God's love has been poured into our hearts by the Holy Spirit, who has been given to us. ✦ You haven't received the spirit of slaves that leads you into fear again. Instead, you have received the spirit of God's adopted children by which we call out, "Abba! Father!" The Spirit himself testifies with our spirit that we are God's children. ✦ Those who believe in the Son of God have the testimony of God in them. ✦ God has shown us his love by sending his only Son into the world so that we could have life through him. ✦ Through the blood of his Son, we are set free from our sins. God forgives our failures because of his overflowing kindness. ✦ He did this through Christ Jesus out of his generosity to us in order to show his extremely rich kindness in the world to come. ✦ Dear friends, if this is the way God loved us, we must also love each other.

*1 John 4:7; Romans 5:5; Romans 8:15–16; 1 John 5:10; 1 John 4:9; Ephesians 1:7; Ephesians 2:7; 1 John 4:11*

## EVENING READING

Insults have broken my heart.

"Isn't this the carpenter's son?" ✦ "Can anything good come from Nazareth?" ✦ "Aren't we right when we say that you're a Samaritan and that you're possessed by a demon?" ✦ "He forces demons out of people with the help of the ruler of demons." ✦ "Look at him! He's a glutton and a drunk, a friend of tax collectors and sinners!" ✦ "It is enough for a student to become like his teacher and a slave like his owner. If they have called the owner of the house Beelzebul, they will certainly call the family members the same name." ✦ God is pleased if a person is aware of him while enduring the pains of unjust suffering. . . . God called you to endure suffering because Christ suffered for you. He left you an example so that you could follow in his footsteps. Christ never committed any sin. He never spoke deceitfully. Christ never verbally abused those who verbally abused him. When he suffered, he didn't make any threats but left everything to the one who judges fairly. ✦ If you are insulted because of the name of Christ, you are blessed because the Spirit of glory—the Spirit of God—is resting on you.

*Psalm 69:20; Matthew 13:55; John 1:46; John 8:48; Matthew 9:34; Matthew 11:19; Matthew 10:25; 1 Peter 2:19, 21–23; 1 Peter 4:14*

## MORNING READING

I want men to offer prayers everywhere. They should raise their hands in prayer after putting aside their anger and any quarrels they have with anyone.

"The true worshipers will worship the Father in spirit and truth. The Father is looking for people like that to worship him. God is a spirit. Those who worship him must worship in spirit and truth." ✦ Then you will call, and the LORD will answer. You will cry for help, and he will say, "Here I am!" ✦ "Whenever you pray, forgive anything you have against anyone." ✦ No one can please God without faith. Whoever goes to God must believe that God exists and that he rewards those who seek him. ✦ When you ask for something, don't have any doubts. A person who has doubts is like a wave that is blown by the wind and tossed by the sea. A person who has doubts shouldn't expect to receive anything from the Lord. ✦ If I had thought about doing anything sinful, the Lord would not have listened to me. ✦ My dear children, I'm writing this to you so that you will not sin. Yet, if anyone does sin, we have Jesus Christ, who has God's full approval. He speaks on our behalf when we come into the presence of the Father. He is the payment for our sins, and not only for our sins, but also for the sins of the whole world.

*1 Timothy 2:8; John 4:23–24; Isaiah 58:9; Mark 11:25; Hebrews 11:6; James 1:6–7; Psalm 66:18; 1 John 2:1–2*

## EVENING READING

My heart is pounding. I have lost my strength.

Listen to my cry for help, O God. Pay attention to my prayer. From the ends of the earth, I call to you when I begin to lose heart. Lead me to the rock that is high above me. ✦ [The Lord Jesus] told me: "My kindness is all you need. My power is strongest when you are weak." So I will brag even more about my weaknesses in order that Christ's power will live in me. ✦ When [Peter] noticed how strong the wind was, he became afraid and started to sink. He shouted, "Lord, save me!" Immediately, Jesus reached out, caught hold of him, and said, "You have so little faith! Why did you doubt?" ✦ If you faint in a crisis, you are weak. ✦ He gives strength to those who grow tired and increases the strength of those who are weak. ✦ The eternal God is your shelter, and his everlasting arms support you. ✦ We ask him to strengthen you by his glorious might with all the power you need to patiently endure everything with joy.

*Psalm 38:10; Psalm 61:1–2; 2 Corinthians 12:9–10; Matthew 14:30–31; Proverbs 24:10; Isaiah 40:29; Deuteronomy 33:27; Colossians 1:11*

## Morning Reading

What it means to share his suffering.

It is enough for a student to become like his teacher and a slave like his owner. ✦ He was despised and rejected by people. He was a man of sorrows, familiar with suffering. He was despised like one from whom people turn their faces, and we didn't consider him to be worth anything. ✦ "In the world you'll have trouble." ✦ "You don't have anything in common with the world. I chose you from the world, and that's why the world hates you." ✦ I looked for sympathy, but there was none. ✦ At my first hearing no one stood up in my defense. Everyone abandoned me. ✦ "Foxes have holes, and birds have nests, but the Son of Man has nowhere to sleep." ✦ We don't have a permanent city here on earth, but we are looking for the city that we will have in the future. ✦ We must run the race that lies ahead of us and never give up. We must focus on Jesus, the source and goal of our faith. He saw the joy ahead of him, so he endured death on the cross and ignored the disgrace it brought him. Then he received the highest position in heaven, the one next to the throne of God.

*Philippians 3:10; Matthew 10:25; Isaiah 53:3; John 16:33; John 15:19; Psalm 69:20; 2 Timothy 4:16; Matthew 8:20; Hebrews 13:14; Hebrews 12:1–2*

## Evening Reading

They won the victory over him because of the blood of the lamb.

Who will accuse those whom God has chosen? God has approved of them. Who will condemn them? Christ has died. ✦ "Blood is needed to make peace with me." ✦ I am the Lord. But the blood on your houses will be a sign for your protection. When I see the blood, I will pass over you. ✦ So those who are believers in Christ Jesus can no longer be condemned. ✦ One of the leaders asked me, "Who are these people wearing white robes, and where did they come from?" . . . Then he told me, "These are the people who are coming out of the terrible suffering." They have washed their robes and made them white in the blood of the lamb. ✦ Glory and power forever and ever belong to the one who loves us and has freed us from our sins by his blood and has made us a kingdom, priests for God his Father. Amen.

*Revelation 12:11; Romans 8:33–34; Leviticus 17:11; Exodus 12:12–13; Romans 8:1; Revelation 7:13–14; Revelation 1:5–6*

## MORNING READING

"He will wipe every tear from their eyes.
There won't be any more death. There won't be any grief,
crying, or pain, because the first things have disappeared."

He will swallow up death forever. The Almighty Lord will wipe away tears from every face, and he will remove the disgrace of his people from the whole earth. The Lord has spoken. ✦ Your sun will no longer go down, nor will your moon disappear. The Lord will be your everlasting light, and your days of sadness will be over. ✦ No one who lives in Zion will say, "I'm sick." The sins of its inhabitants will be forgiven. ✦ Screaming and crying will no longer be heard in the city. ✦ They will have no sorrow or grief. ✦ I want to reclaim them from death. Death, I want to be a plague to you. Grave, I want to destroy you. ✦ The last enemy he will destroy is death. ✦ Then the teaching of Scripture will come true: "Death is turned into victory!" ✦ Things that can't be seen last forever.

*Revelation 21:4; Isaiah 25:8; Isaiah 60:20; Isaiah 33:24; Isaiah 65:19; Isaiah 35:10; Hosea 13:14; 1 Corinthians 15:26; 1 Corinthians 15:54; 2 Corinthians 4:18*

## EVENING READING

God has brought us back to life together with Christ Jesus.

"Don't be afraid! . . . I am alive." ✦ "Father, I want those you have given to me to be with me, to be where I am." ✦ We are parts of his body. ✦ He is also the head of the church, which is his body. He is the beginning, the first to come back to life. ✦ God has made you complete in Christ. Christ is in charge of every ruler and authority. ✦ Since all of these sons and daughters have flesh and blood, Jesus took on flesh and blood to be like them. He did this so that by dying he would destroy the one who had power over death (that is, the devil). In this way he would free those who were slaves all their lives because they were afraid of dying. ✦ This body that decays must be changed into a body that cannot decay. This mortal body must be changed into a body that will live forever. When this body that decays is changed into a body that cannot decay, and this mortal body is changed into a body that will live forever, then the teaching of Scripture will come true: "Death is turned into victory!"

*Ephesians 2:6; Revelation 1:17–18; John 17:24; Ephesians 5:30; Colossians 1:18; Colossians 2:10; Hebrews 2:14–15; 1 Corinthians 15:53–54*

## MORNING READING

A servant of Jesus Christ.

"You call me teacher and Lord, and you're right because that's what I am." ✦ "Those who serve me must follow me. My servants will be with me wherever I will be. If people serve me, the Father will honor them." ✦ "Place my yoke over your shoulders, and learn from me, because I am gentle and humble. Then you will find rest for yourselves because my yoke is easy and my burden is light." ✦ These things that I once considered valuable, I now consider worthless for Christ. ✦ Now you have been freed from sin and have become God's slaves. This results in a holy life and, finally, in everlasting life. ✦ "I don't call you servants anymore, because a servant doesn't know what his master is doing. But I've called you friends because I've made known to you everything that I've heard from my Father." ✦ You are no longer slaves but God's children. ✦ Christ has freed us so that we may enjoy the benefits of freedom. Therefore, be firm in this freedom, and don't become slaves again. . . . You were indeed called to be free, brothers and sisters. Don't turn this freedom into an excuse for your corrupt nature to express itself.

*Romans 1:1; John 13:13; John 12:26; Matthew 11:29–30; Philippians 3:7; Romans 6:22; John 15:15; Galatians 4:7; Galatians 5:1, 13*

## EVENING READING

I will praise the LORD, who advises me.

He will be named: Wonderful Counselor. ✦ Advice and priceless wisdom are mine. I, Understanding, have strength. ✦ Your word is a lamp for my feet and a light for my path. ✦ Trust the LORD with all your heart, and do not rely on your own understanding. In all your ways acknowledge him, and he will make your paths smooth. ✦ O LORD, I know that the way humans act is not under their control. Humans do not direct their steps as they walk. ✦ You will hear a voice behind you saying, "This is the way. Follow it, whether it turns to the right or to the left." ✦ Entrust your efforts to the LORD, and your plans will succeed. ✦ He knows the road I take. ✦ The LORD is the one who directs a person's steps. How then can anyone understand his own way? ✦ With your advice you guide me, and in the end you will take me to glory. ✦ "This God is our God forever and ever. He will lead us beyond death."

*Psalm 16:7; Isaiah 9:6; Proverbs 8:14; Psalm 119:105; Proverbs 3:5–6; Jeremiah 10:23; Isaiah 30:21; Proverbs 16:3; Job 23:10; Proverbs 20:24; Psalm 73:24; Psalm 48:14*

## MORNING READING

"I am the Lord your God. Live by my laws.
Obey my rules and follow them."

But because the God who called you is holy you must be holy in every aspect of your life. ✦ Those who say that they live in him must live the same way he lived. ✦ If you know that Christ has God's approval, you also know that everyone who does what God approves of has been born from God. ✦ Circumcision is nothing, and the lack of it is nothing. But keeping what God commands is everything. ✦ If someone obeys all of God's laws except one, that person is guilty of breaking all of them. ✦ By ourselves we are not qualified in any way to claim that we can do anything. Rather, God makes us qualified. ✦ Teach me, O Lord, how to live by your laws. ✦ Work out your salvation with fear and trembling. It is God who produces in you the desires and actions that please him. ✦ The God of peace . . . prepare you to do every good thing he wants. May he work in us through Jesus Christ to do what is pleasing to him.

*Ezekiel 20:19; 1 Peter 1:15; 1 John 2:6; 1 John 2:29; 1 Corinthians 7:19; James 2:10; 2 Corinthians 3:5; Psalm 119:33; Philippians 2:12–13; Hebrews 13:20–21*

## EVENING READING

I have raised up one chosen from the people.

So Jesus helps Abraham's descendants rather than helping angels. Therefore, he had to become like his brothers and sisters. ✦ Above the dome over their heads was something that looked like a throne made of sapphire. On the throne was a figure that looked like a human. ✦ "The Son of Man, who came from heaven." ✦ "Look at my hands and feet, and see that it's really me. Touch me, and see for yourselves. Ghosts don't have flesh and bones, but you can see that I do." ✦ He emptied himself by taking on the form of a servant, by becoming like other humans, by having a human appearance. He humbled himself by becoming obedient to the point of death, death on a cross. This is why God has given him an exceptional honor—the name honored above all other names—so that at the name of Jesus everyone in heaven, on earth, and in the world below will kneel. ✦ Be alert, and strengthen the things that are left which are about to die. I have found that what you are doing has not been completed in the sight of my God.

*Psalm 89:19; Hebrews 2:16–17; Ezekiel 1:26; John 3:13; Luke 24:39; Philippians 2:7–10; Revelation 3:2*

## Morning Reading

"The Father is the source of life,
and he has enabled the Son to be the source of life too."

Our Savior Christ Jesus . . . has destroyed death, and through the Good News he has brought eternal life into full view. ✦ "I am the one who brings people back to life, and I am life itself." ✦ "You will live because I live." ✦ We will remain Christ's partners. ✦ Shared in the Holy Spirit. ✦ You will share in the divine nature. ✦ The first man, Adam, became a living being. The last Adam became a life-giving spirit. ✦ I'm telling you a mystery. Not all of us will die, but we will all be changed. It will happen in an instant, in a split second at the sound of the last trumpet. Indeed, that trumpet will sound, and then the dead will come back to life. They will be changed so that they can live forever. ✦ "Holy, holy, holy is the Lord God Almighty, who was, who is, and who is coming." ✦ The one who lives forever and ever. ✦ God is the blessed and only ruler. He is the King of kings and Lord of lords. He is the only one who cannot die.✦ Worship and glory belong forever to the eternal king, the immortal, invisible, and only God. Amen.

*John 5:26; 2 Timothy 1:10; John 11:25; John 14:19; Hebrews 3:14; Hebrews 6:4; 2 Peter 1:4; 1 Corinthians 15:45; 1 Corinthians 15:51–52; Revelation 4:8; Revelation 4:9; 1 Timothy 6:15–16; 1 Timothy 1:17*

## Evening Reading

We can't allow ourselves to act arrogantly.

Then Gideon said to them, "Do me a favor. Each of you give me the earrings from your loot." (Their enemies, the Ishmaelites, wore gold earrings.) The men of Israel answered, "Yes, we'll give them to you." So they spread out a coat. Each man took the earrings from his loot and dropped them on it. . . . Then Gideon used the gold to make an idol and placed it in his hometown, Ophrah. All Israel chased after it there as though it were a prostitute. It became a trap for Gideon and his family. ✦ Are you looking for great things for yourself? Don't look for them. ✦ Therefore, to keep me from becoming conceited, I am forced to deal with a recurring problem. ✦ Don't act out of selfish ambition or be conceited. Instead, humbly think of others as being better than yourselves. ✦ Love is patient. Love is kind. Love isn't jealous. It doesn't sing its own praises. It isn't arrogant. It isn't rude. It doesn't think about itself. ✦ "Place my yoke over your shoulders, and learn from me."

*Galatians 5:26; Judges 8:24–25, 27; Jeremiah 45:5; 2 Corinthians 12:7; Philippians 2:3; 1 Corinthians 13:4–5; Matthew 11:29*

## MORNING READING

Wash me thoroughly from my guilt.

I will cleanse them from all the sins that they have committed against me. I will forgive them for all the sins that they have committed against me and for rebelling against me. ✦ I will sprinkle clean water on you and make you clean instead of unclean. Then I will cleanse you from all your idols. ✦ No one can enter the kingdom of God without being born of water and the Spirit. ✦ The blood of goats and bulls and the ashes of cows sprinkled on unclean people made their bodies holy and clean. The blood of Christ, who had no defect, does even more. Through the eternal Spirit he offered himself to God and cleansed our consciences from the useless things we had done. Now we can serve the living God. ✦ He saved them because of his reputation so that he could make his mighty power known. ✦ Don't give glory to us, O Lord. Don't give glory to us. Instead, give glory to your name because of your mercy and faithfulness.

*Psalm 51:2; Jeremiah 33:8; Ezekiel 36:25; John 3:5;
Hebrews 9:13–14; Psalm 106:8; Psalm 115:1*

## EVENING READING

The partnership we've had with you in the Good News.

The body is one unit and yet has many parts. As all the parts form one body, so it is with Christ. By one Spirit we were all baptized into one body. Whether we are Jewish or Greek, slave or free, God gave all of us one Spirit to drink. ✦ God faithfully keeps his promises. He called you to be partners with his Son Jesus Christ our Lord. ✦ This is the life we have seen and heard. We are reporting about it to you also so that you, too, can have a relationship with us. Our relationship is with the Father and with his Son Jesus Christ. ✦ If we live in the light in the same way that God is in the light, we have a relationship with each other. And the blood of his Son Jesus cleanses us from every sin. ✦ Jesus looked up to heaven and said . . . "I'm not praying only for them. I'm also praying for those who will believe in me through their message. I pray that all of these people continue to have unity in the way that you, Father, are in me and I am in you. I pray that they may be united with us so that the world will believe that you have sent me."

*Philippians 1:5; 1 Corinthians 12:12–13; 1 Corinthians 1:9;
1 John 1:3; 1 John 1:7; John 17:1, 20–21*

## MORNING READING

Focus on your life and your teaching.

Everyone who enters an athletic contest goes into strict training. They do it to win a temporary crown, but we do it to win one that will be permanent. So I run—but not without a clear goal ahead of me. So I box—but not as if I were just shadow boxing. Rather, I toughen my body with punches and make it my slave so that I will not be disqualified after I have spread the Good News to others. ✦ Put on all the armor that God supplies. In this way you can take a stand against the devil's strategies. This is not a wrestling match against a human opponent. We are wrestling with rulers, authorities, the powers who govern this world of darkness, and spiritual forces that control evil in the heavenly world. ✦ Those who belong to Christ Jesus have crucified their corrupt nature along with its passions and desires. If we live by our spiritual nature, then our lives need to conform to our spiritual nature. ✦ All who are guided by God's Spirit are God's children. ✦ Practice these things. Devote your life to them so that everyone can see your progress.

*1 Timothy 4:16; 1 Corinthians 9:25–27; Ephesians 6:11–12; Galatians 5:24–25; Romans 8:14; 1 Timothy 4:15*

## EVENING READING

Jesus said to her, "Mary!"

Do not be afraid, because I have reclaimed you. I have called you by name; you are mine. ✦ The sheep respond to his voice. He calls his sheep by name. . . . The sheep follow him because they recognize his voice. ✦ I have engraved you on the palms of my hands. Your walls are always in my presence. ✦ In spite of all that, God's people have a solid foundation. These words are engraved on it: "The Lord knows those who belong to him." ✦ We need to hold on to our declaration of faith: We have a superior chief priest who has gone through the heavens. That person is Jesus, the Son of God. ✦ "Take two onyx stones, and engrave on them the names of the sons of Israel. . . . Fasten them on the shoulder straps of the ephod as reminders of who the Israelites are. . . . Make the breastplate for decision-making. . . . Fasten four rows of precious stones on it. . . . The stones correspond to the 12 sons of Israel, by name. . . . They, too, will be over Aaron's heart when he comes into the LORD's presence."

*John 20:16; Isaiah 43:1; John 10:3–4; Isaiah 49:16; 2 Timothy 2:19; Hebrews 4:14; Exodus 28:9, 12, 15, 17, 21, 30*

## Morning Reading

Finally, receive your power from the Lord
and from his mighty strength.

But [the Lord Jesus] told me: "My kindness is all you need. My power is strongest when you are weak." So I will brag even more about my weaknesses in order that Christ's power will live in me. Therefore, I accept weakness, mistreatment, hardship, persecution, and difficulties suffered for Christ. It's clear that when I'm weak, I'm strong. ✦ I will come with the mighty deeds of the Almighty LORD. I will praise your righteousness, yours alone. ✦ The Good News . . . is God's power to save everyone who believes. ✦ I can do everything through Christ who strengthens me. ✦ I work hard and struggle to do this while his mighty power works in me. ✦ Our bodies are made of clay, yet we have the treasure of the Good News in them. This shows that the superior power of this treasure belongs to God and doesn't come from us. ✦ The joy you have in the LORD is your strength. ✦ We ask him to strengthen you by his glorious might with all the power you need to patiently endure everything with joy.

*Ephesians 6:10; 2 Corinthians 12:9–10; Psalm 71:16; Romans 1:16; Philippians 4:13; Colossians 1:29; 2 Corinthians 4:7; Nehemiah 8:10; Colossians 1:11*

## Evening Reading

Jesus Christ our Lord.

"You will name him Jesus [He Saves], because he will save his people from their sins." ✦ He humbled himself by becoming obedient to the point of death, death on a cross. This is why God has given him an exceptional honor—the name honored above all other names—so that at the name of Jesus everyone in heaven, on earth, and in the world below will kneel. ✦ Messiah is the one called Christ. ✦ The Spirit of the Almighty LORD is with me because the LORD has anointed me to deliver good news to humble people. He has sent me to heal those who are brokenhearted, to announce that captives will be set free and prisoners will be released. ✦ The last Adam became a life-giving spirit. . . . The first man was made from the dust of the earth. He came from the earth. The second man came from heaven. ✦ "My Lord and my God!" ✦ "You call me teacher and Lord, and you're right because that's what I am. So if I, your Lord and teacher, have washed your feet, you must wash each other's feet. I've given you an example that you should follow."

*1 Corinthians 1:9; Matthew 1:21; Philippians 2:8–10; John 4:25; Isaiah 61:1; 1 Corinthians 15:45, 47; John 20:28; John 13:13–15*

## MORNING READING

"I'm leaving you peace. I'm giving you my peace.
I don't give you the kind of peace that the world gives."

The world and its evil desires are passing away. ✦ Each person who walks around is like a shadow. They are busy for no reason. They accumulate riches without knowing who will get them. ✦ What did you gain by doing those things? You're ashamed of what you used to do because it ended in death. ✦ The Lord answered her, "Martha, Martha! You worry and fuss about a lot of things. There's only one thing you need. Mary has made the right choice, and that one thing will not be taken away from her." ✦ I don't want you to have any concerns. ✦ "I've told you this so that my peace will be with you. In the world you'll have trouble. But cheer up! I have overcome the world." ✦ May the Lord of peace give you his peace at all times and in every way. ✦ The LORD will bless you and watch over you. The LORD will smile on you and be kind to you. The LORD will look on you with favor and give you peace.

*John 14:27; 1 John 2:17; Psalm 39:6; Romans 6:21; Luke 10:41–42; 1 Corinthians 7:32; John 16:33; 2 Thessalonians 3:16; Numbers 6:24–25*

## EVENING READING

The Spirit also helps us in our weakness.

"The helper, the Holy Spirit." ✦ Don't you know that your body is a temple that belongs to the Holy Spirit? The Holy Spirit, whom you received from God. ✦ It is God who produces in you the desires and actions that please him. ✦ At the same time the Spirit also helps us in our weakness, because we don't know how to pray for what we need. But the Spirit intercedes along with our groans that cannot be expressed in words. The one who searches our hearts knows what the Spirit has in mind. The Spirit intercedes for God's people the way God wants him to. ✦ He certainly knows what we are made of. He bears in mind that we are dust. ✦ He will not break off a damaged cattail. He will not even put out a smoking wick. ✦ "You want to do what's right, but you're weak." ✦ The LORD is my shepherd. I am never in need. He makes me lie down in green pastures. He leads me beside peaceful waters.

*Romans 8:26; John 14:26; 1 Corinthians 6:19; Philippians 2:13; Romans 8:26–27; Psalm 103:14; Isaiah 42:3; Matthew 26:41; Psalm 23:1–2*

## MORNING READING

And fasten them on the shoulder straps of the ephod
as reminders of who the Israelites are.
In this way Aaron will carry their names on his shoulders
as a reminder in the Lord's presence.

But Jesus lives forever, so he serves as a priest forever. That is why he is always able to save those who come to God through him. He can do this because he always lives and intercedes for them. ✦ God can guard you so that you don't fall and so that you can be full of joy as you stand in his glorious presence without fault. ✦ We need to hold on to our declaration of faith: We have a superior chief priest who has gone through the heavens. That person is Jesus, the Son of God. We have a chief priest who is able to sympathize with our weaknesses. He was tempted in every way that we are, but he didn't sin. So we can go confidently to the throne of God's kindness. ✦ "The Lord's beloved people will live securely with him. The Lord will shelter them all day long, since he, too, lives on the mountain slopes."

*Exodus 28:12; Hebrews 7:24–25; Jude 24; Hebrews 4:14–16; Deuteronomy 33:12*

## EVENING READING

That night the king could not sleep.

You keep my eyelids open. ✦ Who is like the Lord our God? He is seated on his high throne. He bends down to look at heaven and earth. ✦ He does whatever he wishes with the army of heaven and with those who live on earth. ✦ Your road went through the sea. Your path went through raging water, but your footprints could not be seen. ✦ Even angry mortals will praise you. You will wear the remainder of their anger. ✦ "The Lord's eyes scan the whole world to find those whose hearts are committed to him and to strengthen them." ✦ We know that all things work together for the good of those who love God. ✦ "Aren't two sparrows sold for a penny? Not one of them will fall to the ground without your Father's permission. Every hair on your head has been counted."

*Esther 6:1; Psalm 77:4; Psalm 113:5–6; Daniel 4:35; Psalm 77:19; Psalm 76:10; 2 Chronicles 16:9; Romans 8:28; Matthew 10:29–30*

## MORNING READING

Don't give God's Holy Spirit any reason to be upset with you.
He has put his seal on you for the day
you will be set free from the world of sin.

The love that the Spirit creates. ✦ "The helper, the Holy Spirit." ✦ In all their troubles he was troubled, and he was the Messenger who saved them. In his love and compassion he reclaimed them. He always held them and carried them in the past. But they rebelled and offended his Holy Spirit. So he turned against them as their enemy; he fought against them. ✦ We know that we live in him and he lives in us because he has given us his Spirit. ✦ You heard and believed the message of truth, the Good News that he has saved you. In him you were sealed with the Holy Spirit whom he promised. This Holy Spirit is the guarantee that we will receive our inheritance. ✦ Live your life as your spiritual nature directs you. Then you will never follow through on what your corrupt nature wants. What your corrupt nature wants is contrary to what your spiritual nature wants, and what your spiritual nature wants is contrary to what your corrupt nature wants. They are opposed to each other. As a result, you don't always do what you intend to do. ✦ The Spirit also helps us in our weakness.

*Ephesians 4:30; Romans 15:30; John 14:26; Isaiah 63:9–10; 1 John 4:13; Ephesians 1:13–14; Galatians 5:16–17; Romans 8:26*

## EVENING READING

"I will go back to my place until they admit that they are guilty.
Then they will search for me."

But your wrongs have separated you from your God, and your sins have made him hide his face. ✦ I opened for my beloved, but my beloved had turned away. He was gone! . . . I looked for him, but I did not find him. I called for him, but he did not answer me. ✦ I was angry because of their sinful greed, so I punished them, hid from them, and remained angry. But they continued to be sinful. I've seen their sinful ways, but I'll heal them. ✦ You have brought this on yourself by abandoning the Lord your God when he led you on his way. ✦ "So he went at once to his father. While he was still at a distance, his father saw him and felt sorry for him. He ran to his son, put his arms around him, and kissed him." ✦ "I will cure them of their unfaithfulness. I will love them freely. I will no longer be angry with them." ✦ If we confess our sins, he forgives them and cleanses us from everything we've done wrong.

*Hosea 5:15; Isaiah 59:2; Song of Songs 5:6; Isaiah 57:17–18; Jeremiah 2:17; Luke 15:20; Hosea 14:4; 1 John 1:9*

## MORNING READING

Your kindness is so great!
You reserve it for those who fear you.

No one has ever heard, no one has paid attention, and no one has seen any god except you. You help those who wait for you. ✦ But as Scripture says: "No eye has seen, no ear has heard, and no mind has imagined the things that God has prepared for those who love him." God has revealed those things to us by his Spirit. ✦ You make the path of life known to me. Complete joy is in your presence. Pleasures are by your side forever. ✦ Your mercy is so precious, O God, that Adam's descendants take refuge in the shadow of your wings. They are refreshed with the rich foods in your house, and you make them drink from the river of your pleasure. Indeed, the fountain of life is with you. In your light we see light. ✦ Godly living helps in every way. Godly living has the promise of life now and in the world to come.

*Psalm 31:19; Isaiah 64:4; 1 Corinthians 2:9–10;*
*Psalm 16:11; Psalm 36:7–9; 1 Timothy 4:8*

## EVENING READING

The Son of God, whose eyes are like flames of fire.

"The human mind is the most deceitful of all things. It is incurable. No one can understand how deceitful it is. I, the LORD, search minds and test hearts. I will reward each person for what he has done. I will reward him for the results of his actions." ✦ You have set our sins in front of you. You have put our secret sins in the light of your presence. ✦ Then the Lord turned and looked directly at Peter. Peter remembered what the Lord had said: "Before a rooster crows today, you will say three times that you don't know me." Then Peter went outside and cried bitterly. ✦ Jesus, however, was wary of these believers. He understood people and didn't need anyone to tell him about human nature. He knew what people were really like. ✦ He certainly knows what we are made of. He bears in mind that we are dust. ✦ He will not break off a damaged cattail. He will not even put out a smoking wick. ✦ The Lord knows those who belong to him. ✦ "I am the good shepherd. I know my sheep as the Father knows me." ✦ "My sheep respond to my voice, and I know who they are. They follow me, and I give them eternal life. They will never be lost, and no one will tear them away from me."

*Revelation 2:18; Jeremiah 17:9–10; Psalm 90:8; Luke 22:61–62; John 2:24–25;*
*Psalm 103:14; Isaiah 42:3; 2 Timothy 2:19; John 10:14; John 10:27–28*

## MORNING READING

The great shepherd of the sheep, our Lord Jesus.

The chief shepherd. ✦ "I am the good shepherd. I know my sheep as the Father knows me. My sheep know me as I know the Father. . . . My sheep respond to my voice, and I know who they are. They follow me, and I give them eternal life. They will never be lost, and no one will tear them away from me." ✦ The Lord is my shepherd. I am never in need. He makes me lie down in green pastures. He leads me beside peaceful waters. He renews my soul. He guides me along the paths of righteousness for the sake of his name. ✦ We have all strayed like sheep. Each one of us has turned to go his own way, and the Lord has laid all our sins on him. ✦ "I am the good shepherd. The good shepherd gives his life for the sheep." ✦ I will look for those that are lost, bring back those that have strayed away, bandage those that are injured, and strengthen those that are sick. ✦ You were like lost sheep. Now you have come back to the shepherd and bishop of your lives.

*Hebrews 13:20; 1 Peter 5:4; John 10:14, 27–28; Psalm 23:1–3; Isaiah 53:6; John 10:11; Ezekiel 34:16; 1 Peter 2:25*

## EVENING READING

The city doesn't need any sun or moon
to give it light because the glory of God gave it light.
The lamb was its lamp.

"At noon, while I was traveling, I saw a light that was brighter than the sun. The light came from the sky and shined around me and those who were with me. . . . I asked, 'Who are you, sir?' " ✦ After six days Jesus took Peter, James, and John (the brother of James) and led them up a high mountain where they could be alone. Jesus' appearance changed in front of them. His face became as bright as the sun and his clothes as white as light. ✦ The sun will no longer be your light during the day, nor will the brightness of the moon give you light, but the Lord will be your everlasting light. Your God will be your glory. Your sun will no longer go down, nor will your moon disappear. The Lord will be your everlasting light, and your days of sadness will be over. ✦ God . . . called you through Christ Jesus to his eternal glory.

*Revelation 21:23; Acts 26:13, 15; Matthew 17:1–2; Isaiah 60:19–20; 1 Peter 5:10*

## May 27

### MORNING READING

The Lord is good. He is a fortress in the day of trouble.
He knows those who seek shelter in him.

"Give thanks to the Lord of Armies because the Lord is good, because his mercy endures forever." ✦ God is our refuge and strength, an ever-present help in times of trouble. ✦ I will say to the Lord, "You are my refuge and my fortress, my God in whom I trust." ✦ Who is like you, a nation saved by the Lord? He is a shield that helps you and a sword that wins your victories. ✦ God's way is perfect! The promise of the Lord has proven to be true. He is a shield to all those who take refuge in him. Who is God but the Lord? Who is a rock other than our God? ✦ If they love God, they are known by God. ✦ God's people have a solid foundation. These words are engraved on it: "The Lord knows those who belong to him," and "Whoever worships the Lord must give up doing wrong." ✦ The Lord knows the way of righteous people, but the way of wicked people will end. ✦ "I am pleased with you, and I know you by name."

*Nahum 1:7; Jeremiah 33:11; Psalm 46:1; Psalm 91:2; Deuteronomy 33:29; 2 Samuel 22:31–32; 1 Corinthians 8:3; 2 Timothy 2:19; Psalm 1:6; Exodus 33:17*

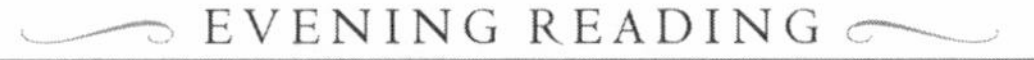

### EVENING READING

I don't want you to have any concerns.

He cares for you. ✦ The Lord's eyes scan the whole world to find those whose hearts are committed to him and to strengthen them. ✦ Taste and see that the Lord is good. Blessed is the person who takes refuge in him. Young lions go hungry and may starve, but those who seek the Lord's help have all the good things they need. ✦ "So I tell you to stop worrying about what you will eat, drink, or wear. Isn't life more than food and the body more than clothes? Look at the birds. They don't plant, harvest, or gather the harvest into barns. Yet, your heavenly Father feeds them. Aren't you worth more than they?" ✦ Never worry about anything. But in every situation let God know what you need in prayers and requests while giving thanks. Then God's peace, which goes beyond anything we can imagine, will guard your thoughts and emotions through Christ Jesus.

*1 Corinthians 7:32; 1 Peter 5:7; 2 Chronicles 16:9; Psalm 34:8, 10; Matthew 6:25–26; Philippians 4:6–7*

## MORNING READING

We look forward to . . . our Savior.

God's saving kindness has appeared for the benefit of all people. It trains us to avoid ungodly lives filled with worldly desires so that we can live self-controlled, moral, and godly lives in this present world. At the same time we can expect what we hope for—the appearance of the glory of our great God and Savior, Jesus Christ. He gave himself for us to set us free from every sin and to cleanse us so that we can be his special people who are enthusiastic about doing good things. ✦ We look forward to what God has promised—a new heaven and a new earth—a place where everything that has God's approval lives. ✦ Christ was sacrificed once to take away the sins of humanity, and after that he will appear a second time. This time he will not deal with sin, but he will save those who eagerly wait for him. ✦ On that day his people will say, "This is our God; we have waited for him, and now he will save us. This is the LORD; we have waited for him. Let us rejoice and be glad because he will save us."

*Philippians 3:20; Titus 2:11–14; 2 Peter 3:13–14; Hebrews 9:28; Isaiah 25:9*

## EVENING READING

Run . . . so that you can win.

A lazy person says, "There's a lion outside! I'll be murdered in the streets!" ✦ We must get rid of everything that slows us down, especially sin that distracts us. We must run the race that lies ahead of us and never give up. We must focus on Jesus, the source and goal of our faith. ✦ We need to cleanse ourselves from everything that contaminates body and spirit and live a holy life in the fear of God. ✦ I run straight toward the goal. ✦ I run—but not without a clear goal ahead of me. . . . I toughen my body with punches and make it my slave so that I will not be disqualified after I have spread the Good News to others. ✦ This world in its present form is passing away. ✦ We look forward to what God has promised—a new heaven and a new earth—a place where everything that has God's approval lives. Therefore, dear friends, with this to look forward to, make every effort. ✦ Your minds must be clear and ready for action. Place your confidence completely in what God's kindness will bring you when Jesus Christ appears again.

*1 Corinthians 9:24; Proverbs 22:13; Hebrews 12:1–2;
2 Corinthians 7:1; Philippians 3:14; 1 Corinthians 9:26–27;
1 Corinthians 7:31; 2 Peter 3:13–14; 1 Peter 1:13*

## MORNING READING

Blood contains life. I have given this blood to you
to make peace with me on the altar.
Blood is needed to make peace with me.

"Look! This is the Lamb of God who takes away the sin of the world." ✦ The blood of the lamb. ✦ The precious blood of Christ, the lamb with no defects or imperfections. ✦ If no blood is shed, no sins can be forgiven. ✦ The blood of his Son Jesus cleanses us from every sin. ✦ He used his own blood. . . . He went into the most holy place and offered this sacrifice once and for all to free us forever. ✦ Brothers and sisters, because of the blood of Jesus we can now confidently go into the holy place. Jesus has opened a new and living way for us to go through the curtain. (The curtain is his own body.) . . . We must continue to hold firmly to our declaration of faith. ✦ You were bought for a price. So bring glory to God in the way you use your body.

*Leviticus 17:11; John 1:29; Revelation 7:14; 1 Peter 1:19; Hebrews 9:22; 1 John 1:7; Hebrews 9:12; Hebrews 10:19–20, 22; 1 Corinthians 6:20*

## EVENING READING

"If only I had wings like a dove—
I would fly away and find rest."

When the sun rose, God made a hot east wind blow. The sun beat down on Jonah's head so that he was about to faint. He wanted to die. So he said, "I'd rather be dead than alive." ✦ Job said . . . "Why give light to one in misery and life to those who find it so bitter, to those who long for death but it never comes—though they dig for it more than for buried treasure?" ✦ The righteous person has many troubles, but the LORD rescues him from all of them. ✦ "I am too deeply troubled now to know how to express my feelings. Should I say, 'Father, save me from this time of suffering'? No! I came for this time of suffering." ✦ He had to become like his brothers and sisters so that he could be merciful. He became like them so that he could serve as a faithful chief priest in God's presence and make peace with God for their sins. Because Jesus experienced temptation when he suffered, he is able to help others when they are tempted.

*Psalm 55:6; Jonah 4:8; Job 3:2, 20–21; Psalm 34:19; John 12:27; Hebrews 2:17–18*

## MORNING READING

So we must make every effort to enter that place of rest.

"Enter through the narrow gate because the gate and road that lead to destruction are wide. . . . But the narrow gate and the road that lead to life are full of trouble. Only a few people find the narrow gate." ✦ "The kingdom of heaven has been forcefully advancing, and forceful people have been seizing it." ✦ "Don't work for food that spoils. Instead, work for the food that lasts into eternal life. This is the food the Son of Man will give you." ✦ Use more effort to make God's calling and choosing of you secure. If you keep doing this, you will never fall away. Then you will also be given the wealth of entering into the eternal kingdom of our Lord and Savior Jesus Christ. ✦ Run like [a competitor], so that you can win. Everyone who enters an athletic contest goes into strict training. They do it to win a temporary crown, but we do it to win one that will be permanent. ✦ Those who entered his place of rest also rested from their work as God did from his. ✦ But the LORD will be your everlasting light. Your God will be your glory.

*Hebrews 4:11; Matthew 7:13–14; Matthew 11:12; John 6:27; 2 Peter 1:10–11; 1 Corinthians 9:24–25; Hebrews 4:10; Isaiah 60:19*

## EVENING READING

"You always hear me."

Jesus looked up and said, "Father, I thank you for hearing me." ✦ "Father, give glory to your name." A voice from heaven said, "I have given it glory, and I will give it glory again." ✦ "Then I said . . . 'I have come to do what you want, my God.'" ✦ "Your will must be done, not mine." ✦ While we are in this world, we are exactly like him. ✦ We are confident that God listens to us if we ask for anything that has his approval. ✦ And receive from him anything we ask. We receive it because we obey his commandments and do what pleases him. ✦ No one can please God without faith. Whoever goes to God must believe that God exists and that he rewards those who seek him. ✦ He always lives and intercedes for them. ✦ We have Jesus Christ, who has God's full approval. He speaks on our behalf when we come into the presence of the Father.

*John 11:42; John 11:41; John 12:28; Hebrews 10:7; Luke 22:42; 1 John 4:17; 1 John 5:14; 1 John 3:22; Hebrews 11:6; Hebrews 7:25; 1 John 2:1*

## MORNING READING

"Your name will no longer be Jacob but Israel [He Struggles With God], because you have struggled with God and with men—and you have won."

When Jacob became a man, he struggled with God. He struggled with the Messenger and won. Jacob cried and pleaded with him. ✦ [Abraham] didn't doubt God's promise out of a lack of faith. Instead, giving honor to God for the promise, he became strong because of faith. ✦ Jesus said to them, "Have faith in God! I can guarantee this truth: This is what will be done for someone who doesn't doubt but believes what he says will happen: He can say to this mountain, 'Be uprooted and thrown into the sea,' and it will be done for him. That's why I tell you to have faith that you have already received whatever you pray for, and it will be yours." ✦ Jesus said to him, "As far as possibilities go, everything is possible for the person who believes." ✦ "You are blessed for believing that the Lord would keep his promise to you." ✦ "Give us more faith."

*Genesis 32:28; Hosea 12:3–4; Romans 4:20; Mark 11:22–24; Mark 9:23; Luke 1:45; Luke 17:5*

## EVENING READING

Dear children, live in Christ.

A person who has doubts is like a wave that is blown by the wind and tossed by the sea. A person who has doubts shouldn't expect to receive anything from the Lord. A person who has doubts is thinking about two different things at the same time and can't make up his mind about anything. ✦ I'm surprised that you're so quickly deserting Christ, who called you in his kindness, to follow a different kind of good news. But what some people are calling good news is not really good news at all. They are confusing you. They want to distort the Good News about Christ. Whoever tells you good news that is different from the Good News we gave you should be condemned to hell, even if he is one of us or an angel from heaven. ✦ Those of you who try to earn God's approval by obeying his laws have been cut off from Christ. You have fallen out of God's favor. . . . You were doing so well. Who stopped you from being influenced by the truth? ✦ Live in me, and I will live in you. A branch cannot produce any fruit by itself. It has to stay attached to the vine. In the same way, you cannot produce fruit unless you live in me. . . . If you live in me and what I say lives in you, then ask for anything you want, and it will be yours. ✦ Certainly, Christ made God's many promises come true. For that reason, because of our message, people also honor God by saying, "Amen!"

*1 John 2:28; James 1:6–8; Galatians 1:6–8; Galatians 5:4, 7; John 15:4, 7; 2 Corinthians 1:20*

## Morning Reading

But the spiritual nature produces . . . patience, kindness.

The Lord, the Lord, a compassionate and merciful God, patient, always faithful and ready to forgive. ✦ I, a prisoner in the Lord, encourage you to live the kind of life which proves that God has called you. Be humble and gentle in every way. Be patient with each other and lovingly accept each other. ✦ Be kind to each other, sympathetic, forgiving each other as God has forgiven you through Christ. ✦ The wisdom that comes from above is first of all pure. Then it is peaceful, gentle, obedient, filled with mercy and good deeds, impartial, and sincere. ✦ Love is patient. Love is kind. ✦ We can't allow ourselves to get tired of living the right way. Certainly, each of us will receive everlasting life at the proper time, if we don't give up. ✦ Brothers and sisters, be patient until the Lord comes again. See how farmers wait for their precious crops to grow. They wait patiently for fall and spring rains. You, too, must be patient. Don't give up hope. The Lord will soon be here.

*Galatians 5:22; Exodus 34:6; Ephesians 4:1–2; Ephesians 4:32; James 3:17; 1 Corinthians 13:4; Galatians 6:9; James 5:7–8*

## Evening Reading

Immanuel . . . "God is with us."

"Does God really live on earth with people? If heaven itself, the highest heaven, cannot hold you." ✦ The Word became human and lived among us. We saw his glory. It was the glory that the Father shares with his only Son, a glory full of kindness and truth. ✦ The mystery that gives us our reverence for God is acknowledged to be great: appeared in his human nature. ✦ In these last days he has spoken to us through his Son. God made his Son responsible for everything. His Son is the one through whom God made the universe. ✦ That Sunday evening, the disciples were together behind locked doors, . . . Jesus stood among them. . . . The disciples were glad to see the Lord. . . . A week later Jesus' disciples were again in the house, and Thomas was with them. Even though the doors were locked, Jesus stood among them and said, "Peace be with you!" Then Jesus said to Thomas, "Put your finger here, and look at my hands. Take your hand, and put it into my side. Stop doubting, and believe." Thomas responded to Jesus, "My Lord and my God!" ✦ A son will be given to us. . . . He will be named . . . Mighty God.

*Matthew 1:23; 2 Chronicles 6:18; John 1:14; 1 Timothy 3:16; Hebrews 1:2; John 20:19–20, 26–28; Isaiah 9:6*

## MORNING READING

This is how you should be dressed when you eat it:
with your belt on. . . . You must eat it in a hurry.
It is the Lord's Passover.

Get up, and go away! This is not a place to rest! ✦ We don't have a permanent city here on earth, but we are looking for the city that we will have in the future. ✦ Therefore, a time of rest and worship exists for God's people. ✦ "Be ready for action, and have your lamps burning. Be like servants waiting to open the door at their master's knock when he returns from a wedding. Blessed are those servants whom the master finds awake when he comes. I can guarantee this truth: He will change his clothes, make them sit down at the table, and serve them. They will be blessed if he comes in the middle of the night or toward morning and finds them awake." ✦ Therefore, your minds must be clear and ready for action. Place your confidence completely in what God's kindness will bring you when Jesus Christ appears again. ✦ I can't consider myself a winner yet. This is what I do: I don't look back. . . . I run straight toward the goal to win the prize that God's heavenly call offers in Christ Jesus. Whoever has a mature faith should think this way.

*Exodus 12:11; Micah 2:10; Hebrews 13:14; Hebrews 4:9;
Luke 12:35–37; 1 Peter 1:13; Philippians 3:13–15*

## EVENING READING

The Lord is my inheritance and my cup.

We are also God's heirs. If we share in Christ's suffering in order to share his glory, we are heirs together with him. ✦ Everything belongs to you. ✦ My beloved is mine. ✦ God's Son . . . loved me and took the punishment for my sins. ✦ The Lord said to Aaron, "You will have no land or property of your own as the other Israelites will have. I am your possession and your property among the Israelites." ✦ As long as I have you, I don't need anyone else in heaven or on earth. My body and mind may waste away, but God remains the foundation of my life and my inheritance forever. ✦ Even though I walk through the dark valley of death, because you are with me, I fear no harm. Your rod and your staff give me courage. ✦ I know whom I trust. I'm convinced that he is able to protect what he had entrusted to me until that day. ✦ O God, you are my God. At dawn I search for you. My soul thirsts for you. My body longs for you in a dry, parched land where there is no water.

*Psalm 16:5; Romans 8:17; 1 Corinthians 3:21; Song of Songs 2:16; Galatians 2:20;
Numbers 18:20; Psalm 73:25–26; Psalm 23:4; 2 Timothy 1:12; Psalm 63:1*

## MORNING READING

"So stay awake, because you don't know the day or the hour."

"Make sure that you don't become drunk, hung over, and worried about life. Then that day could suddenly catch you by surprise like a trap that catches a bird. That day will surprise all people who live on the earth. Be alert at all times. Pray so that you have the power to escape everything that is about to happen and to stand in front of the Son of Man." ✦ The day of the Lord will come like a thief in the night. When people say, "Everything is safe and sound!" destruction will suddenly strike them. It will be as sudden as labor pains come to a pregnant woman. They won't be able to escape. But, brothers and sisters, you don't live in the dark. That day won't take you by surprise as a thief would. You belong to the day and the light not to the night and the dark. Therefore, we must not fall asleep like other people, but we must stay awake and be sober.

*Matthew 25:13; Luke 21:34–36; 1 Thessalonians 5:2–6*

## EVENING READING

"I am God Almighty. Live in my presence with integrity."

It's not that I've already reached the goal or have already completed the course. But I run to win that which Jesus Christ has already won for me. Brothers and sisters, I can't consider myself a winner yet. This is what I do: I don't look back, I lengthen my stride, and I run straight toward the goal to win the prize that God's heavenly call offers in Christ Jesus. ✦ Enoch walked with God; then he was gone because God took him. ✦ Grow in the good will and knowledge of our Lord and Savior Jesus Christ. ✦ As all of us reflect the Lord's glory with faces that are not covered with veils, we are being changed into his image with ever-increasing glory. This comes from the Lord, who is the Spirit. ✦ Jesus looked up to heaven and said, ". . . I'm not asking you to take them out of the world but to protect them from the evil one. I am in them, and you are in me. So they are completely united."

*Genesis 17:1; Philippians 3:12–14; Genesis 5:24;*
*2 Peter 3:18; 2 Corinthians 3:18; John 17:1, 15, 23*

## MORNING READING

This new house will be more glorious than the former,
declares the Lord of Armies. And in this place I will give them peace.

The temple that will be built for the Lord must be magnificent, large, famous, praised, and honored in all other countries. ✦ The Lord's glory had filled the Lord's temple. ✦ Jesus replied, "Tear down this temple, and I'll rebuild it in three days." . . . But the temple Jesus spoke about was his own body. ✦ In fact, the ministry that brings punishment lost its glory because of the superior glory of the other ministry. ✦ The Word became human and lived among us. We saw his glory. It was the glory that the Father shares with his only Son, a glory full of kindness and truth. ✦ In these last days [God] has spoken to us through his Son. God made his Son responsible for everything. His Son is the one through whom God made the universe. ✦ Glory to God in the highest heaven, and on earth peace to those who have his good will! ✦ Prince of Peace. ✦ He is our peace. ✦ Then God's peace, which goes beyond anything we can imagine, will guard your thoughts and emotions through Christ Jesus.

*Haggai 2:9; 1 Chronicles 22:5; 2 Chronicles 7:2; John 2:19, 21; 2 Corinthians 3:10; John 1:14; Hebrews 1:1–2; Luke 2:14; Isaiah 9:6; Ephesians 2:14; Philippians 4:7*

## EVENING READING

Take up the weapons that belong to the light.

Live like the Lord Jesus Christ did. ✦ To gain Christ and to have a relationship with him. This means that I didn't receive God's approval by obeying his laws. The opposite is true! I have God's approval through faith in Christ. This is the approval that comes from God and is based on faith. ✦ Everyone who believes has God's approval through faith in Jesus Christ. ✦ He has wrapped me in the robe of righteousness. ✦ I will come with the mighty deeds of the Almighty Lord. I will praise your righteousness, yours alone. ✦ Once you lived in the dark, but now the Lord has filled you with light. Live as children who have light. . . . Have nothing to do with the useless works that darkness produces. Instead, expose them. . . . Light exposes the true character of everything because light makes everything easy to see. That's why it says: "Wake up, sleeper! Rise from the dead, and Christ will shine on you." So then, be very careful how you live. Don't live like foolish people but like wise people.

*Romans 13:12; Romans 13:14; Philippians 3:8–9; Romans 3:22; Isaiah 61;10; Psalm 71:16; Ephesians 5:8, 11, 13–15*

## MORNING READING

"When you've done everything you're ordered to do, say,
'We're worthless servants. We've only done our duty.' "

So, do we have anything to brag about? Bragging has been eliminated. On what basis was it eliminated? On the basis of our own efforts? No, indeed! Rather, it is eliminated on the basis of faith. ✦ What do you have that wasn't given to you? If you were given what you have, why are you bragging as if it weren't a gift? ✦ God saved you through faith as an act of kindness. You had nothing to do with it. Being saved is a gift from God. It's not the result of anything you've done, so no one can brag about it. God has made us what we are. He has created us in Christ Jesus to live lives filled with good works that he has prepared for us to do. ✦ But God's kindness made me what I am, and that kindness was not wasted on me. Instead, I worked harder than all the others. It was not I who did it, but God's kindness was with me. ✦ Everything is from him and by him and for him. ✦ Everything comes from you. We give you only what has come from your hands. ✦ Do not take me to court for judgment, because there is no one alive who is righteous in your presence.

*Luke 17:10; Romans 3:27; 1 Corinthians 4:7; Ephesians 2:8–10; 1 Corinthians 15:10; Romans 11:36; 1 Chronicles 29:14; Psalm 143:2*

## EVENING READING

He certainly knows what we are made of.
He bears in mind that we are dust.

Then the LORD God formed the man from the dust of the earth, and blew the breath of life into his nostrils. The man became a living being. ✦ I will give thanks to you because I have been so amazingly and miraculously made. Your works are miraculous, and my soul is fully aware of this. My bones were not hidden from you when I was being made in secret, when I was being skillfully woven in an underground workshop. Your eyes saw me when I was only a fetus. Every day of my life was recorded in your book before one of them had taken place. ✦ Don't all of us have the same father? Hasn't the same God created us? ✦ Certainly, we live, move, and exist because of him. ✦ As a father has compassion for his children, so the LORD has compassion for those who fear him. ✦ But he is compassionate. He forgave their sin. He did not destroy them. He restrained his anger many times. He did not display all of his fury. He remembered that they were only flesh and blood, a breeze that blows and does not return.

*Psalm 103:14; Genesis 2:7; Psalm 139:14–16; Malachi 2:10; Acts 17:28; Psalm 103:13; Psalm 78:38–39*

## MORNING READING

Renews you with his love.

The LORD set his heart on you and chose you, even though you didn't outnumber all the other people. You were the smallest of all nations. You were chosen because the LORD loved you. ✦ We love because God loved us first. ✦ You were separated from God. . . . But now Christ has brought you back to God by dying in his physical body. He did this so that you could come into God's presence without sin, fault, or blame. ✦ This is love: not that we have loved God, but that he loved us and sent his Son to be the payment for our sins. ✦ Christ died for us while we were still sinners. This demonstrates God's love for us. ✦ Then a voice from heaven said, "This is my Son, whom I love—my Son with whom I am pleased." ✦ The Father loves me because I give my life in order to take it back again. ✦ His Son is the reflection of God's glory and the exact likeness of God's being. He holds everything together through his powerful words. After he had cleansed people from their sins, he received the highest position, the one next to the Father in heaven.

*Zephaniah 3:17; Deuteronomy 7:7–8; 1 John 4:19; Colossians 1:21–22; 1 John 4:10; Romans 5:8; Matthew 3:17; John 10:17; Hebrews 1:3*

## EVENING READING

A new and living way.

Then Cain left the LORD's presence. ✦ But your wrongs have separated you from your God, and your sins have made him hide his face. ✦ Try to live holy lives, because if you don't, you will not see the Lord. ✦ "I am the way, the truth, and the life. No one goes to the Father except through me." ✦ Christ has destroyed death, and through the Good News he has brought eternal life into full view. ✦ The Holy Spirit used this to show that the way into the most holy place was not open while the tent was still in use. ✦ So he is our peace. In his body he has made Jewish and non-Jewish people one by breaking down the wall of hostility that kept them apart. ✦ Suddenly, the curtain in the temple was split in two from top to bottom. ✦ "But the narrow gate and the road that lead to life are full of trouble. Only a few people find the narrow gate." ✦ You make the path of life known to me. Complete joy is in your presence. Pleasures are by your side forever.

*Hebrews 10:20; Genesis 4:16; Isaiah 59:2; Hebrews 12:14; John 14:6; 2 Timothy 1:10; Hebrews 9:8; Ephesians 2:14; Matthew 27:51; Matthew 7:14; Psalm 16:11*

## MORNING READING

They need to pray all the time and never give up.

"Suppose one of you has a friend. Suppose you go to him at midnight and say, 'Friend, let me borrow three loaves of bread. A friend of mine on a trip has dropped in on me, and I don't have anything to serve him.' Your friend might answer you from inside his house, 'Don't bother me! The door is already locked, and my children are in bed. I can't get up to give you anything.' I can guarantee that although he doesn't want to get up to give you anything, he will get up and give you whatever you need because he is your friend and because you were so bold." ✦ Pray in the Spirit in every situation. Use every kind of prayer and request there is. For the same reason be alert. Use every kind of effort and make every kind of request for all of God's people. ✦ Jacob answered, "I won't let you go until you bless me." . . . The man said, "Because you have struggled with God and with men—and you have won." ✦ Keep praying. Pay attention when you offer prayers of thanksgiving. ✦ At that time Jesus went to a mountain to pray. He spent the whole night in prayer to God.

*Luke 18:1; Luke 11:5–8; Ephesians 6:18;*
*Genesis 32:26, 28; Colossians 4:2; Luke 6:12*

## EVENING READING

Forgive all my sins.

"Come on now, let's discuss this!" says the Lord. "Though your sins are bright red, they will become as white as snow. Though they are dark red, they will become as white as wool. ✦ "Cheer up, friend! Your sins are forgiven." ✦ I alone am the one who is going to wipe away your rebellious actions for my own sake. I will not remember your sins anymore. ✦ "The Son of Man has authority on earth to forgive sins." ✦ Through the blood of his Son, we are set free from our sins. God forgives our failures because of his overflowing kindness. ✦ He saved us, but not because of anything we had done to gain his approval. Instead, because of his mercy he saved us through the washing in which the Holy Spirit gives us new birth and renewal. God poured a generous amount of the Spirit on us through Jesus Christ our Savior. ✦ He forgave all our failures. He did this by erasing the charges that were brought against us by the written laws God had established. He took the charges away by nailing them to the cross. ✦ Praise the Lord, my soul, . . . who forgives all your sins, the one who heals all your diseases.

*Psalm 25:18; Isaiah 1:18; Matthew 9:2; Isaiah 43:25; Matthew 9:6;*
*Ephesians 1:7; Titus 3:5–6; Colossians 2:13–14; Psalm 103:2–3*

## Morning Reading

The Lord made everything he did successful.

Blessed are all who fear the Lord and live his way. You will certainly eat what your own hands have provided. Blessings to you! ✦ Trust the Lord, and do good things. Live in the land, and practice being faithful. Be happy with the Lord, and he will give you the desires of your heart. ✦ I have commanded you, "Be strong and courageous! Don't tremble or be terrified, because the Lord your God is with you wherever you go." ✦ "First, be concerned about his kingdom and what has his approval. Then all these things will be provided for you." ✦ As long as he dedicated his life to serving the Lord, the Lord gave him success. ✦ Be careful that you don't forget the Lord your God. Don't fail to obey his commands, rules, and laws that I'm giving you today. . . . You may say to yourselves, "I became wealthy because of my own ability and strength." ✦ "Isn't the Lord your God with you? Hasn't he given you peace with all your neighbors?"

*Genesis 39:3; Psalm 128:1–2; Psalm 37:3–4; Joshua 1:9; Matthew 6:33; 2 Chronicles 26:5; Deuteronomy 8:11, 17; 1 Chronicles 22:18*

## Evening Reading

"Why do you have these thoughts?"

Abraham didn't weaken. Through faith he regarded the facts: His body was already as good as dead now that he was about a hundred years old, and Sarah was unable to have children. He didn't doubt God's promise out of a lack of faith. Instead, giving honor to God for the promise, he became strong because of faith. ✦ "Is it easier to say to this paralyzed man, 'Your sins are forgiven,' or to say, 'Get up, pick up your cot, and walk'?" ✦ Everything is possible for the person who believes. ✦ "All authority in heaven and on earth has been given to me." ✦ "Why are you such cowards? Don't you have any faith yet?" ✦ "Look at the birds. . . . Your heavenly Father feeds them. Aren't you worth more than they?" ✦ "Why are you discussing among yourselves that you don't have any bread? You have so little faith! Don't you understand yet? Don't you remember the five loaves for the five thousand and how many baskets you filled?" ✦ My God will richly fill your every need in a glorious way through Christ Jesus.

*Mark 2:8; Romans 4:19–20; Mark 2:9; Mark 9:23; Matthew 28:18; Mark 4:40; Matthew 6:26; Matthew 16:8–9; Philippians 4:19*

## MORNING READING

"No human has ever spoken like this man."

You are the most handsome of Adam's descendants. Grace is poured on your lips. That is why God has blessed you forever. ✦ The Almighty LORD will teach me what to say, so I will know how to encourage weary people. ✦ His mouth is sweet in every way. Everything about him is desirable! This is my beloved, and this is my friend. ✦ All the people spoke well of him. They were amazed to hear the gracious words flowing from his lips. ✦ Unlike their scribes, he taught them with authority. ✦ Let Christ's word with all its wisdom and richness live in you. ✦ The word of God as the sword that the Spirit supplies. ✦ God's word is living and active. It is sharper than any two-edged sword. ✦ The weapons we use in our fight are not made by humans. Rather, they are powerful weapons from God. With them we destroy people's defenses, that is, their arguments and all their intellectual arrogance that oppose the knowledge of God. We take every thought captive so that it is obedient to Christ.

*John 7:46; Psalm 45:2; Isaiah 50:4; Song of Songs 5:16; Luke 4:22; Matthew 7:29; Colossians 3:16; Ephesians 6:17; Hebrews 4:12; 2 Corinthians 10:4–5*

## EVENING READING

The triumph of the wicked is short-lived.

You will bruise his heel. ✦ "This is your time, when darkness rules." ✦ Since all of these sons and daughters have flesh and blood, Jesus took on flesh and blood to be like them. He did this so that by dying he would destroy the one who had power over death (that is, the devil). ✦ He stripped the rulers and authorities of their power and made a public spectacle of them as he celebrated his victory in Christ. ✦ Keep your mind clear, and be alert. Your opponent the devil is prowling around like a roaring lion as he looks for someone to devour. Be firm in the faith and resist him. ✦ Resist the devil, and he will run away from you. ✦ The wicked person plots against a righteous one and grits his teeth at him. The Lord laughs at him because he has seen that his time is coming. ✦ The God of peace will quickly crush Satan under your feet. ✦ The devil . . . was thrown into the fiery lake of sulfur. . . . They will be tortured day and night forever and ever.

*Job 20:5; Genesis 3:15; Luke 22:53; Hebrews 2:14; Colossians 2:15; 1 Peter 5:8–9; James 4:7; Psalm 37:12–13; Romans 16:20; Revelation 20:10*

## Morning Reading

"The younger son . . . left for a country far away from home. There he wasted everything he had on a wild lifestyle."

That's what some of you were! But you have been washed and made holy, and you have received God's approval in the name of the Lord Jesus Christ and in the Spirit of our God. ✦ Because of our nature, we deserved God's anger just like everyone else. But God is rich in mercy because of his great love for us. We were dead because of our failures, but he made us alive together with Christ. (It is God's kindness that saved you.) God has brought us back to life together with Christ Jesus and has given us a position in heaven with him. ✦ This is love: not that we have loved God, but that he loved us and sent his Son to be the payment for our sins. ✦ Christ died for us while we were still sinners. . . . If the death of his Son restored our relationship with God while we were still his enemies, we are even more certain that, because of this restored relationship, the life of his Son will save us.

*Luke 15:13; 1 Corinthians 6:11; Ephesians 2:3–6; 1 John 4:10; Romans 5:8, 10*

## Evening Reading

Forgive as the Lord forgave you.

"Two men owed a moneylender some money. One owed him five hundred silver coins, and the other owed him fifty. When they couldn't pay it back, he was kind enough to cancel their debts." ✦ "I canceled your entire debt, because you begged me. Shouldn't you have treated the other servant as mercifully as I treated you?" ✦ "Whenever you pray, forgive anything you have against anyone. Then your Father in heaven will forgive your failures." ✦ As holy people whom God has chosen and loved, be sympathetic, kind, humble, gentle, and patient. Put up with each other, and forgive each other if anyone has a complaint. Forgive as the Lord forgave you. ✦ Then Peter came to Jesus and asked him, "Lord, how often do I have to forgive a believer who wrongs me? Seven times?" Jesus answered him, "I tell you, not just seven times, but seventy times seven."

*Colossians 3:13; Luke 7:41–42; Matthew 18:32–33; Mark 11:25; Colossians 3:12–13; Matthew 18:21–22*

## Morning Reading

"So he went at once to his father.
While he was still at a distance, his father saw him
and felt sorry for him. He ran to his son,
put his arms around him, and kissed him."

The Lord is compassionate, merciful, patient, and always ready to forgive. He will not always accuse us of wrong or be angry with us forever. He has not treated us as we deserve for our sins or paid us back for our wrongs. As high as the heavens are above the earth—that is how vast his mercy is toward those who fear him. As far as the east is from the west—that is how far he has removed our rebellious acts from himself. As a father has compassion for his children, so the Lord has compassion for those who fear him. ✦ You haven't received the spirit of slaves that leads you into fear again. Instead, you have received the spirit of God's adopted children by which we call out, "Abba! Father!" The Spirit himself testifies with our spirit that we are God's children. ✦ You, who were once far away, have been brought near by the blood of Christ. ✦ That is why you are no longer foreigners and outsiders but citizens together with God's people and members of God's family.

*Luke 15:20; Psalm 103:8–13; Romans 8:15–16; Ephesians 2:13; Ephesians 2:19*

## Evening Reading

I am making everything new.

"I can guarantee this truth: No one can see the kingdom of God without being born from above." ✦ Whoever is a believer in Christ is a new creation. The old way of living has disappeared. A new way of living has come into existence. ✦ "I will give you a new heart and put a new spirit in you. I will remove your stubborn hearts and give you obedient hearts." ✦ Remove the old yeast of sin so that you may be a new batch of dough, since you don't actually have the yeast of sin. ✦ You were also taught to become a new person created to be like God, truly righteous and holy. ✦ You will be given a new name that the Lord will announce. ✦ I will create a new heaven and a new earth. Past things will not be remembered. They will not come to mind. ✦ All these things will be destroyed in this way. So think of the kind of holy and godly lives you must live.

*Revelation 21:5; John 3:3; 2 Corinthians 5:17; Ezekiel 36:26;
1 Corinthians 5:7; Ephesians 4:24; Isaiah 62:2; Isaiah 65:17; 2 Peter 3:11*

## MORNING READING

Anything that won't burn—
must be put through fire in order to make it clean.

The LORD your God is testing you to find out if you really love him with all your heart and with all your soul. ✦ He will act like a refiner and a purifier of silver. He will purify Levi's sons and refine them like gold and silver. Then they will bring acceptable offerings to the LORD. ✦ The day will make what each one does clearly visible because fire will reveal it. That fire will determine what kind of work each person has done. ✦ "I will turn my power against you. I will remove your impurities with bleach. I will get rid of all your impurities." ✦ I will now refine them with fire and test them. ✦ You have tested us, O God. You have refined us in the same way silver is refined. . . . You let people ride over our heads. We went through fire and water, but then you brought us out and refreshed us. ✦ When you go through the sea, I am with you. When you go through rivers, they will not sweep you away.

*Numbers 31:23; Deuteronomy 13:3; Malachi 3:3; 1 Corinthians 3:13; Isaiah 1:25; Jeremiah 9:7; Psalm 66:10, 12; Isaiah 43:2*

## EVENING READING

Christ carried our sins in his body
on the cross so that freed from our sins,
we could live a life that has God's approval.

You were taught to change the way you were living. The person you used to be will ruin you through desires that deceive you. However, you were taught to have a new attitude. You were also taught to become a new person created to be like God, truly righteous and holy. ✦ You have died, and your life is hidden with Christ in God. ✦ When we were baptized into his death, we were placed into the tomb with him. As Christ was brought back from death to life by the glorious power of the Father, so we, too, should live a new kind of life. . . . We know that the person we used to be was crucified with him to put an end to sin in our bodies. Because of this we are no longer slaves to sin. The person who has died has been freed from sin. . . . So consider yourselves dead to sin's power but living for God in the power Christ Jesus gives you. Therefore, never let sin rule your physical body so that you obey its desires. Never offer any part of your body to sin's power. No part of your body should ever be used to do any ungodly thing. Instead, offer yourselves to God as people who have come back from death and are now alive. Offer all the parts of your body to God. Use them to do everything that God approves of.

*1 Peter 2:24; Ephesians 4:22–24; Colossians 3:3; Romans 6:4, 6–7, 11–13*

## MORNING READING

Live in me, and I will live in you.

I have been crucified with Christ. I no longer live, but Christ lives in me. The life I now live I live by believing in God's Son, who loved me and took the punishment for my sins. ✦ I know that nothing good lives in me; that is, nothing good lives in my corrupt nature. Although I have the desire to do what is right, I don't do it. . . . What a miserable person I am! Who will rescue me from my dying body? I thank God that our Lord Jesus Christ rescues me! ✦ If Christ lives in you, your bodies are dead because of sin, but your spirits are alive because you have God's approval. ✦ This is on the condition that you continue in faith without being moved from the solid foundation of the hope that the Good News contains. ✦ Now, dear children, live in Christ. Then, when he appears we will have confidence, and when he comes we won't turn from him in shame. ✦ Those who say that they live in him must live the same way he lived.

*John 15:4; Galatians 2:19–20; Romans 7:18, 24–25; Romans 8:10; Colossians 1:23; 1 John 2:28; 1 John 2:6*

## EVENING READING

"Do you believe in the Son of Man?"

The man replied, "Sir, tell me who he is so that I can believe in him." ✦ His Son is the reflection of God's glory and the exact likeness of God's being. ✦ God is the blessed and only ruler. He is the King of kings and Lord of lords. He is the only one who cannot die. He lives in light that no one can come near. No one has seen him, nor can they see him. Honor and power belong to him forever! Amen. ✦ "I am the A and the Z," says the Lord God, the one who is, the one who was, and the one who is coming, the Almighty. ✦ "I believe, Lord." ✦ I know whom I trust. I'm convinced that he is able to protect what he had entrusted to me until that day. ✦ "I am laying a chosen and precious cornerstone in Zion, and the person who believes in him will never be ashamed." This honor belongs to those who believe.

*John 9:35; John 9:36; Hebrews 1:3; 1 Timothy 6:15–16; Revelation 1:8; John 9:38; 2 Timothy 1:12; 1 Peter 2:6–7*

## MORNING READING

Because Christ suffered so much for us,
we can receive so much comfort from him.

What it means to share his suffering. ✦ Be happy as you share Christ's sufferings. Then you will also be full of joy when he appears again in his glory. ✦ If we have died with him, we will live with him. ✦ If we are his children, we are also God's heirs. If we share in Christ's suffering in order to share his glory, we are heirs together with him. ✦ God wouldn't change his plan. He wanted to make this perfectly clear to those who would receive his promise, so he took an oath. God did this so that we would be encouraged. God cannot lie when he takes an oath or makes a promise. These two things can never be changed. Those of us who have taken refuge in him hold on to the confidence we have been given. ✦ God our Father loved us and by his kindness gave us everlasting encouragement and good hope. Together with our Lord Jesus Christ, may he encourage and strengthen you to do and say everything that is good.

*2 Corinthians 1:5; Philippians 3:10; 1 Peter 4:13; 2 Timothy 2:11; Romans 8:17; Hebrews 6:17–18; 2 Thessalonians 2:16–17*

## EVENING READING

"Martha, Martha! You worry and fuss about a lot of things."

"Consider the crows. They don't plant or harvest. . . . Consider how the flowers grow. They never work or spin yarn for clothes. . . . Don't concern yourself about what you will eat or drink, and quit worrying about these things. . . . Your Father knows you need them." ✦ As long as we have food and clothes, we should be satisfied. But people who want to get rich keep falling into temptation. They are trapped by many stupid and harmful desires which drown them in destruction and ruin. Certainly, the love of money is the root of all kinds of evil. Some people who have set their hearts on getting rich have wandered away from the Christian faith and have caused themselves a lot of grief. ✦ "The worries of life, the deceitful pleasures of riches, and the desires for other things take over. They choke the word so that it can't produce anything." ✦ We must get rid of everything that slows us down, especially sin that distracts us. We must run the race that lies ahead of us and never give up.

*Luke 10:41; Luke 12:24, 27, 29–30; 1 Timothy 6:8–10; Mark 4:19; Hebrews 12:1*

## Morning Reading

Some things are hidden. They belong to the Lord our God.
But the things that have been revealed in these teachings belong to us.

O Lord, my heart is not conceited. My eyes do not look down on others. I am not involved in things too big or too difficult for me. Instead, I have kept my soul calm and quiet. My soul is content as a weaned child is content in its mother's arms. ✦ The Lord advises those who fear him. He reveals to them the intent of his promise. ✦ There is a God in heaven who reveals secrets. ✦ "These are only glimpses of what he does. We only hear a whisper of him!" ✦ "I don't call you servants anymore, because a servant doesn't know what his master is doing. But I've called you friends because I've made known to you everything that I've heard from my Father." ✦ "If you love me, you will obey my commandments. I will ask the Father, and he will give you another helper who will be with you forever. That helper is the Spirit of Truth."

*Deuteronomy 29:29; Psalm 131:1–2; Psalm 25:14;*
*Daniel 2:28; Job 26:14; John 15:15; John 14:15–17*

## Evening Reading

The Spirit intercedes for God's people the way God wants him to.

"If you ask the Father for anything in my name, he will give it to you. So far you haven't asked for anything in my name. Ask and you will receive so that you can be completely happy." ✦ Pray in the Spirit in every situation. Use every kind of prayer and request there is. ✦ We are confident that God listens to us if we ask for anything that has his approval. We know that he listens to our requests. So we know that we already have what we ask him for. ✦ It is God's will that you keep away from sexual sin as a mark of your devotion to him. ✦ God didn't call us to be sexually immoral but to be holy. Therefore, whoever rejects this order is not rejecting human authority but God, who gives you his Holy Spirit. ✦ Always be joyful. Never stop praying. Whatever happens, give thanks, because it is God's will in Christ Jesus that you do this. Don't put out the Spirit's fire.

*Romans 8:27; John 16:23–24; Ephesians 6:18; 1 John 5:14–15;*
*1 Thessalonians 4:3; 1 Thessalonians 4:7–8; 1 Thessalonians 5:16–19*

## Morning Reading

Be very careful how you live.
Don't live like foolish people but like wise people.
Make the most of your opportunities because these are evil days.

Carefully follow the commands and teachings that the Lord's servant Moses gave you. Love the Lord your God, follow his directions, and keep his commands. Be loyal to him, and serve him with all your heart and soul. ✦ Be wise in the way you act toward those who are outside the Christian faith. Make the most of your opportunities. Everything you say should be kind and well thought out so that you know how to answer everyone. ✦ Keep away from every kind of evil. ✦ "Since the groom was late, all the bridesmaids became drowsy and fell asleep. At midnight someone shouted, 'The groom is here! Come to meet him!' . . . So stay awake, because you don't know the day or the hour." ✦ Therefore, brothers and sisters, use more effort to make God's calling and choosing of you secure. If you keep doing this, you will never fall away. ✦ Blessed are those servants whom the master finds awake when he comes.

*Ephesians 5:15–16; Joshua 22:5; Colossians 4:5–6;*
*1 Thessalonians 5:22; Matthew 25:5–6, 13; 2 Peter 1:10; Luke 12:37*

## Evening Reading

Hold on to what you have so that no one takes your crown.

"If I only touch his clothes, I'll get well." ✦ A man with a serious skin disease came and bowed down in front of him. The man said to Jesus, "Sir, if you're willing, you can make me clean." Jesus reached out, touched him, and said, "I'm willing. So be clean!" ✦ Faith is the size of a mustard seed. ✦ So don't lose your confidence. It will bring you a great reward. ✦ Continue to work out your salvation with fear and trembling. It is God who produces in you the desires and actions that please him. ✦ First the green blade appears, then the head, then the head full of grain. ✦ Let's learn about the Lord. Let's get to know the Lord. ✦ From the time of John the Baptizer until now, the kingdom of heaven has been forcefully advancing, and forceful people have been seizing it. ✦ Run like them, so that you can win. ✦ I have fought the good fight. I have completed the race. I have kept the faith. The prize that shows I have God's approval is now waiting for me. The Lord, who is a fair judge, will give me that prize on that day.

*Revelation 3:11; Matthew 9:21; Matthew 8:2–3; Matthew 17:20;*
*Hebrews 10:35; Philippians 2:12–13; Mark 4:28; Hosea 6:3;*
*Matthew 11:12; 1 Corinthians 9:24; 2 Timothy 4:7–8*

## MORNING READING

In every situation let God know what you need
in prayers and requests while giving thanks.

I love the LORD because he hears my voice, my pleas for mercy. I will call on him as long as I live because he turns his ear toward me. ✦ "When you pray, don't ramble like heathens who think they'll be heard if they talk a lot." ✦ At the same time the Spirit also helps us in our weakness, because we don't know how to pray for what we need. But the Spirit intercedes along with our groans that cannot be expressed in words. ✦ I want men to offer prayers everywhere. They should raise their hands in prayer after putting aside their anger and any quarrels they have with anyone. ✦ Pray in the Spirit in every situation. Use every kind of prayer and request there is. For the same reason be alert. Use every kind of effort and make every kind of request for all of God's people. ✦ "I can guarantee again that if two of you agree on anything here on earth, my Father in heaven will accept it."

*Philippians 4:6; Psalm 116:1–2; Matthew 6:7; Romans 8:26; 1 Timothy 2:8; Ephesians 6:18; Matthew 18:19*

## EVENING READING

Everything that you have made will give thanks to you,
O LORD, and your faithful ones will praise you.

Praise the LORD, my soul! Praise his holy name, all that is within me. Praise the LORD, my soul, and never forget all the good he has done. ✦ I will thank the LORD at all times. My mouth will always praise him. ✦ I will bless you every day. I will praise your name forever and ever. ✦ My lips will praise you because your mercy is better than life itself. So I will thank you as long as I live. I will lift up my hands to pray in your name. You satisfy my soul with the richest foods. My mouth will sing your praise with joyful lips. ✦ "My soul praises the Lord's greatness! My spirit finds its joy in God, my Savior." ✦ "Our Lord and God, you deserve to receive glory, honor, and power because you created everything. Everything came into existence and was created because of your will."

*Psalm 145:10; Psalm 103:1–2; Psalm 34:1; Psalm 145:2; Psalm 63:3–5; Luke 1:46–47; Revelation 4:11*

## MORNING READING

"After you put into the ark the words of my promise
which I will give you, place the throne of mercy on top . . .
whenever I meet with you."

The Holy Spirit used this to show that the way into the most holy place was not open while the tent was still in use. ✦ Then Jesus loudly cried out once again and gave up his life. Suddenly, the curtain in the temple was split in two from top to bottom. ✦ Brothers and sisters, because of the blood of Jesus we can now confidently go into the holy place. Jesus has opened a new and living way for us to go through the curtain. (The curtain is his own body.) . . . We have been sprinkled with his blood to free us from a guilty conscience, and our bodies have been washed with clean water. So we must continue to come to him with a sincere heart and strong faith. ✦ So we can go confidently to the throne of God's kindness to receive mercy and find kindness, which will help us at the right time. ✦ They receive God's approval freely by an act of his kindness through the price Christ Jesus paid to set us free from sin. God showed that Christ is the throne of mercy where God's approval is given through faith in Christ's blood. In his patience God waited to deal with sins committed in the past. ✦ So Jewish and non-Jewish people can go to the Father in one Spirit.

*Exodus 25:21–22; Hebrews 9:8; Matthew 27:50–51;
Hebrews 10:19–20, 22; Hebrews 4:16; Romans 3:24–25; Ephesians 2:18*

## EVENING READING

Faith as the size of a mustard seed.

Barak said to [Deborah], "If you go with me, I'll go. But if you don't go with me, I won't go." . . . So on that day, God used the people of Israel to crush the power of King Jabin of Canaan. ✦ Gideon . . . did what the Lord had told him to do. However, he didn't do anything during the day. He was too afraid of his father's family and the men of the city, so he did it at night. . . . Then Gideon said to God, "You said that you would rescue Israel through me. . . . Let me make one more test." . . . During the night, God did what Gideon asked. ✦ You only have a little strength, but you have paid attention to my word and have not denied my name. ✦ Who despised the day when little things began to happen? ✦ We always have to thank God for you, brothers and sisters. It's right to do this because your faith is showing remarkable growth and your love for each other is increasing. ✦ "Give us more faith." ✦ I will be like dew to the people of Israel. They will blossom like flowers. They will be firmly rooted like cedars from Lebanon. They will be like growing branches. They will be beautiful like olive trees. They will be fragrant like cedars from Lebanon.

*Matthew 17:20; Judges 4:8, 23; Judges 6:27, 36, 39–40; Revelation 3:8;
Zechariah 4:10; 2 Thessalonians 1:3; Luke 17:5; Hosea 14:5–6*

## Morning Reading

Try to live holy lives, because if you don't, you will not see the Lord.

"No one can see the kingdom of God without being born from above." ✦ Nothing unclean, no one who does anything detestable, and no liars will ever enter it. ✦ There is no blemish on you. ✦ Be holy because I, the Lord your God, am holy. ✦ Because you are children who obey God, don't live the kind of lives you once lived. Once you lived to satisfy your desires because you didn't know any better. But because the God who called you is holy you must be holy in every aspect of your life. Scripture says, "Be holy, because I am holy." So if you call God your Father, live your time as temporary residents on earth in fear. ✦ You were taught to change the way you were living. The person you used to be will ruin you through desires that deceive you. However, you were taught to have a new attitude. You were also taught to become a new person created to be like God, truly righteous and holy. ✦ Before the creation of the world, he chose us through Christ to be holy and perfect in his presence.

*Hebrews 12:14; John 3:3; Revelation 21:27; Song of Songs 4:7; Leviticus 19:2; 1 Peter 1:14–17; Ephesians 4:22–24; Ephesians 1:4*

## Evening Reading

Gold purified in fire.

"Anyone who gave up his home, brothers, sisters, mother, father, children, or fields because of me and the Good News will certainly receive a hundred times as much here in this life. They will certainly receive homes, brothers, sisters, mothers, children and fields, along with persecutions. But in the world to come they will receive eternal life." ✦ Dear friends, don't be surprised by the fiery troubles that are coming in order to test you. Don't feel as though something strange is happening to you. ✦ You have to suffer different kinds of trouble for a little while now. The purpose of these troubles is to test your faith as fire tests how genuine gold is. Your faith is more precious than gold, and by passing the test, it gives praise, glory, and honor to God. This will happen when Jesus Christ appears again. ✦ God, who shows you his kindness and who has called you through Christ Jesus to his eternal glory, will restore you, strengthen you, make you strong, and support you as you suffer for a little while. ✦ "In the world you'll have trouble. But cheer up! I have overcome the world."

*Revelation 3:18; Mark 10:29–30; 1 Peter 4:12; 1 Peter 1:6–7; 1 Peter 5:10; John 16:33*

## MORNING READING

"Take this child, nurse him for me, and I will pay you."

"Work in my vineyard, and I'll give you whatever is right." ✦ "Whoever gives you a cup of water to drink because you belong to Christ will certainly not lose his reward." ✦ A generous person will be made rich, and whoever satisfies others will himself be satisfied. ✦ God is fair. He won't forget what you've done or the love you've shown for him. You helped his holy people, and you continue to help them. ✦ Each will receive a reward for his own work. ✦ "Then the people who have God's approval will reply to him, 'Lord, when did we see you hungry and feed you or see you thirsty and give you something to drink? When did we see you as a stranger and take you into our homes or see you in need of clothes. . . . The king will answer them, 'I can guarantee this truth: Whatever you did for one of my brothers or sisters, no matter how unimportant they seemed, you did for me.' " ✦ "Come, my Father has blessed you! Inherit the kingdom prepared for you from the creation of the world."

*Exodus 2:9; Matthew 20:4; Mark 9:41; Proverbs 11:25; Hebrews 6:10; 1 Corinthians 3:8; Matthew 25:37–38, 40; Matthew 25:34*

## EVENING READING

You watch me when I travel and when I rest.

Then Jacob woke up from his sleep and exclaimed, "Certainly, the LORD is in this place, and I didn't know it!" Filled with awe, he said, "How awe-inspiring this place is! Certainly, this is the house of God and the gateway to heaven!" ✦ "The LORD's eyes scan the whole world to find those whose hearts are committed to him and to strengthen them." ✦ I fall asleep in peace the moment I lie down because you alone, O LORD, enable me to live securely. ✦ You, O LORD, are my refuge! You have made the Most High your home. No harm will come to you. No sickness will come near your house. He will put his angels in charge of you to protect you in all your ways. ✦ When you lie down, you will not be afraid. As you lie there, your sleep will be sweet. ✦ The LORD gives food to those he loves while they sleep.

*Psalm 139:3; Genesis 28:16–17; 2 Chronicles 16:9; Psalm 4:8; Psalm 91:9–11; Proverbs 3:24; Psalm 127:2*

## MORNING READING

Christ suffered for you. He left you an example
so that you could follow in his footsteps.

"The Son of Man . . . didn't come so that others could serve him. He came to serve and to give his life as a ransom for many people." ✦ Whoever wants to be most important among you will be a slave for everyone. ✦ Jesus went everywhere and did good things. ✦ Help carry each other's burdens. In this way you will follow Christ's teachings. ✦ The gentleness and kindness of Christ. ✦ Don't act out of selfish ambition or be conceited. Instead, humbly think of others as being better than yourselves. ✦ "Father, forgive them. They don't know what they're doing." ✦ Be kind to each other, sympathetic, forgiving each other as God has forgiven you through Christ. ✦ Those who say that they live in him must live the same way he lived. ✦ We must focus on Jesus, the source and goal of our faith. He saw the joy ahead of him, so he endured death on the cross and ignored the disgrace it brought him. Then he received the highest position in heaven, the one next to the throne of God.

*1 Peter 2:21; Mark 10:45; Mark 10:44; Acts 10:38; Galatians 6:2; 2 Corinthians 10:1; Philippians 2:3; Luke 23:34; Ephesians 4:32; 1 John 2:6; Hebrews 12:2*

## EVENING READING

I looked for him, but I did not find him.
I called for him, but he did not answer me.

[Joshua said,] "Lord, what else can I say after Israel ran away from its enemy?" . . . The LORD said to Joshua, "Get up! What are you doing bowing on the ground? Israel has sinned. . . . They have taken what I claimed for myself and put it among their own goods." ✦ The LORD is not too weak to save or his ear too deaf to hear. But your wrongs have separated you from your God, and your sins have made him hide his face so that he doesn't hear you. ✦ If I had thought about doing anything sinful, the Lord would not have listened to me. ✦ Dear friends, if our conscience doesn't condemn us, we can boldly look to God and receive from him anything we ask. We receive it because we obey his commandments and do what pleases him.

*Song of Songs 5:6; Joshua 7:8, 10–11; Isaiah 59:1–2; Psalm 66:18; 1 John 3:21–22*

# June 22

## MORNING READING

You have died, and your life is hidden with Christ in God.

We have died. So how can we still live under sin's influence? ✦ I no longer live, but Christ lives in me. The life I now live I live by believing in God's Son, who loved me and took the punishment for my sins. ✦ He died for all people so that those who live should no longer live for themselves but for the man who died and was brought back to life for them. . . . Whoever is a believer in Christ is a new creation. The old way of living has disappeared. A new way of living has come into existence. ✦ We are in the one who is real, his Son Jesus Christ. ✦ I pray that all of these people continue to have unity in the way that you, Father, are in me and I am in you. I pray that they may be united with us. ✦ You are Christ's body and each of you is an individual part of it. ✦ You will live because I live. ✦ I will give some of the hidden manna to everyone who wins the victory. I will also give each person a white stone with a new name written on it, a name that is known only to the person who receives it.

*Colossians 3:3; Romans 6:2; Galatians 2:20; 2 Corinthians 5:15, 17; 1 John 5:20; John 17:21; 1 Corinthians 12:27; John 14:19; Revelation 2:17*

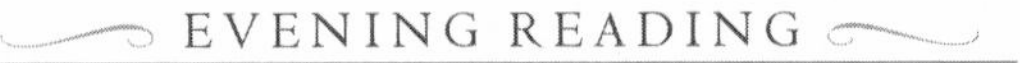

## EVENING READING

"See how much Jesus loved him."

He died for all people. ✦ The greatest love you can show is to give your life for your friends. ✦ He always lives and intercedes for them. ✦ "I'm going to prepare a place for you." ✦ "I will come again. Then I will bring you into my presence so that you will be where I am." ✦ "Father, I want those you have given to me to be with me, to be where I am." ✦ Jesus loved his own who were in the world, and he loved them to the end. ✦ We love because God loved us first. ✦ Clearly, Christ's love guides us. We are convinced of the fact that one man has died for all people. Therefore, all people have died. He died for all people so that those who live should no longer live for themselves but for the man who died and was brought back to life for them. ✦ "If you obey my commandments, you will live in my love. I have obeyed my Father's commandments, and in that way I live in his love."

*John 11:36; 2 Corinthians 5:15; John 15:13; Hebrews 7:25; John 14:2; John 14:3; John 17:24; John 13:1; 1 John 4:19; 2 Corinthians 5:14–15; John 15:10*

## MORNING READING

"I will ask the Father, and he will give you another helper, . . . the Spirit of Truth."

"It's good for you that I'm going away. If I don't go away, the helper won't come to you. But if I go, I will send him to you." ✦ The Spirit himself testifies with our spirit that we are God's children. ✦ You haven't received the spirit of slaves that leads you into fear again. Instead, you have received the spirit of God's adopted children by which we call out, "Abba! Father!" ✦ The Spirit also helps us in our weakness, because we don't know how to pray for what we need. But the Spirit intercedes along with our groans that cannot be expressed in words. ✦ May God, the source of hope, fill you with joy and peace through your faith in him. Then you will overflow with hope by the power of the Holy Spirit. ✦ We're not ashamed to have this confidence, because God's love has been poured into our hearts by the Holy Spirit, who has been given to us. ✦ We know that we live in him and he lives in us because he has given us his Spirit.

*John 14:16–17; John 16:7; Romans 8:16; Romans 8:15; Romans 8:26; Romans 15:13; Romans 5:5; 1 John 4:13*

## EVENING READING

"Shouldn't I try to look for a home that would be good for you?"

Therefore, a time of rest and worship exists for God's people. ✦ My people will live in a peaceful place, in safe homes and quiet places of rest. ✦ There the wicked stop their raging. There the weary are able to rest. ✦ "Let them rest from their hard work." ✦ Where Jesus went before us on our behalf. He has become the chief priest forever in the way Melchizedek was a priest. ✦ "Come to me, all who are tired from carrying heavy loads, and I will give you rest. Place my yoke over your shoulders, and learn from me, because I am gentle and humble. Then you will find rest for yourselves because my yoke is easy and my burden is light." ✦ You can be saved by returning to me. You can have rest. You can be strong by being quiet and by trusting me. ✦ The Lord is my shepherd. I am never in need. He makes me lie down in green pastures. He leads me beside peaceful waters.

*Ruth 3:1; Hebrews 4:9; Isaiah 32:18; Job 3:17; Revelation 14:13; Hebrews 6:20; Matthew 11:28–30; Isaiah 30:15; Psalm 23:1–2*

## MORNING READING

The ark of the LORD's promise went ahead of them
a distance of three days' journey to find them a place to rest.

My future is in your hands. ✦ He chooses our inheritance for us. ✦ O LORD, lead me in your righteousness. . . . Make your way in front of me smooth. ✦ Entrust your ways to the LORD. Trust him, and he will act on your behalf. ✦ In all your ways acknowledge him, and he will make your paths smooth. ✦ You will hear a voice behind you saying, "This is the way. Follow it, whether it turns to the right or to the left." ✦ The LORD is my shepherd. I am never in need. He makes me lie down in green pastures. He leads me beside peaceful waters. ✦ As a father has compassion for his children, so the LORD has compassion for those who fear him. He certainly knows what we are made of. He bears in mind that we are dust. ✦ "Your heavenly Father certainly knows you need all of them." ✦ Turn all your anxiety over to God because he cares for you.

*Numbers 10:33; Psalm 31:15; Psalm 47:4; Psalm 5:8; Psalm 37:5; Proverbs 3:6; Isaiah 30:21; Psalm 23:1–2; Psalm 103:13–14; Matthew 6:32; 1 Peter 5:7*

## EVENING READING

They said to him, "Rabbi . . . where are you staying?"
Jesus told them, "Come, and you will see."

"My Father's house has many rooms. If that were not true, would I have told you that I'm going to prepare a place for you? If I go to prepare a place for you, I will come again. Then I will bring you into my presence so that you will be where I am." ✦ "I will allow everyone who wins the victory to sit with me on my throne." ✦ The High and Lofty One lives forever, and his name is holy. This is what he says: I live in a high and holy place. But I am with those who are crushed and humble. I will renew the spirit of those who are humble and the courage of those who are crushed. ✦ "Look, I'm standing at the door and knocking. If anyone listens to my voice and opens the door, I'll come in and we'll eat together." ✦ "And remember that I am always with you until the end of time." ✦ Your mercy is so precious, O God, that Adam's descendants take refuge in the shadow of your wings.

*John 1:38–39; John 14:2–3; Revelation 3:21; Isaiah 57:15; Revelation 3:20; Matthew 28:20; Psalm 36:7*

## MORNING READING

When Christ appears we will be like him
because we will see him as he is.

He gave the right to become God's children to everyone who believed in him. ✦ Through his glory and integrity he has given us his promises that are of the highest value. Through these promises you will share in the divine nature because you have escaped the corruption that sinful desires cause in the world. ✦ No one has ever heard, no one has paid attention, and no one has seen any god except you. You help those who wait for you. ✦ Now we see a blurred image in a mirror. Then we will see very clearly. Now my knowledge is incomplete. Then I will have complete knowledge as God has complete knowledge of me. ✦ Through [Christ's] power to bring everything under his authority, he will change our humble bodies and make them like his glorified body. ✦ I will see your face when I am declared innocent. When I wake up, I will be satisfied with seeing you.

*1 John 3:2; John 1:12; 2 Peter 1:4; Isaiah 64:4;
1 Corinthians 13:12; Philippians 3:21; Psalm 17:15*

## EVENING READING

"The man who is my friend,"
declares the LORD of Armies.

All of God lives in Christ's body. ✦ "I set a boy above warriors. I have raised up one chosen from the people." ✦ "I have trampled alone in the winepress. No one was with me." ✦ The mystery that gives us our reverence for God is acknowledged to be great: He appeared in his human nature. ✦ A child will be born for us. A son will be given to us. The government will rest on his shoulders. He will be named: Wonderful Counselor, Mighty God, Everlasting Father, Prince of Peace. ✦ His Son is the reflection of God's glory and the exact likeness of God's being. He holds everything together through his powerful words. After he had cleansed people from their sins, he received the highest position, the one next to the Father in heaven. ✦ God said about his Son, "Your throne, O God, is forever and ever." ✦ "All of God's angels must worship him." ✦ King of kings and Lord of lords.

*Zechariah 13:7; Colossians 2:9; Psalm 89:19; Isaiah 63:3; 1 Timothy 3:16;
Isaiah 9:6; Hebrews 1:3; Hebrews 1:8; Hebrews 1:6; Revelation 19:16*

## Morning Reading

Jabez prayed to the God of Israel,
"Please bless me. . . . May your power . . . free me from evil . . ."
God gave him what he prayed for.

It is the LORD's blessing that makes a person rich, and hard work adds nothing to it. ✦ If he keeps quiet, who can condemn him? If he hides his face, who can see him? ✦ Victory belongs to the LORD! May your blessing rest on your people. ✦ Your kindness is so great! You reserve it for those who fear you. Adam's descendants watch as you show it to those who take refuge in you. ✦ "I'm not asking you to take them out of the world but to protect them from the evil one." ✦ "Ask, and you will receive. Search, and you will find. Knock, and the door will be opened for you. Everyone who asks will receive. The one who searches will find, and for the one who knocks, the door will be opened." ✦ The LORD protects the souls of his servants. All who take refuge in him will never be condemned.

*1 Chronicles 4:10; Proverbs 10:22; Job 34:29; Psalm 3:8; Psalm 31:19; John 17:15; Matthew 7:7–8; Psalm 34:22*

## Evening Reading

Future generations must keep watch on this night,
since it is dedicated to the LORD.

On the night he was betrayed, the Lord Jesus took bread and spoke a prayer of thanksgiving. He broke the bread and said, "This is my body, which is given for you. Do this to remember me." When supper was over, he did the same with the cup. He said, "This cup is the new promise made with my blood. Every time you drink from it, do it to remember me." ✦ [Jesus] knelt down, and prayed. . . . So he prayed very hard in anguish. His sweat became like drops of blood falling to the ground. ✦ The time was about six o'clock in the morning on the Friday of the Passover festival. . . . So the soldiers took Jesus . . . to a location called The Skull. (In Hebrew this place is called *Golgotha*.) The soldiers crucified Jesus. ✦ Christ, our Passover lamb, has been sacrificed. So we must not celebrate our festival.

*Exodus 12:42; 1 Corinthians 11:23–25; Luke 22:41, 44; John 19:14, 16–18; 1 Corinthians 5:7–8*

## MORNING READING

"Who is able to endure it?"

But who will be able to endure the day he comes? Who will be able to survive on the day he appears? He is like a purifying fire and like a cleansing soap. ✦ After these things I saw a large crowd from every nation, tribe, people, and language. No one was able to count how many people there were. They were standing in front of the throne and the lamb. They were wearing white robes, holding palm branches in their hands. . . . "These are the people who are coming out of the terrible suffering. They have washed their robes and made them white in the blood of the lamb. . . . They will never be hungry or thirsty again. Neither the sun nor any burning heat will ever overcome them. The lamb in the center near the throne will be their shepherd. He will lead them to springs filled with the water of life, and God will wipe every tear from their eyes." ✦ So those who are believers in Christ Jesus can no longer be condemned. ✦ Christ has freed us so that we may enjoy the benefits of freedom. Therefore, be firm in this freedom, and don't become slaves again.

*Revelation 6:17; Malachi 3:2;*
*Revelation 7:9, 14, 16–17; Romans 8:1; Galatians 5:1*

## EVENING READING

Do not take me to court for judgment,
because there is no one alive
who is righteous in your presence.

"Come on now, let's discuss this!" says the LORD. "Though your sins are bright red, they will become as white as snow. Though they are dark red, they will become as white as wool. ✦ Let them come to me for protection. Let them make peace with me. Yes, let them make peace with me. ✦ Be in harmony and at peace with God. ✦ Now that we have God's approval by faith, we have peace with God because of what our Lord Jesus Christ has done. ✦ Yet, we know that people don't receive God's approval because of their own efforts to live according to a set of standards, but only by believing in Jesus Christ. So we also believed in Jesus Christ in order to receive God's approval by faith in Christ and not because of our own efforts. ✦ Not one person can have God's approval by following Moses' Teachings. Moses' Teachings show what sin is. ✦ However, everyone who believes in Jesus receives God's approval. ✦ Thank God that he gives us the victory through our Lord Jesus Christ.

*Psalm 143:2; Isaiah 1:18; Isaiah 27:5; Job 22:21; Romans 5:1;*
*Galatians 2:16; Romans 3:20; Acts 13:39; 1 Corinthians 15:57*

## MORNING READING

I know that my defender lives.

If the death of his Son restored our relationship with God while we were still his enemies, we are even more certain that, because of this restored relationship, the life of his Son will save us. ✦ But Jesus lives forever, so he serves as a priest forever. That is why he is always able to save those who come to God through him. He can do this because he always lives and intercedes for them. ✦ "You will live because I live." ✦ If Christ is our hope in this life only, we deserve more pity than any other people. But now Christ has come back from the dead. He is the very first person of those who have died to come back to life. ✦ "Then a Savior will come to Zion, to those in Jacob who turn from rebellion," declares the LORD. ✦ Through the blood of his Son, we are set free from our sins. God forgives our failures because of his overflowing kindness. ✦ Realize that you weren't set free from the worthless life handed down to you from your ancestors by a payment of silver or gold which can be destroyed. Rather, the payment that freed you was the precious blood of Christ, the lamb with no defects or imperfections.

*Job 19:25; Romans 5:10; Hebrews 7:24–25; John 14:19; 1 Corinthians 15:19–20; Isaiah 59:20; Ephesians 1:7; 1 Peter 1:18–19*

## EVENING READING

The Spirit says clearly that in later times some believers will desert the Christian faith. They will follow spirits that deceive.

"So pay attention to how you listen!" ✦ Let Christ's word with all its wisdom and richness live in you. ✦ In addition to all these, take the Christian faith as your shield. With it you can put out all the flaming arrows of the evil one. ✦ There is lasting peace for those who love your teachings. Nothing can make those people stumble. ✦ How sweet the taste of your promise is! It tastes sweeter than honey. From your guiding principles I gain understanding. That is why I hate every path that leads to lying. ✦ Your word is a lamp for my feet and a light for my path. ✦ I have more insight than all my teachers, because your written instructions are in my thoughts. ✦ Even Satan disguises himself as an angel of light. ✦ Whoever tells you good news that is different from the Good News we gave you should be condemned to hell, even if he is one of us or an angel from heaven.

*1 Timothy 4:1; Luke 8:18; Colossians 3:16; Ephesians 6:16; Psalm 119:165; Psalm 119:103–4; Psalm 119:105; Psalm 119:99; 2 Corinthians 11:14; Galatians 1:8*

## MORNING READING

Obeying his commandments isn't difficult.

"My Father wants all those who see the Son and believe in him to have eternal life." ✦ [We] receive from him anything we ask. We receive it because we obey his commandments and do what pleases him. ✦ "My yoke is easy and my burden is light." ✦ "If you love me, you will obey my commandments. . . . Whoever knows and obeys my commandments is the person who loves me. Those who love me will have my Father's love, and I, too, will love them and show myself to them." ✦ Blessed is the one who finds wisdom and the one who obtains understanding. . . . Wisdom's ways are pleasant ways, and all its paths lead to peace. ✦ There is lasting peace for those who love your teachings. Nothing can make those people stumble. ✦ I take pleasure in God's standards in my inner being. ✦ This is his commandment: to believe in his Son, the one named Jesus Christ, and to love each other as he commanded us. ✦ Love never does anything that is harmful to a neighbor. Therefore, love fulfills Moses' Teachings.

*1 John 5:3; John 6:40; 1 John 3:22; Matthew 11:30; John 14:15, 21; Proverbs 3:13, 17; Psalm 119:165; Romans 7:22; 1 John 3:23; Romans 13:10*

## EVENING READING

Do not remember the sins of my youth or my rebellious ways.

I made your rebellious acts disappear like a thick cloud and your sins like the morning mist. ✦ I alone am the one who is going to wipe away your rebellious actions for my own sake. I will not remember your sins anymore. ✦ "Come on now, let's discuss this!" says the Lord. "Though your sins are bright red, they will become as white as snow. Though they are dark red, they will become as white as wool." ✦ "I will no longer hold their sins against them." ✦ You will throw all our sins into the deep sea. ✦ You have saved me and kept me from the rotting pit. You have thrown all my sins behind you. ✦ Who is a God like you? You forgive sin. . . . You will not be angry forever, because you would rather show mercy. ✦ To the one who loves us and has freed us from our sins by his blood.

*Psalm 25:7; Isaiah 44:22; Isaiah 43:25; Isaiah 1:18; Jeremiah 31:34; Micah 7:19; Isaiah 38:17; Micah 7:18; Revelation 1:5*

## MORNING READING

I correct and discipline everyone I love.

"My child, pay attention when the Lord disciplines you. Don't give up when he corrects you. The Lord disciplines everyone he loves. He severely disciplines everyone he accepts as his child." ✦ The Lord warns the one he loves, even as a father warns a son with whom he is pleased. ✦ God injures, but he bandages. He beats you up, but his hands make you well. ✦ Be humbled by God's power so that when the right time comes he will honor you. ✦ I have tested you in the furnace of suffering. ✦ He does not willingly bring suffering or grief to anyone. ✦ He has not treated us as we deserve for our sins or paid us back for our wrongs. As high as the heavens are above the earth—that is how vast his mercy is toward those who fear him. As far as the east is from the west—that is how far he has removed our rebellious acts from himself. As a father has compassion for his children, so the Lord has compassion for those who fear him. He certainly knows what we are made of. He bears in mind that we are dust.

*Revelation 3:19; Hebrews 12:5–6; Proverbs 3:12; Job 5:18; 1 Peter 5:6; Isaiah 48:10; Lamentations 3:33; Psalm 103:10–14*

## EVENING READING

Since God is in heaven and you are on earth,
limit the number of your words.

"When you pray, don't ramble like heathens who think they'll be heard if they talk a lot. Don't be like them. Your Father knows what you need before you ask him." ✦ They . . . called on the name of Baal from morning until noon. They said, "Baal, answer us!" ✦ "Two men went into the temple courtyard to pray. One was a Pharisee, and the other was a tax collector. The Pharisee stood up and prayed, 'God, I thank you that I'm not like other people! I'm not a robber or a dishonest person. I haven't committed adultery. I'm not even like this tax collector.' . . . But the tax collector was standing at a distance. He wouldn't even look up to heaven. Instead, he became very upset, and he said, 'God, be merciful to me, a sinner!' I can guarantee that this tax collector went home with God's approval, but the Pharisee didn't." ✦ "Lord, teach us to pray."

*Ecclesiastes 5:2; Matthew 6:7–8; 1 Kings 18:26; Luke 18:10–11, 13–14; Luke 11:1*

## MORNING READING

But the spiritual nature produces . . . goodness.

Imitate God, since you are the children he loves. ✦ "Love your enemies, and pray for those who persecute you. In this way you show that you are children of your Father in heaven. He makes his sun rise on people whether they are good or evil. He lets rain fall on them whether they are just or unjust." ✦ "Be merciful as your Father is merciful." ✦ Light produces everything that is good, that has God's approval, and that is true. ✦ When God our Savior made his kindness and love for humanity appear, he saved us, but not because of anything we had done to gain his approval. Instead, because of his mercy he saved us through the washing in which the Holy Spirit gives us new birth and renewal. God poured a generous amount of the Spirit on us through Jesus Christ our Savior. ✦ The LORD is good to everyone and has compassion for everything that he has made. ✦ God didn't spare his own Son but handed him over to death for all of us. So he will also give us everything along with him.

*Galatians 5:22; Ephesians 5:1; Matthew 5:44–45; Luke 6:36; Ephesians 5:9; Titus 3:4–6; Psalm 145:9; Romans 8:32*

## EVENING READING

Ebenezer . . . "Until now the LORD has helped us."

When I was weak, he saved me. ✦ Thank the LORD! He has heard my prayer for mercy! The LORD is my strength and my shield. My heart trusted him, so I received help. My heart is triumphant; I give thanks to him with my song. ✦ It is better to depend on the LORD than to trust mortals. It is better to depend on the LORD than to trust influential people. ✦ Blessed are those who receive help from the God of Jacob. Their hope rests on the LORD their God. ✦ He led them on a road that went straight to an inhabited city. ✦ Every single good promise that the LORD had given the nation of Israel came true. ✦ Then Jesus said to [the disciples], "When I sent you out without a wallet, traveling bag, or sandals, you didn't lack anything, did you?" "Not a thing!" they answered. ✦ You have been my help. In the shadow of your wings, I sing joyfully.

*1 Samuel 7:12; Psalm 116:6; Psalm 28:6–7; Psalm 118:8–9; Psalm 146:5; Psalm 107:7; Joshua 21:45; Luke 22:35; Psalm 63:7*

## MORNING READING

"These are the rules for the Passover:
No foreigner may eat the Passover meal."

Those who serve at the tent have no right to eat what is sacrificed at our altar. ✦ "No one can see the kingdom of God without being born from above." ✦ At that time you were without Christ. You were excluded from citizenship in Israel, and the pledges God made in his promise were foreign to you. You had no hope and were in the world without God. But now through Christ Jesus you, who were once far away, have been brought near by the blood of Christ. ✦ So he is our peace. In his body he has made Jewish and non-Jewish people one. . . . He brought an end to the commandments and demands found in Moses' Teachings so that he could take Jewish and non-Jewish people and create one new humanity in himself. So he made peace. ✦ You are no longer foreigners and outsiders but citizens together with God's people and members of God's family. ✦ "Look, I'm standing at the door and knocking. If anyone listens to my voice and opens the door, I'll come in and we'll eat together."

*Exodus 12:43; Hebrews 13:10; John 3:3; Ephesians 2:12–13; Ephesians 2:14–15; Ephesians 2:19; Revelation 3:20*

## EVENING READING

[Jesus] prayed the same prayer a third time.

During his life on earth, Jesus prayed to God, who could save him from death. He prayed and pleaded with loud crying and tears. ✦ Let's learn about the LORD. Let's get to know the LORD. ✦ Pray continually. ✦ Pray in the Spirit in every situation. Use every kind of prayer and request there is. For the same reason be alert. Use every kind of effort and make every kind of request for all of God's people. ✦ In every situation let God know what you need in prayers and requests while giving thanks. Then God's peace, which goes beyond anything we can imagine, will guard your thoughts and emotions through Christ Jesus. ✦ "But let your will be done rather than mine." ✦ We are confident that God listens to us if we ask for anything that has his approval. ✦ Be happy with the LORD, and he will give you the desires of your heart. Entrust your ways to the LORD. Trust him, and he will act on your behalf.

*Matthew 26:44; Hebrews 5:7; Hosea 6:3; Romans 12:12; Ephesians 6:18; Philippians 4:6–7; Matthew 26:39; 1 John 5:14; Psalm 37:4–5*

## MORNING READING

If we are his children, we are also God's heirs. . . .
We are heirs together with [Christ].

If you belong to Christ, then you are Abraham's descendants and heirs, as God promised. ✦ Consider this: The Father has given us his love. He loves us so much that we are actually called God's dear children. ✦ So you are no longer slaves but God's children. Since you are God's children, God has also made you heirs. ✦ Because of his love he had already decided to adopt us through Jesus Christ. ✦ "Father, I want those you have given to me to be with me, to be where I am. I want them to see my glory, which you gave me because you loved me before the world was made." ✦ I will give authority over the nations to everyone who wins the victory and continues to do what I want until the end. ✦ I will allow everyone who wins the victory to sit with me on my throne, as I have won the victory and have sat down with my Father on his throne.

*Romans 8:17; Galatians 3:29; 1 John 3:1; Galatians 4:7; Ephesians 1:5; John 17:24; Revelation 2:26; Revelation 3:21*

## EVENING READING

God chose what the world considers ordinary and what it despises.

"All of these men who are speaking are Galileans." ✦ [Jesus] saw two brothers . . . throwing a net into the sea because they were fishermen. Jesus said to them, "Come, follow me!" ✦ After they found out that Peter and John had no education or special training, they were surprised to see how boldly they spoke. They realized that these men had been with Jesus. ✦ I didn't speak my message with persuasive intellectual arguments. I spoke my message with a show of spiritual power so that your faith would not be based on human wisdom but on God's power. ✦ You didn't choose me, but I chose you. I have appointed you to go, to produce fruit that will last. ✦ "I am the vine. You are the branches. Those who live in me while I live in them will produce a lot of fruit. But you can't produce anything without me." ✦ Our bodies are made of clay, yet we have the treasure of the Good News in them. This shows that the superior power of this treasure belongs to God and doesn't come from us.

*1 Corinthians 1:28; Acts 2:7; Matthew 4:18–19; Acts 4:13; 1 Corinthians 2:4–5; John 15:16; John 15:5; 2 Corinthians 4:7*

## MORNING READING

Near [Jesus] at the table.

As a mother comforts her child, so will I comfort you. ✦ Some people brought little children to Jesus to have him hold them. But the disciples told the people not to do that. . . . Jesus put his arms around the children and blessed them by placing his hands on them. ✦ Jesus called his disciples and said, "I feel sorry for the people. They have been with me three days now and have nothing to eat. I don't want to send them away hungry, or they may become exhausted on their way home." ✦ We have a chief priest who is able to sympathize with our weaknesses. He was tempted in every way that we are, but he didn't sin. ✦ In his love and compassion he reclaimed them. ✦ "I will not leave you all alone. I will come back to you." ✦ Can a woman forget her nursing child? Will she have no compassion on the child from her womb? Although mothers may forget, I will not forget you. ✦ "The lamb in the center near the throne will be their shepherd. He will lead them to springs filled with the water of life, and God will wipe every tear from their eyes."

*John 13:23; Isaiah 66:13; Mark 10:13, 16; Matthew 15:32; Hebrews 4:15; Isaiah 63:9; John 14:18; Isaiah 49:15; Revelation 7:17*

## EVENING READING

Jesus Christ, who has God's full approval. . . . the payment for our sins.

"The angels should have their wings spread above the throne of mercy, overshadowing it. They should face each other, looking at the throne of mercy. After you put into the ark the words of my promise which I will give you, place the throne of mercy on top. I will be above the throne of mercy between the angels whenever I meet with you and give you all my commands for the Israelites." ✦ Indeed, his salvation is near those who fear him. . . . Mercy and truth have met. Righteousness and peace have kissed. ✦ O LORD, who would be able to stand if you kept a record of sins? But with you there is forgiveness so that you can be feared. ✦ O Israel, put your hope in the LORD, because with the LORD there is mercy and with him there is unlimited forgiveness. He will rescue Israel from all its sins. ✦ Because all people have sinned, they have fallen short of God's glory. They receive God's approval freely by an act of his kindness through the price Christ Jesus paid to set us free from sin. God showed that Christ is the throne of mercy where God's approval is given through faith in Christ's blood. In his patience God waited to deal with sins committed in the past.

*1 John 2:1–2; Exodus 25:20–22; Psalm 85:9–10; Psalm 130:3–4; Psalm 130:7–8; Romans 3:23–25*

## Morning Reading

We have known and believed that God loves us.

God is rich in mercy because of his great love for us. We were dead because of our failures, but he made us alive together with Christ. (It is God's kindness that saved you.) God has brought us back to life together with Christ Jesus and has given us a position in heaven with him. He did this through Christ Jesus out of his generosity to us in order to show his extremely rich kindness in the world to come. ✦ God loved the world this way: He gave his only Son so that everyone who believes in him will not die but will have eternal life. ✦ God didn't spare his own Son but handed him over to death for all of us. So he will also give us everything along with him. ✦ The Lord is good to everyone and has compassion for everything that he has made. ✦ We love because God loved us first. ✦ "You are blessed for believing that the Lord would keep his promise to you."

*1 John 4:16; Ephesians 2:4–7; John 3:16; Romans 8:32; Psalm 145:9; 1 John 4:19; Luke 1:45*

## Evening Reading

Don't be arrogant, but be friendly to humble people.

My brothers and sisters, practice your faith in our glorious Lord Jesus Christ by not favoring one person over another. ✦ Didn't God choose poor people in the world to become rich in faith and to receive the kingdom that he promised to those who love him? ✦ People should be concerned about others and not just about themselves. ✦ As long as we have food and clothes, we should be satisfied. But people who want to get rich keep falling into temptation. They are trapped by many stupid and harmful desires which drown them in destruction and ruin. ✦ But God chose what the world considers nonsense to put wise people to shame. God chose what the world considers weak to put what is strong to shame. God chose what the world considers ordinary and what it despises—what it considers to be nothing—in order to destroy what it considers to be something. As a result, no one can brag in God's presence. ✦ O Lord, my heart is not conceited. My eyes do not look down on others.

*Romans 12:16; James 2:1; James 2:5; 1 Corinthians 10:24; 1 Timothy 6:8–9; 1 Corinthians 1:27–29; Psalm 131:1*

## Morning Reading

Everything you say should be kind.

Like golden apples in silver settings, so is a word spoken at the right time. Like a gold ring and a fine gold ornament, so is constructive criticism to the ear of one who listens. ✦ Don't say anything that would hurt another person. Instead, speak only what is good so that you can give help wherever it is needed. That way, what you say will help those who hear you. ✦ "Good people do the good things that are in them. But evil people do the evil things that are in them." ✦ "By your words you will be declared innocent." ✦ The words of wise people bring healing. ✦ Then those who feared the Lord spoke to one another, and the Lord paid attention and listened. A book was written in his presence to be a reminder to those who feared the Lord and respected his name. ✦ If you will speak what is worthwhile and not what is worthless, you will stand in my presence. ✦ Indeed, the more your faith, your ability to speak, your knowledge, your dedication, and your love for us increase, the more we want you to participate in this work of God's kindness.

*Colossians 4:6; Proverbs 25:11–12; Ephesians 4:29; Matthew 12:35; Matthew 12:37; Proverbs 12:18; Malachi 3:16; Jeremiah 15:19; 2 Corinthians 8:7*

## Evening Reading

I see your mercy in front of me.

The Lord is merciful, compassionate, patient, and always ready to forgive. ✦ In this way you show that you are children of your Father in heaven. He makes his sun rise on people whether they are good or evil. He lets rain fall on them whether they are just or unjust. ✦ Imitate God, since you are the children he loves. Live in love as Christ also loved us. He gave his life for us as an offering and sacrifice, a soothing aroma to God. ✦ Be kind to each other, sympathetic, forgiving each other as God has forgiven you through Christ. ✦ Love each other with a warm love that comes from the heart. After all, you have purified yourselves by obeying the truth. As a result you have a sincere love for each other. ✦ Christ's love guides us. ✦ Rather, love your enemies, help them, and lend to them without expecting to get anything back. Then you will have a great reward. You will be the children of the Most High God. After all, he is kind to unthankful and evil people. Be merciful as your Father is merciful.

*Psalm 26:3; Psalm 145:8; Matthew 5:45; Ephesians 5:1–2; Ephesians 4:32; 1 Peter 1:22; 2 Corinthians 5:14; Luke 6:35–36*

## Morning Reading

Then the Spirit led Jesus into the desert to be tempted by the devil.

During his life on earth, Jesus prayed to God, who could save him from death. He prayed and pleaded with loud crying and tears, and he was heard because of his devotion to God. Although Jesus was the Son of God, he learned to be obedient through his sufferings. After he had finished his work, he became the source of eternal salvation for everyone who obeys him. ✦ We have a chief priest who is able to sympathize with our weaknesses. He was tempted in every way that we are, but he didn't sin. ✦ There isn't any temptation that you have experienced which is unusual for humans. God, who faithfully keeps his promises, will not allow you to be tempted beyond your power to resist. But when you are tempted, he will also give you the ability to endure the temptation as your way of escape. ✦ "My kindness is all you need. My power is strongest when you are weak."

*Matthew 4:1; Hebrews 5:7–9; Hebrews 4:15; 1 Corinthians 10:13; 2 Corinthians 12:9*

## Evening Reading

"The Son of Man . . . didn't come
so that others could serve him.
He came to serve and to give his life
as a ransom for many people."

The blood of goats and bulls and the ashes of cows sprinkled on unclean people made their bodies holy and clean. The blood of Christ, who had no defect, does even more. Through the eternal Spirit he offered himself to God and cleansed our consciences from the useless things we had done. Now we can serve the living God. ✦ He was led like a lamb to the slaughter. ✦ "I give my life for my sheep. . . . No one takes my life from me. I give my life of my own free will. I have the authority to give my life, and I have the authority to take my life back again." ✦ "Blood contains life. I have given this blood to you to make peace with me on the altar. Blood is needed to make peace with me." ✦ If no blood is shed, no sins can be forgiven. ✦ Christ died for us while we were still sinners. This demonstrates God's love for us. Since Christ's blood has now given us God's approval, we are even more certain that Christ will save us from God's anger.

*Matthew 20:28; Hebrews 9:13–14; Isaiah 53:7; John 10:15, 18; Leviticus 17:11; Hebrews 9:22; Romans 5:8–9*

## MORNING READING

God is faithful and reliable.
If we confess our sins, he forgives them and cleanses us from everything we've done wrong.

I admit that I am rebellious. My sin is always in front of me. I have sinned against you, especially you. ✦ "[The Prodigal Son] went at once to his father. While he was still at a distance, his father saw him and felt sorry for him. He ran to his son, put his arms around him, and kissed him." ✦ I made your rebellious acts disappear like a thick cloud and your sins like the morning mist. Come back to me, because I have reclaimed you. ✦ Your sins are forgiven through Christ. ✦ God has forgiven you through Christ. ✦ He is a God of justice, a God who approves of people who believe in Jesus. ✦ I will sprinkle clean water on you and make you clean. ✦ They will walk with me in white clothes because they deserve it. ✦ This Son of God is Jesus Christ, who came by water and blood. He didn't come with water only, but with water and with blood.

*1 John 1:9; Psalm 51:3–4; Luke 15:20; Isaiah 44:22; 1 John 2:12; Ephesians 4:32; Romans 3:26; Ezekiel 36:25; Revelation 3:4; 1 John 5:6*

## EVENING READING

Are wicked rulers . . . able to be your partners?

Our relationship is with the Father and with his Son Jesus Christ. ✦ Dear friends, now we are God's children. What we will be isn't completely clear yet. We do know that when Christ appears we will be like him because we will see him as he is. So all people who have this confidence in Christ keep themselves pure, as Christ is pure. ✦ "The ruler of this world has no power over me." ✦ A chief priest who is holy, innocent, pure, set apart from sinners. ✦ This is not a wrestling match against a human opponent. We are wrestling with rulers, authorities, the powers who govern this world of darkness, and spiritual forces that control evil in the heavenly world. ✦ This present world and its spiritual ruler. This ruler continues to work in people who refuse to obey God. ✦ We know that those who have been born from God don't go on sinning. Rather, the Son of God protects them, and the evil one can't harm them. We know that we are from God, and that the whole world is under the control of the evil one.

*Psalm 94:20; 1 John 1:3; 1 John 3:2–3; John 14:30; Hebrews 7:26; Ephesians 6:12; Ephesians 2:2; 1 John 5:18–19*

## MORNING READING

"See, I have taken your sin away from you,
and I will dress you in fine clothing."

Blessed is the person whose disobedience is forgiven and whose sin is pardoned. ✦ We've all become unclean. ✦ I know that nothing good lives in me; that is, nothing good lives in my corrupt nature. Although I have the desire to do what is right, I don't do it. ✦ Clearly, all of you who were baptized in Christ's name have clothed yourselves with Christ. ✦ You've gotten rid of the person you used to be and the life you used to live, and you've become a new person. This new person is continually renewed in knowledge to be like its Creator. ✦ I didn't receive God's approval by obeying his laws. . . . I have God's approval through faith in Christ. ✦ "Bring out the best robe, and put it on him." ✦ This fine linen represents the things that God's holy people do that have his approval. ✦ I will find joy in the LORD. I will delight in my God. He has dressed me in the clothes of salvation. He has wrapped me in the robe of righteousness.

*Zechariah 3:4; Psalm 32:1; Isaiah 64:6; Romans 7:18; Galatians 3:27; Colossians 3:9–10; Philippians 3:9; Luke 15:22; Revelation 19:8; Isaiah 61:10*

## EVENING READING

The day will make what each one does clearly visible.

Don't judge anything before the appointed time. Wait until the Lord comes. He will also bring to light what is hidden in the dark and reveal people's motives. Then each person will receive praise from God. ✦ Why do you criticize or despise other Christians? Everyone will stand in front of God to be judged. ✦ All of us will have to give an account of ourselves to God. So let's stop criticizing each other. Instead, you should decide never to do anything that would make other Christians have doubts or lose their faith. ✦ God, through Christ Jesus, will judge people's secret thoughts. ✦ "The Father doesn't judge anyone. He has entrusted judgment entirely to the Son. . . . He has also given the Son authority to pass judgment because he is the Son of Man." ✦ You, God, are great and mighty. Your name is the LORD of Armies. You make wise plans and do mighty things. You see everything the descendants of Adam do. You reward them for the way they live and for what they do.

*1 Corinthians 3:13; 1 Corinthians 4:5; Romans 14:10; Romans 14:12–13; Romans 2:16; John 5:22, 27; Jeremiah 32:18–19*

## Morning Reading

"A student is not better than his teacher."

"You call me teacher and Lord, and you're right because that's what I am." ✦ "It is enough for a student to become like his teacher and a slave like his owner." ✦ "If they persecuted me, they will also persecute you. If they did what I said, they will also do what you say." ✦ "I have given them your message. But the world has hated them because they don't belong to the world any more than I belong to the world." ✦ Think about Jesus, who endured opposition from sinners, so that you don't become tired and give up. You struggle against sin, but your struggles haven't killed you. ✦ We must get rid of everything that slows us down, especially sin that distracts us. We must run the race that lies ahead of us and never give up. We must focus on Jesus, the source and goal of our faith. He saw the joy ahead of him, so he endured death on the cross and ignored the disgrace it brought him. Then he received the highest position in heaven, the one next to the throne of God. ✦ Since Christ has suffered physically, take the same attitude that he had.

*Matthew 10:24; John 13:13; Matthew 10:25; John 15:20; John 17:14; Hebrews 12:3–4; Hebrews 12:1–2; 1 Peter 4:1*

## Evening Reading

My son, give me your heart.

"If only they would fear me and obey all my commandments as long as they live! Then things would go well for them and their children forever." ✦ God can see how twisted your thinking is. ✦ This is so because the corrupt nature has a hostile attitude toward God. It refuses to place itself under the authority of God's standards because it can't. Those who are under the control of the corrupt nature can't please God. ✦ First, they gave themselves to the Lord. ✦ Hezekiah . . . dedicated his life to serving God. Whatever he did for the worship in God's temple, he did wholeheartedly, and he succeeded. ✦ Guard your heart more than anything else, because the source of your life flows from it. ✦ Whatever you do, do it wholeheartedly as though you were working for your real master and not merely for humans. ✦ Obey like slaves who belong to Christ, who have a deep desire to do what God wants them to do. Serve eagerly as if you were serving your heavenly master and not merely serving human masters. ✦ I will eagerly pursue your commandments because you continue to increase my understanding.

*Proverbs 23:26; Deuteronomy 5:29; Acts 8:21; Romans 8:7–8; 2 Corinthians 8:5; 2 Chronicles 31:21; Proverbs 4:23; Colossians 3:23; Ephesians 6:6–7; Psalm 119:32*

## MORNING READING

I am with you, and I will save you and rescue you.

Can loot be taken away from mighty men or prisoners be freed from conquerors? This is what the LORD says: Prisoners will be freed from mighty men. Loot will be taken away from tyrants. I will fight your enemies, and I will save your children. I will make your oppressors eat their own flesh, and they will become drunk on their own blood as though it were new wine. Then all humanity will know that I am the LORD, who saves you, the Mighty One of Jacob, who reclaims you. ✦ Don't be afraid, because I am with you. Don't be intimidated; I am your God. I will strengthen you. I will help you. I will support you with my victorious right hand. ✦ We have a chief priest who is able to sympathize with our weaknesses. He was tempted in every way that we are, but he didn't sin. ✦ Because Jesus experienced temptation when he suffered, he is able to help others when they are tempted. ✦ A person's steps are directed by the LORD, and the LORD delights in his way. When he falls, he will not be thrown down headfirst because the LORD holds on to his hand.

*Jeremiah 15:20; Isaiah 49:24–26; Isaiah 41:10; Hebrews 4:15; Hebrews 2:18; Psalm 37:23–24*

## EVENING READING

He gave plenty to drink to those who were thirsty.
He filled those who were hungry with good food.

Certainly you have tasted that the Lord is good! ✦ O God, you are my God. At dawn I search for you. My soul thirsts for you. My body longs for you in a dry, parched land where there is no water. So I look for you in the holy place to see your power and your glory. ✦ My soul longs and yearns for the LORD's courtyards. My whole body shouts for joy to the living God. ✦ I would like to leave this life and be with Christ. That's by far the better choice. ✦ When I wake up, I will be satisfied with seeing you. ✦ "They will never be hungry or thirsty again. Neither the sun nor any burning heat will ever overcome them. The lamb in the center near the throne will be their shepherd. He will lead them to springs filled with the water of life, and God will wipe every tear from their eyes." ✦ They are refreshed with the rich foods in your house, and you make them drink from the river of your pleasure. ✦ "My people will be filled with my blessings," declares the LORD.

*Psalm 107:9; 1 Peter 2:3; Psalm 63:1–2; Psalm 84:2; Philippians 1:23; Psalm 17:15; Revelation 7:16–17; Psalm 36:8; Jeremiah 31:14*

## Morning Reading

"My presence will go with you, and I will give you peace."

"Be strong and courageous. Don't tremble! Don't be afraid of them! The Lord your God is the one who is going with you. He won't abandon you or leave you. . . . The Lord is the one who is going ahead of you. He will be with you. He won't abandon you or leave you. So don't be afraid or terrified." ✦ "I have commanded you, 'Be strong and courageous! Don't tremble or be terrified, because the Lord your God is with you wherever you go.' " ✦ In all your ways acknowledge him, and he will make your paths smooth. ✦ Don't love money. . . . God has said, "I will never abandon you or leave you." So we can confidently say, "The Lord is my helper. I will not be afraid. What can mortals do to me?" ✦ God makes us qualified. ✦ Don't allow us to be tempted. ✦ O Lord, I know that the way humans act is not under their control. Humans do not direct their steps as they walk. ✦ My future is in your hands.

*Exodus 33:14; Deuteronomy 31:6, 8; Joshua 1:9; Proverbs 3:6; Hebrews 13:5–6; 2 Corinthians 3:5; Matthew 6:13; Jeremiah 10:23; Psalm 31:15*

## Evening Reading

We must also consider how to encourage each other to show love and to do good things.

How painful an honest discussion can be! ✦ I'm trying to refresh your memory. ✦ Then those who feared the Lord spoke to one another, and the Lord paid attention and listened. A book was written in his presence to be a reminder to those who feared the Lord and respected his name. ✦ "If two of you agree on anything here on earth, my Father in heaven will accept it." ✦ Then the Lord God said, "It is not good for the man to be alone." ✦ Two people are better than one because together they have a good reward for their hard work. If one falls, the other can help his friend get up. But how tragic it is for the one who is all alone when he falls. There is no one to help him get up. ✦ You should decide never to do anything that would make other Christians have doubts or lose their faith. ✦ Help carry each other's burdens. In this way you will follow Christ's teachings. ✦ Brothers and sisters, if a person gets trapped by wrongdoing, those of you who are spiritual should help that person turn away from doing wrong. Do it in a gentle way. At the same time watch yourself so that you also are not tempted.

*Hebrews 10:24; Job 6:25; 2 Peter 3:1; Malachi 3:16; Matthew 18:19; Genesis 2:18; Ecclesiastes 4:9–10; Romans 14:13; Galatians 6:2; Galatians 6:1*

## MORNING READING

I am my beloved's, and he longs for me.

I know whom I trust. I'm convinced that he is able to protect what he had entrusted to me until that day. ✦ I am convinced that nothing can ever separate us from God's love which Christ Jesus our Lord shows us. We can't be separated by death or life, by angels or rulers, by anything in the present or anything in the future, by forces or powers in the world above or in the world below, or by anything else in creation. ✦ "I watched over them, and none of them, except one person, became lost." ✦ The LORD takes pleasure in his people. ✦ Delighted in the human race. ✦ But God is rich in mercy because of his great love for us. ✦ "The greatest love you can show is to give your life for your friends." ✦ You were bought for a price. So bring glory to God in the way you use your body. ✦ If we live, we honor the Lord, and if we die, we honor the Lord. So whether we live or die, we belong to the Lord.

*Song of Songs 7:10; 2 Timothy 1:12; Romans 8:38–39; John 17:12; Psalm 149:4; Proverbs 8:31; Ephesians 2:4; John 15:13; 1 Corinthians 6:20; Romans 14:8*

## EVENING READING

Search the LORD's book, and read it.

Take these words of mine to heart and keep them in mind. Write them down, tie them around your wrist, and wear them as headbands as a reminder. ✦ Never stop reciting these teachings. You must think about them night and day so that you will faithfully do everything written in them. Only then will you prosper and succeed. ✦ The teachings of his God are in his heart. His feet do not slip. ✦ I have avoided cruelty because of your word. ✦ I have treasured your promise in my heart so that I may not sin against you. ✦ So we regard the words of the prophets as confirmed beyond all doubt. You're doing well by paying attention to their words. Continue to pay attention as you would to a light that shines in a dark place as you wait for day to come and the morning star to rise in your hearts. ✦ That we would have confidence through the endurance and encouragement which the Scriptures give us.

*Isaiah 34:16; Deuteronomy 11:18; Joshua 1:8; Psalm 37:31; Psalm 17:4; Psalm 119:11; 2 Peter 1:19; Romans 15:4*

## MORNING READING

"Your mouth says what comes from inside you."

Let Christ's word with all its wisdom and richness live in you. ✦ Guard your heart more than anything else, because the source of your life flows from it. ✦ The tongue has the power of life and death. ✦ The mouth of the righteous person reflects on wisdom. His tongue speaks what is fair. The teachings of his God are in his heart. His feet do not slip. ✦ Don't say anything that would hurt another person. Instead, speak only what is good so that you can give help wherever it is needed. That way, what you say will help those who hear you. ✦ We cannot stop talking about what we've seen and heard. ✦ I kept my faith even when I said, "I am suffering terribly." ✦ "So I will acknowledge in front of my Father in heaven that person who acknowledges me in front of others." ✦ By believing you receive God's approval, and by declaring your faith you are saved.

*Matthew 12:34; Colossians 3:16; Proverbs 4:23; Proverbs 18:21; Psalm 37:30–31; Ephesians 4:29; Acts 4:20; Psalm 116:10; Matthew 10:32; Romans 10:10*

## EVENING READING

I hope to visit you very soon. Then we can talk things over personally.

If only you would split open the heavens and come down! ✦ As a deer longs for flowing streams, so my soul longs for you, O God. My soul thirsts for God, for the living God. When may I come to see God's face? ✦ Come away quickly, my beloved. Run like a gazelle or a young stag on the mountains of spices. ✦ We, however, are citizens of heaven. We look forward to the Lord Jesus Christ coming from heaven as our Savior. ✦ We can expect what we hope for—the appearance of the glory of our great God and Savior, Jesus Christ. ✦ God our Savior and Christ Jesus our confidence. ✦ Although you have never seen Christ, you love him. ✦ The one who is testifying to these things says, "Yes, I'm coming soon!" Amen! Come, Lord Jesus! ✦ On that day his people will say, "This is our God; we have waited for him, and now he will save us. This is the Lord; we have waited for him. Let us rejoice and be glad because he will save us."

*3 John 14; Isaiah 64:1; Psalm 42:1–2; Song of Songs 8:14; Philippians 3:20; Titus 2:13; 1 Timothy 1:1; 1 Peter 1:8; Revelation 22:20; Isaiah 25:9*

## MORNING READING

"Let your will be done on earth as it is done in heaven."

Praise the Lord, all his angels, you mighty beings who carry out his orders and are ready to obey his spoken orders. Praise the Lord, all his armies, his servants who carry out his will. ✦ "I haven't come from heaven to do what I want to do. I've come to do what the one who sent me wants me to do." ✦ "I am happy to do your will, O my God." Your teachings are deep within me. ✦ "Father, if this cup cannot be taken away unless I drink it, let your will be done." ✦ "Not everyone who says to me, 'Lord, Lord!' will enter the kingdom of heaven, but only the person who does what my Father in heaven wants." ✦ People who merely listen to laws from God don't have God's approval. Rather, people who do what those laws demand will have God's approval. ✦ If you understand all of this, you are blessed whenever you follow my example. ✦ Whoever knows what is right but doesn't do it is sinning. ✦ Don't become like the people of this world. Instead, change the way you think. Then you will always be able to determine what God really wants—what is good, pleasing, and perfect.

*Matthew 6:10; Psalm 103:20–21; John 6:38; Psalm 40:8; Matthew 26:42; Matthew 7:21; Romans 2:13; John 13:17; James 4:17; Romans 12:2*

## EVENING READING

The ear tests words like the tongue tastes food.

Dear friends, don't believe all people who say that they have the Spirit. Instead, test them. See whether the spirit they have is from God, because there are many false prophets in the world. ✦ "Stop judging by outward appearance! Instead, judge correctly." ✦ I'm talking to intelligent people. Judge for yourselves what I'm saying. ✦ Let Christ's word with all its wisdom and richness live in you. ✦ Let the person who has ears listen to what the Spirit says. ✦ Spiritual people evaluate everything. ✦ "Pay attention to what you're listening to!" ✦ I know what you have done. . . . You have tested those who call themselves apostles but are not apostles. You have discovered that they are liars. ✦ Test everything. Hold on to what is good. ✦ "He calls his sheep by name and leads them out of the pen. After he has brought out all his sheep, he walks ahead of them. The sheep follow him because they recognize his voice. They won't follow a stranger. Instead, they will run away from a stranger because they don't recognize his voice."

*Job 34:3; 1 John 4:1; John 7:24; 1 Corinthians 10:15; Colossians 3:16; Revelation 2:29; 1 Corinthians 2:15; Mark 4:24; Revelation 2:2; 1 Thessalonians 5:21; John 10:3–5*

## MORNING READING

You will be my kingdom of priests and my holy nation.

"You were slaughtered. You bought people with your blood to be God's own. They are from every tribe, language, people, and nation. You made them a kingdom and priests for our God." ✦ You are chosen people, a royal priesthood, a holy nation, people who belong to God. You were chosen to tell about the excellent qualities of God, who called you out of darkness into his marvelous light. ✦ You will be called the priests of the Lord. You will be called the servants of our God. ✦ Priests of God and Christ. ✦ Brothers and sisters, you are holy partners in a heavenly calling. So look carefully at Jesus, the apostle and chief priest about whom we make our declaration of faith. ✦ Through Jesus we should always bring God a sacrifice of praise, that is, words that acknowledge him. ✦ God has made us what we are. He has created us in Christ Jesus to live lives filled with good works that he has prepared for us to do. ✦ God's temple is holy. You are that holy temple!

*Exodus 19:6; Revelation 5:9–10; 1 Peter 2:9; Isaiah 61:6; Revelation 20:6; Hebrews 3:1; Hebrews 13:15; Ephesians 2:10; 1 Corinthians 3:17*

## EVENING READING

We prayed to our God and set guards to protect us day and night.

"Stay awake, and pray that you won't be tempted." ✦ Keep praying. Pay attention when you offer prayers of thanksgiving. ✦ Turn all your anxiety over to God because he cares for you. Keep your mind clear, and be alert. Your opponent the devil is prowling around like a roaring lion as he looks for someone to devour. Be firm in the faith and resist him. ✦ "Why do you call me Lord but don't do what I tell you?" ✦ Do what God's word says. Don't merely listen to it, or you will fool yourselves. ✦ Why are you crying out to me? Tell the Israelites to start moving. ✦ Never worry about anything. But in every situation let God know what you need in prayers and requests while giving thanks. Then God's peace, which goes beyond anything we can imagine, will guard your thoughts and emotions through Christ Jesus.

*Nehemiah 4:9; Matthew 26:41; Colossians 4:2; 1 Peter 5:7–9; Luke 6:46; James 1:22; Exodus 14:15; Philippians 4:6–7*

## MORNING READING

"You are a merciful and compassionate God, patient, and always ready to forgive and to reconsider your threats of destruction."

"Lord, let your power be as great as when you said, 'The LORD . . . patient, forever loving. . . . He forgives wrongdoing and disobedience. . . . He never lets the guilty go unpunished, punishing children . . . for their parents' sins to the third and fourth generation. . . .'" ✦ Do not hold the crimes of our ancestors against us. Reach out to us soon with your compassion, because we are helpless. Help us, O God, our savior, for the glory of your name. Rescue us, and forgive our sins for the honor of your name. ✦ Do something, LORD, for the sake of your name, even though our sins testify against us. We have been unfaithful and have sinned against you. . . . O LORD, we realize our wickedness and the wrongs done by our ancestors. We have sinned against you. ✦ O LORD, who would be able to stand if you kept a record of sins? But with you there is forgiveness so that you can be feared.

*Jonah 4:2; Numbers 14:17–18; Psalm 79:8–9; Jeremiah 14:7, 20; Psalm 130:3–4*

## EVENING READING

Saved through a life of spiritual devotion and faith in the truth.

Awake, north wind! Come, south wind! Blow on my garden! Let its spices flow from it. ✦ When you became distressed in a godly way, look at how much devotion it caused you to have. You were ready to clear yourselves of the charges against you. ✦ Light produces everything that is good, that has God's approval, and that is true. Determine which things please the Lord. ✦ The Father . . . will give you another helper. ✦ God's love has been poured into our hearts by the Holy Spirit, who has been given to us. ✦ But the spiritual nature produces love, joy, peace. ✦ While they were being severely tested by suffering, their overflowing joy, along with their extreme poverty, has made them even more generous. ✦ There is only one Spirit who does all these things by giving what God wants to give to each person.

*2 Thessalonians 2:13; Song of Songs 4:16; 2 Corinthians 7:11; Ephesians 5:9–10; John 14:16; Romans 5:5; Galatians 5:22; 2 Corinthians 8:2; 1 Corinthians 12:11*

## MORNING READING

"He calls his sheep by name and leads them out of the pen."

God's people have a solid foundation. These words are engraved on it: "The Lord knows those who belong to him," and "Whoever worships the Lord must give up doing wrong." ✦ "Many will say to me on that day, 'Lord, Lord, didn't we prophesy in your name? Didn't we force out demons and do many miracles by the power and authority of your name?' Then I will tell them publicly, 'I've never known you. Get away from me, you evil people.' " ✦ The Lord knows the way of righteous people, but the way of wicked people will end. ✦ I have engraved you on the palms of my hands. Your walls are always in my presence. ✦ Wear me as a signet ring on your heart, as a ring on your hand. ✦ The Lord is good. He is a fortress in the day of trouble. He knows those who seek shelter in him. ✦ "I'm going to prepare a place for you . . . If I go to prepare a place for you, I will come again. Then I will bring you into my presence so that you will be where I am."

*John 10:3; 2 Timothy 2:19; Matthew 7:22–23; Psalm 1:6; Isaiah 49:16; Song of Songs 8:6; Nahum 1:7; John 14:2–3*

## EVENING READING

"She did what she could."

"This poor widow has given more than all the others." ✦ "Whoever gives you a cup of water to drink because you belong to Christ will certainly not lose his reward." ✦ Since you are willing to do this, remember that people are accepted if they give what they are able to give. God doesn't ask for what they don't have. ✦ We must show love through actions that are sincere, not through empty words. ✦ Suppose a believer, whether a man or a woman, needs clothes or food and one of you tells that person, "God be with you! Stay warm, and make sure you eat enough." If you don't provide for that person's physical needs, what good does it do? ✦ The farmer who plants a few seeds will have a very small harvest. But the farmer who plants because he has received God's blessings will receive a harvest of God's blessings in return. ✦ Each of you should give whatever you have decided. You shouldn't be sorry that you gave or feel forced to give, since God loves a cheerful giver. ✦ "That's the way it is with you. When you've done everything you're ordered to do, say, 'We're worthless servants. We've only done our duty.' "

*Mark 14:8; Luke 21:3; Mark 9:41; 2 Corinthians 8:12; 1 John 3:18; James 2:15–16; 2 Corinthians 9:6; 2 Corinthians 9:7; Luke 17:10*

## Morning Reading

"The Almighty has done great things to me.
His name is holy."

"Who is like you among the gods, O Lord? Who is like you? You are glorious because of your holiness and awe-inspiring because of your splendor. You perform miracles." ✦ No god is like you, O Lord. No one can do what you do. ✦ Lord, who won't fear and praise your name? You are the only holy one. ✦ "Let your name be kept holy." ✦ "Praise the Lord God of Israel! He has come to take care of his people." ✦ Who is this coming from Bozrah in Edom with his clothes stained bright red? Who is this dressed in splendor, going forward with great strength? "It is I, the Lord. I am coming to announce my victory. I am powerful enough to save you." ✦ "I set a boy above warriors. I have raised up one chosen from the people." ✦ Glory belongs to God, whose power is at work in us. By this power he can do infinitely more than we can ask or imagine. Glory belongs to God.

*Luke 1:49; Exodus 15:11; Psalm 86:8; Revelation 15:4; Matthew 6:9; Luke 1:68; Isaiah 63:1; Psalm 89:19; Ephesians 3:20–21*

## Evening Reading

Dew on Mount Hermon.

Mount Siyon (that is, Mount Hermon). ✦ That is where the Lord promised the blessing of eternal life. ✦ I will be like dew to the people of Israel. They will blossom like flowers. They will be firmly rooted like cedars from Lebanon. ✦ Let my teachings come down like raindrops. Let my words drip like dew, like gentle rain on grass, like showers on green plants. ✦ "Rain and snow come down from the sky. They do not go back again until they water the earth. They make it sprout and grow so that it produces seed for farmers and food for people to eat. My word, which comes from my mouth, is like the rain and snow. It will not come back to me without results. It will accomplish whatever I want and achieve whatever I send it to do." ✦ "God gives him the Spirit without limit." ✦ Each of us has received one gift after another because of all that the Word is. ✦ It is like fine, scented oil on the head, running down the beard—down Aaron's beard—running over the collar of his robes.

*Psalm 133:3; Deuteronomy 4:48; Psalm 133:3; Hosea 14:5; Deuteronomy 32:2; Isaiah 55:10–11; John 3:34; John 1:16; Psalm 133:2*

## Morning Reading

"They don't belong to the world any more than I belong to the world."

He was despised and rejected by people. He was a man of sorrows, familiar with suffering. ✦ "In the world you'll have trouble. But cheer up! I have overcome the world." ✦ We need a chief priest who is holy, innocent, pure, set apart from sinners. ✦ Then you will be blameless and innocent. You will be God's children without any faults among people who are crooked and corrupt. ✦ Jesus went everywhere and did good things, such as healing everyone who was under the devil's power. Jesus did these things because God was with him. ✦ Whenever we have the opportunity, we have to do what is good for everyone, especially for the family of believers. ✦ The real light, which shines on everyone, was coming into the world. ✦ "You are light for the world. A city cannot be hidden when it is located on a hill. . . . Let your light shine in front of people. Then they will see the good that you do and praise your Father in heaven."

*John 17:16; Isaiah 53:3; John 16:33; Hebrews 7:26; Philippians 2:15; Acts 10:38; Galatians 6:10; John 1:9; Matthew 5:14, 16*

## Evening Reading

A cheerful heart has a continual feast.

"The joy you have in the Lord is your strength." ✦ God's kingdom does not consist of what a person eats or drinks. Rather, God's kingdom consists of God's approval and peace, as well as the joy that the Holy Spirit gives. ✦ Be filled with the Spirit by reciting psalms, hymns, and spiritual songs for your own good. Sing and make music to the Lord with your hearts. Always thank God the Father for everything in the name of our Lord Jesus Christ. ✦ Through Jesus we should always bring God a sacrifice of praise, that is, words that acknowledge him. ✦ Even if the fig tree does not bloom and the vines have no grapes, even if the olive tree fails to produce and the fields yield no food, even if the sheep pen is empty and the stalls have no cattle—even then, I will be happy with the Lord. I will truly find joy in God, who saves me. ✦ People think we are sad although we're always glad. ✦ We also brag when we are suffering.

*Proverbs 15:15; Nehemiah 8:10; Romans 14:17; Ephesians 5:18–20; Hebrews 13:15; Habakkuk 3:17–18; 2 Corinthians 6:10; Romans 5:3*

## MORNING READING

Is there any value in being circumcised?

There are all kinds of advantages. ✦ Be circumcised by the LORD, and get rid of the foreskins of your hearts. ✦ If they humble their uncircumcised hearts and accept their guilt, I will remember my promise to Jacob, Isaac, and Abraham. I will also remember the land. ✦ Christ became a servant for the Jewish people to reveal God's truth. As a result, he fulfilled God's promise to the ancestors of the Jewish people. ✦ In him you were also circumcised. It was not a circumcision performed by human hands. But it was a removal of the corrupt nature in the circumcision performed by Christ. . . . You were once dead because of your failures and your uncircumcised corrupt nature. But God made you alive with Christ when he forgave all our failures. ✦ You were taught to change the way you were living. The person you used to be will ruin you through desires that deceive you. However, you were taught to have a new attitude. You were also taught to become a new person created to be like God, truly righteous and holy.

*Romans 3:1; Romans 3:2; Jeremiah 4:4; Leviticus 26:41–42; Romans 15:8; Colossians 2:11, 13; Ephesians 4:22–24*

## EVENING READING

The curtain in the temple was split in two from top to bottom.

On the night he was betrayed, the Lord Jesus took bread and spoke a prayer of thanksgiving. He broke the bread and said, "This is my body, which is given for you. Do this to remember me." ✦ "The bread I will give to bring life to the world is my flesh." ✦ Jesus told them, ". . . If you don't eat the flesh of the Son of Man and drink his blood, you don't have the source of life in you. Those who eat my flesh and drink my blood have eternal life, and I will bring them back to life on the last day. . . . Those who eat my flesh and drink my blood live in me, and I live in them. The Father who has life sent me, and I live because of the Father. So those who feed on me will live because of me." . . . Jesus was aware that his disciples were criticizing his message. So Jesus asked them, "Did what I say make you lose faith? What if you see the Son of Man go where he was before? Life is spiritual. Your physical existence doesn't contribute to that life." ✦ We can now confidently go into the holy place. Jesus has opened a new and living way for us to go through the curtain. (The curtain is his own body.) . . . So we must continue to come to him.

*Matthew 27:51; 1 Corinthians 11:23–24; John 6:51; John 6:53–54, 56–57, 61–63; Hebrews 10:19–20, 22*

## MORNING READING

When he died, he died once and for all to sin's power.
But now he lives, and he lives for God.

He was counted with sinners. ✦ Christ was sacrificed once to take away the sins of humanity. ✦ Christ carried our sins in his body on the cross so that freed from our sins, we could live a life that has God's approval. His wounds have healed you. ✦ With one sacrifice he accomplished the work of setting them apart for God forever. ✦ Jesus lives forever, so he serves as a priest forever. That is why he is always able to save those who come to God through him. He can do this because he always lives and intercedes for them. ✦ Christ died for us while we were still sinners. This demonstrates God's love for us. Since Christ's blood has now given us God's approval, we are even more certain that Christ will save us from God's anger. ✦ Since Christ has suffered physically, take the same attitude that he had. (A person who has suffered physically no longer sins.) That way you won't be guided by sinful human desires as you live the rest of your lives on earth. Instead, you will be guided by what God wants you to do.

*Romans 6:10; Isaiah 53:12; Hebrews 9:28; 1 Peter 2:24;*
*Hebrews 10:14; Hebrews 7:24–25; Romans 5:8–9; 1 Peter 4:1–2*

## EVENING READING

Remain in God's love.

"Live in me, and I will live in you. A branch cannot produce any fruit by itself. It has to stay attached to the vine. In the same way, you cannot produce fruit unless you live in me. I am the vine. You are the branches. Those who live in me while I live in them will produce a lot of fruit. But you can't produce anything without me." ✦ The spiritual nature produces love. ✦ "You give glory to my Father when you produce a lot of fruit and therefore show that you are my disciples. I have loved you the same way the Father has loved me. So live in my love. If you obey my commandments, you will live in my love. I have obeyed my Father's commandments, and in that way I live in his love." ✦ Whoever obeys what Christ says is the kind of person in whom God's love is perfected. That's how we know we are in Christ. ✦ "Love each other as I have loved you. This is what I'm commanding you to do." ✦ Christ died for us while we were still sinners. This demonstrates God's love for us. ✦ God is love. Those who live in God's love live in God, and God lives in them.

*Jude 21; John 15:4–5; Galatians 5:22; John 15:8–10;*
*1 John 2:5; John 15:12; Romans 5:8; 1 John 4:16*

## MORNING READING

Then the end will come.

"No one knows when that day or hour will come. Even the angels in heaven and the Son don't know. Only the Father knows. Be careful! Watch! You don't know the exact time. . . . I'm telling everyone what I'm telling you: 'Be alert!' " ✦ The Lord isn't slow to do what he promised, as some people think. Rather, he is patient for your sake. He doesn't want to destroy anyone but wants all people to have an opportunity to turn to him and change the way they think and act. ✦ The Lord will soon be here. . . . The judge is standing at the door. ✦ "Yes, I'm coming soon!" ✦ All these things will be destroyed in this way. So think of the kind of holy and godly lives you must live. ✦ The end of everything is near. Therefore, practice self-control, and keep your minds clear so that you can pray. ✦ "Be ready for action, and have your lamps burning. Be like servants waiting to open the door at their master's knock when he returns from a wedding."

*1 Corinthians 15:24; Mark 13:32–33, 37; 2 Peter 3:9; James 5:8–9; Revelation 22:20; 2 Peter 3:11; 1 Peter 4:7; Luke 12:35–36*

## EVENING READING

Brothers and sisters, pray for us.

If you are sick, call for the church leaders. Have them pray for you and anoint you with olive oil in the name of the Lord. (Prayers offered in faith will save those who are sick, and the Lord will cure them.) . . . Pray for each other so that you will be healed. Prayers offered by those who have God's approval are effective. Elijah was human like us. Yet, when he prayed that it wouldn't rain, no rain fell on the ground for three-and-a-half years. Then he prayed again. It rained, and the ground produced crops. ✦ Pray in the Spirit in every situation. Use every kind of prayer and request there is. For the same reason be alert. Use every kind of effort and make every kind of request for all of God's people. ✦ I always mention you every time I pray. ✦ [Epaphras] . . . always prays intensely for you. He prays that you will continue to be mature and completely convinced of everything that God wants.

*1 Thessalonians 5:25; James 5:14–18; Ephesians 6:18; Romans 1:9–10; Colossians 4:12*

## MORNING READING

Patient in trouble.

"He is the LORD. May he do what he thinks is right." ✦ Even if I were right, I could not answer him. I would have to plead for mercy from my judge. ✦ "The LORD has given, and the LORD has taken away! May the name of the LORD be praised." ✦ "We accept the good that God gives us. Shouldn't we also accept the bad?" ✦ Jesus cried. ✦ He was a man of sorrows, familiar with suffering. . . . He certainly has taken upon himself our suffering and carried our sorrows. ✦ "The Lord disciplines everyone he loves. He severely disciplines everyone he accepts as his child." . . . We don't enjoy being disciplined. It always seems to cause more pain than joy. But later on, those who learn from that discipline have peace that comes from doing what is right. ✦ We ask him to strengthen you by his glorious might with all the power you need to patiently endure everything with joy. ✦ "In the world you'll have trouble. But cheer up! I have overcome the world."

*Romans 12:12; 1 Samuel 3:18; Job 9:15; Job 1:21; Job 2:10; John 11:35; Isaiah 53:3–4; Hebrews 12:6, 11; Colossians 1:11; John 16:33*

## EVENING READING

He didn't doubt God's promise out of a lack of faith.

"Have faith in God! . . . This is what will be done for someone who doesn't doubt but believes what he says will happen: He can say to this mountain, 'Be uprooted and thrown into the sea,' and it will be done for him. That's why I tell you to have faith that you have already received whatever you pray for, and it will be yours." ✦ No one can please God without faith. Whoever goes to God must believe that God exists and that he rewards those who seek him. ✦ When God tested Abraham, faith led him to offer his son Isaac. Abraham, the one who received the promises from God, was willing to offer his only son as a sacrifice. God had said to him, "Through Isaac your descendants will carry on your name." Abraham believed that God could bring Isaac back from the dead. ✦ [Abraham] was absolutely confident that God would do what he promised. ✦ "Is anything too hard for the LORD?" ✦ "Everything is possible for God." ✦ "[Lord,] give us more faith."

*Romans 4:20; Mark 11:22–24; Hebrews 11:6; Hebrews 11:17–19; Romans 4:21; Genesis 18:14; Matthew 19:26; Luke 17:5*

## MORNING READING

We know that we have passed from death to life.

"Those who listen to what I say and believe in the one who sent me will have eternal life. They won't be judged because they have already passed from death to life." ✦ The person who has the Son has this life. The person who doesn't have the Son of God doesn't have this life. ✦ God establishes us, together with you, in a relationship with Christ. He has also anointed us. In addition, he has put his seal of ownership on us and has given us the Spirit as his guarantee. ✦ This is how we will know that we belong to the truth and how we will be reassured in his presence. . . . Dear friends, if our conscience doesn't condemn us, we can boldly look to God. ✦ We know that we are from God, and that the whole world is under the control of the evil one. ✦ You were once dead because of your failures and sins. ✦ He made us alive together with Christ. (It is God's kindness that saved you.) ✦ God has rescued us from the power of darkness and has brought us into the kingdom of his Son, whom he loves.

*1 John 3:14; John 5:24; 1 John 5:12; 2 Corinthians 1:21–22; 1 John 3:19, 21; 1 John 5:19; Ephesians 2:1; Ephesians 2:5; Colossians 1:13*

## EVENING READING

You make the path of life known to me.

"This is what the LORD says: I am going to give you the choice of life or death." ✦ "I will go on teaching you the way that is good and right." ✦ "I am the way, the truth, and the life. No one goes to the Father except through me." ✦ "Follow me." ✦ There is a way that seems right to a person, but eventually it ends in death. ✦ "The gate and road that lead to destruction are wide. Many enter through the wide gate. But the narrow gate and the road that lead to life are full of trouble. Only a few people find the narrow gate." ✦ A highway will be there, a roadway. It will be called the Holy Road. Sinners won't travel on it. It will be for those who walk on it. Godless fools won't wander onto it. ✦ Let's learn about the LORD. Let's get to know the LORD. ✦ "My Father's house has many rooms. If that were not true, would I have told you that I'm going to prepare a place for you?"

*Psalm 16:11; Jeremiah 21:8; 1 Samuel 12:23; John 14:6; Matthew 4:19; Proverbs 14:12; Matthew 7:13–14; Isaiah 35:8; Hosea 6:3; John 14:2*

## Morning Reading

Faith led Abraham to obey when God called him
to go to a place that he would receive as an inheritance.

He chooses our inheritance for us. ✦ He guarded them, took care of them, and protected them because they were helpless. Like an eagle that stirs up its nest, hovers over its young, spreads its wings to catch them, and carries them on its feathers, so the Lord alone led his people. No foreign god was with him. ✦ I am the Lord your God. I teach you what is best for you. I lead you where you should go. ✦ Is there any teacher like him? ✦ Our lives are guided by faith, not by sight. ✦ We don't have a permanent city here on earth, but we are looking for the city that we will have in the future. ✦ Dear friends, since you are foreigners and temporary residents in the world, I'm encouraging you to keep away from the desires of your corrupt nature. These desires constantly attack you. ✦ Get up, and go away! This is not a place to rest! It will be destroyed, completely destroyed, because it offends me.

*Hebrews 11:8; Psalm 47:4; Deuteronomy 32:10–12; Isaiah 48:17; Job 36:22; 2 Corinthians 5:7; Hebrews 13:14; 1 Peter 2:11; Micah 2:10*

## Evening Reading

Give thanks to him as you remember how holy he is.

The heavens are not pure in his sight, how much less will he trust the one who is disgusting and corrupt, the one who drinks wickedness like water. ✦ The stars aren't pure in his sight. How much less pure is a mortal—who is only a maggot. ✦ "Who is like you among the gods, O Lord? Who is like you? You are glorious because of your holiness." ✦ "Holy, holy, holy is the Lord of Armies!" ✦ Because the God who called you is holy you must be holy in every aspect of your life. Scripture says, "Be holy, because I am holy." ✦ We can become holy like him. ✦ God's temple is holy. You are that holy temple! ✦ Think of the kind of holy and godly lives you must live. . . . without spiritual stains or blemishes. ✦ Don't say anything that would hurt another person. Instead, speak only what is good so that you can give help wherever it is needed. That way, what you say will help those who hear you. Don't give God's Holy Spirit any reason to be upset with you. He has put his seal on you for the day you will be set free from the world of sin.

*Psalm 97:12; Job 15:15–16; Job 25:5–6; Exodus 15:11; Isaiah 6:3; 1 Peter 1:15–16; Hebrews 12:10; 1 Corinthians 3:17; 2 Peter 3:11, 14; Ephesians 4:29–30*

## Morning Reading

It is Christ who is God's image.

Then the Lord's glory will be revealed and all people will see it together. ✦ No one has ever seen God. God's only Son, the one who is closest to the Father's heart, has made him known. ✦ The Word became human and lived among us. We saw his glory. It was the glory that the Father shares with his only Son, a glory full of kindness and truth. ✦ "The person who has seen me has seen the Father." ✦ His Son is the reflection of God's glory and the exact likeness of God's being. ✦ He appeared in his human nature. ✦ His Son paid the price to free us, which means that our sins are forgiven. He is the image of the invisible God, the firstborn of all creation. ✦ He already knew his people and had already appointed them to have the same form as the image of his Son. Therefore, his Son is the firstborn among many children. ✦ As we have worn the likeness of the man who was made from the dust of the earth, we will also wear the likeness of the man who came from heaven.

*2 Corinthians 4:4; Isaiah 40:5; John 1:18; John 1:14; John 14:9; Hebrews 1:3; 1 Timothy 3:16; Colossians 1:14–15; Romans 8:29; 1 Corinthians 15:49*

## Evening Reading

You armed me with strength for battle.

When I'm weak, I'm strong. ✦ Asa called on the Lord his God. He said, "Lord, there is no one except you who can help those who are not strong so that they can fight against a large army. Help us, Lord our God, because we are depending on you. In your name we go against this large crowd. You are the Lord our God. Don't let anyone successfully oppose you." ✦ When Jehoshaphat cried out, the Lord helped him. God drew them away from him. ✦ It is better to depend on the Lord than to trust mortals. It is better to depend on the Lord than to trust influential people. ✦ No king achieves a victory with a large army. No warrior rescues himself by his own great strength. Horses are not a guarantee for victory. Their great strength cannot help someone escape. ✦ This is not a wrestling match against a human opponent. We are wrestling with rulers, authorities, the powers who govern this world of darkness, and spiritual forces that control evil in the heavenly world. For this reason, take up all the armor that God supplies.

*Psalm 18:39; 2 Corinthians 12:10; 2 Chronicles 14:11; 2 Chronicles 18:31; Psalm 118:8–9; Psalm 33:16–17; Ephesians 6:12–13*

## Morning Reading

Live in love.

"I'm giving you a new commandment: Love each other in the same way that I have loved you." ✦ Above all, love each other warmly, because love covers many sins. ✦ Love covers every wrong. ✦ "Whenever you pray, forgive anything you have against anyone. Then your Father in heaven will forgive your failures." ✦ Love your enemies, help them, and lend to them without expecting to get anything back. ✦ Do not be happy when your enemy falls, and do not feel glad when he stumbles. ✦ Don't pay people back with evil for the evil they do to you, or ridicule those who ridicule you. Instead, bless them, because you were called to inherit a blessing. ✦ As much as it is possible, live in peace with everyone. ✦ Be kind to each other, sympathetic, forgiving each other as God has forgiven you through Christ. ✦ Dear children, we must show love through actions that are sincere, not through empty words.

*Ephesians 5:2; John 13:34; 1 Peter 4:8; Proverbs 10:12; Mark 11:25; Luke 6:35; Proverbs 24:17; 1 Peter 3:9; Romans 12:18; Ephesians 4:32; 1 John 3:18*

## Evening Reading

Let God know what you need in prayers and requests.

"Abba! Father! You can do anything. Take this cup of suffering away from me. But let your will be done rather than mine." ✦ I am forced to deal with a recurring problem. That problem, Satan's messenger, torments me to keep me from being conceited. I begged the Lord three times to take it away from me. But he told me: "My kindness is all you need. My power is strongest when you are weak." So I will brag even more about my weaknesses in order that Christ's power will live in me. ✦ I pour out my complaints in his presence and tell him my troubles. ✦ Though [Hannah] was resentful, she prayed to the Lord while she cried. She made this vow, "Lord of Armies, if you will look at my misery, remember me, and give me a boy, then I will give him to you for as long as he lives." . . . The Lord remembered her. ✦ We don't know how to pray for what we need. ✦ He chooses our inheritance for us.

*Philippians 4:6; Mark 14:36; 2 Corinthians 12:7–9; Psalm 142:2; 1 Samuel 1:10–11, 19; Romans 8:26; Psalm 47:4*

## MORNING READING

If only you would split open the heavens and come down!

Come away quickly, my beloved. Run like a gazelle or a young stag on the mountains of spices. ✦ We, who have the Spirit as the first of God's gifts, also groan inwardly. We groan as we eagerly wait for our adoption, the freeing of our bodies from sin. ✦ O Lord, bend your heaven low, and come down. Touch the mountains, and they will smoke. ✦ "Jesus, who was taken from you to heaven, will come back in the same way that you saw him go to heaven." ✦ He will appear a second time. This time he will not deal with sin, but he will save those who eagerly wait for him. ✦ On that day his people will say, "This is our God; we have waited for him, and now he will save us. This is the Lord; we have waited for him. Let us rejoice and be glad because he will save us." ✦ The one who is testifying to these things says, "Yes, I'm coming soon!" Amen! Come, Lord Jesus! ✦ The appearance of the glory of our great God and Savior, Jesus Christ. ✦ We, however, are citizens of heaven.

*Isaiah 64:1; Song of Songs 8:14; Romans 8:23; Psalm 144:5; Acts 1:11; Hebrews 9:28; Isaiah 25:9; Revelation 22:20; Titus 2:13; Philippians 3:20*

## EVENING READING

You have given me the inheritance
that belongs to those who fear your name.

"No weapon that has been made to be used against you will succeed. You will have an answer for anyone who accuses you. This is the inheritance of the Lord's servants. Their victory comes from me," declares the Lord. ✦ The Messenger of the Lord camps around those who fear him, and he rescues them. Taste and see that the Lord is good. Blessed is the person who takes refuge in him. Fear the Lord, you holy people who belong to him. Those who fear him are never in need. Young lions go hungry and may starve, but those who seek the Lord's help have all the good things they need. ✦ Your boundary lines mark out pleasant places for me. Indeed, my inheritance is something beautiful. ✦ "The Sun of Righteousness will rise with healing in his wings for you people who fear my name. You will go out and leap like calves let out of a stall." ✦ God didn't spare his own Son but handed him over to death for all of us. So he will also give us everything along with him.

*Psalm 61:5; Isaiah 54:17; Psalm 34:7–10; Psalm 16:6; Malachi 4:2; Romans 8:32*

## MORNING READING

Focus on the things that are above—
where Christ holds the highest position.

Acquire wisdom. Acquire understanding. ✦ The wisdom that comes from above. ✦ The deep ocean says, "[Wisdom] isn't in me." The sea says, "It isn't with me." ✦ When we were baptized into his death, we were placed into the tomb with him. As Christ was brought back from death to life by the glorious power of the Father, so we, too, should live a new kind of life. If we've become united with him in a death like his, certainly we will also be united with him when we come back to life as he did. ✦ We must get rid of everything that slows us down, especially sin that distracts us. We must run the race that lies ahead of us and never give up. ✦ But God is rich in mercy because of his great love for us. We were dead because of our failures, but he made us alive together with Christ. (It is God's kindness that saved you.) God has brought us back to life together with Christ Jesus and has given us a position in heaven with him. ✦ They are looking for their own country. ✦ Search for the LORD, all you humble people in the land who carry out his justice. Search for what is right. Search for humility.

*Colossians 3:1; Proverbs 4:5; James 3:17; Job 28:14; Romans 6:4–5; Hebrews 12:1; Ephesians 2:4–6; Hebrews 11:14; Zephaniah 2:3*

## EVENING READING

Nicodemus, who had previously visited Jesus.

Peter followed [Jesus] at a distance. ✦ Many rulers believed in Jesus. However, they wouldn't admit it publicly because the Pharisees would have thrown them out of the synagogue. They were more concerned about what people thought of them than about what God thought of them. ✦ A person's fear sets a trap for him, but one who trusts the LORD is safe. ✦ "I will never turn away anyone who comes to me." ✦ He will not break off a damaged cattail. He will not even put out a smoking wick. ✦ Faith . . . the size of a mustard seed. ✦ God didn't give us a cowardly spirit but a spirit of power, love, and good judgment. So never be ashamed to tell others about our Lord. ✦ Now, dear children, live in Christ. Then, when he appears we will have confidence, and when he comes we won't turn from him in shame. ✦ "So I will acknowledge in front of my Father in heaven that person who acknowledges me in front of others."

*John 7:50; Matthew 26:58; John 12:42–43; Proverbs 29:25; John 6:37; Isaiah 42:3; Matthew 17:20; 2 Timothy 1:7–8; 1 John 2:28; Matthew 10:32*

## MORNING READING

Join me in suffering like a good soldier of Christ Jesus.

I made him a witness to people, a leader and a commander for people. ✦ God is the one for whom and through whom everything exists. Therefore, while God was bringing many sons and daughters to glory, it was the right time to bring Jesus, the source of their salvation, to the end of his work through suffering. ✦ "We must suffer a lot to enter the kingdom of God." ✦ This is not a wrestling match against a human opponent. We are wrestling with rulers, authorities, the powers who govern this world of darkness, and spiritual forces that control evil in the heavenly world. For this reason, take up all the armor that God supplies. ✦ Of course we are human, but we don't fight like humans. The weapons we use in our fight are not made by humans. Rather, they are powerful weapons from God. With them we destroy people's defenses. ✦ God, who shows you his kindness and who has called you through Christ Jesus to his eternal glory, will restore you, strengthen you, make you strong, and support you as you suffer for a little while.

*2 Timothy 2:3; Isaiah 55:4; Hebrews 2:10; Acts 14:22; Ephesians 6:12–13; 2 Corinthians 10:3–4; 1 Peter 5:10*

## EVENING READING

The unity that the Spirit gives.

There is one body and one Spirit. ✦ Jewish and non-Jewish people can go to the Father in one Spirit. That is why you are no longer foreigners and outsiders but citizens together with God's people and members of God's family. You are built on the foundation of the apostles and prophets. Christ Jesus himself is the cornerstone. In him all the parts of the building fit together and grow into a holy temple in the Lord. Through him you, also, are being built in the Spirit together with others into a place where God lives. ✦ See how good and pleasant it is when brothers and sisters live together in harmony! It is like fine, scented oil on the head, running down the beard—down Aaron's beard—running over the collar of his robes. ✦ Love each other with a warm love that comes from the heart. After all, you have purified yourselves by obeying the truth. As a result you have a sincere love for each other.

*Ephesians 4:3; Ephesians 4:4; Ephesians 2:18–22; Psalm 133:1–2; 1 Peter 1:22*

## MORNING READING

The spiritual nature produces . . . faithfulness.

God saved you through faith as an act of kindness. You had nothing to do with it. Being saved is a gift from God. ✦ No one can please God without faith. Whoever goes to God must believe that God exists and that he rewards those who seek him. ✦ Those who believe in him won't be condemned. But those who don't believe are already condemned because they don't believe in God's only Son. ✦ "I believe! Help my lack of faith." ✦ Whoever obeys what Christ says is the kind of person in whom God's love is perfected. That's how we know we are in Christ. ✦ Faith which does nothing is useless. ✦ Indeed, our lives are guided by faith, not by sight. ✦ I have been crucified with Christ. I no longer live, but Christ lives in me. The life I now live I live by believing in God's Son, who loved me and took the punishment for my sins. ✦ Although you have never seen Christ, you love him. You don't see him now, but you believe in him. You are extremely happy with joy and praise that can hardly be expressed in words as you obtain the salvation that is the goal of your faith.

*Galatians 5:22; Ephesians 2:8; Hebrews 11:6; John 3:18; Mark 9:24; 1 John 2:5; James 2:20; 2 Corinthians 5:7; Galatians 2:19–20; 1 Peter 1:8–9*

## EVENING READING

The Lord is compassionate and merciful.

As a father has compassion for his children, so the LORD has compassion for those who fear him. ✦ The LORD is merciful and compassionate. He provides food for those who fear him. He always remembers his promise. ✦ Your guardian will not fall asleep. Indeed, the Guardian of Israel never rests or sleeps. ✦ Like an eagle that stirs up its nest, hovers over its young, spreads its wings to catch them, and carries them on its feathers, so the LORD alone led his people. No foreign god was with him. ✦ His compassion is never limited. It is new every morning. His faithfulness is great. ✦ When Jesus got out of the boat, he saw a large crowd. He felt sorry for them and cured their sick people. ✦ Jesus Christ is the same yesterday, today, and forever. ✦ Every hair on your head has been counted. ✦ "Aren't two sparrows sold for a penny? Not one of them will fall to the ground without your Father's permission. Don't be afraid! You are worth more than many sparrows."

*James 5:11; Psalm 103:13; Psalm 111:4–5; Psalm 121:3–4; Deuteronomy 32:11–12; Lamentations 3:22–23; Matthew 14:14; Hebrews 13:8; Matthew 10:30; Matthew 10:29, 31*

## MORNING READING

The lamb who was slaughtered before the creation of the world.

Your animal must be a one-year-old male that has no defects. . . . "Then at dusk, all the assembled people from the community of Israel must slaughter their animals. They must take some of the blood and put it on the sides and tops of the doorframes of the houses where they will eat the animals. . . . But the blood on your houses will be a sign for your protection. When I see the blood, I will pass over you. ✦ The sprinkled blood. ✦ Christ, our Passover lamb, has been sacrificed. ✦ Jesus, who was given over to death by a plan that God had determined in advance. ✦ Before the world began, God planned that Christ Jesus would show us God's kindness. ✦ Through the blood of his Son, we are set free from our sins. ✦ Since Christ has suffered physically, take the same attitude that he had. (A person who has suffered physically no longer sins.) That way you won't be guided by sinful human desires as you live the rest of your lives on earth. Instead, you will be guided by what God wants you to do.

*Revelation 13:8; Exodus 12:5–7, 13; Hebrews 12:24; 1 Corinthians 5:7; Acts 2:23; 2 Timothy 1:9; Ephesians 1:7; 1 Peter 4:1–2*

## EVENING READING

I have trampled alone in the winepress.

Who is like you among the gods, O LORD? Who is like you? You are glorious because of your holiness and awe-inspiring because of your splendor. You perform miracles. ✦ He sees that there's no one to help. He's astounded that there's no one to intercede. So with his own power he wins a victory. His righteousness supports him. ✦ Christ carried our sins in his body on the cross. ✦ Becoming cursed instead of us. ✦ Sing a new song to the LORD because he has done miraculous things. His right hand and his holy arm have gained victory for him. ✦ He stripped the rulers and authorities of their power and made a public spectacle of them as he celebrated his victory in Christ. ✦ He will see and be satisfied because of his suffering. My righteous servant will acquit many people because of what he has learned through suffering. He will carry their sins as a burden. ✦ I must march on with strength! ✦ The one who loves us gives us an overwhelming victory in all these difficulties. ✦ They won the victory over him because of the blood of the lamb and the word of their testimony.

*Isaiah 63:3; Exodus 15:11; Isaiah 59:16; 1 Peter 2:24; Galatians 3:13; Psalm 98:1; Colossians 2:15; Isaiah 53:11; Judges 5:21; Romans 8:37; Revelation 12:11*

## MORNING READING

"For those who fear him, his mercy lasts."

Your kindness is so great! You reserve it for those who fear you. Adam's descendants watch as you show it to those who take refuge in you. You hide them in the secret place of your presence from those who scheme against them. You keep them in a shelter, safe from quarrelsome tongues. ✦ So if you call God your Father, live your time as temporary residents on earth in fear. He is the God who judges all people by what they have done, and he doesn't play favorites. ✦ The Lord is near to everyone who prays to him, to every faithful person who prays to him. He fills the needs of those who fear him. He hears their cries for help and saves them. ✦ You had a change of heart and humbled yourself in front of the Lord. . . . You also tore your clothes in distress and cried in front of me. So I will listen to you, declares the Lord. ✦ I will pay attention to those who are humble and sorry for their sins and who tremble at my word. ✦ The Lord is near to those whose hearts are humble. He saves those whose spirits are crushed.

*Luke 1:50; Psalm 31:19–20; 1 Peter 1:17;*
*Psalm 145:18–19; 2 Kings 22:19; Isaiah 66:2; Psalm 34:18*

## EVENING READING

I will honor those who honor me.

"So I will acknowledge in front of my Father in heaven that person who acknowledges me in front of others." ✦ "The person who loves his father or mother more than me does not deserve to be my disciple. The person who loves a son or daughter more than me does not deserve to be my disciple. Whoever doesn't take up his cross and follow me doesn't deserve to be my disciple. The person who tries to preserve his life will lose it, but the person who loses his life for me will preserve it." ✦ Blessed are those who endure when they are tested. When they pass the test, they will receive the crown of life that God has promised to those who love him. ✦ Don't be afraid of what you are going to suffer. . . . Be faithful until death, and I will give you the crown of life. ✦ Our suffering is light and temporary and is producing for us an eternal glory that is greater than anything we can imagine. ✦ Praise, glory, and honor to God. This will happen when Jesus Christ appears again.

*1 Samuel 2:30; Matthew 10:32; Matthew 10:37–39;*
*James 1:12; Revelation 2:10; 2 Corinthians 4:17; 1 Peter 1:7*

## MORNING READING

[Jesus] said, "It is finished!"
Then he bowed his head and died.

Jesus, the source and goal of our faith. ✦ "On earth I have given you glory by finishing the work you gave me to do." ✦ We have been set apart as holy because Jesus Christ did what God wanted him to do by sacrificing his body once and for all. Every day each priest performed his religious duty. He offered the same type of sacrifice again and again. Yet, these sacrifices could never take away sins. However, this chief priest made one sacrifice for sins, and this sacrifice lasts forever. Then he received the highest position in heaven. Since that time, he has been waiting for his enemies to be made his footstool. With one sacrifice he accomplished the work of setting them apart for God forever. ✦ He did this by erasing the charges that were brought against us by the written laws God had established. He took the charges away by nailing them to the cross. ✦ "The Father loves me because I give my life in order to take it back again. No one takes my life from me. I give my life of my own free will. I have the authority to give my life, and I have the authority to take my life back again." ✦ "The greatest love you can show is to give your life for your friends."

*John 19:30; Hebrews 12:2; John 17:4; Hebrews 10:10–14; Colossians 2:14; John 10:17–18; John 15:13*

## EVENING READING

He reached down from high above and took hold of me.
He pulled me out of the raging water.

He pulled me out of a horrible pit, out of the mud and clay. He set my feet on a rock and made my steps secure. ✦ You were once dead because of your failures and sins. You followed the ways of this present world. . . . All of us once lived among these people, and followed the desires of our corrupt nature. We did what our corrupt desires and thoughts wanted us to do. ✦ Listen to my cry for help, O God. Pay attention to my prayer. From the ends of the earth, I call to you when I begin to lose heart. ✦ "I called to the Lord in my distress, and he answered me. From the depths of my watery grave I cried for help, and you heard my cry. You threw me into the deep, into the depths of the sea, and water surrounded me. All the whitecaps on your waves have swept over me. ✦ We went through fire and water, but then you brought us out and refreshed us. ✦ When you go through the sea, I am with you. When you go through rivers, they will not sweep you away.

*Psalm 18:16; Psalm 40:2; Ephesians 2:1–3; Psalm 61:1–2; Jonah 2:2–3; Psalm 66:12; Isaiah 43:2*

## Morning Reading

Live a new kind of life.

You once offered all the parts of your body as slaves to sexual perversion and disobedience. This led you to live disobedient lives. Now, in the same way, offer all the parts of your body as slaves that do what God approves of. This leads you to live holy lives. ✦ Brothers and sisters, in view of all we have just shared about God's compassion, I encourage you to offer your bodies as living sacrifices, dedicated to God and pleasing to him. This kind of worship is appropriate for you. Don't become like the people of this world. Instead, change the way you think. Then you will always be able to determine what God really wants—what is good, pleasing, and perfect. ✦ Whoever is a believer in Christ is a new creation. The old way of living has disappeared. A new way of living has come into existence. ✦ Certainly, it doesn't matter whether a person is circumcised or not. Rather, what matters is being a new creation. Peace and mercy will come to rest on all those who conform to this principle. ✦ So I tell you and encourage you in the Lord's name not to live any longer like other people in the world. Their minds are set on worthless things. . . . But that is not what you learned from Christ's teachings. You have certainly heard his message and have been taught his ways. The truth is in Jesus. . . . You were also taught to become a new person created to be like God, truly righteous and holy.

*Romans 6:4; Romans 6:19; Romans 12:1–2; 2 Corinthians 5:17; Galatians 6:15–16; Ephesians 4:17, 20–21, 24*

## Evening Reading

"Let your will be done."

O Lord, I know that the way humans act is not under their control. Humans do not direct their steps as they walk. ✦ "Let your will be done rather than mine." ✦ Instead, I have kept my soul calm and quiet. My soul is content as a weaned child is content in its mother's arms. ✦ At the same time the Spirit also helps us in our weakness, because we don't know how to pray for what we need. But the Spirit intercedes along with our groans that cannot be expressed in words. The one who searches our hearts knows what the Spirit has in mind. The Spirit intercedes for God's people the way God wants him to. ✦ "You don't realize what you're asking." ✦ He gave them what they asked for. He also gave them a degenerative disease. ✦ These things have become examples for us so that we won't desire what is evil, as they did. ✦ I don't want you to have any concerns. ✦ With perfect peace you will protect those whose minds cannot be changed, because they trust you.

*Matthew 26:42; Jeremiah 10:23; Matthew 26:39; Psalm 131:2; Romans 8:26–27; Matthew 20:22; Psalm 106:15; 1 Corinthians 10:6; 1 Corinthians 7:32; Isaiah 26:3*

## MORNING READING

The LORD warns the one he loves.

See, I am the only God. There are no others. I kill, and I make alive. I wound, and I heal, and no one can rescue you from my power. ✦ I know the plans that I have for you, declares the LORD. They are plans for peace and not disaster, plans to give you a future filled with hope. ✦ "My thoughts are not your thoughts, and my ways are not your ways," declares the LORD. ✦ "That is why I'm going to win her back. I will lead her into the desert. I will speak tenderly to her." ✦ The LORD your God was disciplining you as parents discipline their children. ✦ We don't enjoy being disciplined. It always seems to cause more pain than joy. But later on, those who learn from that discipline have peace that comes from doing what is right. ✦ Be humbled by God's power so that when the right time comes he will honor you. ✦ I know that your regulations are fair, O LORD, and that you were right to make me suffer.

*Proverbs 3:12; Deuteronomy 32:39; Jeremiah 29:11; Isaiah 55:8; Hosea 2:14; Deuteronomy 8:5; Hebrews 12:11; 1 Peter 5:6; Psalm 119:75*

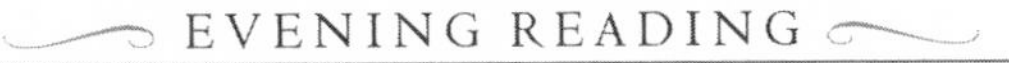

## EVENING READING

The earth and everything it contains are the LORD's.

"She doesn't believe that I gave her grain, new wine, and olive oil. I gave her plenty of silver and gold, but she used it to make statues of Baal. That is why I will take back my grain when it has ripened and my new wine when it's in season. I will take away the wool and the linen." ✦ Everything comes from you. We give you only what has come from your hands. To you we are all like our ancestors—foreigners without permanent homes. Our days are as fleeting as shadows on the ground. There's no hope for them. "LORD, our God, all this wealth . . . is yours." ✦ Everything is from him and by him and for him. Glory belongs to him forever! Amen! ✦ God . . . richly provides us with everything to enjoy. ✦ Everything God created is good. Nothing should be rejected if it is received with prayers of thanks. The word of God and prayer set it apart as holy. ✦ My God will richly fill your every need in a glorious way through Christ Jesus.

*Psalm 24:1; Hosea 2:8–9; 1 Chronicles 29:14–16; Romans 11:36; 1 Timothy 6:17; 1 Timothy 4:4–5; Philippians 4:19*

## MORNING READING

"The helper, the Holy Spirit, whom the Father will send in my name."

"If you only knew what God's gift is and who is asking you for a drink, you would have asked him for a drink. He would have given you living water." ✦ "Even though you're evil, you know how to give good gifts to your children. So how much more will your Father in heaven give the Holy Spirit to those who ask him?" ✦ "I can guarantee this truth: If you ask the Father for anything in my name, he will give it to you. So far you haven't asked for anything in my name. Ask and you will receive so that you can be completely happy." ✦ You don't have the things you want, because you don't pray for them. ✦ "When the Spirit of Truth comes, he will guide you into the full truth. He won't speak on his own. He will speak what he hears and will tell you about things to come. He will give me glory, because he will tell you what I say." ✦ But they rebelled and offended his Holy Spirit. So he turned against them as their enemy; he fought against them.

*John 14:26; John 4:10; Luke 11:13; John 16:23–24; James 4:2; John 16:13–14; Isaiah 63:10*

## EVENING READING

"What do you think about the Messiah?"

Lift your heads, you gates. Be lifted, you ancient doors, so that the king of glory may come in. Who, then, is this king of glory? The Lord of Armies is the king of glory! ✦ On his clothes and his thigh he has a name written: King of kings and Lord of lords. ✦ This honor belongs to those who believe. But to those who don't believe: "The stone that the builders rejected has become the cornerstone." ✦ Our message is that Christ was crucified. This offends Jewish people and makes no sense to people who are not Jewish. But to those Jews and Greeks who are called, he is Christ, God's power and God's wisdom. ✦ I consider everything else worthless because I'm much better off knowing Christ Jesus my Lord. It's because of him that I think of everything as worthless. I threw it all away in order to gain Christ. ✦ "Lord, you know everything. You know that I love you."

*Matthew 22:42; Psalm 24:9–10; Revelation 19:16; 1 Peter 2:7; 1 Corinthians 1:23–24; Philippians 3:8; John 21:17*

# August 8

## MORNING READING

But the path of righteous people is like the light of dawn
that becomes brighter and brighter until it reaches midday.

It's not that I've already reached the goal or have already completed the course. But I run to win that which Jesus Christ has already won for me. ✦ Let's learn about the LORD. Let's get to know the LORD. ✦ "Then the people who have God's approval will shine like the sun in their Father's kingdom." ✦ As all of us reflect the Lord's glory with faces that are not covered with veils, we are being changed into his image with ever-increasing glory. This comes from the Lord, who is the Spirit. ✦ But when what is complete comes, then what is incomplete will no longer be used. . . . Now we see a blurred image in a mirror. Then we will see very clearly. Now my knowledge is incomplete. Then I will have complete knowledge as God has complete knowledge of me. ✦ Dear friends, now we are God's children. What we will be isn't completely clear yet. We do know that when Christ appears we will be like him because we will see him as he is. So all people who have this confidence in Christ keep themselves pure, as Christ is pure.

*Proverbs 4:18; Philippians 3:12; Hosea 6:3; Matthew 13:43; 2 Corinthians 3:18; 1 Corinthians 13:10, 12; 1 John 3:2–3*

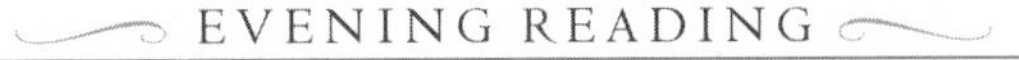

## EVENING READING

"Whoever calls on the name of the Lord will be saved."

"I will never turn away anyone who comes to me." ✦ [The thief on the cross] said, "Jesus, remember me when you enter your kingdom." Jesus said to him, "I can guarantee this truth: Today you will be with me in paradise." ✦ Jesus stopped and called them. "What do you want me to do for you?" he asked. They told him, "Lord, we want you to give us our eyesight back." Jesus felt sorry for them, so he touched their eyes. Their sight was restored at once, and they followed him. ✦ "Even though you're evil, you know how to give good gifts to your children. So how much more will your Father in heaven give the Holy Spirit to those who ask him?" ✦ I will put my Spirit in you. ✦ This is what the Almighty LORD says: I will also let the people of Israel ask me to make them as numerous as sheep. ✦ We are confident that God listens to us if we ask for anything that has his approval. We know that he listens to our requests. So we know that we already have what we ask him for.

*Romans 10:13; John 6:37; Luke 23:42–43; Matthew 20:32–34; Luke 11:13; Ezekiel 36:27; Ezekiel 36:37; 1 John 5:14–15*

## MORNING READING

You are beautiful in every way, my true love.
There is no blemish on you.

Your whole head is infected. Your whole heart is failing. From the bottom of your feet to the top of your head there is no healthy spot left on your body—only bruises, sores, and fresh wounds. They haven't been cleansed, bandaged, or soothed with oil. ✦ We've all become unclean, and all our righteous acts are like permanently stained rags. ✦ I know that nothing good lives in me; that is, nothing good lives in my corrupt nature. ✦ You have been washed and made holy, and you have received God's approval in the name of the Lord Jesus Christ and in the Spirit of our God. ✦ The daughter of the king is glorious inside the palace. ✦ Your beauty was perfect because I gave you my glory, declares the Almighty LORD. ✦ Let the kindness of the Lord our God be with us. ✦ "These are the people who . . . have washed their robes and made them white in the blood of the lamb." ✦ A glorious church, without any kind of stain or wrinkle—holy and without faults. ✦ God has made you complete in Christ.

*Song of Songs 4:7; Isaiah 1:5–6; Isaiah 64:6; Romans 7:18; 1 Corinthians 6:11; Psalm 45:13; Ezekiel 16:14; Psalm 90:17; Revelation 7:14; Ephesians 5:27; Colossians 2:10*

## EVENING READING

Broken cisterns that can't hold water.

[Eve] became pregnant and gave birth to Cain. She said, "I have gotten the man that the LORD promised." ✦ [Men] said, "Let's build a city for ourselves and a tower with its top in the sky. . . . So the LORD scattered them. ✦ Lot chose the whole Jordan Plain for himself. ✦ The whole Jordan Plain was well-watered like the LORD's garden or like Egypt. . . . The people who lived in Sodom were very wicked. ✦ I've used my mind to understand wisdom and knowledge as well as madness and stupidity. Now I know that this is like trying to catch the wind. With a lot of wisdom comes a lot of heartache. The greater your knowledge, the greater your pain. ✦ I accomplished some great things: I built houses for myself. I planted vineyards for myself. . . . I also gathered silver and gold for myself. . . . But when I turned to look at all that I had accomplished and all the hard work I had put into it, I saw that it was all pointless. It was like trying to catch the wind. ✦ "Whoever is thirsty must come to me to drink." ✦ He gave plenty to drink to those who were thirsty. He filled those who were hungry with good food. ✦ Keep your mind on things above, not on worldly things.

*Jeremiah 2:13; Genesis 4:1; Genesis 11:4, 8; Genesis 13:11; Genesis 13:10, 13; Ecclesiastes 1:17–18; Ecclesiastes 2:4, 8, 11; John 7:37; Psalm 107:9; Colossians 3:2*

## MORNING READING

I'm not asking you to take them out of the world
but to protect them from the evil one.

Then you will be blameless and innocent. You will be God's children without any faults among people who are crooked and corrupt. You will shine like stars among them in the world. ✦ "You are salt for the earth . . . light for the world . . . Let your light shine in front of people. Then they will see the good that you do and praise your Father in heaven." ✦ "I kept you from sinning against me." ✦ The Lord is faithful and will strengthen you and protect you against the evil one. ✦ I didn't do that, because I feared God. ✦ In order to free us from this present evil world, Christ took the punishment for our sins, because that was what our God and Father wanted. ✦ God can guard you so that you don't fall and so that you can be full of joy as you stand in his glorious presence without fault. Before time began, now, and for eternity glory, majesty, power, and authority belong to the only God, our Savior, through Jesus Christ our Lord. Amen.

*John 17:15; Philippians 2:15; Matthew 5:13–14, 16; Genesis 20:6; 2 Thessalonians 3:3; Nehemiah 5:15; Galatians 1:4; Jude 24–25*

## EVENING READING

One who trusts the LORD is safe.

The LORD is honored because he lives on high. ✦ The LORD is high above all the nations. His glory is above the heavens. . . . He lifts the poor from the dust. He lifts the needy from a garbage heap. He seats them with influential people. ✦ But God is rich in mercy because of his great love for us. We were dead because of our failures, but he made us alive together with Christ. (It is God's kindness that saved you.) God has brought us back to life together with Christ Jesus and has given us a position in heaven with him. ✦ God didn't spare his own Son but handed him over to death for all of us. So he will also give us everything along with him. ✦ I am convinced that nothing can ever separate us from God's love which Christ Jesus our Lord shows us. We can't be separated by death or life, by angels or rulers, by anything in the present or anything in the future, by forces or powers in the world above or in the world below, or by anything else in creation.

*Proverbs 29:25; Isaiah 33:5; Psalm 113:4, 7–8; Ephesians 2:4–6; Romans 8:32; Romans 8:38–39*

## MORNING READING

By dying he would destroy the one who had power over death.

Christ has destroyed death, and through the Good News he has brought eternal life into full view. ✦ He will swallow up death forever. The Almighty LORD will wipe away tears from every face, and he will remove the disgrace of his people from the whole earth. The LORD has spoken. ✦ When this body that decays is changed into a body that cannot decay, and this mortal body is changed into a body that will live forever, then the teaching of Scripture will come true: "Death is turned into victory! Death, where is your victory? Death, where is your sting?" Sin gives death its sting, and God's standards give sin its power. Thank God that he gives us the victory through our Lord Jesus Christ. ✦ God didn't give us a cowardly spirit but a spirit of power, love, and good judgment. ✦ Even though I walk through the dark valley of death, because you are with me, I fear no harm. Your rod and your staff give me courage.

*Hebrews 2:14; 2 Timothy 1:10; Isaiah 25:8;*
*1 Corinthians 15:54–57; 2 Timothy 1:7; Psalm 23:4*

## EVENING READING

"What is the way to the place where light lives?"

God is light, and there isn't any darkness in him. ✦ "As long as I'm in the world, I'm light for the world." ✦ If we say, "We have a relationship with God" and yet live in the dark, we're lying. We aren't being truthful. But if we live in the light in the same way that God is in the light, we have a relationship with each other. And the blood of his Son Jesus cleanses us from every sin. ✦ The Father, who has made you able to share the light, which is what God's people inherit. God has rescued us from the power of darkness and has brought us into the kingdom of his Son, whom he loves. His Son paid the price to free us, which means that our sins are forgiven. ✦ You belong to the day and the light not to the night and the dark. ✦ "You are light for the world. A city cannot be hidden when it is located on a hill. . . . Let your light shine in front of people. Then they will see the good that you do and praise your Father in heaven."

*Job 38:19; 1 John 1:5; John 9:5; 1 John 1:6–7;*
*Colossians 1:12–14; 1 Thessalonians 5:5; Matthew 5:14, 16*

## MORNING READING

The Lord will not reject such people forever.
Even if he makes us suffer, he will have compassion.

Don't be afraid, my servant Jacob," declares the LORD. "I am with you. . . . I will not completely destroy you. I will correct you with justice." ✦ "I abandoned you for one brief moment, but I will bring you back with unlimited compassion. I hid my face from you for a moment in a burst of anger, but I will have compassion on you with everlasting kindness," says the LORD your defender. . . . The mountains may move, and the hills may shake, but my kindness will never depart from you. My promise of peace will never change," says the LORD, who has compassion on you. "You suffering, comfortless, storm-ravaged city! I will rebuild your city with precious stones. I will reset your foundations with sapphires." ✦ I have sinned against the LORD. So I will endure his fury until he takes up my cause and wins my case. He will bring me into the light, and I will see his victory.

*Lamentations 3:31–32; Jeremiah 46:28; Isaiah 54:7–8, 10–11; Micah 7:9*

## EVENING READING

God chose what the world considers weak
to put what is strong to shame.

Then the people of Israel cried out to the LORD for help. The LORD sent a savior to rescue them. It was Ehud, a left-handed man. . . . After Ehud came Shamgar, son of Anath. He killed 600 Philistines with a sharp stick used for herding oxen. So he, too, rescued Israel. ✦ The LORD turned to [Gideon] and said, "You will rescue Israel from Midian with the strength you have. I am sending you." Gideon said to him, "Excuse me, sir! How can I rescue Israel? Look at my whole family. It's the weakest one in Manasseh. And me? I'm the least important member of my family." ✦ The LORD said to Gideon, "You have too many men with you for me. . . . Israel might brag and say, 'We saved ourselves.'" ✦ You won't succeed by might or by power, but by my Spirit, says the LORD of Armies. ✦ Finally, receive your power from the Lord and from his mighty strength.

*1 Corinthians 1:27; Judges 3:15, 31; Judges 6:14–15;
Judges 7:2; Zechariah 4:6; Ephesians 6:10*

## MORNING READING

He has prepared a city for them.

"If I go to prepare a place for you, I will come again. Then I will bring you into my presence so that you will be where I am." ✦ An inheritance that can't be destroyed or corrupted and can't fade away. That inheritance is kept in heaven for you. ✦ We don't have a permanent city here on earth, but we are looking for the city that we will have in the future. ✦ "Jesus, who was taken from you to heaven, will come back in the same way that you saw him go to heaven." ✦ Brothers and sisters, be patient until the Lord comes again. See how farmers wait for their precious crops to grow. They wait patiently for fall and spring rains. You, too, must be patient. Don't give up hope. The Lord will soon be here. ✦ "Yet, the one who is coming will come soon. He will not delay." ✦ We who are still alive will be taken in the clouds to meet the Lord in the air. In this way we will always be with the Lord. So then, comfort each other with these words!

*Hebrews 11:16; John 14:3; 1 Peter 1:4; Hebrews 13:14; Acts 1:11; James 5:7–8; Hebrews 10:37; 1 Thessalonians 4:17–18*

## EVENING READING

God chose what the world considers ordinary and what it despises.

Stop deceiving yourselves! People who continue to commit sexual sins, who worship false gods, those who commit adultery, homosexuals, or thieves, those who are greedy or drunk, who use abusive language, or who rob people will not inherit the kingdom of God. That's what some of you were! But you have been washed and made holy, and you have received God's approval in the name of the Lord Jesus Christ and in the Spirit of our God. ✦ You were once dead because of your failures and sins. You followed the ways of this present world. . . . All of us once lived among these people, and followed the desires of our corrupt nature. We did what our corrupt desires and thoughts wanted us to do. So, because of our nature, we deserved God's anger just like everyone else. ✦ Because of his mercy he saved us through the washing in which the Holy Spirit gives us new birth and renewal. God poured a generous amount of the Spirit on us through Jesus Christ our Savior. ✦ "My thoughts are not your thoughts, and my ways are not your ways," declares the Lord.

*1 Corinthians 1:28; 1 Corinthians 6:9–11; Ephesians 2:1–3; Titus 3:5–6; Isaiah 55:8*

## MORNING READING

"The joy you have in the LORD is your strength."

Sing with joy, you heavens! Rejoice, you earth! Break into shouts of joy, you mountains! The LORD has comforted his people and will have compassion on his humble people. ✦ "Look! God is my Savior. I am confident and unafraid, because the LORD is my strength and my song. He is my Savior." ✦ The LORD is my strength and my shield. My heart trusted him, so I received help. My heart is triumphant; I give thanks to him with my song. ✦ I will find joy in the LORD. I will delight in my God. He has dressed me in the clothes of salvation. He has wrapped me in the robe of righteousness like a bridegroom with a priest's turban, like a bride with her jewels. ✦ So Christ Jesus gives me the right to brag about what I'm doing for God. ✦ In addition, our Lord Jesus Christ lets us continue to brag about God. After all, it is through Christ that we now have this restored relationship with God. ✦ I will be happy with the LORD. I will truly find joy in God, who saves me.

*Nehemiah 8:10; Isaiah 49:13; Isaiah 12:2; Psalm 28:7; Isaiah 61:10; Romans 15:17; Romans 5:11; Habakkuk 3:18*

## EVENING READING

"He has made a lasting promise to me,
with every detail arranged and assured."

I know whom I trust. I'm convinced that he is able to protect what he had entrusted to me until that day. ✦ Praise the God and Father of our Lord Jesus Christ! Through Christ, God has blessed us with every spiritual blessing that heaven has to offer. Before the creation of the world, he chose us through Christ to be holy and perfect in his presence. Because of his love he had already decided to adopt us through Jesus Christ. ✦ We know that all things work together for the good of those who love God—those whom he has called according to his plan. This is true because he already knew his people and had already appointed them to have the same form as the image of his Son. Therefore, his Son is the firstborn among many children. He also called those whom he had already appointed. He approved of those whom he had called, and he gave glory to those whom he had approved of.

*2 Samuel 23:5; 2 Timothy 1:12; Ephesians 1:3–5; Romans 8:28–30*

## MORNING READING

May this God of peace prepare you to do
every good thing he wants.

Make sure that you improve. Accept my encouragement. Share the same attitude and live in peace. The God of love and peace will be with you. ✦ God saved you through faith as an act of kindness. You had nothing to do with it. Being saved is a gift from God. It's not the result of anything you've done, so no one can brag about it. ✦ Every good present and every perfect gift comes from above, from the Father who made the sun, moon, and stars. The Father doesn't change like the shifting shadows produced by the sun and the moon. ✦ Work out your salvation with fear and trembling. It is God who produces in you the desires and actions that please him. ✦ Change the way you think. Then you will always be able to determine what God really wants—what is good, pleasing, and perfect. ✦ Jesus Christ will fill your lives with everything that God's approval produces. Your lives will then bring glory and praise to God. ✦ By ourselves we are not qualified in any way to claim that we can do anything. Rather, God makes us qualified.

*Hebrews 13:21; 2 Corinthians 13:11; Ephesians 2:8–9; James 1:17; Philippians 2:12–13; Romans 12:2; Philippians 1:11; 2 Corinthians 3:5*

## EVENING READING

"I'm going to win her back.
I will lead her into the desert.
I will speak tenderly to her."

The Lord says, "Get away from unbelievers. Separate yourselves from them. Have nothing to do with anything unclean. Then I will welcome you." The Lord Almighty says, "I will be your Father, and you will be my sons and daughters." ✦ Since we have these promises, dear friends, we need to cleanse ourselves from everything that contaminates body and spirit and live a holy life in the fear of God. ✦ Jesus suffered outside the gates of Jerusalem. He suffered to make the people holy with his own blood. So we must go to him outside the camp and endure the insults he endured. ✦ [Jesus] said to them, "Let's go to a place where we can be alone to rest for a while." ✦ The Lord is my shepherd. I am never in need. He makes me lie down in green pastures. He leads me beside peaceful waters. He renews my soul. He guides me along the paths of righteousness for the sake of his name.

*Hosea 2:14; 2 Corinthians 6:17–18; 2 Corinthians 7:1; Hebrews 13:12–13; Mark 6:31; Psalm 23:1–3*

## MORNING READING

The temple that will be built for the Lord must be magnificent.

You come to him as living stones, a spiritual house that is being built into a holy priesthood. ✦ Don't you know that you are God's temple and that God's Spirit lives in you? If anyone destroys God's temple, God will destroy him because God's temple is holy. You are that holy temple! ✦ Don't you know that your body is a temple that belongs to the Holy Spirit? The Holy Spirit, whom you received from God, lives in you. You don't belong to yourselves. You were bought for a price. So bring glory to God in the way you use your body. ✦ Can God's temple contain false gods? Clearly, we are the temple of the living God. As God said, "I will live and walk among them. I will be their God, and they will be my people." ✦ You are built on the foundation of the apostles and prophets. Christ Jesus himself is the cornerstone. In him all the parts of the building fit together and grow into a holy temple in the Lord. Through him you, also, are being built in the Spirit together with others into a place where God lives.

*1 Chronicles 22:5; 1 Peter 2:5; 1 Corinthians 3:16–17;*
*1 Corinthians 6:19–20; 2 Corinthians 6:16; Ephesians 2:20–22*

## EVENING READING

He existed before everything.

The amen, . . . the source of God's creation. ✦ [Jesus] is also the head of the church, which is his body. He is the beginning, the first to come back to life so that he would have first place in everything. ✦ "The Lord already possessed me long ago, when his way began, before any of his works. I was appointed from everlasting from the first, before the earth began. . . . When he set up the heavens, I was there. When he traced the horizon on the surface of the ocean, when he established the skies above, when he determined the currents in the ocean, when he set a limit for the sea so the waters would not overstep his command, . . . I was beside him as a master craftsman. I made him happy day after day, I rejoiced in front of him all the time." ✦ "From the first day I was the one who did this." ✦ The lamb who was slaughtered before the creation of the world. ✦ Jesus, the source and goal of our faith. He saw the joy ahead of him, so he endured death on the cross and ignored the disgrace it brought him. Then he received the highest position in heaven, the one next to the throne of God.

*Colossians 1:17; Revelation 3:14; Colossians 1:18;*
*Proverbs 8:22–23, 27–30; Isaiah 43:13; Revelation 13:8; Hebrews 12:2*

## Morning Reading

Pray for each other so that you will be healed.

Abraham asked, "Consider now, if I may be so bold as to ask you, although I'm only dust and ashes, what if there are 45 innocent people? Will you destroy the whole city because of 5 fewer people?" The Lord answered, "I will not destroy it if I find 45 there." ✦ "Father, forgive them. They don't know what they're doing." ✦ "Pray for those who persecute you." ✦ "I pray for them. I'm not praying for the world but for those you gave me, because they are yours. . . . I'm not praying only for them. I'm also praying for those who will believe in me through their message." ✦ Help carry each other's burdens. In this way you will follow Christ's teachings. ✦ Prayers offered by those who have God's approval are effective. Elijah was human like us. Yet, when he prayed that it wouldn't rain, no rain fell on the ground for three-and-a-half years.

*James 5:16; Genesis 18:27–28; Luke 23:34; Matthew 5:44; John 17:9, 20; Galatians 6:2; James 5:16–17*

## Evening Reading

Human life is as short-lived as grass.
It blossoms like a flower in the field.
When the wind blows over the flower, it disappears,
and there is no longer any sign of it.

Teach us to number each of our days so that we may grow in wisdom. ✦ "What good does it do for people to win the whole world yet lose their lives?" ✦ "Yes, people are like grass. Grass dries up, and flowers wither, but the word of our God will last forever." ✦ The world and its evil desires are passing away. But the person who does what God wants lives forever. ✦ Listen, now is God's acceptable time! Now is the day of salvation! ✦ Those who use the things in this world should do so but not depend on them. It is clear that this world in its present form is passing away. ✦ We must also consider how to encourage each other to show love and to do good things. We should not stop gathering together with other believers, as some of you are doing. Instead, we must continue to encourage each other even more as we see the day of the Lord coming.

*Psalm 103:15–16; Psalm 90:12; Mark 8:36; Isaiah 40:7–8; 1 John 2:17; 2 Corinthians 6:2; 1 Corinthians 7:31; Hebrews 10:24–25*

## MORNING READING

What kind of god is there in heaven or on earth
who can do the deeds and the mighty acts you have done?

Who in the skies can compare with the Lord? Who among the heavenly beings is like the Lord? . . . O Lord God of Armies, who is like you? Mighty Lord, even your faithfulness surrounds you. ✦ No god is like you, O Lord. No one can do what you do. ✦ You've done this great thing because of your promise and your own desire. You made it known to me. "That is why you are great, Lord God. There is no one like you, and there is no other god except you, as we have heard with our own ears." ✦ As Scripture says: "No eye has seen, no ear has heard, and no mind has imagined the things that God has prepared for those who love him." God has revealed those things to us by his Spirit. ✦ Some things are hidden. They belong to the Lord our God. But the things that have been revealed in these teachings belong to us and to our children forever.

*Deuteronomy 3:24; Psalm 89:6, 8; Psalm 86:8;
2 Samuel 7:21–22; 1 Corinthians 2:9–10; Deuteronomy 29:29*

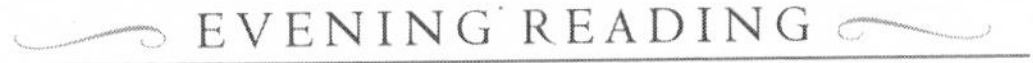

## EVENING READING

"Whoever brags must brag about what the Lord has done."

Don't let wise people brag about their wisdom. Don't let strong people brag about their strength. Don't let rich people brag about their riches. If they want to brag, they should brag that they understand and know me. ✦ I consider everything else worthless because I'm much better off knowing Christ Jesus my Lord. It's because of him that I think of everything as worthless. I threw it all away in order to gain Christ. ✦ I'm not ashamed of the Good News. It is God's power to save everyone who believes. ✦ So Christ Jesus gives me the right to brag about what I'm doing for God. ✦ As long as I have you, I don't need anyone else in heaven or on earth. ✦ "My heart finds joy in the Lord. . . . I rejoice because you saved me." ✦ Don't give glory to us, O Lord. Don't give glory to us. Instead, give glory to your name because of your mercy and faithfulness.

*1 Corinthians 1:31; Jeremiah 9:23–24; Philippians 3:8; Romans 1:16;
Romans 15:17; Psalm 73:25; 1 Samuel 2:1; Psalm 115:1*

## MORNING READING

Because the God who called you is holy
you must be holy in every aspect of your life.

We comforted you and encouraged you. Yet, we insisted that you should live in a way that proves you belong to the God who calls you into his kingdom and glory. ✦ You were chosen to tell about the excellent qualities of God, who called you out of darkness into his marvelous light. ✦ Once you lived in the dark, but now the Lord has filled you with light. Live as children who have light. Light produces everything that is good, that has God's approval, and that is true. Determine which things please the Lord. Have nothing to do with the useless works that darkness produces. Instead, expose them for what they are. ✦ Jesus Christ will fill your lives with everything that God's approval produces. Your lives will then bring glory and praise to God. ✦ "Let your light shine in front of people. Then they will see the good that you do and praise your Father in heaven." ✦ So, whether you eat or drink, or whatever you do, do everything to the glory of God.

*1 Peter 1:15; 1 Thessalonians 2:11–12; 1 Peter 2:9; Ephesians 5:8–11; Philippians 1:11; Matthew 5:16; 1 Corinthians 10:31*

## EVENING READING

Ask me about what is going to happen to my children!
Are you going to give me orders concerning my handiwork?

[The Lord says,] I will give you a new heart and put a new spirit in you. I will remove your stubborn hearts and give you obedient hearts. I will put my Spirit in you. I will enable you to live by my laws, and you will obey my rules. . . . This is what the Almighty LORD says: I will also let the people of Israel ask me to make them as numerous as sheep. ✦ "I can guarantee again that if two of you agree on anything here on earth, my Father in heaven will accept it. Where two or three have come together in my name, I am there among them." ✦ "Have faith in God! I can guarantee this truth: This is what will be done for someone who doesn't doubt but believes what he says will happen: He can say to this mountain, 'Be uprooted and thrown into the sea,' and it will be done for him."

*Isaiah 45:11; Ezekiel 36:26–27, 37; Matthew 18:19–20; Mark 11:22–23*

## Morning Reading

God is not like people. He tells no lies.
He is not like humans. He doesn't change his mind.

The Father who made the sun, moon, and stars. The Father doesn't change like the shifting shadows produced by the sun and the moon. ✦ Jesus Christ is the same yesterday, today, and forever. ✦ His truth is your shield and armor. ✦ God wouldn't change his plan. He wanted to make this perfectly clear to those who would receive his promise, so he took an oath. God did this so that we would be encouraged. God cannot lie when he takes an oath or makes a promise. These two things can never be changed. Those of us who have taken refuge in him hold on to the confidence we have been given. ✦ He is a faithful God, who keeps his promise and is merciful to thousands of generations of those who love him and obey his commands. ✦ Every path of the Lord is one of mercy and truth for those who cling to his promise and written instructions. ✦ Blessed are those who receive help from the God of Jacob. Their hope rests on the Lord their God, who made heaven, earth, the sea, and everything in them. The Lord remains faithful forever.

*Numbers 23:19; James 1:17; Hebrews 13:8; Psalm 91:4; Hebrews 6:17–18; Deuteronomy 7:9; Psalm 25:10; Psalm 146:5–6*

## Evening Reading

If you faint in a crisis, you are weak.

He gives strength to those who grow tired and increases the strength of those who are weak. ✦ "My kindness is all you need. My power is strongest when you are weak." ✦ When you call to me, I will answer you. I will be with you when you are in trouble. I will save you and honor you. ✦ The eternal God is your shelter, and his everlasting arms support you. He will force your enemies out of your way. ✦ I looked for sympathy, but there was none. I looked for people to comfort me, but I found no one. ✦ Every chief priest is chosen from humans to represent them in front of God. . . . The chief priest can be gentle with people who are ignorant and easily deceived. . . . So Christ . . . Although Jesus was the Son of God, he learned to be obedient through his sufferings. After he had finished his work, he became the source of eternal salvation for everyone who obeys him. ✦ He certainly has taken upon himself our suffering and carried our sorrows.

*Proverbs 24:10; Isaiah 40:29; 2 Corinthians 12:9; Psalm 91:15; Deuteronomy 33:27; Psalm 69:20; Hebrews 5:1–2, 5, 8–9; Isaiah 53:4*

## MORNING READING

You are my inheritance, O Lord.

Everything belongs to you. . . . You belong to Christ, and Christ belongs to God. ✦ Our great God and Savior, Jesus Christ . . . gave himself for us. ✦ [God] has made Christ the head of everything for the good of the church. ✦ Christ loved the church and gave his life for it. . . . Then he could present it to himself as a glorious church, without any kind of stain or wrinkle—holy and without faults. ✦ My soul will boast about the Lord. ✦ I will find joy in the Lord. I will delight in my God. He has dressed me in the clothes of salvation. He has wrapped me in the robe of righteousness. ✦ As long as I have you, I don't need anyone else in heaven or on earth. My body and mind may waste away, but God remains the foundation of my life and my inheritance forever. ✦ I said to the Lord, "You are my Lord. Without you, I have nothing good." ✦ The Lord is my inheritance and my cup. You are the one who determines my destiny. Your boundary lines mark out pleasant places for me. Indeed, my inheritance is something beautiful.

*Psalm 119:57; 1 Corinthians 3:21, 23; Titus 2:13–14; Ephesians 1:22; Ephesians 5:25, 27; Psalm 34:2; Isaiah 61:10; Psalm 73:25–26; Psalm 16:2; Psalm 16:5–6*

## EVENING READING

There is a way that seems right to a person,
but eventually it ends in death.

Whoever trusts his own heart is a fool. ✦ Your word is a lamp for my feet and a light for my path. ✦ I have avoided cruelty because of your word. In spite of what others have done. ✦ One of your people, claiming to be a prophet or to have prophetic dreams, may predict a miraculous sign or an amazing thing. What he predicts may even take place. But don't listen to that prophet or dreamer if he says, "Let's worship and serve other gods." (Those gods may be gods you've never heard of.) The Lord your God is testing you to find out if you really love him with all your heart and with all your soul. Worship the Lord your God, fear him, obey his commands, listen to what he says, serve him, and be loyal to him. ✦ "I will instruct you. I will teach you the way that you should go. I will advise you as my eyes watch over you."

*Proverbs 14:12; Proverbs 28:26; Psalm 119:105; Psalm 17:4; Deuteronomy 13:1–4; Psalm 32:8*

## MORNING READING

We don't live to honor ourselves, and we don't die to honor ourselves.

If we live, we honor the Lord, and if we die, we honor the Lord. So whether we live or die, we belong to the Lord. ✦ People should be concerned about others and not just about themselves. ✦ You were bought for a price. So bring glory to God in the way you use your body. ✦ I will speak very boldly and honor Christ in my body, now as always, whether I live or die. Christ means everything to me in this life, and when I die I'll have even more. If I continue to live in this life, my work will produce more results. I don't know which I would prefer. I find it hard to choose between the two. I would like to leave this life and be with Christ. That's by far the better choice. ✦ When I tried to obey the law's standards, those laws killed me. As a result, I live in a relationship with God. I have been crucified with Christ. I no longer live, but Christ lives in me. The life I now live I live by believing in God's Son, who loved me and took the punishment for my sins.

*Romans 14:7; Romans 14:8; 1 Corinthians 10:24;*
*1 Corinthians 6:20; Philippians 1:20–23; Galatians 2:19–20*

## EVENING READING

God gave Solomon . . .
a mind as limitless as the sand on the seashore.

"Look, someone greater than Solomon is here!" ✦ Prince of Peace. ✦ Finding someone who would die for a godly person is rare. Maybe someone would have the courage to die for a good person. Christ died for us while we were still sinners. This demonstrates God's love for us. ✦ Although he was in the form of God and equal with God, he did not take advantage of this equality. Instead, he emptied himself by taking on the form of a servant, by becoming like other humans, by having a human appearance. He humbled himself by becoming obedient to the point of death, death on a cross. ✦ Christ's love . . . goes far beyond any knowledge. ✦ Christ, God's power and God's wisdom. ✦ God has hidden all the treasures of wisdom and knowledge in Christ. ✦ The immeasurable wealth of Christ. ✦ You are partners with Christ Jesus because of God. Jesus has become our wisdom sent from God, our righteousness, our holiness, and our ransom from sin.

*1 Kings 4:29; Matthew 12:42; Isaiah 9:6; Romans 5:7–8;*
*Philippians 2:6–8; Ephesians 3:19; 1 Corinthians 1:24;*
*Colossians 2:3; Ephesians 3:8; 1 Corinthians 1:30*

## MORNING READING

"I love you with an everlasting love.
So I will continue to show you my kindness."

We always have to thank God for you, brothers and sisters. You are loved by the Lord and we thank God that in the beginning he chose you to be saved through a life of spiritual devotion and faith in the truth. With this in mind he called you by the Good News which we told you so that you would obtain the glory of our Lord Jesus Christ. ✦ God saved us and called us to be holy, not because of what we had done, but because of his own plan and kindness. Before the world began, God planned that Christ Jesus would show us God's kindness. ✦ Your eyes saw me when I was only a fetus. Every day of my life was recorded in your book before one of them had taken place. ✦ God loved the world this way: He gave his only Son so that everyone who believes in him will not die but will have eternal life. ✦ This is love: not that we have loved God, but that he loved us and sent his Son to be the payment for our sins.

*Jeremiah 31:3; 2 Thessalonians 2:13–14;
2 Timothy 1:9; Psalm 139:16; John 3:16; 1 John 4:10*

## EVENING READING

I made you and will continue to care for you.

The Lord created Jacob and formed Israel. Now, this is what the Lord says: Do not be afraid, because I have reclaimed you. I have called you by name; you are mine. When you go through the sea, I am with you. When you go through rivers, they will not sweep you away. ✦ Even when you're old, I'll take care of you. Even when your hair turns gray, I'll support you. ✦ Like an eagle that stirs up its nest, hovers over its young, spreads its wings to catch them, and carries them on its feathers, so the Lord alone led his people. ✦ In his love and compassion he reclaimed them. He always held them and carried them in the past. ✦ Jesus Christ is the same yesterday, today, and forever. ✦ I am convinced that . . . we can't be separated [from God's love] by . . . powers in the world above or in the world below, or by anything else in creation. ✦ Can a woman forget her nursing child? Will she have no compassion on the child from her womb? Although mothers may forget, I will not forget you.

*Isaiah 46:4; Isaiah 43:1–2; Isaiah 46:4; Deuteronomy 32:11–12;
Isaiah 63:9; Hebrews 13:8; Romans 8:38–39; Isaiah 49:15*

## MORNING READING

I know how much they're suffering.

He was a man of sorrows, familiar with suffering. ✦ [Christ] is able to sympathize with our weaknesses. ✦ "He took away our weaknesses and removed our diseases." ✦ Jesus sat down by the well because he was tired from traveling. ✦ When Jesus saw her crying, and the Jews who were crying with her, he was deeply moved and troubled. . . . Jesus cried. ✦ Because Jesus experienced temptation when he suffered, he is able to help others when they are tempted. ✦ "The Lord looked down from his holy place high above. From heaven he looked at the earth. He heard the groans of the prisoners and set free those who were condemned to death. ✦ He knows the road I take. When he tests me, I'll come out as pure as gold. ✦ When I begin to lose hope, you already know what I am experiencing. ✦ Whoever touches you touches the apple of his eye. ✦ In all their troubles he was troubled, and he was the Messenger who saved them. In his love and compassion he reclaimed them. He always held them and carried them in the past.

*Exodus 3:7; Isaiah 53:3; Hebrews 4:15; Matthew 8:17; John 4:6; John 11:33, 35; Hebrews 2:18; Psalm 102:19–20; Job 23:10; Psalm 142:3; Zechariah 2:8; Isaiah 63:9*

## EVENING READING

"We must do what the one who sent me wants us to do while it is day."

A lazy person craves food and there is none, but the appetite of hard-working people is satisfied. ✦ Whoever satisfies others will himself be satisfied. ✦ "My food is to do what the one who sent me wants me to do and to finish the work he has given me. Don't you say, 'In four more months the harvest will be here'? I'm telling you to look and see that the fields are ready to be harvested. The person who harvests the crop is already getting paid. He is gathering grain for eternal life. So the person who plants the grain and the person who harvests it are happy together." ✦ "The kingdom of heaven is like a landowner who went out at daybreak to hire workers for his vineyard. After agreeing to pay the workers the usual day's wages, he sent them to work in his vineyard." ✦ Be ready to spread the word whether or not the time is right. Point out errors, warn people, and encourage them. Be very patient when you teach. ✦ "Invest this money until I come back." ✦ I worked harder than all the others. It was not I who did it, but God's kindness was with me.

*John 9:4; Proverbs 13:4; Proverbs 11:25; John 4:34–36; Matthew 20:1–2; 2 Timothy 4:2; Luke 19:13; 1 Corinthians 15:10*

## MORNING READING

Look to the rock from which you were cut
and to the quarry from which you were dug.

Indeed, I was born guilty. ✦ "No one who saw you felt sorry enough for you to do any of these things. But you were thrown into an open field. You were rejected when you were born. Then I went by you and saw you kicking around in your own blood. I said to you, 'Live.'" ✦ He pulled me out of a horrible pit, out of the mud and clay. He set my feet on a rock and made my steps secure. He placed a new song in my mouth, a song of praise to our God. ✦ At the right time, while we were still helpless, Christ died for ungodly people. Finding someone who would die for a godly person is rare. Maybe someone would have the courage to die for a good person. Christ died for us while we were still sinners. This demonstrates God's love for us. ✦ But God is rich in mercy because of his great love for us. We were dead because of our failures, but he made us alive together with Christ. (It is God's kindness that saved you.)

*Isaiah 51:1; Psalm 51:5; Ezekiel 16:5–6;*
*Psalm 40:2–3; Romans 5:6–8; Ephesians 2:4–5*

## EVENING READING

I will find joy in the Lord.
I will delight in my God.

I will thank the Lord at all times. My mouth will always praise him. My soul will boast about the Lord. Those who are oppressed will hear it and rejoice. Praise the Lord's greatness with me. Let us highly honor his name together. ✦ The Lord grants favor and honor. He does not hold back any blessing from those who live innocently. O Lord of Armies, blessed is the person who trusts you. ✦ Praise the Lord, my soul! Praise his holy name, all that is within me. ✦ If you are happy, sing psalms. ✦ Be filled with the Spirit by reciting psalms, hymns, and spiritual songs for your own good. Sing and make music to the Lord with your hearts. Always thank God the Father for everything in the name of our Lord Jesus Christ. ✦ Sing to God in your hearts. ✦ Around midnight Paul and Silas were praying and singing hymns of praise to God. The other prisoners were listening to them. ✦ Always be joyful in the Lord! I'll say it again: Be joyful!

*Isaiah 61:10; Psalm 34:1–3; Psalm 84:11–12; Psalm 103:1; James 5:13;*
*Ephesians 5:18–20; Colossians 3:16; Acts 16:25; Philippians 4:4*

## MORNING READING

Make a flower-shaped medallion out of pure gold,
and engrave on it (as on a signet ring): Holy to the LORD.

Try to live holy lives, because if you don't, you will not see the Lord. ✦ "God is a spirit. Those who worship him must worship in spirit and truth." ✦ We've all become unclean, and all our righteous acts are like permanently stained rags. ✦ "I will show my holiness among those who come to me. I will show my glory to all the people." ✦ "This is a regulation of the temple: The whole area all the way around the top of the mountain is most holy." ✦ O LORD, holiness is what makes your house beautiful for days without end. ✦ "I'm dedicating myself to this holy work I'm doing for them so that they, too, will use the truth to be holy." ✦ We have a superior chief priest who has gone through the heavens. That person is Jesus, the Son of God. We have a chief priest who is able to sympathize with our weaknesses. . . . So we can go confidently to the throne of God's kindness to receive mercy and find kindness, which will help us at the right time.

*Exodus 28:36; Hebrews 12:14; John 4:24; Isaiah 64:6; Leviticus 10:3; Ezekiel 43:12; Psalm 93:5; John 17:19; Hebrews 4:14–16*

## EVENING READING

My cup overflows.

Taste and see that the LORD is good. Blessed is the person who takes refuge in him. Fear the LORD, you holy people who belong to him. Those who fear him are never in need. Young lions go hungry and may starve, but those who seek the LORD's help have all the good things they need. ✦ His compassion is never limited. It is new every morning. His faithfulness is great. ✦ The LORD is my inheritance and my cup. You are the one who determines my destiny. Your boundary lines mark out pleasant places for me. Indeed, my inheritance is something beautiful. ✦ Whether . . . the world, life or death, present or future things, everything belongs to you. ✦ Praise the God and Father of our Lord Jesus Christ! Through Christ, God has blessed us with every spiritual blessing that heaven has to offer. ✦ I've learned to be content in whatever situation I'm in. ✦ A godly life brings huge profits to people who are content with what they have. ✦ My God will richly fill your every need in a glorious way through Christ Jesus.

*Psalm 23:5; Psalm 34:8–10; Lamentations 3:22–23; Psalm 16:5–6; 1 Corinthians 3:22; Ephesians 1:3; Philippians 4:11; 1 Timothy 6:6; Philippians 4:19*

## August 27

### Morning Reading

Your word is a lamp for my feet and a light for my path.

I have avoided cruelty because of your word. In spite of what others have done, my steps have remained firmly in your paths. My feet have not slipped. ✦ When you walk around, they will lead you. When you lie down, they will watch over you. When you wake up, they will talk to you because the command is a lamp, the teachings are a light. ✦ You will hear a voice behind you saying, "This is the way. Follow it, whether it turns to the right or to the left." ✦ "I am the light of the world. Whoever follows me will have a life filled with light and will never live in the dark." ✦ Continue to pay attention [to the words of the prophets] as you would to a light that shines in a dark place. ✦ Now we see a blurred image in a mirror. Then we will see very clearly. Now my knowledge is incomplete. Then I will have complete knowledge as God has complete knowledge of me. ✦ There will be no more night, and they will not need any light from lamps or the sun because the Lord God will shine on them. They will rule as kings forever and ever.

*Psalm 119:105; Psalm 17:4–5; Proverbs 6:22–23; Isaiah 30:21; John 8:12; 2 Peter 1:19; 1 Corinthians 13:12; Revelation 22:5*

### Evening Reading

"How can you sleep? Get up."

This is not a place to rest! It will be destroyed, completely destroyed. ✦ Keep your mind on things above, not on worldly things. ✦ When riches increase, do not depend on them. ✦ So dedicate your hearts and lives to serving the Lord your God. ✦ "Why are you sleeping? Get up, and pray that you won't be tempted." ✦ "Make sure that you don't become drunk, hung over, and worried about life. Then that day could suddenly catch you by surprise." ✦ "Since the groom was late, all the bridesmaids became drowsy and fell asleep." ✦ "Yet, the one who is coming will come soon. He will not delay." ✦ It's time for you to wake up. Our salvation is nearer now than when we first became believers. ✦ "Therefore, be alert, because you don't know when the owner of the house will return. It could be in the evening or at midnight or at dawn or in the morning. Make sure he doesn't come suddenly and find you asleep."

*Jonah 1:6; Micah 2:10; Colossians 3:2; Psalm 62:10; 1 Chronicles 22:12; Luke 22:46; Luke 21:34; Matthew 25:5; Hebrews 10:37; Romans 13:11; Mark 13:35–36*

## MORNING READING

"The one accusing our brothers and sisters,
the one accusing them day and night in the presence of our God,
has been thrown out."

"They won the victory over him because of the blood of the lamb and the word of their testimony." ✦ Who will accuse those whom God has chosen? God has approved of them. Who will condemn them? Christ has died, and more importantly, he was brought back to life. Christ has the highest position in heaven. Christ also intercedes for us. ✦ He stripped the rulers and authorities of their power and made a public spectacle of them as he celebrated his victory in Christ. ✦ That by dying he would destroy the one who had power over death (that is, the devil). In this way he would free those who were slaves all their lives because they were afraid of dying. ✦ The one who loves us gives us an overwhelming victory in all these difficulties. ✦ Put on all the armor that God supplies. In this way you can take a stand against the devil's strategies. . . . Also take salvation as your helmet and the word of God as the sword that the Spirit supplies. ✦ Thank God that he gives us the victory through our Lord Jesus Christ.

*Revelation 12:10; Revelation 12:11; Romans 8:33–34; Colossians 2:15; Hebrews 2:14–15; Romans 8:37; Ephesians 6:11, 17; 1 Corinthians 15:57*

## EVENING READING

The tree of life.

God has given us eternal life, and this life is found in his Son. ✦ He gave his only Son so that everyone who believes in him will not die but will have eternal life. ✦ "In the same way that the Father brings back the dead and gives them life, the Son gives life to anyone he chooses. . . . The Father is the source of life, and he has enabled the Son to be the source of life too." ✦ "I will give the privilege of eating from the tree of life, which stands in the paradise of God, to everyone who wins the victory." ✦ Between the street of the city and the river there was a tree of life visible from both sides. It produced 12 kinds of fruit. Each month had its own fruit. The leaves of the tree will heal the nations. ✦ Blessed is the one who finds wisdom. . . . Long life is in wisdom's right hand. . . . Wisdom is a tree of life for those who take firm hold of it. Those who cling to it are blessed. ✦ Jesus has become our wisdom.

*Genesis 2:9; 1 John 5:11; John 3:16; John 5:21, 26; Revelation 2:7; Revelation 22:2; Proverbs 3:13, 16, 18; 1 Corinthians 1:30*

## Morning Reading

Blessed is the person who trusts the Lord.

[Abraham] didn't doubt God's promise out of a lack of faith. Instead, giving honor to God for the promise, he became strong because of faith and was absolutely confident that God would do what he promised. ✦ So the Israelites were humbled at that time, and the men of Judah won because they trusted the Lord God of their ancestors. ✦ God is our refuge and strength, an ever-present help in times of trouble. That is why we are not afraid even when the earth quakes or the mountains topple into the depths of the sea. ✦ It is better to depend on the Lord than to trust mortals. It is better to depend on the Lord than to trust influential people. ✦ A person's steps are directed by the Lord, and the Lord delights in his way. When he falls, he will not be thrown down headfirst because the Lord holds on to his hand. ✦ Taste and see that the Lord is good. Blessed is the person who takes refuge in him. Fear the Lord, you holy people who belong to him. Those who fear him are never in need.

*Proverbs 16:20; Romans 4:20–21; 2 Chronicles 13:18; Psalm 46:1–2; Psalm 118:8–9; Psalm 37:23–24; Psalm 34:8–9*

## Evening Reading

I fall asleep in peace the moment I lie down
because you alone, O Lord, enable me to live securely.

You do not need to fear terrors of the night. ✦ He will cover you with his feathers, and under his wings you will find refuge. ✦ "The way a hen gathers her chicks under her wings!" ✦ He will not let you fall. Your guardian will not fall asleep. Indeed, the Guardian of Israel never rests or sleeps. The Lord is your guardian. The Lord is the shade over your right hand. ✦ I would like to be a guest in your tent forever and to take refuge under the protection of your wings. ✦ Even the darkness is not too dark for you. Night is as bright as day. Darkness and light are the same to you. ✦ God didn't spare his own Son but handed him over to death for all of us. So he will also give us everything along with him. ✦ You belong to Christ, and Christ belongs to God. ✦ I am confident and unafraid.

*Psalm 4:8; Psalm 91:5; Psalm 91:4; Matthew 23:37; Psalm 121:3–5; Psalm 61:4; Psalm 139:12; Romans 8:32; 1 Corinthians 3:23; Isaiah 12:2*

## MORNING READING

The king held out the golden scepter that was in his hand to Esther. Esther went up to him and touched the top of the scepter.

When he cries out to me, I will listen because I am compassionate. ✦ We have known and believed that God loves us. God is love. Those who live in God's love live in God, and God lives in them. God's love has reached its goal in us. So we look ahead with confidence to the day of judgment. While we are in this world, we are exactly like him with regard to love. No fear exists where his love is. Rather, perfect love gets rid of fear, because fear involves punishment. The person who lives in fear doesn't have perfect love. We love because God loved us first. ✦ We have been sprinkled with his blood to free us from a guilty conscience, and our bodies have been washed with clean water. So we must continue to come to him with a sincere heart and strong faith. ✦ So Jewish and non-Jewish people can go to the Father in one Spirit. ✦ We can go to God with bold confidence through faith in Christ. ✦ So we can go confidently to the throne of God's kindness to receive mercy and find kindness, which will help us at the right time.

*Esther 5:2; Exodus 22:27; 1 John 4:16–19; Hebrews 10:22; Ephesians 2:18; Ephesians 3:12; Hebrews 4:16*

## EVENING READING

When the Israelites saw [the manna], they asked each other, "What is this?" because they didn't know what it was.

The mystery that gives us our reverence for God is acknowledged to be great: He appeared in his human nature. ✦ "God's bread is the man who comes from heaven and gives life to the world." ✦ "Your ancestors ate the manna in the desert and died. . . . I am the living bread that came from heaven. Whoever eats this bread will live forever. The bread I will give to bring life to the world is my flesh. . . . My flesh is true food, and my blood is true drink." ✦ Some gathered more, some less. . . . Those who had gathered less didn't have too little. . . . Each morning they gathered as much food as they could eat. ✦ "Don't ever worry and say, 'What are we going to eat?' or 'What are we going to drink?' . . . Your heavenly Father certainly knows you need all of them. But first, be concerned about his kingdom and what has his approval. Then all these things will be provided for you."

*Exodus 16:15; 1 Timothy 3:16; John 6:33; John 6:49, 51, 55; Exodus 16:17–18, 21; Matthew 6:31–33*

## Morning Reading

Even after many failures, the gift brought God's approval.

"Though your sins are bright red, they will become as white as snow. Though they are dark red, they will become as white as wool." ✦ I alone am the one who is going to wipe away your rebellious actions for my own sake. I will not remember your sins anymore. Remind me of what happened. Let us argue our case together. State your case so that you can prove you are right. ✦ I made your rebellious acts disappear like a thick cloud and your sins like the morning mist. Come back to me, because I have reclaimed you. ✦ God loved the world this way: He gave his only Son so that everyone who believes in him will not die but will have eternal life. ✦ There is no comparison between God's gift and Adam's failure. If humanity died as the result of one person's failure, it is certainly true that God's kindness and the gift given through the kindness of one person, Jesus Christ, have been showered on humanity. ✦ That's what some of you were! But you have been washed and made holy, and you have received God's approval in the name of the Lord Jesus Christ and in the Spirit of our God.

*Romans 5:16; Isaiah 1:18; Isaiah 43:25–26; Isaiah 44:22; John 3:16; Romans 5:15; 1 Corinthians 6:11*

## Evening Reading

"Invest this money until I come back."

"[The Son of Man] is like a man who went on a trip. As he left home, he put his servants in charge. He assigned work to each one and ordered the guard to be alert." ✦ "He gave one man ten thousand dollars, another four thousand dollars, and another two thousand dollars. Each was given money based on his ability. Then the man went on his trip." ✦ "We must do what the one who sent me wants us to do while it is day. The night when no one can do anything is coming." ✦ "Didn't you realize that I had to be in my Father's house?" ✦ He left you an example so that you could follow in his footsteps. ✦ Be ready to spread the word whether or not the time is right. Point out errors, warn people, and encourage them. Be very patient when you teach. ✦ The day will make what each one does clearly visible because fire will reveal it. ✦ So, then, brothers and sisters, don't let anyone move you off the foundation of your faith. Always excel in the work you do for the Lord. You know that the hard work you do for the Lord is not pointless.

*Luke 19:13; Mark 13:34; Matthew 25:15; John 9:4; Luke 2:49; 1 Peter 2:21; 2 Timothy 4:2; 1 Corinthians 3:13; 1 Corinthians 15:58*

## MORNING READING

But the spiritual nature produces . . . gentleness.

Humble people again will find joy in the LORD. The poorest of people will find joy in the Holy One of Israel. ✦ "Unless you change and become like little children, you will never enter the kingdom of heaven. Whoever becomes like this little child is the greatest in the kingdom of heaven." ✦ Beauty expresses itself in a gentle and quiet attitude which God considers precious. ✦ [Love] doesn't sing its own praises. It isn't arrogant. ✦ Pursue . . . gentleness. ✦ "Place my yoke over your shoulders, and learn from me, because I am gentle and humble." ✦ He was abused and punished, but he didn't open his mouth. He was led like a lamb to the slaughter. He was like a sheep that is silent when its wool is cut off. He didn't open his mouth. ✦ God called you to endure suffering because Christ suffered for you. He left you an example so that you could follow in his footsteps. Christ never committed any sin. He never spoke deceitfully. Christ never verbally abused those who verbally abused him. . . . [He] left everything to the one who judges fairly.

*Galatians 5:22–23; Isaiah 29:19; Matthew 18:3–4; 1 Peter 3:4; 1 Corinthians 13:4; 1 Timothy 6:11; Matthew 11:29; Isaiah 53:7; 1 Peter 2:21–23*

## EVENING READING

"Those who want to come with me must say no to the things they want, pick up their crosses every day, and follow me."

Our lives demonstrate that we are God's servants. . . . we are praised and dishonored, as we are slandered and honored. ✦ Those who try to live a godly life because they believe in Christ Jesus will be persecuted. ✦ Brothers and sisters, if I am still preaching that circumcision is necessary, why am I still being persecuted? In that case the cross wouldn't be offensive anymore. ✦ If I were still trying to please people, I would not be Christ's servant. ✦ If you are insulted because of the name of Christ, you are blessed. . . . If you suffer, you shouldn't suffer for being a murderer, thief, criminal, or troublemaker. If you suffer for being a Christian, don't feel ashamed, but praise God for being called that name. ✦ God has given you the privilege not only to believe in Christ but also to suffer for him. ✦ We are convinced of the fact that one man has died for all people. Therefore, all people have died. He died for all people so that those who live should no longer live for themselves but for the man who died and was brought back to life for them. ✦ If we endure, we will rule with him.

*Luke 9:23; 2 Corinthians 6:4, 8; 2 Timothy 3:12; Galatians 5:11; Galatians 1:10; 1 Peter 4:14–16; Philippians 1:29; 2 Corinthians 5:14–15; 2 Timothy 2:12*

## MORNING READING

Wait with hope for the LORD.
Be strong, and let your heart be courageous.

Don't you know? Haven't you heard? The eternal God, the LORD, the Creator of the ends of the earth, doesn't grow tired or become weary. His understanding is beyond reach. He gives strength to those who grow tired and increases the strength of those who are weak. ✦ Don't be afraid, because I am with you. Don't be intimidated; I am your God. I will strengthen you. I will help you. I will support you with my victorious right hand. ✦ You have been a refuge for the poor, a refuge for the needy in their distress, a shelter from the rain, and shade from the heat. (A tyrant's breath is like a rainstorm against a wall.) ✦ You know that such testing of your faith produces endurance. Endure until your testing is over. Then you will be mature and complete, and you won't need anything. ✦ So don't lose your confidence. It will bring you a great reward. You need endurance so that after you have done what God wants you to do, you can receive what he has promised.

*Psalm 27:14; Isaiah 40:28–29; Isaiah 41:10;*
*Isaiah 25:4; James 1:3–4; Hebrews 10:35–36*

## EVENING READING

He makes me lie down in green pastures.

The wicked are like the churning sea. It isn't quiet. . . . "There is no peace for the wicked," says my God. ✦ "Come to me, all who are tired from carrying heavy loads, and I will give you rest." ✦ Surrender yourself to the LORD. ✦ Those who entered his place of rest also rested from their work as God did from his. ✦ Don't get carried away by all kinds of unfamiliar teachings. Gaining inner strength from God's kindness is good for us. ✦ Then we will no longer be little children, tossed and carried about by all kinds of teachings that change like the wind. We will no longer be influenced by people who use cunning and clever strategies to lead us astray. Instead, as we lovingly speak the truth, we will grow up completely in our relationship to Christ, who is the head. ✦ I want to sit in his shadow. His fruit tastes sweet to me. He leads me into a banquet room and looks at me with love.

*Psalm 23:2; Isaiah 57:20–21; Matthew 11:28; Psalm 37:7;*
*Hebrews 4:10; Hebrews 13:9; Ephesians 4:14–15; Song of Songs 2:3–4*

## MORNING READING

"No sourdough or yeast should be seen anywhere in your territory."

To fear the LORD is to hate evil. ✦ Keep away from every kind of evil. ✦ Make sure that everyone has kindness from God so that bitterness doesn't take root and grow up to cause trouble that corrupts many of you. ✦ If I had thought about doing anything sinful, the Lord would not have listened to me. ✦ Don't you know that a little yeast spreads through the whole batch of dough? Remove the old yeast of sin so that you may be a new batch of dough, since you don't actually have the yeast of sin. Christ, our Passover lamb, has been sacrificed. So we must not celebrate our festival with the old yeast of sin or with the yeast of vice and wickedness. Instead, we must celebrate it with the bread of purity and truth that has no yeast. ✦ With this in mind, individuals must determine whether what they are doing is proper when they eat the bread and drink from the cup. ✦ "Whoever worships the Lord must give up doing wrong." ✦ We need a chief priest who is holy, innocent, pure, set apart from sinners. ✦ You know that Christ appeared in order to take away our sins. He isn't sinful.

*Exodus 13:7; Proverbs 8:13; 1 Thessalonians 5:22; Hebrews 12:15; Psalm 66:18; 1 Corinthians 5:6–8; 1 Corinthians 11:28; 2 Timothy 2:19; Hebrews 7:26; 1 John 3:5*

## EVENING READING

"You certainly won't die!" the snake told the woman. . . .
"Your eyes will be opened. You'll be like God, knowing good and evil."

I'm afraid that as the snake deceived Eve by its tricks, so your minds may somehow be lured away from your sincere and pure devotion to Christ. ✦ Receive your power from the Lord and from his mighty strength. Put on all the armor that God supplies. In this way you can take a stand against the devil's strategies. . . . For this reason, take up all the armor that God supplies. Then you will be able to take a stand during these evil days. Once you have overcome all obstacles, you will be able to stand your ground. So then, take your stand! Fasten truth around your waist like a belt. Put on God's approval as your breastplate. Put on your shoes so that you are ready to spread the Good News that gives peace. In addition to all these, take the Christian faith as your shield. With it you can put out all the flaming arrows of the evil one. Also take salvation as your helmet and the word of God as the sword that the Spirit supplies. ✦ I don't want Satan to outwit us. After all, we are not ignorant about Satan's scheming.

*Genesis 3:4–5; 2 Corinthians 11:3; Ephesians 6:10–11, 13–17; 2 Corinthians 2:11*

## MORNING READING

"Stay here, my daughter."

"Be careful, stay calm, and don't be afraid." ✦ Let go of your concerns! Then you will know that I am God. ✦ "Didn't I tell you that if you believe, you would see God's glory?" ✦ Then arrogant people will be brought down, and high and mighty people will be humbled. On that day the LORD alone will be honored. ✦ Mary sat at the Lord's feet and listened to him talk. . . . [Jesus said,] "Mary has made the right choice, and that one thing will not be taken away from her." ✦ "You can be saved by returning to me. You can have rest. You can be strong by being quiet and by trusting me." ✦ Think about this on your bed and remain quiet. ✦ Surrender yourself to the LORD, and wait patiently for him. Do not be preoccupied with an evildoer who succeeds in his way when he carries out his schemes. ✦ He is not afraid of bad news. His heart remains secure, full of confidence in the LORD. ✦ "Whoever believes in him will not worry."

*Ruth 3:18; Isaiah 7:4; Psalm 46:10; John 11:40; Isaiah 2:17; Luke 10:39, 42; Isaiah 30:15; Psalm 4:4; Psalm 37:7; Psalm 112:7–8; Isaiah 28:16*

## EVENING READING

"You don't know now what I'm doing. You will understand later."

Remember that for 40 years the LORD your God led you on your journey in the desert. He did this in order to humble you and test you. He wanted to know whether or not you would wholeheartedly obey his commands. ✦ "I went by you again and looked at you. You were old enough to make love to. . . . I promised to love you, and I exchanged marriage vows with you. You became mine," declares the Almighty LORD. ✦ The Lord disciplines everyone he loves. ✦ Dear friends, don't be surprised by the fiery troubles that are coming in order to test you. Don't feel as though something strange is happening to you, but be happy as you share Christ's sufferings. Then you will also be full of joy when he appears again in his glory. ✦ Our suffering is light and temporary and is producing for us an eternal glory that is greater than anything we can imagine. We don't look for things that can be seen but for things that can't be seen.

*John 13:7; Deuteronomy 8:2; Ezekiel 16:8; Hebrews 12:6; 1 Peter 4:12–13; 2 Corinthians 4:17–18*

## MORNING READING

The body is one unit and yet has many parts, . . . so it is with Christ.

He is also the head of the church, which is his body. ✦ Head of everything for the good of the church. The church is Christ's body and completes him as he fills everything in every way. ✦ We are parts of his body. ✦ "You prepared a body for me." ✦ Your eyes saw me when I was only a fetus. Every day of my life was recorded in your book before one of them had taken place. ✦ They belonged to you, and you gave them to me. ✦ Before the creation of the world, he chose us through Christ to be holy and perfect in his presence. ✦ He already knew his people and had already appointed them to have the same form as the image of his Son. ✦ Grow up completely in our relationship to Christ, who is the head. He makes the whole body fit together and unites it through the support of every joint. As each and every part does its job, he makes the body grow so that it builds itself up in love.

*1 Corinthians 12:12; Colossians 1:18; Ephesians 1:22–23; Ephesians 5:30; Hebrews 10:5; Psalm 139:16; John 17:6; Ephesians 1:4; Romans 8:29; Ephesians 4:15–16*

## EVENING READING

The fountain of life-giving water.

Your mercy is so precious, O God, that Adam's descendants take refuge in the shadow of your wings. They are refreshed with the rich foods in your house, and you make them drink from the river of your pleasure. Indeed, the fountain of life is with you. ✦ This is what the Lord God says: My servants will eat, but you will be hungry. My servants will drink, but you will be thirsty. ✦ "Those who drink the water that I will give them will never become thirsty again. In fact, the water I will give them will become in them a spring that gushes up to eternal life." ✦ Jesus said this about the Spirit, whom his believers would receive. ✦ "Listen! Whoever is thirsty, come to the water!" ✦ The Spirit and the bride say, "Come!" Let those who hear this say, "Come!" Let those who are thirsty come! Let those who want the water of life take it as a gift.

*Jeremiah 2:13; Psalm 36:7–9; Isaiah 65:13; John 4:14; John 7:39; Isaiah 55:1; Revelation 22:17*

## MORNING READING

Let us raise our hearts and hands to God in heaven.

Who is like the Lord our God? He is seated on his high throne. He bends down to look at heaven and earth. ✦ To you, O Lord, I lift my soul. ✦ I stretch out my hands to you in prayer. Like parched land, my soul thirsts for you. . . . Do not hide your face from me, or I will be like those who go into the pit. Let me hear about your mercy in the morning, because I trust you. Let me know the way that I should go, because I long for you. ✦ My lips will praise you because your mercy is better than life itself. So I will thank you as long as I live. I will lift up my hands to pray in your name. ✦ Give me joy, O Lord, because I lift my soul to you. You, O Lord, are good and forgiving, full of mercy toward everyone who calls out to you. ✦ "I will do anything you ask the Father in my name."

*Lamentations 3:41; Psalm 113:5–6; Psalm 25:1; Psalm 143:6–8; Psalm 63:3–4; Psalm 86:4–5; John 14:13*

## EVENING READING

"Watchman, how much of the night is left?"

It's time for you to wake up. Our salvation is nearer now than when we first became believers. The night is almost over, and the day is near. So we should get rid of the things that belong to the dark and take up the weapons that belong to the light. ✦ "Learn from the story of the fig tree. When its branch becomes tender and it sprouts leaves, you know that summer is near. In the same way, when you see all these things, you know that he is near, at the door." ✦ "The earth and the heavens will disappear, but my words will never disappear." ✦ I wait for the Lord, my soul waits, and with hope I wait for his word. My soul waits for the Lord more than those who watch for the morning, more than those who watch for the morning. ✦ The one who is testifying to these things says, "Yes, I'm coming soon!" Amen! Come, Lord Jesus! ✦ "So stay awake, because you don't know the day or the hour."

*Isaiah 21:11; Romans 13:11–12; Matthew 24:32–33; Matthew 24:35; Psalm 130:5–6; Revelation 22:20; Matthew 25:13*

## MORNING READING

Be happy in your confidence.

The hope which is kept safe for you in heaven. ✦ If Christ is our hope in this life only, we deserve more pity than any other people. ✦ "We must suffer a lot to enter the kingdom of God." ✦ "So those who do not carry their crosses and follow me cannot be my disciples." ✦ You know that we're destined to suffer persecution. ✦ Always be joyful in the Lord! I'll say it again: Be joyful! ✦ May God, the source of hope, fill you with joy and peace through your faith in him. Then you will overflow with hope by the power of the Holy Spirit. ✦ Praise the God and Father of our Lord Jesus Christ! God has given us a new birth because of his great mercy. We have been born into a new life that has a confidence which is alive because Jesus Christ has come back to life. . . . Although you have never seen Christ, you love him. You don't see him now, but you believe in him. You are extremely happy with joy and praise that can hardly be expressed in words. ✦ Through Christ we can approach God and stand in his favor. So we brag because of our confidence that we will receive glory from God.

*Romans 12:12; Colossians 1:5; 1 Corinthians 15:19; Acts 14:22; Luke 14:27; 1 Thessalonians 3:3; Philippians 4:4; Romans 15:13; 1 Peter 1:3, 8; Romans 5:2*

## EVENING READING

I am oppressed and needy. May the Lord think of me.

I know the plans that I have for you, declares the LORD. They are plans for peace and not disaster. ✦ "My thoughts are not your thoughts, and my ways are not your ways," declares the LORD. "Just as the heavens are higher than the earth, so my ways are higher than your ways, and my thoughts are higher than your thoughts." ✦ How precious are your thoughts concerning me, O God! How vast in number they are! If I try to count them, there would be more of them than there are grains of sand. When I wake up, I am still with you. ✦ How spectacular are your works, O LORD! How very deep are your thoughts! ✦ You have done many miraculous things, O LORD my God. You have made many wonderful plans for us. ✦ You were not in powerful positions or in the upper social classes. ✦ Didn't God choose poor people in the world to become rich in faith and to receive the kingdom? ✦ We have nothing although we possess everything. ✦ The immeasurable wealth of Christ.

*Psalm 40:17; Jeremiah 29:11; Isaiah 55:8–9; Psalm 139:17–18; Psalm 92:5; Psalm 40:5; 1 Corinthians 1:26; James 2:5; 2 Corinthians 6:10; Ephesians 3:8*

## MORNING READING

"You have been weighed on a scale and found to be too light."

The LORD is a God of knowledge, and he weighs our actions. ✦ What is important to humans is disgusting to God. ✦ "God does not see as humans see. Humans look at outward appearances, but the LORD looks into the heart." ✦ Make no mistake about this: You can never make a fool out of God. Whatever you plant is what you'll harvest. If you plant in the soil of your corrupt nature, you will harvest destruction. But if you plant in the soil of your spiritual nature, you will harvest everlasting life. ✦ What good will it do for people to win the whole world and lose their lives? Or what will a person give in exchange for life? ✦ These things that I once considered valuable, I now consider worthless for Christ. ✦ Yet, you desire truth and sincerity. ✦ You have probed my heart. You have confronted me at night. You have tested me like silver, but you found nothing wrong.

*Daniel 5:27; 1 Samuel 2:3; Luke 16:15; 1 Samuel 16:7; Galatians 6:7–8; Matthew 16:26; Philippians 3:7; Psalm 51:6; Psalm 17:3*

## EVENING READING

Christ is the first.

"A single grain of wheat doesn't produce anything unless it is planted in the ground and dies. If it dies, it will produce a lot of grain." ✦ If the first handful of dough is holy, the whole batch of dough is holy. If the root is holy, the branches are holy. ✦ But now Christ has come back from the dead. He is the very first person of those who have died to come back to life. ✦ If we've become united with him in a death like his, certainly we will also be united with him when we come back to life as he did. ✦ The Lord Jesus Christ, . . . through his power to bring everything under his authority, . . . will change our humble bodies and make them like his glorified body. ✦ The first to come back to life. ✦ Does the Spirit of the one who brought Jesus back to life live in you? Then the one who brought Christ back to life will also make your mortal bodies alive by his Spirit who lives in you. ✦ "I am the one who brings people back to life, and I am life itself. Those who believe in me will live even if they die."

*1 Corinthians 15:23; John 12:24; Romans 11:16; 1 Corinthians 15:20; Romans 6:5; Philippians 3:20–21; Colossians 1:18; Romans 8:11; John 11:25*

## MORNING READING

He fed hungry people with good food.
He sent rich people away with nothing.

You say, "I'm rich. I'm wealthy. I don't need anything." Yet, you do not realize that you are miserable, pitiful, poor, blind, and naked. I advise you: Buy gold purified in fire from me so that you may be rich. . . . I correct and discipline everyone I love. Take this seriously, and change the way you think and act. ✦ "Blessed are those who hunger and thirst for God's approval. They will be satisfied." ✦ "The poor and needy are looking for water, but there is none. Their tongues are parched with thirst. I, the LORD, will answer them. I, the God of Israel, will not abandon them." ✦ I am the LORD your God. . . . Open your mouth wide, and I will fill it. ✦ Why do you spend money on what cannot nourish you and your wages on what does not satisfy you? Listen carefully to me: Eat what is good, and enjoy the best foods. ✦ "I am the bread of life. Whoever comes to me will never become hungry, and whoever believes in me will never become thirsty."

*Luke 1:53; Revelation 3:17–19; Matthew 5:6;*
*Isaiah 41:17; Psalm 81:10; Isaiah 55:2; John 6:35*

## EVENING READING

But my feet had almost stumbled.
They had almost slipped.

When I said, "My feet are slipping," your mercy, O LORD, continued to hold me up. ✦ Then the Lord said, "Simon, Simon, listen! Satan has demanded to have you apostles for himself. He wants to separate you from me as a farmer separates wheat from husks. But I have prayed for you, Simon, that your faith will not fail." ✦ A righteous person may fall seven times, but he gets up again. ✦ When he falls, he will not be thrown down headfirst because the LORD holds on to his hand. ✦ Don't laugh at me, my enemies. Although I've fallen, I will get up. Although I sit in the dark, the LORD is my light. ✦ "He will keep you safe from six troubles, and when the seventh one comes, no harm will touch you." ✦ If anyone does sin, we have Jesus Christ, who has God's full approval. He speaks on our behalf when we come into the presence of the Father. ✦ That is why he is always able to save those who come to God through him. He can do this because he always lives and intercedes for them.

*Psalm 73:2; Psalm 94:18; Luke 22:31–32; Proverbs 24:16;*
*Psalm 37:24; Micah 7:8; Job 5:19; 1 John 2:1; Hebrews 7:25*

## MORNING READING

I will give them the same attitude and the same purpose
so that they will fear me as long as they live.
This will be for their own good.

I will give you a new heart and put a new spirit in you. ✦ The LORD is good and decent. That is why he teaches sinners the way they should live. He leads humble people to do what is right, and he teaches them his way. Every path of the LORD is one of mercy and truth for those who cling to his promise and written instructions. ✦ "I pray that all of these people continue to have unity in the way that you, Father, are in me and I am in you. I pray that they may be united with us so that the world will believe that you have sent me." ✦ I . . . encourage you to live the kind of life which proves that God has called you. Be humble and gentle in every way. . . . Through the peace that ties you together, do your best to maintain the unity that the Spirit gives. There is one body and one Spirit. In the same way you were called to share one hope. There is one Lord, one faith, one baptism, one God and Father of all, who is over everything, through everything, and in everything.

*Jeremiah 32:39; Ezekiel 36:26; Psalm 25:8–10; John 17:21; Ephesians 4:1–6*

## EVENING READING

The strength of those who wait with hope
in the LORD will be renewed.

When I'm weak, I'm strong. ✦ My God has become my strength. ✦ But he told me: "My kindness is all you need. My power is strongest when you are weak." So I will brag even more about my weaknesses in order that Christ's power will live in me. ✦ Let them come to me for protection. ✦ Turn your burdens over to the LORD, and he will take care of you. ✦ His arms remained limber because of the help of the Mighty One of Jacob. ✦ I won't let you go until you bless me. ✦ "You come to me with sword and spear and javelin, but I come to you in the name of the LORD of Armies, the God of the army of Israel, whom you have insulted." ✦ O LORD, attack those who attack me. Fight against those who fight against me. Use your shields, both small and large. Arise to help me.

*Isaiah 40:31; 2 Corinthians 12:10; Isaiah 49:5; 2 Corinthians 12:9; Isaiah 27:5; Psalm 55:22; Genesis 49:24; Genesis 32:26; 1 Samuel 17:45; Psalm 35:1–2*

## MORNING READING

Don't become like the people of this world.
Instead, change the way you think.

Never follow a crowd in doing wrong. ✦ You unfaithful people! Don't you know that love for this evil world is hatred toward God? Whoever wants to be a friend of this world is an enemy of God. ✦ Can right and wrong be partners? Can light have anything in common with darkness? Can Christ agree with the devil? Can a believer share life with an unbeliever? Can God's temple contain false gods? ✦ Don't love the world and what it offers. Those who love the world don't have the Father's love in them. . . . The world and its evil desires are passing away. But the person who does what God wants lives forever. ✦ You followed the ways of this present world and its spiritual ruler. This ruler continues to work in people who refuse to obey God. ✦ But that is not what you learned from Christ's teachings. You have certainly heard his message and have been taught his ways. The truth is in Jesus.

*Romans 12:2; Exodus 23:2; James 4:4; 2 Corinthians 6:14–16; 1 John 2:15, 17; Ephesians 2:2; Ephesians 4:20–21*

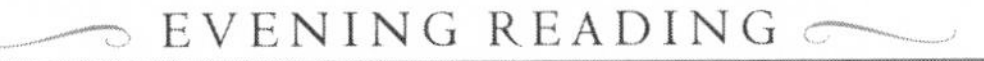

## EVENING READING

People go to do their work, to do their tasks until evening.

By the sweat of your brow, you will produce food to eat until you return to the ground. ✦ While we were with you, we gave you the order: "Whoever doesn't want to work shouldn't be allowed to eat." ✦ Make it your goal to live quietly, do your work, and earn your own living, as we ordered you. ✦ Whatever presents itself for you to do, do it with all your might, because there is no work, planning, knowledge, or skill in the grave where you're going. ✦ "The night when no one can do anything is coming." ✦ We can't allow ourselves to get tired of living the right way. Certainly, each of us will receive everlasting life at the proper time, if we don't give up. ✦ Always excel in the work you do for the Lord. You know that the hard work you do for the Lord is not pointless. ✦ Therefore, a time of rest and worship exists for God's people. ✦ We worked hard all day under a blazing sun. ✦ He will say to them, "This is a place for comfort. This is a place of rest for those who are tired. This is a place for them to rest." But they weren't willing to listen.

*Psalm 104:23; Genesis 3:19; 2 Thessalonians 3:10; 1 Thessalonians 4:11; Ecclesiastes 9:10; John 9:4; Galatians 6:9; 1 Corinthians 15:58; Hebrews 4:9; Matthew 20:12; Isaiah 28:12*

## MORNING READING

I've seen their sinful ways, but I'll heal them.

I am the LORD, who heals you. ✦ O LORD, you have examined me, and you know me. You alone know when I sit down and when I get up. You read my thoughts from far away. You watch me when I travel and when I rest. You are familiar with all my ways. ✦ You have set our sins in front of you. You have put our secret sins in the light of your presence. ✦ No creature can hide from God. Everything is uncovered and exposed for him to see. We must answer to him. ✦ "Come on now, let's discuss this!" says the LORD. "Though your sins are bright red, they will become as white as snow. Though they are dark red, they will become as white as wool." ✦ He will have pity on them and say, "Free them from going into the pit. I have found a ransom." ✦ He was wounded for our rebellious acts. He was crushed for our sins. He was punished so that we could have peace, and we received healing from his wounds. ✦ He has sent me to heal those who are brokenhearted. ✦ "Your faith has made you well. Go in peace! Be cured from your illness."

*Isaiah 57:18; Exodus 15:26; Psalm 139:1–3; Psalm 90:8; Hebrews 4:13; Isaiah 1:18; Job 33:24; Isaiah 53:5; Isaiah 61:1; Mark 5:34*

## EVENING READING

The LORD is on my side.

The LORD will answer you in times of trouble. The name of the God of Jacob will protect you. He will send you help from his holy place and support you from Zion. . . . We will joyfully sing about your victory. We will wave our flags in the name of our God. The LORD will fulfill all your requests. . . . Some rely on chariots and others on horses, but we will boast in the name of the LORD our God. They will sink to their knees and fall, but we will rise and stand firm. ✦ He will come like a rushing stream. The wind of the LORD pushes him. ✦ There isn't any temptation that you have experienced which is unusual for humans. God, who faithfully keeps his promises, will not allow you to be tempted beyond your power to resist. But when you are tempted, he will also give you the ability to endure the temptation as your way of escape. ✦ If God is for us, who can be against us? ✦ The LORD is on my side. I am not afraid. ✦ If our God, whom we honor, can save us from a blazing furnace and from your power, he will.

*Psalm 118:7; Psalm 20:1–2, 5, 7–8; Isaiah 59:19; 1 Corinthians 10:13; Romans 8:31; Psalm 118:6; Daniel 3:17*

## MORNING READING

"Whoever is thirsty must come to me to drink."

My soul longs and yearns for the LORD's courtyards. My whole body shouts for joy to the living God. ✦ O God, you are my God. At dawn I search for you. My soul thirsts for you. My body longs for you in a dry, parched land where there is no water. So I look for you in the holy place to see your power and your glory. ✦ "Listen! Whoever is thirsty, come to the water! Whoever has no money can come, buy, and eat! Come, buy wine and milk. You don't have to pay; it's free!" ✦ The Spirit and the bride say, "Come!" Let those who hear this say, "Come!" Let those who are thirsty come! Let those who want the water of life take it as a gift. ✦ "Those who drink the water that I will give them will never become thirsty again. In fact, the water I will give them will become in them a spring that gushes up to eternal life." ✦ "My blood is true drink." ✦ Eat, my friends! Drink and become intoxicated with expressions of love!

*John 7:37; Psalm 84:2; Psalm 63:1–2; Isaiah 55:1; Revelation 22:17; John 4:14; John 6:55; Song of Songs 5:1*

## EVENING READING

"You are salt for the earth."

Beauty . . . can't be destroyed. ✦ You have been born again, not from a seed that can be destroyed, but through God's everlasting word that can't be destroyed. ✦ "Those who believe in me will live even if they die." ✦ "They are God's children who have come back to life." ✦ The immortal God. ✦ But if God's Spirit lives in you, you are under the control of your spiritual nature, not your corrupt nature. Whoever doesn't have the Spirit of Christ doesn't belong to him. However, if Christ lives in you, your bodies are dead because of sin, but your spirits are alive because you have God's approval. Does the Spirit of the one who brought Jesus back to life live in you? Then the one who brought Christ back to life will also make your mortal bodies alive by his Spirit who lives in you. ✦ When the body is planted, it decays. When it comes back to life, it cannot decay. ✦ "Have salt within you, and live in peace with one another." ✦ Don't say anything that would hurt another person. Instead, speak only what is good so that you can give help wherever it is needed. That way, what you say will help those who hear you.

*Matthew 5:13; 1 Peter 3:4; 1 Peter 1:23; John 11:25; Luke 20:36; Romans 1:23; Romans 8:9–11; 1 Corinthians 15:42; Mark 9:50; Ephesians 4:29*

## MORNING READING

I alone am the one who comforts you.

Praise the God and Father of our Lord Jesus Christ! He is the Father who is compassionate and the God who gives comfort. He comforts us whenever we suffer. That is why whenever other people suffer, we are able to comfort them by using the same comfort we have received from God. ✦ As a father has compassion for his children, so the Lord has compassion for those who fear him. He certainly knows what we are made of. He bears in mind that we are dust. ✦ As a mother comforts her child, so will I comfort you. ✦ Turn all your anxiety over to God because he cares for you. ✦ You, O Lord, are a compassionate and merciful God. You are patient, always faithful and ready to forgive. ✦ "That helper is the Spirit of Truth." ✦ The Spirit also helps us in our weakness. ✦ He will wipe every tear from their eyes. There won't be any more death. There won't be any grief, crying, or pain, because the first things have disappeared.

*Isaiah 51:12; 2 Corinthians 1:3–4; Psalm 103:13–14; Isaiah 66:13; 1 Peter 5:7; Psalm 86:15; John 14:17; Romans 8:26; Revelation 21:4*

## EVENING READING

He called you to be partners with his Son Jesus Christ our Lord.

He received honor and glory from God the Father and when the voice of our majestic God spoke these words to him: "This is my Son, whom I love and in whom I delight." ✦ The Father has given us his love. He loves us so much that we are actually called God's dear children. ✦ Imitate God, since you are the children he loves. ✦ If we are his children, we are also God's heirs. ✦ His Son is the reflection of God's glory and the exact likeness of God's being. ✦ Let your light shine in front of people. Then they will see the good that you do and praise your Father in heaven. ✦ Jesus, the source and goal of our faith. He saw the joy ahead of him, so he endured death on the cross and ignored the disgrace it brought him. ✦ "I say these things while I'm still in the world so that they will have the same joy that I have." ✦ Because Christ suffered so much for us, we can receive so much comfort from him.

*1 Corinthians 1:9; 2 Peter 1:17; 1 John 3:1; Ephesians 5:1; Romans 8:17; Hebrews 1:3; Matthew 5:16; Hebrews 12:2; John 17:13; 2 Corinthians 1:5*

## MORNING READING

Sin shouldn't have power over you because
you're not controlled by laws, but by God's favor.

Then what is the implication? Should we sin because we are not controlled by laws but by God's favor? That's unthinkable! ✦ In the same way, brothers and sisters, you have died to the laws in Moses' Teachings through Christ's body. You belong to someone else, the one who was brought back to life. As a result, we can do what God wants. ✦ I have God's teachings. I'm really subject to Christ's teachings. ✦ Sin gives death its sting, and God's standards give sin its power. Thank God that he gives us the victory through our Lord Jesus Christ. ✦ The standards of the Spirit, who gives life through Christ Jesus, have set you free from the standards of sin and death. ✦ "Whoever lives a sinful life is a slave to sin." ✦ "If the Son sets you free, you will be absolutely free." ✦ Christ has freed us so that we may enjoy the benefits of freedom. Therefore, be firm in this freedom, and don't become slaves again.

*Romans 6:14; Romans 6:15; Romans 7:4; 1 Corinthians 9:21;
1 Corinthians 15:56–57; Romans 8:2; John 8:34; John 8:36; Galatians 5:1*

## EVENING READING

A person who has doubts is thinking about two different things . . .
and can't make up his mind about anything.

"Whoever starts to plow and looks back is not fit for the kingdom of God." ✦ Whoever goes to God must believe that God exists and that he rewards those who seek him. ✦ When you ask for something, don't have any doubts. A person who has doubts is like a wave that is blown by the wind and tossed by the sea. A person who has doubts shouldn't expect to receive anything from the Lord. ✦ That's why I tell you to have faith that you have already received whatever you pray for, and it will be yours. ✦ Then we will no longer be little children, tossed and carried about by all kinds of teachings that change like the wind. We will no longer be influenced by people who use cunning and clever strategies to lead us astray. Instead, as we lovingly speak the truth, we will grow up completely in our relationship to Christ, who is the head. ✦ Live in me. ✦ Don't let anyone move you off the foundation of your faith. Always excel in the work you do for the Lord. You know that the hard work you do for the Lord is not pointless.

*James 1:8; Luke 9:62; Hebrews 11:6; James 1:6–7; Mark 11:24;
Ephesians 4:14–15; John 15:4; 1 Corinthians 15:58*

## MORNING READING

The LORD weighs hearts.

The LORD knows the way of righteous people, but the way of wicked people will end. ✦ The LORD will show who belongs to him, who is holy. ✦ "Your Father sees what you do in private. He will reward you." ✦ Examine me, O God, and know my mind. Test me, and know my thoughts. See whether I am on an evil path. Then lead me on the everlasting path. ✦ No fear exists where his love is. Rather, perfect love gets rid of fear. ✦ You know all my desires, O Lord, and my groaning has not been hidden from you. ✦ When I begin to lose hope, you already know what I am experiencing. ✦ The one who searches our hearts knows what the Spirit has in mind. The Spirit intercedes for God's people the way God wants him to. ✦ God's people have a solid foundation. These words are engraved on it: "The Lord knows those who belong to him," and "Whoever worships the Lord must give up doing wrong."

*Proverbs 21:2; Psalm 1:6; Numbers 16:5; Matthew 6:4; Psalm 139:23–24; 1 John 4:18; Psalm 38:9; Psalm 142:3; Romans 8:27; 2 Timothy 2:19*

## EVENING READING

Weeping may last for the night,
but there is a song of joy in the morning.

So that these troubles don't disturb any of you. You know that we're destined to suffer persecution. In fact, when we were with you, we told you ahead of time that we were going to suffer persecution. ✦ "My peace will be with you. In the world you'll have trouble. But cheer up! I have overcome the world." ✦ When I wake up, I will be satisfied with seeing you. ✦ The night is almost over, and the day is near. ✦ "He is like the morning light as the sun rises, like a morning without clouds, like the brightness after a rainstorm. The rain makes the grass grow from the earth." ✦ He will swallow up death forever. The Almighty LORD will wipe away tears from every face. ✦ "There won't be any more death. There won't be any grief, crying, or pain, because the first things have disappeared." ✦ Then, together with them, we who are still alive will be taken in the clouds to meet the Lord in the air. In this way we will always be with the Lord. So then, comfort each other with these words!

*Psalm 30:5; 1 Thessalonians 3:3–4; John 16:33; Psalm 17:15; Romans 13:12; 2 Samuel 23:4; Isaiah 25:8; Revelation 21:4; 1 Thessalonians 4:17–18*

## MORNING READING

"He will not break off a damaged cattail."

The sacrifice pleasing to God is a broken spirit. O God, you do not despise a broken and sorrowful heart. ✦ He is the healer of the brokenhearted. He is the one who bandages their wounds. ✦ The High and Lofty One lives forever, and his name is holy. This is what he says: I live in a high and holy place. But I am with those who are crushed and humble. I will renew the spirit of those who are humble and the courage of those who are crushed. I will not accuse you forever. I will not be angry with you forever. Otherwise, the spirits, the lives of those I've made. would grow faint in my presence. ✦ I will look for those that are lost, bring back those that have strayed away, bandage those that are injured, and strengthen those that are sick. ✦ Strengthen your tired arms and weak knees. Keep walking along straight paths so that your injured leg won't get worse. Instead, let it heal. ✦ Your God . . . will come and rescue you.

*Matthew 12:20; Psalm 51:17; Psalm 147:3; Isaiah 57:15–16; Ezekiel 34:16; Hebrews 12:12–13; Isaiah 35:4*

## EVENING READING

Taste and see that the LORD is good.
Blessed is the person who takes refuge in him.

The person in charge tasted the water that had become wine. He didn't know where it had come from. . . . The person in charge called the groom and said to him, "Everyone serves the best wine first. When people are drunk, the host serves cheap wine. But you have saved the best wine for now." ✦ The ear tests words like the tongue tastes food. ✦ I believed; therefore, I spoke. ✦ I know whom I trust. ✦ I want to sit in his shadow. His fruit tastes sweet to me. ✦ God, who is very kind to you. ✦ God didn't spare his own Son but handed him over to death for all of us. So he will also give us everything along with him. ✦ Desire God's pure word as newborn babies desire milk. Then you will grow in your salvation. Certainly you have tasted that the Lord is good! ✦ But let all who take refuge in you rejoice. Let them sing with joy forever.

*Psalm 34:8; John 2:9–10; Job 34:3; 2 Corinthians 4:13; 2 Timothy 1:12; Song of Songs 2:3; Romans 2:4; Romans 8:32; 1 Peter 2:2–3; Psalm 5:11*

## Morning Reading

Uncover my eyes so that I may see the miraculous things in your teachings.

Then he opened their minds to understand the Scriptures. ✦ "Knowledge about the mysteries of the kingdom of heaven has been given to you. But it has not been given to the crowd." ✦ "I praise you, Father, Lord of heaven and earth, for hiding these things from wise and intelligent people and revealing them to little children. Yes, Father, this is what pleased you." ✦ Now, we didn't receive the spirit that belongs to the world. Instead, we received the Spirit who comes from God so that we could know the things which God has freely given us. ✦ How precious are your thoughts concerning me, O God! How vast in number they are! If I try to count them, there would be more of them than there are grains of sand. ✦ God's riches, wisdom, and knowledge are so deep that it is impossible to explain his decisions or to understand his ways. Who knows how the Lord thinks? Who can become his adviser? Everything is from him and by him and for him. Glory belongs to him forever! Amen!

*Psalm 119:18; Luke 24:45; Matthew 13:11; Matthew 11:25–26; 1 Corinthians 2:12; Psalm 139:17–18; Romans 11:33–34, 36*

## Evening Reading

En Hakkore [Spring of the One Who Calls Out].

"If you only knew what God's gift is and who is asking you for a drink, you would have asked him for a drink. He would have given you living water." ✦ Jesus was standing in the temple courtyard. He said loudly, "Whoever is thirsty must come to me to drink." . . . Jesus said this about the Spirit, whom his believers would receive. ✦ "Test me in this way," says the LORD of Armies. "See if I won't open the windows of heaven for you and flood you with blessings." ✦ "Even though you're evil, you know how to give good gifts to your children. So how much more will your Father in heaven give the Holy Spirit to those who ask him?" ✦ "Ask, and you will receive. Search, and you will find. Knock, and the door will be opened for you." ✦ Because you are God's children, God has sent the Spirit of his Son into us to call out, "Abba! Father!" ✦ You haven't received the spirit of slaves that leads you into fear again. Instead, you have received the spirit of God's adopted children by which we call out, "Abba! Father!"

*Judges 15:19; John 4:10; John 7:37, 39; Malachi 3:10; Luke 11:13; Luke 11:9; Galatians 4:6; Romans 8:15*

## Morning Reading

God, who shows you his kindness.

I will call out my name "the Lord." I will be kind to anyone I want to. ✦ Then he will have pity on them and say, "Free them from going into the pit. I have found a ransom." ✦ They receive God's approval freely by an act of his kindness through the price Christ Jesus paid to set us free from sin. God showed that Christ is the throne of mercy where God's approval is given through faith in Christ's blood. In his patience God waited to deal with sins committed in the past. ✦ Kindness and truth came into existence through Jesus Christ. ✦ God saved you through faith as an act of kindness. You had nothing to do with it. Being saved is a gift from God. ✦ Good will, mercy, and peace from God the Father and Christ Jesus our Lord. ✦ God's favor has been given to each of us. It was measured out to us by Christ who gave it. ✦ Each of you as a good manager must use the gift that God has given you to serve others. ✦ But God shows us even more kindness. Scripture says, "God opposes arrogant people, but he is kind to humble people." ✦ Grow in the good will and knowledge of our Lord and Savior Jesus Christ. Glory belongs to him now and for that eternal day! Amen.

*1 Peter 5:10; Exodus 33:19; Job 33:24; Romans 3:24–25; John 1:17; Ephesians 2:8; 1 Timothy 1:2; Ephesians 4:7; 1 Peter 4:10; James 4:6; 2 Peter 3:18*

## Evening Reading

I look up toward the mountains. Where can I find help?
My help comes from the Lord, the maker of heaven and earth.

As the mountains surround Jerusalem, so the Lord surrounds his people now and forever. ✦ I look up to you, to the one who sits enthroned in heaven. As servants depend on their masters, as a maid depends on her mistress, so we depend on the Lord our God until he has pity on us. ✦ You have been my help. In the shadow of your wings, I sing joyfully. ✦ You're our God. Won't you judge them? We don't have the strength to face this large crowd that is attacking us. We don't know what to do, so we're looking to you. ✦ My eyes are always on the Lord. He removes my feet from traps. ✦ Our help is in the name of the Lord, the maker of heaven and earth.

*Psalm 121:1–2; Psalm 125:2; Psalm 123:1–2; Psalm 63:7; 2 Chronicles 20:12; Psalm 25:15; Psalm 124:8*

## MORNING READING

Blessed is the one who finds wisdom
and the one who obtains understanding.

Whoever finds [wisdom] finds life and obtains favor from the LORD. ✦ This is what the LORD says: Don't let wise people brag about their wisdom. Don't let strong people brag about their strength. Don't let rich people brag about their riches. If they want to brag, they should brag that they understand and know me. ✦ The fear of the LORD is the beginning of wisdom. ✦ These things that I once considered valuable, I now consider worthless for Christ. It's far more than that! I consider everything else worthless because I'm much better off knowing Christ Jesus my Lord. It's because of him that I think of everything as worthless. I threw it all away in order to gain Christ. ✦ God has hidden all the treasures of wisdom and knowledge in Christ. ✦ Advice and priceless wisdom are mine. I, Understanding, have strength. ✦ Jesus has become our wisdom sent from God, our righteousness, our holiness, and our ransom from sin. ✦ A winner of souls is wise.

*Proverbs 3:13; Proverbs 8:35; Jeremiah 9:23–24; Proverbs 9:10; Philippians 3:7–8; Colossians 2:3; Proverbs 8:14; 1 Corinthians 1:30; Proverbs 11:30*

## EVENING READING

Beggars although we make many people spiritually rich.

You know about the kindness of our Lord Jesus Christ. He was rich, yet for your sake he became poor in order to make you rich through his poverty. ✦ Each of us has received one gift after another because of all that the Word is. ✦ My God will richly fill your every need in a glorious way through Christ Jesus. ✦ God will give you his constantly overflowing kindness. Then, when you always have everything you need, you can do more and more good things. ✦ Didn't God choose poor people in the world to become rich in faith and to receive the kingdom that he promised to those who love him? ✦ Not many of you were wise from a human point of view. You were not in powerful positions or in the upper social classes. But God chose what the world considers nonsense to put wise people to shame. God chose what the world considers weak to put what is strong to shame. ✦ Our bodies are made of clay, yet we have the treasure of the Good News in them. This shows that the superior power of this treasure belongs to God and doesn't come from us.

*2 Corinthians 6:10; 2 Corinthians 8:9; John 1:16; Philippians 4:19; 2 Corinthians 9:8; James 2:5; 1 Corinthians 1:26–27; 2 Corinthians 4:7*

## MORNING READING

We know that all things work together for
the good of those who love God.

Even angry mortals will praise you. You will wear the remainder of their anger. ✦ Even though you planned evil against me, God planned good to come out of it. ✦ Everything belongs to you. Whether . . . the world, life or death, present or future things, everything belongs to you. You belong to Christ, and Christ belongs to God. ✦ All this is for your sake so that, as God's kindness overflows in the lives of many people, it will produce even more thanksgiving to the glory of God. That is why we are not discouraged. Though outwardly we are wearing out, inwardly we are renewed day by day. Our suffering is light and temporary and is producing for us an eternal glory that is greater than anything we can imagine. ✦ My brothers and sisters, be very happy when you are tested in different ways. You know that such testing of your faith produces endurance. Endure until your testing is over. Then you will be mature and complete, and you won't need anything.

*Romans 8:28; Psalm 76:10; Genesis 50:20;
1 Corinthians 3:21–23; 2 Corinthians 4:15–17; James 1:2–4*

## EVENING READING

The Holy Spirit's presence be with all of you!

"I will ask the Father, and he will give you another helper who will be with you forever. That helper is the Spirit of Truth. The world cannot accept him, because it doesn't see or know him. You know him, because he lives with you and will be in you." ✦ "He won't speak on his own. He will speak what he hears and will tell you about things to come. He will give me glory, because he will tell you what I say." ✦ God's love has been poured into our hearts by the Holy Spirit, who has been given to us. ✦ The person who unites himself with the Lord becomes one spirit with him. . . . Don't you know that your body is a temple that belongs to the Holy Spirit? The Holy Spirit, whom you received from God, lives in you. You don't belong to yourselves. ✦ Don't give God's Holy Spirit any reason to be upset with you. He has put his seal on you for the day you will be set free from the world of sin. ✦ The Spirit also helps us in our weakness, because we don't know how to pray for what we need. But the Spirit intercedes along with our groans that cannot be expressed in words.

*2 Corinthians 13:14; John 14:16–17; John 16:13–14;
Romans 5:5; 1 Corinthians 6:17, 19; Ephesians 4:30; Romans 8:26*

## MORNING READING

May my thoughts be pleasing to him.
I will find joy in the LORD.

Like an apple tree among the trees in the forest, so is my beloved among the young men. I want to sit in his shadow. His fruit tastes sweet to me. ✦ Who in the skies can compare with the LORD? Who among the heavenly beings is like the LORD? ✦ My beloved is dazzling yet ruddy. He stands out among 10,000 men. ✦ "A valuable pearl." ✦ The ruler over the kings of the earth. ✦ His head is the finest gold. His hair is wavy, black as a raven. ✦ The head of everything. ✦ He is also the head of the church, which is his body. ✦ His cheeks are like a garden of spices, a garden that produces scented herbs. ✦ It couldn't be kept a secret.✦ His lips are lilies that drip with myrrh. ✦ "No human has ever spoken like this man." ✦ His form is like Lebanon, choice as the cedars. ✦ Smile on me. ✦ Let the light of your presence shine on us, O LORD.

*Psalm 104:34; Song of Songs 2:3; Psalm 89:6; Song of Songs 5:10; Matthew 13:46; Revelation 1:5; Song of Songs 5:11; Ephesians 1:22; Colossians 1:18; Song of Songs 5:13; Mark 7:24; Song of Songs 5:13; John 7:46; Song of Songs 5:15; Psalm 31:16; Psalm 4:6*

## EVENING READING

"Father, if it's possible, let this cup of suffering be taken away from me.
But let your will be done rather than mine."

"I am too deeply troubled now to know how to express my feelings. Should I say, 'Father, save me from this time of suffering'? No! I came for this time of suffering." ✦ "I haven't come from heaven to do what I want to do. I've come to do what the one who sent me wants me to do." ✦ He humbled himself by becoming obedient to the point of death, death on a cross. ✦ During his life on earth, Jesus prayed to God, who could save him from death. He prayed and pleaded with loud crying and tears, and he was heard because of his devotion to God. Although Jesus was the Son of God, he learned to be obedient through his sufferings. ✦ "Don't you think that I could call on my Father to send more than twelve legions of angels to help me now?" ✦ "Scripture says that the Messiah would suffer and that he would come back to life on the third day. Scripture also says that by the authority of Jesus people would be told to turn to God and change the way they think and act so that their sins will be forgiven. This would be told to people from all nations, beginning in the city of Jerusalem."

*Matthew 26:39; John 12:27; John 6:38; Philippians 2:8; Hebrews 5:7–8; Matthew 26:53; Luke 24:46–47*

## MORNING READING

Our God hasn't abandoned us.

Dear friends, don't be surprised by the fiery troubles that are coming in order to test you. Don't feel as though something strange is happening to you. ✦ Endure your discipline. God corrects you as a father corrects his children. All children are disciplined by their fathers. If you aren't disciplined like the other children, you aren't part of the family. ✦ The LORD your God is testing you to find out if you really love him with all your heart and with all your soul. ✦ For the sake of his great name, the LORD will not abandon his people, because the LORD wants to make you his people. ✦ Can a woman forget her nursing child? Will she have no compassion on the child from her womb? Although mothers may forget, I will not forget you. ✦ Blessed are those who receive help from the God of Jacob. Their hope rests on the LORD their God. ✦ "Won't God give his chosen people justice when they cry out to him for help day and night? Is he slow to help them? I can guarantee that he will give them justice quickly."

*Ezra 9:9; 1 Peter 4:12; Hebrews 12:7–8; Deuteronomy 13:3; 1 Samuel 12:22; Isaiah 49:15; Psalm 146:5; Luke 18:7–8*

## EVENING READING

Everyone who wins the victory will inherit these things.

If Christ is our hope in this life only, we deserve more pity than any other people. ✦ These men were longing for a better country—a heavenly country. That is why God is not ashamed to be called their God. He has prepared a city for them. ✦ We have been born into a new life which has an inheritance that can't be destroyed or corrupted and can't fade away. That inheritance is kept in heaven for you. ✦ Everything belongs to you; . . . the world, life or death, present or future things, everything belongs to you. ✦ "No eye has seen, no ear has heard, and no mind has imagined the things that God has prepared for those who love him." God has revealed those things to us by his Spirit. ✦ Be careful that you don't destroy what we've worked for, but that you receive your full reward. ✦ We must get rid of everything that slows us down, especially sin that distracts us. We must run the race that lies ahead of us and never give up.

*Revelation 21:7; 1 Corinthians 15:19; Hebrews 11:16; 1 Peter 1:4; 1 Corinthians 3:21–22; 1 Corinthians 2:9–10; 2 John 8; Hebrews 12:1*

## MORNING READING

Being united with God is my highest good.

O LORD, I love the house where you live, the place where your glory dwells. ✦ One day in your courtyards is better than a thousand anywhere else. I would rather stand in the entrance to my God's house than live inside wicked people's homes. ✦ Blessed is the person you choose and invite to live with you in your courtyards. We will be filled with good food from your house, from your holy temple. ✦ The LORD is good to those who wait for him, to anyone who seeks help from him. ✦ The LORD is waiting to be kind to you. He rises to have compassion on you. The LORD is a God of justice. Blessed are all those who wait for him. ✦ Brothers and sisters, because of the blood of Jesus we can now confidently go into the holy place. Jesus has opened a new and living way for us. . . . We have been sprinkled with his blood to free us from a guilty conscience, and our bodies have been washed with clean water.

*Psalm 73:28; Psalm 26:8; Psalm 84:10; Psalm 65:4; Lamentations 3:25; Isaiah 30:18; Hebrews 10:19–20, 22*

## EVENING READING

You know about the kindness of our Lord Jesus Christ.

The Word became human and lived among us. We saw his glory. It was the glory that the Father shares with his only Son, a glory full of kindness and truth. ✦ You are the most handsome of Adam's descendants. Grace is poured on your lips. ✦ All the people spoke well of him. They were amazed to hear the gracious words flowing from his lips. ✦ You have tasted that the Lord is good! ✦ Those who believe in the Son of God have the testimony of God in them. ✦ We know what we're talking about, and we confirm what we've seen. ✦ Taste and see that the LORD is good. Blessed is the person who takes refuge in him. ✦ I want to sit in his shadow. His fruit tastes sweet to me. ✦ But he told me: "My kindness is all you need. My power is strongest when you are weak." ✦ God's favor has been given to each of us. It was measured out to us by Christ who gave it. ✦ Each of you as a good manager must use the gift that God has given you to serve others.

*2 Corinthians 8:9; John 1:14; Psalm 45:2; Luke 4:22; 1 Peter 2:3; 1 John 5:10; John 3:11; Psalm 34:8; Song of Songs 2:3; 2 Corinthians 12:9; Ephesians 4:7; 1 Peter 4:10*

## MORNING READING

Endure until your testing is over.
Then you will be mature and complete,
and you won't need anything.

You have to suffer different kinds of trouble for a little while now. The purpose of these troubles is to test your faith as fire tests how genuine gold is. Your faith is more precious than gold, and by passing the test, it gives praise, glory, and honor to God. This will happen when Jesus Christ appears again. ✦ We also brag when we are suffering. We know that suffering creates endurance, endurance creates character, and character creates confidence. ✦ It is good to continue to hope and wait silently for the Lord to save us. ✦ You have a better and more permanent possession. So don't lose your confidence. It will bring you a great reward. You need endurance so that after you have done what God wants you to do, you can receive what he has promised. ✦ God our Father loved us and by his kindness gave us everlasting encouragement and good hope. Together with our Lord Jesus Christ, may he encourage and strengthen you to do and say everything that is good.

*James 1:4; 1 Peter 1:6–7; Romans 5:3–4;*
*Lamentations 3:26; Hebrews 10:34–36; 2 Thessalonians 2:16–17*

## EVENING READING

God, through Christ Jesus, will judge people's secret thoughts.

Don't judge anything before the appointed time. Wait until the Lord comes. He will also bring to light what is hidden in the dark and reveal people's motives. Then each person will receive praise from God. ✦ "The Father doesn't judge anyone. He has entrusted judgment entirely to the Son. . . . He has also given the Son authority to pass judgment because he is the Son of Man." ✦ The Son of God, whose eyes are like flames of fire. ✦ Then wicked people ask, "What does God know?" "Does the Most High know anything?" ✦ When you did these things, I remained silent. That made you think I was like you. I will argue my point with you and lay it all out for you to see. ✦ "Nothing has been covered that will not be exposed. Whatever is secret will be made known." ✦ You know all my desires, O Lord, and my groaning has not been hidden from you. ✦ Examine me, O Lord, and test me. Look closely into my heart and mind.

*Romans 2:16; 1 Corinthians 4:5; John 5:22, 27; Revelation 2:18;*
*Psalm 73:11; Psalm 50:21; Luke 12:2; Psalm 38:9; Psalm 26:2*

## MORNING READING

He is a faithful God, who does no wrong.
He is honorable and reliable.

The one who judges fairly. ✦ All of us must appear in front of Christ's judgment seat. Then all people will receive what they deserve for the good or evil they have done while living in their bodies. ✦ All of us will have to give an account of ourselves to God. ✦ The person who sins will die. ✦ "Arise, sword, against my shepherd, against the man who is my friend," declares the LORD of Armies. "Strike the shepherd." ✦ The LORD has laid all our sins on him. ✦ Mercy and truth have met. Righteousness and peace have kissed. ✦ Mercy triumphs over judgment. ✦ The payment for sin is death, but the gift that God freely gives is everlasting life found in Christ Jesus our Lord. ✦ There is no other righteous God and Savior besides me. ✦ He is a God of justice, a God who approves of people who believe in Jesus. ✦ They receive God's approval freely by an act of his kindness through the price Christ Jesus paid to set us free from sin.

*Deuteronomy 32:4; 1 Peter 2:23; 2 Corinthians 5:10; Romans 14:12; Ezekiel 18:4; Zechariah 13:7; Isaiah 53:6; Psalm 85:10; James 2:13; Romans 6:23; Isaiah 45:21; Romans 3:26; Romans 3:24*

## EVENING READING

"Death is turned into victory!"

Thank God that he gives us the victory through our Lord Jesus Christ. ✦ Since all of these sons and daughters have flesh and blood, Jesus took on flesh and blood to be like them. He did this so that by dying he would destroy the one who had power over death (that is, the devil). In this way he would free those who were slaves all their lives because they were afraid of dying. ✦ If we have died with Christ, we believe that we will also live with him. We know that Christ, who was brought back to life, will never die again. Death no longer has any power over him. When he died, he died once and for all to sin's power. But now he lives, and he lives for God. ✦ So consider yourselves dead to sin's power but living for God in the power Christ Jesus gives you. ✦ The one who loves us gives us an overwhelming victory in all these difficulties.

*1 Corinthians 15:54; 1 Corinthians 15:57; Hebrews 2:14–15; Romans 6:8–10; Romans 6:11; Romans 8:37*

## MORNING READING

Be humbled by God's power so that
when the right time comes he will honor you.

Everyone with a conceited heart is disgusting to the LORD. Certainly, such a person will not go unpunished. ✦ You are our Father. We are the clay, and you are our potter. We are the work of your hands. Don't be too angry, LORD. Don't remember our sin forever. Now look, we are all your people. ✦ "You disciplined me, and I was disciplined. I was like a young, untrained calf. Turn me, and I will be turned, because you are the LORD my God. After I was turned around, I changed the way I thought and acted. After I was taught a lesson, I hung my head in shame. I was so ashamed and humiliated, because of all the stupid things I have done ever since I was young." ✦ It is good for people to endure burdens when they're young. ✦ Certainly, sorrow doesn't come from the soil, and trouble doesn't sprout from the ground. But a person is born for trouble as surely as sparks fly up from a fire.

*1 Peter 5:6; Proverbs 16:5; Isaiah 64:8–9; Jeremiah 31:18–19; Lamentations 3:27; Job 5:6–7*

## EVENING READING

"Did God really say . . . ?"

The tempter came to him and said, "If you are the Son of God, tell these stones to become loaves of bread." Jesus answered, "Scripture says . . . Scripture says . . . Scripture says" . . . Then the devil left him. ✦ The man of God said, "I'm not allowed to go back with you. I'm not allowed to eat or drink with you. When the LORD spoke to me, he told me not to eat or drink there or go back on the road I took to get there." The old prophet said, "I'm also a prophet, like you. An angel spoke the word of the LORD to me. He said, 'Bring him home with you so that he may have something to eat and drink.' " (But the old prophet was lying.) The man of God went back with him and ate and drank in his home. . . . When the old prophet who had brought the man of God back from the road heard about it, he said, "It's the man of God who rebelled against the words from the LORD's mouth! The LORD gave him to the lion. It tore him to pieces and killed him as the word of the LORD had told him." ✦ Whoever tells you good news that is different from the Good News we gave you should be condemned to hell, even if he is one of us or an angel from heaven. ✦ I have treasured your promise in my heart so that I may not sin against you.

*Genesis 3:1; Matthew 4:3–4, 7, 10–11; 1 Kings 13:16–19, 26; Galatians 1:8; Psalm 119:11*

## MORNING READING

Whenever they use my name to bless the Israelites,
I will bless them."

We have become like those whom you never ruled, like those who are not called by your name. ✦ O LORD, our God, you are not the only master to rule us, but we acknowledge only you. ✦ All the people in the world will see that you are the LORD's people, and they will be afraid of you. ✦ For the sake of his great name, the LORD will not abandon his people, because the LORD wants to make you his people. ✦ "Listen to us, Lord. Forgive us, Lord. Pay attention, and act. Don't delay! Do this for your sake, my God, because your city and your people are called by your name." ✦ Help us, O God, our savior, for the glory of your name. Rescue us, and forgive our sins for the honor of your name. Why should the nations be allowed to say, "Where is their God?" ✦ The name of the LORD is a strong tower. A righteous person runs to it and is safe.

*Numbers 6:27; Isaiah 63:19; Isaiah 26:13; Deuteronomy 28:10; 1 Samuel 12:22; Daniel 9:19; Psalm 79:9–10; Proverbs 18:10*

## EVENING READING

The heavens declare the glory of God,
and the sky displays what his hands have made.

From the creation of the world, God's invisible qualities, his eternal power and divine nature, have been clearly observed in what he made. ✦ "He has given evidence of his existence." ✦ One day tells a story to the next. One night shares knowledge with the next without talking, without words, without their voices being heard. ✦ When I look at your heavens, the creation of your fingers, the moon and the stars that you have set in place—what is a mortal that you remember him or the Son of Man that you take care of him? ✦ The sun has one kind of splendor, the moon has another kind of splendor, and the stars have still another kind of splendor. Even one star differs in splendor from another star. That is how it will be when the dead come back to life. ✦ Those who are wise will shine like the brightness on the horizon. Those who lead many people to righteousness will shine like the stars forever and ever.

*Psalm 19:1; Romans 1:20; Acts 14:17; Psalm 19:2–3; Psalm 8:3–4; 1 Corinthians 15:41–42; Daniel 12:3*

## MORNING READING

We understand what love is when
we realize that Christ gave his life for us.

Christ's love, which goes far beyond any knowledge. ✦ "The greatest love you can show is to give your life for your friends." ✦ You know about the kindness of our Lord Jesus Christ. He was rich, yet for your sake he became poor in order to make you rich through his poverty. ✦ Dear friends, if this is the way God loved us, we must also love each other. ✦ Be kind to each other, sympathetic, forgiving each other as God has forgiven you through Christ. ✦ Put up with each other, and forgive each other if anyone has a complaint. Forgive as the Lord forgave you. ✦ "It's the same way with the Son of Man. He didn't come so that others could serve him. He came to serve and to give his life as a ransom for many people." ✦ Christ suffered for you. He left you an example so that you could follow in his footsteps. ✦ "You must wash each other's feet. I've given you an example that you should follow." ✦ We must give our lives for other believers.

*1 John 3:16; Ephesians 3:19; John 15:13; 2 Corinthians 8:9; 1 John 4:11; Ephesians 4:32; Colossians 3:13; Mark 10:45; 1 Peter 2:21; John 13:14–15; 1 John 3:16*

## EVENING READING

The Son does exactly what the Father does.

The Lord gives wisdom. From his mouth come knowledge and understanding. ✦ "I will give you words and wisdom that none of your enemies will be able to oppose or prove wrong." ✦ Wait with hope for the Lord. Be strong, and let your heart be courageous. ✦ "My kindness is all you need. My power is strongest when you are weak." ✦ Those who have been called, who are loved by God the Father. ✦ Jesus, who makes people holy, and all those who are made holy have the same Father. That is why Jesus isn't ashamed to call them brothers and sisters. ✦ "I fill heaven and earth!" declares the Lord. ✦ He fills everything in every way. ✦ I alone am the Lord, and there is no savior except me. ✦ "He really is the savior of the world." ✦ Good will and peace from God the Father and from Christ Jesus our Savior are yours!

*John 5:19; Proverbs 2:6; Luke 21:15; Psalm 27:14; 2 Corinthians 12:9; Jude 1; Hebrews 2:11; Jeremiah 23:24; Ephesians 1:23; Isaiah 43:11; John 4:42; Titus 1:4*

## MORNING READING

"He knows the road I take. When he tests me,
I'll come out as pure as gold."

He certainly knows what we are made of. ✦ He does not willingly bring suffering or grief to anyone. ✦ God's people have a solid foundation. These words are engraved on it: "The Lord knows those who belong to him," and "Whoever worships the Lord must give up doing wrong." In a large house there are not only objects made of gold and silver, but also those made of wood and clay. Some objects are honored when they are used; others aren't. Those who stop associating with dishonorable people will be honored. They will be set apart for the master's use, prepared to do good things. ✦ He will act like a refiner and a purifier of silver. He will purify Levi's sons and refine them like gold and silver. Then they will bring acceptable offerings to the Lord. ✦ "I will refine them as silver is refined. . . . They will call on me, and I will answer them. I will say, 'They are my people.' They will reply, 'The Lord is our God.' "

*Job 23:10; Psalm 103:14; Lamentations 3:33;
2 Timothy 2:19–21; Malachi 3:3; Zechariah 13:9*

## EVENING READING

Make your ways known to me, O Lord,
and teach me your paths.

Moses said to the Lord, . . . "If you really are pleased with me, show me your ways so that I can know you and so that you will continue to be pleased with me." . . . The Lord answered, "My presence will go with you, and I will give you peace." ✦ He let Moses know his ways. He let the Israelites know the things he had done. ✦ He leads humble people to do what is right, and he teaches them his way. . . . Who, then, is this person that fears the Lord? He is the one whom the Lord will teach which path to choose. ✦ Trust the Lord with all your heart, and do not rely on your own understanding. In all your ways acknowledge him, and he will make your paths smooth. ✦ You make the path of life known to me. Complete joy is in your presence. Pleasures are by your side forever. ✦ The Lord says, "I will instruct you. I will teach you the way that you should go." ✦ The path of righteous people is like the light of dawn that becomes brighter and brighter until it reaches midday.

*Psalm 25:4; Exodus 33:12–14; Psalm 103:7; Psalm 25:9, 12;
Proverbs 3:5–6; Psalm 16;11; Psalm 32:8; Proverbs 4:18*

## MORNING READING

The spiritual nature produces . . . self-control.

Everyone who enters an athletic contest goes into strict training. They do it to win a temporary crown, but we do it to win one that will be permanent. So I run—but not without a clear goal ahead of me. So I box—but not as if I were just shadow boxing. Rather, I toughen my body with punches and make it my slave so that I will not be disqualified after I have spread the Good News to others. ✦ Don't get drunk on wine, which leads to wild living. Instead, be filled with the Spirit. ✦ "Those who want to come with me must say no to the things they want, pick up their crosses, and follow me." ✦ We must not fall asleep like other people, but we must stay awake and be sober. People who sleep, sleep at night; people who get drunk, get drunk at night. Since we belong to the day, we must be sober. We must put on faith and love as a breastplate and the hope of salvation as a helmet. ✦ It trains us to avoid ungodly lives filled with worldly desires so that we can live self-controlled, moral, and godly lives in this present world. At the same time we can expect what we hope for—the appearance of the glory of our great God and Savior, Jesus Christ.

*Galatians 5:22–23; 1 Corinthians 9:25–27; Ephesians 5:18; Matthew 16:24; 1 Thessalonians 5:6–8; Titus 2:12–13*

## EVENING READING

Grow up completely in our relationship to Christ, who is the head.

"The ground produces grain by itself. First the green blade appears, then the head, then the head full of grain." ✦ Until all of us are united in our faith and in our knowledge about God's Son, until we become mature, until we measure up to Christ, who is the standard. ✦ They measure themselves by themselves and compare themselves to themselves, they show how foolish they are. . . . "Whoever brags should brag about what the Lord has done." It isn't the person who makes his own recommendation who receives approval, but the person whom the Lord recommends. ✦ The body that casts the shadow belongs to Christ. Let no one who delights in false humility and the worship of angels tell you that you don't deserve a prize. Such a person, whose sinful mind fills him with arrogance, gives endless details of the visions he has seen. He doesn't hold on to Christ, the head. Christ makes the whole body grow as God wants it to, through support and unity given by the joints and ligaments. ✦ Grow in the good will and knowledge of our Lord and Savior Jesus Christ.

*Ephesians 4:15; Mark 4:28; Ephesians 4:13; 2 Corinthians 10:12, 17–18; Colossians 2:17–19; 2 Peter 3:18*

## MORNING READING

The goat will take all their sins away to a deserted place.
The man must release the goat in the desert.

As far as the east is from the west—that is how far he has removed our rebellious acts from himself. ✦ "In those days and at that time," declares the Lord, "people will look for Israel's crimes, but they will find none. They will look for Judah's sins, but none will be found. I will forgive the faithful few whom I have spared." ✦ You will throw all our sins into the deep sea. ✦ Who is a God like you? You forgive sin. ✦ We have all strayed like sheep. Each one of us has turned to go his own way, and the Lord has laid all our sins on him. . . . He will carry their sins as a burden. So I will give him a share among the mighty, and he will divide the prize with the strong, because he poured out his life in death and he was counted with sinners. He carried the sins of many. He intercedes for those who are rebellious. ✦ "This is the Lamb of God who takes away the sin of the world."

*Leviticus 16:22; Psalm 103:12; Jeremiah 50:20;*
*Micah 7:19; Micah 7:18; Isaiah 53:6, 11–12; John 1:29*

## EVENING READING

Who says that you are any better than other people?
What do you have that wasn't given to you?

God's kindness made me what I am. ✦ God decided to give us life through the word of truth to make us his most important creatures. ✦ Therefore, God's choice does not depend on a person's desire or effort, but on God's mercy. ✦ So, do we have anything to brag about? Bragging has been eliminated. ✦ Jesus has become our wisdom sent from God, our righteousness, our holiness, and our ransom from sin. As Scripture says, "Whoever brags must brag about what the Lord has done." ✦ You were once dead because of your failures and sins. You followed the ways of this present world and its spiritual ruler. This ruler continues to work in people who refuse to obey God. All of us once lived among these people, and followed the desires of our corrupt nature. We did what our corrupt desires and thoughts wanted us to do. So, because of our nature, we deserved God's anger just like everyone else. ✦ You have been washed and made holy, and you have received God's approval in the name of the Lord Jesus Christ and in the Spirit of our God.

*1 Corinthians 4:7; 1 Corinthians 15:10; James 1:18; Romans 9:16;*
*Romans 3:27; 1 Corinthians 1:30–31; Ephesians 2:1–3; 1 Corinthians 6:11*

## Morning Reading

To the one who loves us and has freed us
from our sins by his blood.

Raging water cannot extinguish love, and rivers will never wash it away. ✦ Love is as overpowering as death. ✦ "The greatest love you can show is to give your life for your friends." ✦ Christ carried our sins in his body on the cross so that freed from our sins, we could live a life that has God's approval. His wounds have healed you. ✦ Through the blood of his Son, we are set free from our sins. God forgives our failures because of his overflowing kindness. ✦ You have been washed and made holy, and you have received God's approval in the name of the Lord Jesus Christ and in the Spirit of our God. ✦ However, you are chosen people, a royal priesthood, a holy nation, people who belong to God. You were chosen to tell about the excellent qualities of God, who called you out of darkness into his marvelous light. ✦ Brothers and sisters, in view of all we have just shared about God's compassion, I encourage you to offer your bodies as living sacrifices, dedicated to God and pleasing to him. This kind of worship is appropriate for you.

*Revelation 1:5; Song of Songs 8:7; Song of Songs 8:6; John 15:13; 1 Peter 2:24; Ephesians 1:7; 1 Corinthians 6:11; 1 Peter 2:9; Romans 12:1*

## Evening Reading

There are different ways of serving,
and yet the same Lord is served.

These were all the commanders in charge of King David's property: for the royal treasuries Azmaveth, son of Adiel; for the goods in the fields, cities, villages, and watchtowers Jonathan, son of Uzziah; for the farm workers in the fields Ezri, son of Chelub; for the vineyards Shimei from Ramah; . . . for the flocks Jaziz of Hagar. ✦ In the church God has appointed first apostles, next prophets, third teachers, then those who perform miracles, then those who have the gift of healing, then those who help others, those who are managers, and those who can speak in a number of languages. ✦ There is only one Spirit who does all these things by giving what God wants to give to each person. ✦ Each of you as a good manager must use the gift that God has given you to serve others. Whoever speaks must speak God's words. Whoever serves must serve with the strength God supplies so that in every way God receives glory through Jesus Christ. Glory and power belong to Jesus Christ forever and ever!

*1 Corinthians 12:5; 1 Chronicles 27:25–27, 31; 1 Corinthians 12:28; 1 Corinthians 12:11; 1 Peter 4:10–11*

## MORNING READING

[Moses'] face was shining from speaking with the LORD,
but he didn't know it.

Don't give glory to us, O LORD. Don't give glory to us. Instead, give glory to your name. ✦ "Lord, when did we see you hungry and feed you or see you thirsty and give you something to drink?" ✦ Humbly think of others as being better than yourselves. ✦ Serve each other with humility. ✦ Jesus' appearance changed in front of them. His face became as bright as the sun and his clothes as white as light. ✦ Everyone who sat in the council stared at [Stephen] and saw that his face looked like an angel's face. ✦ "I have given them the glory that you gave me." ✦ As all of us reflect the Lord's glory with faces that are not covered with veils, we are being changed into his image with ever-increasing glory. This comes from the Lord, who is the Spirit. ✦ "You are light for the world. A city cannot be hidden when it is located on a hill. No one lights a lamp and puts it under a basket. Instead, everyone who lights a lamp puts it on a lamp stand. Then its light shines on everyone in the house."

*Exodus 34:29; Psalm 115:1; Matthew 25:37; Philippians 2:3; 1 Peter 5:5; Matthew 17:2; Acts 6:15; John 17:22; 2 Corinthians 3:18; Matthew 5:14–15*

## EVENING READING

There are different types of work to do,
but the same God produces every gift in every person.

Some men from Manasseh had deserted Saul's army to join David. . . . They helped David fight raiding parties because they were all warriors, commanders in the army. ✦ The evidence of the Spirit's presence is given to each person for the common good of everyone. ✦ From Issachar's descendants there were 200 leaders who understood the times and knew what Israel should do. ✦ The Spirit gives one person the ability to speak with wisdom. The same Spirit gives another person the ability to speak with knowledge. ✦ From Zebulun there were 50,000 experienced soldiers. They were equipped for battle with every kind of weapon. Their loyalty was unquestioned. ✦ A person who has doubts is thinking about two different things at the same time and can't make up his mind about anything. ✦ The body should not be divided but rather that all of its parts should feel the same concern for each other. If one part of the body suffers, all the other parts share its suffering. If one part is praised, all the others share in its happiness. ✦ There is one Lord, one faith, one baptism.

*1 Corinthians 12:6; 1 Chronicles 12:19, 21; 1 Corinthians 12:7; 1 Chronicles 12:32; 1 Corinthians 12:8; 1 Chronicles 12:33; James 1:8; 1 Corinthians 12:25–26; Ephesians 4:5*

## MORNING READING

"Call on me in times of trouble.
I will rescue you, and you will honor me."

Why are you discouraged, my soul? Why are you so restless? Put your hope in God, because I will still praise him. He is my savior and my God. ✦ You have heard the desire of oppressed people, O LORD. You encourage them. You pay close attention to them. ✦ You, O Lord, are good and forgiving, full of mercy toward everyone who calls out to you. ✦ Jacob said to his family, . . . "Let's go to Bethel. I will make an altar there to God, who answered me when I was troubled and who has been with me wherever I've gone." ✦ Praise the LORD, my soul, and never forget all the good he has done. ✦ I love the LORD because he hears my voice, my pleas for mercy. I will call on him as long as I live because he turns his ear toward me. The ropes of death became tangled around me. The horrors of the grave took hold of me. I experienced pain and agony. But I kept calling on the name of the LORD.

*Psalm 50:15; Psalm 42:11; Psalm 10:17; Psalm 86:5;
Genesis 35:2–3; Psalm 103:2; Psalm 116:1–4*

## EVENING READING

"Yet, the one who is coming will come soon.
He will not delay."

"Write the vision. Make it clear on tablets so that anyone can read it quickly. The vision will still happen at the appointed time. It hurries toward its goal. It won't be a lie. If it's delayed, wait for it. It will certainly happen. It won't be late." ✦ Dear friends, don't ignore this fact: One day with the Lord is like a thousand years, and a thousand years are like one day. The Lord isn't slow to do what he promised, as some people think. Rather, he is patient for your sake. He doesn't want to destroy anyone but wants all people to have an opportunity to turn to him and change the way they think and act. ✦ You, O Lord, are a compassionate and merciful God. You are patient, always faithful and ready to forgive. ✦ If only you would split open the heavens and come down! . . . No one has ever heard, no one has paid attention, and no one has seen any god except you. You help those who wait for you.

*Hebrews 10:37; Habakkuk 2:2–3; 2 Peter 3:8–9; Psalm 86:15; Isaiah 64:1, 4*

## Morning Reading

"The Lord our God, the Almighty, has become king."

"I know that you can do everything." ✦ "The things that are impossible for people to do are possible for God to do." ✦ Everyone who lives on earth is nothing compared to him. He does whatever he wishes with the army of heaven and with those who live on earth. There is no one who can oppose him or ask him, "What are you doing?" ✦ "No one can rescue people from my power. When I do something, who can undo it?" ✦ "Abba! Father! You can do anything." ✦ [Jesus] said to [the blind men], "Do you believe that I can do this?" "Yes, Lord," they answered. He touched their eyes and said, "What you have believed will be done for you!" ✦ A man with a serious skin disease came and bowed down in front of him. The man said to Jesus, "Sir, if you're willing, you can make me clean." Jesus reached out, touched him, and said, "I'm willing. So be clean!" ✦ Mighty God. ✦ "All authority in heaven and on earth has been given to me." ✦ Some rely on chariots and others on horses, but we will boast in the name of the Lord our God. ✦ Be strong and courageous. Don't be frightened or terrified. . . . Someone greater is on our side.

*Revelation 19:6; Job 42:2; Luke 18:27; Daniel 4:35; Isaiah 43:13; Mark 14:36; Matthew 9:28–29; Matthew 8:2–3; Isaiah 9:6; Matthew 28:18; Psalm 20:7; 2 Chronicles 32:7*

## Evening Reading

"What did the Lord tell you?"

You mortals, the Lord has told you what is good. This is what the Lord requires from you: to do what is right, to love mercy, and to live humbly with your God. ✦ The Lord wants you to obey his commands and laws that I'm giving you today for your own good. ✦ Certainly, there is a curse on all who rely on their own efforts to live according to a set of standards because Scripture says, "Whoever doesn't obey everything that is written in Moses' Teachings is cursed." No one receives God's approval by obeying the law's standards since, "The person who has God's approval will live by faith." . . . [The laws] were added to identify what wrongdoing is. Moses' laws did this until the descendant to whom the promise was given came. ✦ In the past God spoke to our ancestors at many different times and in many different ways through the prophets. In these last days he has spoken to us through his Son. ✦ "Speak, Lord. I'm listening."

*1 Samuel 3:17; Micah 6:8; Deuteronomy 10:13; Galatians 3:10–11, 19; Hebrews 1:1–2; 1 Samuel 3:9*

## MORNING READING

He leads humble people to do what is right,
and he teaches them his way.

"Blessed are those who are gentle." ✦ I saw something else under the sun. The race isn't won by fast runners, or the battle by heroes. Wise people don't necessarily have food. Intelligent people don't necessarily have riches, and skilled people don't necessarily receive special treatment. ✦ A person may plan his own journey, but the LORD directs his steps. ✦ I look up to you, to the one who sits enthroned in heaven. As servants depend on their masters, as a maid depends on her mistress, so we depend on the LORD our God. ✦ Let me know the way that I should go, because I long for you. ✦ You're our God. Won't you judge them? We don't have the strength to face this large crowd that is attacking us. We don't know what to do, so we're looking to you. ✦ If any of you needs wisdom to know what you should do, you should ask God, and he will give it to you. God is generous to everyone and doesn't find fault with them. ✦ "When the Spirit of Truth comes, he will guide you into the full truth."

*Psalm 25:9; Matthew 5:5; Ecclesiastes 9:11; Proverbs 16:9; Psalm 123:1–2; Psalm 143:8; 2 Chronicles 20:12; James 1:5; John 16:13*

## EVENING READING

Almighty LORD, . . .
with your blessing my house will be blessed forever.

You, LORD, have blessed it. It will be blessed forever. ✦ It is the LORD's blessing that makes a person rich, and hard work adds nothing to it. ✦ We should remember the words that the Lord Jesus said, "Giving gifts is more satisfying than receiving them." ✦ "When you give a banquet, invite the poor, the handicapped, the lame, and the blind. Then you will be blessed because they don't have any way to pay you back. You will be paid back when those who have God's approval come back to life." ✦ "Come, my Father has blessed you! Inherit the kingdom prepared for you from the creation of the world. I was hungry, and you gave me something to eat. I was thirsty, and you gave me something to drink. I was a stranger, and you took me into your home. I needed clothes, and you gave me something to wear. I was sick, and you took care of me. I was in prison, and you visited me." ✦ Blessed is the one who has concern for helpless people. The LORD will rescue him in times of trouble. ✦ The LORD God is a sun and shield.

*2 Samuel 7:29; 1 Chronicles 17:27; Proverbs 10:22; Acts 20:35; Luke 14:13–14; Matthew 25:34–36; Psalm 41:1; Psalm 84:11*

## Morning Reading

I will not be afraid. What can mortals do to me?

What will separate us from the love Christ has for us? Can trouble, distress, persecution, hunger, nakedness, danger, or violent death separate us from his love? . . . The one who loves us gives us an overwhelming victory in all these difficulties. ✦ "You don't need to be afraid of those who kill the body. After that they can't do anything more. I'll show you the one you should be afraid of. Be afraid of the one who has the power to throw you into hell after killing you. I'm warning you to be afraid of him." ✦ "Blessed are those who are persecuted for doing what God approves of. The kingdom of heaven belongs to them. Blessed are you when people insult you, persecute you, lie, and say all kinds of evil things about you because of me. Rejoice and be glad because you have a great reward in heaven!" ✦ But I don't place any value on my own life. I want to finish the race I'm running. ✦ I will speak about your written instructions in the presence of kings and not feel ashamed.

*Hebrews 13:6; Romans 8:35, 37; Luke 12:4–5; Matthew 5:10–12; Acts 20:24; Psalm 119:46*

## Evening Reading

He set my feet on a rock.

That rock was Christ. ✦ Simon Peter answered, "You are the Messiah, the Son of the living God!" . . . "You are Peter, and I can guarantee that on this rock I will build my church. And the gates of hell will not overpower it." ✦ No one else can save us. Indeed, we can be saved only by the power of the one named Jesus and not by any other person. ✦ We must continue to come to him with a sincere heart and strong faith. We must continue to hold firmly to our declaration of faith. ✦ When you ask for something, don't have any doubts. A person who has doubts is like a wave that is blown by the wind and tossed by the sea. ✦ What will separate us from the love Christ has for us? Can trouble, distress, persecution, hunger, nakedness, danger, or violent death separate us from his love? . . . The one who loves us gives us an overwhelming victory in all these difficulties. . . . We can't be separated [from the love of God] by death or life, by angels or rulers, by anything in the present or anything in the future, by forces or powers in the world above or in the world below, or by anything else in creation.

*Psalm 40:2; 1 Corinthians 10:4; Matthew 16:16, 18; Acts 4:12; Hebrews 10:22–23; James 1:6; Romans 8:35, 37, 39*

## MORNING READING

But you are a forgiving God,
one who is compassionate [and] merciful.

The Lord isn't slow to do what he promised, as some people think. Rather, he is patient for your sake. He doesn't want to destroy anyone but wants all people to have an opportunity to turn to him and change the way they think and act. . . . Think of our Lord's patience as an opportunity for us to be saved. ✦ I was treated with mercy so that Christ Jesus could use me, the foremost sinner, to demonstrate his patience. This patience serves as an example for those who would believe in him and live forever. ✦ Everything written long ago was written to teach us so that we would have confidence through the endurance and encouragement which the Scriptures give us. ✦ Do you have contempt for God, who is very kind to you, puts up with you, and deals patiently with you? Don't you realize that it is God's kindness that is trying to lead you to him and change the way you think and act? ✦ Tear your hearts, not your clothes. Return to the Lord your God. He is merciful and compassionate, patient, and always ready to forgive and to change his plans about disaster.

*Nehemiah 9:17; 2 Peter 3:9, 15; 1 Timothy 1:16;
Romans 15:4; Romans 2:4; Joel 2:13*

## EVENING READING

The promises of the Lord are pure.

Your promise has been thoroughly tested, and I love it. ✦ The instructions of the Lord are correct. They make the heart rejoice. The command of the Lord is radiant. It makes the eyes shine. ✦ "Every word of God has proven to be true. He is a shield to those who come to him for protection. Do not add to his words, or he will reprimand you, and you will be found to be a liar." ✦ I have treasured your promise in my heart so that I may not sin against you. I want to reflect on your guiding principles and study your ways. ✦ Finally, brothers and sisters, keep your thoughts on whatever is right or deserves praise: things that are true, honorable, fair, pure, acceptable, or commendable. ✦ Desire God's pure word as newborn babies desire milk. Then you will grow in your salvation. ✦ We don't go around selling an impure word of God like many others. The opposite is true. As Christ's spokesmen and in God's presence, we speak the pure message that comes from God. ✦ We don't distort God's word.

*Psalm 12:6; Psalm 119:140; Psalm 19:8; Proverbs 30:5–6; Psalm 119:11, 15;
Philippians 4:8; 1 Peter 2:2; 2 Corinthians 2:17; 2 Corinthians 4:2*

## MORNING READING

All the family in heaven and on earth.

One God and Father of all, who is over everything, through everything, and in everything. ✦ You are all God's children by believing in Christ Jesus. ✦ He planned to bring all of history to its goal in Christ. Then Christ would be the head of everything in heaven and on earth. ✦ Jesus isn't ashamed to call them brothers and sisters. ✦ Pointing with his hand at his disciples, [Jesus] said, "Look, here are my mother and my brothers. Whoever does what my Father in heaven wants is my brother and sister and mother." ✦ "Go to my brothers and sisters and tell them, 'I am going to my Father and your Father, to my God and your God.' " ✦ I saw under the altar the souls of those who had been slaughtered because of God's word and the testimony they had given about him. . . . Each of the souls was given a white robe. They were told to rest a little longer until all their coworkers, the other Christians, would be killed as they had been killed. ✦ God planned to give us something very special so that we would gain eternal life with them.

*Ephesians 3:15; Ephesians 4:6; Galatians 3:26; Ephesians 1:10; Hebrews 2:11; Matthew 12:49–50; John 20:17; Revelation 6:9, 11; Hebrews 11:40*

## EVENING READING

"This is how you should pray:
Our Father in heaven, let your name be kept holy."

Jesus looked up to heaven and said, "Father." ✦ "My Father and your Father, to my God and your God." ✦ You are all God's children by believing in Christ Jesus. ✦ You haven't received the spirit of slaves that leads you into fear again. Instead, you have received the spirit of God's adopted children by which we call out, "Abba! Father!" The Spirit himself testifies with our spirit that we are God's children. ✦ Because you are God's children, God has sent the Spirit of his Son into us to call out, "Abba! Father!" So you are no longer slaves but God's children. ✦ "When that day comes, you won't ask me any more questions. I can guarantee this truth: If you ask the Father for anything in my name, he will give it to you. So far you haven't asked for anything in my name. Ask and you will receive so that you can be completely happy." ✦ I will welcome you." The Lord Almighty says, "I will be your Father, and you will be my sons and daughters.

*Matthew 6:9; John 17:1; John 20:17; Galatians 3:26; Romans 8:15–16; Galatians 4:6–7; John 16:23–24; 2 Corinthians 6:17–18*

## Morning Reading

Do not be so far away from me. Trouble is near.

How long, O Lord? Will you forget me forever? How long will you hide your face from me? How long must I make decisions alone with sorrow in my heart day after day? ✦ Do not hide your face from me. Do not angrily turn me away. You have been my help. Do not leave me! Do not abandon me, O God, my savior! ✦ When you call to me, I will answer you. I will be with you when you are in trouble. I will save you and honor you. ✦ The Lord is near to everyone who prays to him, to every faithful person who prays to him. He fills the needs of those who fear him. He hears their cries for help and saves them. ✦ "I will not leave you all alone. I will come back to you." ✦ "I am always with you until the end of time." ✦ God is our refuge and strength, an ever-present help in times of trouble. ✦ My soul waits calmly for God alone. My salvation comes from him. . . . Wait calmly for God alone, my soul, because my hope comes from him.

*Psalm 22:11; Psalm 13:1–2; Psalm 27:9; Psalm 91:15; Psalm 145:18–19; John 14:18; Matthew 28:20; Psalm 46:1; Psalm 62:1, 5*

## Evening Reading

"Let your name be kept holy."

(Never worship any other god, because the Lord is a God who does not tolerate rivals. In fact, he is known for not tolerating rivals.) ✦ "Who is like you among the gods, O Lord? Who is like you? You are glorious because of your holiness and awe-inspiring because of your splendor. You perform miracles." ✦ "Holy, holy, holy is the Lord God Almighty." ✦ Worship the Lord in his holy splendor. ✦ I saw the Lord sitting on a high and lofty throne. The bottom of his robe filled the temple. Angels were standing above him. Each had six wings: With two they covered their faces, with two they covered their feet, and with two they flew. They called to each other and said, "Holy, holy, holy is the Lord of Armies! The whole earth is filled with his glory." . . . "Oh, no! I'm doomed. Every word that passes through my lips is sinful." ✦ "I had heard about you with my own ears, but now I have seen you with my own eyes. That is why I take back what I said, and I sit in dust and ashes to show that I am sorry." ✦ The blood of his Son Jesus cleanses us from every sin. ✦ That we can become holy like him. ✦ We can now confidently go into the holy place. . . . So we must continue to come to him with a sincere heart and strong faith.

*Matthew 6:9; Exodus 34:14; Exodus 15:11; Revelation 4:8; 1 Chronicles 16:29; Isaiah 6:1–3, 5; Job 42:5–6; 1 John 1:7; Hebrews 12:10; Hebrews 10:19, 22*

## MORNING READING

God was using Christ to restore his relationship with humanity. He didn't hold people's faults against them.

God was pleased to have all of himself live in Christ. God was also pleased to bring everything on earth and in heaven back to himself through Christ. He did this by making peace through Christ's blood sacrificed on the cross. ✦ Mercy and truth have met. Righteousness and peace have kissed. ✦ I know the plans that I have for you, declares the Lord. They are plans for peace and not disaster. ✦ "Come on now, let's discuss this!" says the Lord. "Though your sins are bright red, they will become as white as snow. Though they are dark red, they will become as white as wool." ✦ Who is a God like you? You forgive sin. ✦ "Be in harmony and at peace with God." ✦ Work out your salvation with fear and trembling. It is God who produces in you the desires and actions that please him. ✦ O Lord, you will establish peace for us, since you have done everything for us.

*2 Corinthians 5:19; Colossians 1:19–20; Psalm 85:10; Jeremiah 29:11; Isaiah 1:18; Micah 7:18; Job 22:21; Philippians 2:12–13; Isaiah 26:12*

## EVENING READING

"Let your kingdom come."

"At the time of those kings, the God of heaven will establish a kingdom that will never be destroyed. No other people will be permitted to rule it. It will smash all the other kingdoms and put an end to them. But it will be established forever." ✦ "A stone was cut out, but not by humans." ✦ You won't succeed by might or by power, but by my Spirit, says the Lord of Armies. ✦ "People can't observe the coming of the kingdom of God. They can't say, 'Here it is!' or 'There it is!' You see, the kingdom of God is within you." ✦ "The mystery about the kingdom of God has been given directly to you." ✦ "The kingdom of God is like a man who scatters seeds on the ground. He sleeps at night and is awake during the day. The seeds sprout and grow, although the man doesn't know how. . . . As soon as the grain is ready, he cuts it with a sickle, because harvest time has come." ✦ "You, too, must be ready because the Son of Man will return when you least expect him." ✦ The Spirit and the bride say, "Come!" Let those who hear this say, "Come!"

*Matthew 6:10; Daniel 2:44; Daniel 2:34; Zechariah 4:6; Luke 17:20–21; Mark 4:11; Mark 4:26–27, 29; Matthew 24:44; Revelation 22:17*

## Morning Reading

God has heard everything that you said
ever since the first day you decided to humble yourself
in front of your God so that you could learn to understand things.

The High and Lofty One lives forever, and his name is holy. This is what he says: I live in a high and holy place. But I am with those who are crushed and humble. I will renew the spirit of those who are humble and the courage of those who are crushed. ✦ The sacrifice pleasing to God is a broken spirit. O God, you do not despise a broken and sorrowful heart. ✦ Even though the Lord is high above, he sees humble people close up, and he recognizes arrogant people from a distance. ✦ Be humbled by God's power so that when the right time comes he will honor you. ✦ Scripture says, "God opposes arrogant people, but he is kind to humble people." So place yourselves under God's authority. ✦ You, O Lord, are good and forgiving, full of mercy toward everyone who calls out to you. Open your ears to my prayer, O Lord. Pay attention when I plead for mercy. When I am in trouble, I call out to you because you answer me.

*Daniel 10:12; Isaiah 57:15; Psalm 51:17; Psalm 138:6; 1 Peter 5:6; James 4:6–7; Psalm 86:5–7*

## Evening Reading

"Let your will be done on earth as it is done in heaven."

Understand what the Lord wants. ✦ "Your Father in heaven does not want one of these little ones to be lost." ✦ It is God's will that you keep away from sexual sin as a mark of your devotion to him. ✦ That way you won't be guided by sinful human desires as you live the rest of your lives on earth. Instead, you will be guided by what God wants you to do. ✦ God decided to give us life through the word of truth. . . . So get rid of all immoral behavior. ✦ "Be holy, because I am holy." ✦ [Jesus said,] "Whoever does what God wants is my brother and sister and mother." ✦ "Everyone who hears what I say and obeys it will be like a wise person who built a house on rock. Rain poured, and floods came. Winds blew and beat against that house. But it did not collapse, because its foundation was on rock." ✦ The world and its evil desires are passing away. But the person who does what God wants lives forever.

*Matthew 6:10; Ephesians 5:17; Matthew 18:14; 1 Thessalonians 4:3; 1 Peter 4:2; James 1:18, 21; 1 Peter 1:16; Mark 3:34–35; Matthew 7:24–25; 1 John 2:17*

## MORNING READING

Christ died and came back to life so that
he would be the Lord of both the living and the dead.

Yet, it was the Lord's will to crush him with suffering. When the Lord has made his life a sacrifice for our wrongdoings, he will see his descendants for many days. The will of the Lord will succeed through him. He will see and be satisfied because of his suffering. My righteous servant will acquit many people because of what he has learned through suffering. He will carry their sins as a burden. ✦ "Didn't the Messiah have to suffer these things and enter into his glory?" ✦ We are convinced of the fact that one man has died for all people. Therefore, all people have died. He died for all people so that those who live should no longer live for themselves but for the man who died and was brought back to life for them. ✦ "All the people of Israel should know beyond a doubt that God made Jesus, whom you crucified, both Lord and Christ." ✦ He is the lamb who was known long ago before the world existed, but for your good he became publicly known in the last period of time. Through him you believe in God.

*Romans 14:9; Isaiah 53:10–11; Luke 24:26;*
*2 Corinthians 5:14–15; Acts 2:36; 1 Peter 1:20–21*

## EVENING READING

"Give us our daily bread today."

I have been young, and now I am old, but I have never seen a righteous person abandoned or his descendants begging for food. ✦ He will have plenty of food and a dependable supply of water. ✦ Ravens brought [Elijah] bread and meat in the morning and in the evening. And he drank from the stream. ✦ My God will richly fill your every need in a glorious way through Christ Jesus. ✦ Be happy with what you have because God has said, "I will never abandon you or leave you." ✦ He made you suffer from hunger and then fed you with manna . . . to teach you that a person cannot live on bread alone but on every word that the Lord speaks. ✦ "I can guarantee this truth: Moses didn't give you bread from heaven, but my Father gives you the true bread from heaven. God's bread is the man who comes from heaven and gives life to the world." They said to him, "Sir, give us this bread all the time."

*Matthew 6:11; Psalm 37:25; Isaiah 33:16; 1 Kings 17:6;*
*Philippians 4:19; Hebrews 13:5; Deuteronomy 8:3; John 6:32–34*

## MORNING READING

God is my stronghold.

The LORD is my rock and my fortress and my Savior, my God, my rock in whom I take refuge, my shield, the strength of my salvation, my stronghold, my refuge, and my Savior. ✦ The LORD is my strength and my shield. My heart trusted him, so I received help. My heart is triumphant; give thanks to him with my song. ✦ Those in the east will fear his glory. He will come like a rushing stream. ✦ "The Lord is my helper. I will not be afraid. What can mortals do to me?" ✦ The LORD is my light and my salvation. Who is there to fear? The LORD is my life's fortress. Who is there to be afraid of? ✦ As the mountains surround Jerusalem, so the LORD surrounds his people now and forever. ✦ You have been my help. In the shadow of your wings, I sing joyfully. ✦ For the sake of your name, lead me and guide me.

*Psalm 59:9; 2 Samuel 22:2–3; Psalm 28:7; Isaiah 59:19; Hebrews 13:6; Psalm 27:1; Psalm 125:2; Psalm 63:7; Psalm 31:3*

## EVENING READING

"Forgive us as we forgive others."

Then Peter came to Jesus and asked him, "Lord, how often do I have to forgive a believer who wrongs me? Seven times?" Jesus answered him, "I tell you, not just seven times, but seventy times seven." ✦ "Then his master sent for him and said to him, 'You evil servant! I canceled your entire debt, because you begged me. Shouldn't you have treated the other servant as mercifully as I treated you?' His master was so angry that he handed him over to the torturers until he would repay everything that he owed. That is what my Father in heaven will do to you if each of you does not sincerely forgive other believers." ✦ Be kind to each other, sympathetic, forgiving each other as God has forgiven you through Christ. ✦ God made you alive with Christ when he forgave all our failures. He did this by erasing the charges that were brought against us by the written laws God had established. He took the charges away by nailing them to the cross. ✦ Forgive as the Lord forgave you.

*Matthew 6:12; Matthew 18:21–22; Matthew 18:32–35; Ephesians 4:32; Colossians 2:13–14; Colossians 3:13*

## Morning Reading

Don't be lazy in showing your devotion.
Use your energy to serve the Lord.

Whatever presents itself for you to do, do it with all your might, because there is no work, planning, knowledge, or skill in the grave where you're going. ✦ Whatever you do, do it wholeheartedly as though you were working for your real master and not merely for humans. You know that your real master will give you an inheritance as your reward. It is Christ, your real master, whom you are serving. ✦ You know that your heavenly master will reward all of us for whatever good we do. ✦ "We must do what the one who sent me wants us to do while it is day. The night when no one can do anything is coming." ✦ "Didn't you realize that I had to be in my Father's house?" ✦ "Devotion for your house will consume me." ✦ Brothers and sisters, use more effort to make God's calling and choosing of you secure. If you keep doing this, you will never fall away. ✦ We want each of you to prove that you're working hard so that you will remain confident until the end. Then, instead of being lazy, you will imitate those who are receiving the promises through faith and patience. ✦ Run . . . so that you can win [the prize].

*Romans 12:11; Ecclesiastes 9:10; Colossians 3:23–24; Ephesians 6:8; John 9:4; Luke 2:49; John 2:17; 2 Peter 1:10; Hebrews 6:11–12; 1 Corinthians 9:24*

## Evening Reading

"Don't allow us to be tempted.
Instead, rescue us from the evil one."

Whoever trusts his own heart is a fool. Whoever walks in wisdom will survive. ✦ When someone is tempted, he shouldn't say that God is tempting him. God can't be tempted by evil, and God doesn't tempt anyone. Everyone is tempted by his own desires as they lure him away and trap him. ✦ The Lord says, "Get away from unbelievers. Separate yourselves from them. Have nothing to do with anything unclean. Then I will welcome you." ✦ Lot . . . saw that the whole Jordan Plain was well-watered like the Lord's garden. . . . Lot chose the whole Jordan Plain for himself. . . . (The people who lived in Sodom were very wicked. They committed terrible sins against the Lord.) ✦ God rescued Lot, a man who had his approval. Lot was distressed by the lifestyle of people who had no principles and lived in sexual freedom. . . . [The Lord] knows how to rescue godly people when they are tested. ✦ The servant will be successful because the Lord makes him successful.

*Matthew 6:13; Proverbs 28:26; James 1:13–14; 2 Corinthians 6:17; Genesis 13:10–11, 13; 2 Peter 2:7, 9; Romans 14:4*

## MORNING READING

They find joy in your name all day long.
They are joyful in your righteousness.

"Certainly, righteousness and strength are found in the LORD alone." All who are angry with him will come to him and be ashamed. All the descendants of Israel will be declared righteous, and they will praise the LORD. ✦ Be glad and find joy in the LORD, you righteous people. Sing with joy, all whose motives are decent. ✦ Now, the way to receive God's approval has been made plain in a way other than Moses' Teachings. Moses' Teachings and the Prophets tell us this. Everyone who believes has God's approval through faith in Jesus Christ. . . . He waited so that he could display his approval at the present time. This shows that he is a God of justice, a God who approves of people who believe in Jesus. ✦ Always be joyful in the Lord! I'll say it again: Be joyful! ✦ Although you have never seen Christ, you love him. You don't see him now, but you believe in him. You are extremely happy with joy and praise that can hardly be expressed in words.

*Psalm 89:16; Isaiah 45:24–25; Psalm 32:11;
Romans 3:21–22, 26; Philippians 4:4; 1 Peter 1:8*

## EVENING READING

Glory and power forever and ever belong to the one who loves us
. . . and has made us a kingdom, priests for God his Father.

The LORD rules as king! He is clothed with majesty. . . . Your throne was set in place a long time ago. You are eternal. ✦ The LORD . . . has great strength. ✦ If God is for us, who can be against us? ✦ Our God, whom we honor, can save us. ✦ "My Father, who gave them to me, is greater than everyone else, and no one can tear them away from my Father." ✦ The one who is in you is greater than the one who is in the world. ✦ Don't give glory to us, O LORD. Don't give glory to us. Instead, give glory to your name ✦ "Greatness, power, splendor, glory, and majesty are yours, LORD, because everything in heaven and on earth is yours. The kingdom is yours, LORD, and you are honored as head of all things. . . . Our God, we thank you and praise your wonderful name. But who am I and who are my people that you enable us to give so generously? Everything comes from you. We give you only what has come from your hands."

*Revelation 1:5–6; Psalm 93:1–2; Nahum 1:3; Romans 8:31; Daniel 3:17;
John 10:29; 1 John 4:4; Psalm 115:1; 1 Chronicles 29:11, 13–14*

## MORNING READING

One of the soldiers stabbed Jesus' side with his spear, and blood and water immediately came out.

"Here is the blood which seals the promise that the Lord has made to you." ✦ "Blood contains life. I have given this blood to you to make peace with me on the altar." ✦ The blood of bulls and goats cannot take away sins. ✦ [Jesus] said to them, "This is my blood, the blood of the promise. It is poured out for many people." ✦ He used his own blood, not the blood of goats and bulls, for the sacrifice. He went into the most holy place and offered this sacrifice once and for all to free us forever. ✦ Making peace through Christ's blood sacrificed on the cross. ✦ Realize that you weren't set free from the worthless life handed down to you from your ancestors by a payment of silver or gold . . . Rather, the payment that freed you was the precious blood of Christ, the lamb with no defects or imperfections, . . . publicly known in the last period of time. ✦ I will sprinkle clean water on you and make you clean instead of unclean. Then I will cleanse you from all your idols. ✦ We have been sprinkled with his blood to free us from a guilty conscience, and our bodies have been washed with clean water. So we must continue to come to him with a sincere heart and strong faith.

*John 19:34; Exodus 24:8; Leviticus 17:11; Hebrews 10:4; Mark 14:24; Hebrews 9:12; Colossians 1:20; 1 Peter 1:18–20; Ezekiel 36:25; Hebrews 10:22*

## EVENING READING

Amen.

"So be it! . . . The Lord your God says so too." ✦ Whoever asks for a blessing in the land will be blessed by the God of Truth. Whoever swears an oath in the land will swear by the God of Truth. Past troubles are forgotten. They are hidden from my eyes. ✦ God made a promise to Abraham. Since he had no one greater on whom to base his oath, he based it on himself. . . . When people take oaths, they base their oaths on someone greater than themselves. Their oaths guarantee what they say and end all arguments. God wouldn't change his plan. He wanted to make this perfectly clear to those who would receive his promise, so he took an oath. God did this so that we would be encouraged. . . . Those of us who have taken refuge in him hold on to the confidence we have been given. ✦ The amen, the witness who is faithful and true. ✦ Certainly, Christ made God's many promises come true. For that reason, because of our message, people also honor God by saying, "Amen!" ✦ Thank the Lord God, the God of Israel, who alone does miracles. Thanks be to his glorious name forever. Amen and amen!

*Romans 15:33; 1 Kings 1:36; Isaiah 65:16; Hebrews 6:13, 16–18; Revelation 3:14; 2 Corinthians 1:20; Psalm 72:18–19*

## Morning Reading

The Lord will be your confidence.
He will keep your foot from getting caught.

Even angry mortals will praise you. You will wear the remainder of their anger. ✦ The king's heart is like streams of water. Both are under the Lord's control. He turns them in any direction he chooses. ✦ When a person's ways are pleasing to the Lord, he makes even his enemies to be at peace with him. ✦ I wait for the Lord, my soul waits, and with hope I wait for his word. My soul waits for the Lord more than those who watch for the morning, more than those who watch for the morning. ✦ I went to the Lord for help. He answered me and rescued me from all my fears. ✦ The eternal God is your shelter, and his everlasting arms support you. He will force your enemies out of your way and tell you to destroy them. ✦ Blessed is the person who trusts the Lord. The Lord will be his confidence. ✦ What can we say about all of this? If God is for us, who can be against us?

*Proverbs 3:26; Psalm 76:10; Proverbs 21:1; Proverbs 16:7; Psalm 130:5–6; Psalm 34:4; Deuteronomy 33:27; Jeremiah 17:7; Romans 8:31*

## Evening Reading

Encouragement . . . comfort from love . . . spiritual relationships.

"A person who is born of a woman is short-lived and is full of trouble. He comes up like a flower; then he withers. He is like a fleeting shadow; he doesn't stay long." ✦ My body and mind may waste away, but God remains the foundation of my life and my inheritance forever. ✦ "I will ask the Father, and he will give you another helper who will be with you forever . . . the Holy Spirit, whom the Father will send in my name." ✦ Praise the God and Father of our Lord Jesus Christ! He is the Father who is compassionate and the God who gives comfort. He comforts us whenever we suffer. That is why whenever other people suffer, we are able to comfort them by using the same comfort we have received from God. ✦ We believe that Jesus died and came back to life. We also believe that, through Jesus, God will bring back those who have died. . . . In this way we will always be with the Lord. So then, comfort each other with these words!

*Philippians 2:1; Job 14:1–2; Psalm 73:26; John 14:16, 26; 2 Corinthians 1:3–4; 1 Thessalonians 4:14, 17–18*

## MORNING READING

I take pleasure in God's standards in my inner being.

Oh, how I love your teachings! They are in my thoughts all day long. ✦ Your words were found, and I devoured them. Your words are my joy and my heart's delight. ✦ I want to sit in his shadow. His fruit tastes sweet to me. ✦ I have not left his commands behind. I have treasured his words in my heart. ✦ I am happy to do your will, O my God. Your teachings are deep within me. ✦ "My food is to do what the one who sent me wants me to do and to finish the work he has given me." ✦ The instructions of the LORD are correct. They make the heart rejoice. The command of the LORD is radiant. It makes the eyes shine. . . . They are more desirable than gold, even the finest gold. They are sweeter than honey, even the drippings from a honeycomb. ✦ Do what God's word says. Don't merely listen to it, or you will fool yourselves. If someone listens to God's word but doesn't do what it says, he is like a person who looks at his face in a mirror, studies his features, goes away, and immediately forgets what he looks like.

*Romans 7:22; Psalm 119:97; Jeremiah 15:16; Song of Songs 2:3; Job 23:12; Psalm 40:8; John 4:34; Psalm 19:8, 10; James 1:22–24*

## EVENING READING

May the LORD your God accept you.

What should I bring when I come into the LORD's presence, when I bow in front of the God of heaven? Should I bring him year-old calves as burnt offerings? Will the LORD be pleased with thousands of rams or with endless streams of olive oil? Should I give him my firstborn child because of my rebellious acts? Should I give him my young child for my sin? You mortals, the LORD has told you what is good. This is what the LORD requires from you: to do what is right, to love mercy, and to live humbly with your God. ✦ We've all become unclean, and all our righteous acts are like permanently stained rags. ✦ Not one person has God's approval. . . . Because all people have sinned, they have fallen short of God's glory. They receive God's approval freely by an act of his kindness through the price Christ Jesus paid to set us free from sin. God showed that Christ is the throne of mercy where God's approval is given through faith in Christ's blood. In his patience God waited to deal with sins committed in the past. He waited so that he could display his approval at the present time. This shows that he is a God of justice, a God who approves of people who believe in Jesus. ✦ The kindness he had given us in his dear Son. ✦ God has made you complete in Christ.

*2 Samuel 24:23; Micah 6:6–8; Isaiah 64:6; Romans 3:10, 23–26; Ephesians 1:6; Colossians 2:10*

## MORNING READING

Each of us has received one gift after another.

"This is my Son, whom I love and with whom I am pleased." ✦ Consider this: The Father has given us his love. He loves us so much that we are actually called God's dear children. ✦ God made his Son responsible for everything. His Son is the one through whom God made the universe. ✦ If we are his children, we are also God's heirs. If we share in Christ's suffering in order to share his glory, we are heirs together with him. ✦ "The Father and I are one. . . . The Father is in me and that I am in the Father." ✦ "I am going to my Father and your Father, to my God and your God." ✦ "I am in them, and you are in me. So they are completely united." ✦ The church is Christ's body and completes him as he fills everything in every way. ✦ Since we have these promises, dear friends, we need to cleanse ourselves from everything that contaminates body and spirit and live a holy life in the fear of God.

*John 1:16; Matthew 17:5; 1 John 3:1; Hebrews 1:2; Romans 8:17; John 10:30, 38; John 20:17; John 17:23; Ephesians 1:22–23; 2 Corinthians 7:1*

## EVENING READING

"Slaves are not superior to their owners,
and messengers are not superior to the people who send them.
If you understand all of this,
you are blessed whenever you follow my example."

Then a quarrel broke out among the disciples. They argued about who should be considered the greatest. Jesus said to them, "The kings of nations have power over their people, and those in authority call themselves friends of the people. But you're not going to be that way! Rather, the greatest among you must be like the youngest, and your leader must be like a servant. Who's the greatest, the person who sits at the table or the servant? Isn't it really the person who sits at the table? But I'm among you as a servant." ✦ "It's the same way with the Son of Man. He didn't come so that others could serve him. He came to serve and to give his life as a ransom for many people." ✦ The Father had put everything in Jesus' control. Jesus knew that. He also knew that he had come from God and was going back to God. So he got up from the table, removed his outer clothes, took a towel, and tied it around his waist. Then he poured water into a basin and began to wash the disciples' feet and dry them with the towel that he had tied around his waist.

*John 13:16–17; Luke 22:24–27; Matthew 20:28; John 13:3–5*

## MORNING READING

My heart is confident, O God.

The Lord is my light and my salvation. Who is there to fear? The Lord is my life's fortress. Who is there to be afraid of? ✦ With perfect peace you will protect those whose minds cannot be changed, because they trust you. ✦ He is not afraid of bad news. His heart remains secure, full of confidence in the Lord. His heart is steady, and he is not afraid. In the end he will look triumphantly at his enemies. ✦ Even when I am afraid, I still trust you. ✦ He hides me in his shelter when there is trouble. He keeps me hidden in his tent. He sets me high on a rock. Now my head will be raised above my enemies who surround me. I will offer sacrifices with shouts of joy in his tent. I will sing and make music to praise the Lord. ✦ God, who shows you his kindness and who has called you through Christ Jesus to his eternal glory, will restore you, strengthen you, make you strong, and support you as you suffer for a little while. Power belongs to him forever.

*Psalm 108:1; Psalm 27:1; Isaiah 26:3; Psalm 112:7–8; Psalm 56:3; Psalm 27:5–6; 1 Peter 5:10–11*

## EVENING READING

The Lord has set his throne in heaven.
His kingdom rules everything.

The dice are thrown, but the Lord determines every outcome. ✦ If there is a disaster in a city, hasn't the Lord done it? ✦ I am the Lord, and there is no other. There is no other God besides me. I will strengthen you, although you don't know me, so that from the east to the west people will know that there is no God except me. I am the Lord, and there is no other. I make light and create darkness. I make blessings and create disasters. I, the Lord, do all these things. ✦ He does whatever he wishes with the army of heaven and with those who live on earth. There is no one who can oppose him or ask him, "What are you doing?" ✦ If God is for us, who can be against us? ✦ Christ must rule until God has put every enemy under his control. ✦ "Don't be afraid, little flock. Your Father is pleased to give you the kingdom."

*Psalm 103:19; Proverbs 16:33; Amos 3:6; Isaiah 45:5–7; Daniel 4:35; Romans 8:31; 1 Corinthians 15:25; Luke 12:32*

## MORNING READING

"Life is not about having a lot of material possessions."

The little that the righteous person has is better than the wealth of many wicked people. ✦ Better to have a little with the fear of the LORD than great treasure and turmoil. ✦ A godly life brings huge profits to people who are content with what they have. . . . But people who want to get rich keep falling into temptation. ✦ Don't give me either poverty or riches. Feed me only the food I need, or I may feel satisfied and deny you and say, 'Who is the LORD?' or I may become poor and steal and give the name of my God a bad reputation. ✦ "Give us our daily bread today." ✦ "Stop worrying about what you will eat, drink, or wear. Isn't life more than food and the body more than clothes?" ✦ Jesus said to [his disciples], "When I sent you out without a wallet, traveling bag, or sandals, you didn't lack anything, did you?" "Not a thing!" they answered. ✦ Don't love money. Be happy with what you have because God has said, "I will never abandon you or leave you."

*Luke 12:15; Psalm 37:16; Proverbs 15:16; 1 Timothy 6:6, 8; Proverbs 30:8–9; Matthew 6:11; Matthew 6:25; Luke 22:35; Hebrews 13:5*

## EVENING READING

"Life is spiritual."

This is what Scripture says: "The first man, Adam, became a living being." The last Adam became a life-giving spirit." ✦ "Flesh and blood give birth to flesh and blood, but the Spirit gives birth to things that are spiritual." ✦ He saved us through the washing in which the Holy Spirit gives us new birth and renewal. ✦ Whoever doesn't have the Spirit of Christ doesn't belong to him. However, if Christ lives in you, your bodies are dead because of sin, but your spirits are alive because you have God's approval. Does the Spirit of the one who brought Jesus back to life live in you? Then the one who brought Christ back to life will also make your mortal bodies alive by his Spirit who lives in you. ✦ I no longer live, but Christ lives in me. The life I now live I live by believing in God's Son. ✦ So consider yourselves dead to sin's power but living for God in the power Christ Jesus gives you.

*John 6:63; 1 Corinthians 15:45; John 3:6; Titus 3:5; Romans 8:9–11; Galatians 2:20; Romans 6:11*

## MORNING READING

"I have been banished from your sight.
Will I ever see your holy temple again?"

Zion said, "The LORD has abandoned me. My Lord has forgotten me." Can a woman forget her nursing child? Will she have no compassion on the child from her womb? Although mothers may forget, I will not forget you." ✦ I have forgotten what happiness is. I said, "I've lost my strength to live and my hope in the LORD." ✦ Wake up! Why are you sleeping, O Lord? Awake! Do not reject us forever! ✦ Jacob, why do you complain? Israel, why do you say, "My way is hidden from the LORD, and my rights are ignored by my God"? ✦ I hid my face from you for a moment in a burst of anger, but I will have compassion on you with everlasting kindness," says the LORD your defender. ✦ Why are you discouraged, my soul? Why are you so restless? Put your hope in God, because I will still praise him. He is my savior and my God. ✦ In every way we're troubled, but we aren't crushed by our troubles. We're frustrated, but we don't give up. We're persecuted, but we're not abandoned. We're captured, but we're not killed.

*Jonah 2:4; Isaiah 49:14–15; Lamentations 3:17–18; Psalm 44:23; Isaiah 40:27; Isaiah 54:8; Psalm 43:5; 2 Corinthians 4:8–9*

## EVENING READING

"The poor and needy are looking for water, but there is none.
Their tongues are parched with thirst.
I, the LORD, will answer them."

Many are saying, "Who can show us anything good?" ✦ What do people get from all of their hard work and struggles under the sun? Their entire life is filled with pain, and their work is unbearable. Even at night their minds don't rest. ✦ Everything was pointless. It was like trying to catch the wind. ✦ They have abandoned me, the fountain of life-giving water. They have also dug their own cisterns, broken cisterns that can't hold water. ✦ "Everyone whom the Father gives me will come to me. I will never turn away anyone who comes to me." ✦ I will pour water on thirsty ground and rain on dry land. ✦ "Blessed are those who hunger and thirst for God's approval. They will be satisfied." ✦ O God, you are my God. At dawn I search for you. My soul thirsts for you. My body longs for you in a dry, parched land where there is no water.

*Isaiah 41:17; Psalm 4:6; Ecclesiastes 2:22–23; Ecclesiastes 2:17; Jeremiah 2:13; John 6:37; Isaiah 44:3; Matthew 5:6; Psalm 63:1*

## Morning Reading

"Remember that I am always with you until the end of time."

"If two of you agree on anything here on earth, my Father in heaven will accept it. Where two or three have come together in my name, I am there among them." ✦ "Whoever knows and obeys my commandments is the person who loves me. Those who love me will have my Father's love, and I, too, will love them and show myself to them." ✦ Judas (not Iscariot) asked Jesus, "Lord, what has happened that you are going to reveal yourself to us and not to the world?" Jesus answered him, "Those who love me will do what I say. My Father will love them, and we will go to them and make our home with them." ✦ God can guard you so that you don't fall and so that you can be full of joy as you stand in his glorious presence without fault. Before time began, now, and for eternity glory, majesty, power, and authority belong to the only God, our Savior, through Jesus Christ our Lord. Amen.

*Matthew 28:20; Matthew 18:19–20; John 14:21; John 14:22–23; Jude 24–25*

## Evening Reading

The end of everything is near.

I saw a large, white throne and the one who was sitting on it. The earth and the sky fled from his presence. ✦ By God's word, the present heaven and earth are designated to be burned. They are being kept until the day ungodly people will be judged and destroyed. ✦ God is our refuge and strength, an ever-present help in times of trouble. That is why we are not afraid even when the earth quakes or the mountains topple into the depths of the sea. Water roars and foams, and mountains shake at the surging waves. ✦ "You will hear of wars and rumors of wars. Don't be alarmed!" ✦ We still have a building from God. It is an eternal house in heaven that isn't made by human hands. ✦ But we look forward to . . . a new heaven and a new earth—a place where everything that has God's approval lives. Therefore, dear friends, with this to look forward to, make every effort to have him find you at peace, without spiritual stains or blemishes.

*1 Peter 4:7; Revelation 20:11; 2 Peter 3:7; Psalm 46:1–3;*
*Matthew 24:6; 2 Corinthians 5:1; 2 Peter 3:13–14*

## MORNING READING

The Lord rules as king.

"Don't you fear me?" asks the Lord. "Don't you tremble in my presence? I made the sand a boundary for the sea, a permanent barrier that it cannot cross. Although the waves toss continuously, they can't break through. Although they roar, they can't cross it." ✦ The authority to reward someone does not come from the east, from the west, or even from the wilderness. God alone is the judge. He punishes one person and rewards another. ✦ He changes times and periods of history. He removes kings and establishes them. He gives wisdom to those who are wise and knowledge to those who have insight. ✦ "You will hear of wars and rumors of wars. Don't be alarmed!" ✦ If God is for us, who can be against us? ✦ "Aren't two sparrows sold for a penny? Not one of them will fall to the ground without your Father's permission. Every hair on your head has been counted. Don't be afraid! You are worth more than many sparrows."

*Psalm 99:1; Jeremiah 5:22; Psalm 75:6–7; Daniel 2:21; Matthew 24:6; Romans 8:31; Matthew 10:29–31*

## EVENING READING

Keep watch over the door of my lips.

John replied, "Master, we saw someone forcing demons out of a person by using the power and authority of your name. We tried to stop him because he was not one of us." Jesus said to him, "Don't stop him! Whoever isn't against you is for you." ✦ James and John . . . asked, "Lord, do you want us to call down fire from heaven to burn [the Samaritan village] up?" But he turned and corrected them. ✦ A young man ran and told Moses, "Eldad and Medad are prophesying in the camp." So Joshua, son of Nun, . . . spoke up and said, "Stop them, sir!" But Moses asked him, "Do you think you need to stand up for me? I wish all the Lord's people were prophets and that the Lord would put his Spirit on them." ✦ But the spiritual nature produces love, joy, peace, patience, kindness, goodness, faithfulness, gentleness, and self-control. . . . Those who belong to Christ Jesus have crucified their corrupt nature along with its passions and desires. If we live by our spiritual nature, then our lives need to conform to our spiritual nature. We can't allow ourselves to act arrogantly and to provoke or envy each other.

*Malachi 2:15; Luke 9:49–50; Luke 9:54–55; Numbers 11:27–29; Galatians 5:22–26*

## Morning Reading

"He took away our weaknesses and removed our diseases."

The priest will order someone to get two living, clean birds, some cedar wood, red yarn, and a hyssop sprig to use for the cleansing. Then the priest will order someone to kill one bird over a clay bowl containing fresh water. The priest will take the living bird, the cedar wood, the red yarn, and the hyssop sprig and dip them and the living bird in the blood of the bird that was killed over the fresh water. He will sprinkle the blood seven times on the one to be cleansed and will declare that person clean. Then he will let the living bird fly away into the open country. ✦ One day Jesus was in a city where there was a man covered with a serious skin disease. When the man saw Jesus, he bowed with his face to the ground. He begged Jesus, "Sir, if you want to, you can make me clean." ✦ Jesus felt sorry for him, reached out, touched him, and said, "I'm willing. So be clean!" Immediately, his skin disease went away, and he was clean.

*Matthew 8:17; Leviticus 14:4–7; Luke 5:12; Mark 1:41–42*

## Evening Reading

Whomever you bless is blessed.

"Blessed are those who recognize they are spiritually helpless. The kingdom of heaven belongs to them. Blessed are those who mourn. They will be comforted. Blessed are those who are gentle. They will inherit the earth. Blessed are those who hunger and thirst for God's approval. They will be satisfied. Blessed are those who show mercy. They will be treated mercifully. Blessed are those whose thoughts are pure. They will see God. Blessed are those who make peace. They will be called God's children. Blessed are those who are persecuted for doing what God approves of. The kingdom of heaven belongs to them. Blessed are you when people insult you, persecute you, lie, and say all kinds of evil things about you because of me. Rejoice and be glad because you have a great reward in heaven! The prophets who lived before you were persecuted in these ways." ✦ "Blessed are those who hear and obey God's word." ✦ "Blessed are those who wash their robes so that they may have the right to the tree of life and may go through the gates into the city."

*Numbers 22:6; Matthew 5:3–12; Luke 11:28; Revelation 22:14*

## MORNING READING

He sees that there's no one to help.
He's astounded that there's no one to intercede.
So with his own power he wins a victory.

You were not pleased with sacrifices and offerings. You have dug out two ears for me. You did not ask for burnt offerings or sacrifices for sin. Then I said, "I have come! (It is written about me in the scroll of the book.) I am happy to do your will, O my God." Your teachings are deep within me. ✦ "I give my life in order to take it back again. No one takes my life from me. I give my life of my own free will. I have the authority to give my life, and I have the authority to take my life back again." ✦ There is no other God except me. There is no other righteous God and Savior besides me. Turn to me and be saved, all who live at the ends of the earth, because I am God, and there is no other. ✦ "We can be saved only by the power of the one named Jesus and not by any other person." ✦ You know about the kindness of our Lord Jesus Christ. He was rich, yet for your sake he became poor in order to make you rich through his poverty.

*Isaiah 59:16; Psalm 40:6–8; John 10:17–18;*
*Isaiah 45:21–22; Acts 4:12; 2 Corinthians 8:9*

## EVENING READING

The enemy's power.

Keep your mind clear, and be alert. Your opponent the devil is prowling around like a roaring lion as he looks for someone to devour. ✦ Resist the devil, and he will run away from you. ✦ Put on all the armor that God supplies. In this way you can take a stand against the devil's strategies. This is not a wrestling match against a human opponent. We are wrestling with rulers, authorities, the powers who govern this world of darkness, and spiritual forces that control evil in the heavenly world. For this reason, take up all the armor that God supplies. Then you will be able to take a stand during these evil days. Once you have overcome all obstacles, you will be able to stand your ground. So then, take your stand! Fasten truth around your waist like a belt. Put on God's approval as your breastplate. Put on your shoes so that you are ready to spread the Good News that gives peace. In addition to all these, take the Christian faith as your shield. With it you can put out all the flaming arrows of the evil one. ✦ Don't laugh at me, my enemies. Although I've fallen, I will get up. Although I sit in the dark, the Lord is my light.

*Luke 10:19; 1 Peter 5:8; James 4:7; Ephesians 6:11–16; Micah 7:8*

## Morning Reading

Everything about him is desirable!

May my thoughts be pleasing to him. ✦ My beloved . . . stands out among 10,000 men. ✦ "[Jesus is] a chosen and precious cornerstone in Zion, and the person who believes in him will never be ashamed." ✦ You are the most handsome of Adam's descendants. Grace is poured on your lips. ✦ This is why God has given [Jesus] an exceptional honor—the name honored above all other names. ✦ God was pleased to have all of himself live in Christ. ✦ Although you have never seen Christ, you love him. You don't see him now, but you believe in him. You are extremely happy with joy and praise that can hardly be expressed in words. ✦ I consider everything else worthless because I'm much better off knowing Christ Jesus my Lord. It's because of him that I think of everything as worthless. I threw it all away in order to gain Christ and to have a relationship with him. This means that I didn't receive God's approval by obeying his laws. The opposite is true! I have God's approval through faith in Christ. This is the approval that comes from God and is based on faith.

*Song of Songs 5:16; Psalm 104:34; Song of Songs 5:10; 1 Peter 2:6; Psalm 45:2; Philippians 2:9; Colossians 1:19; 1 Peter 1:8; Philippians 3:8–9*

## Evening Reading

David found strength in the Lord his God.

"Lord, to what person could we go? Your words give eternal life." ✦ I know whom I trust. I'm convinced that he is able to protect what he had entrusted to me until that day. ✦ I called on the Lord in my distress. I cried to my God for help. He heard my voice from his temple, and my cry for help reached his ears. ✦ On the day when I faced disaster, they confronted me, but the Lord came to my defense. He brought me out to a wide-open place. He rescued me because he was pleased with me. ✦ I will thank the Lord at all times. My mouth will always praise him. My soul will boast about the Lord. Those who are oppressed will hear it and rejoice. Praise the Lord's greatness with me. Let us highly honor his name together. I went to the Lord for help. He answered me and rescued me from all my fears. . . . Taste and see that the Lord is good. Blessed is the person who takes refuge in him.

*1 Samuel 30:6; John 6:68; 2 Timothy 1:12; Psalm 18:6; Psalm 18:18–19; Psalm 34:1–4, 8*

## MORNING READING

"It is good to continue to hope and wait silently
for the Lord to save us."

Has God forgotten to be merciful? Has he locked up his compassion because of his anger? ✦ When I was panic-stricken, I said, "I have been cut off from your sight." But you heard my pleas for mercy when I cried out to you for help. ✦ "Won't God give his chosen people justice when they cry out to him for help day and night? Is he slow to help them? I can guarantee that he will give them justice quickly." ✦ Wait for the Lord, and he will save you. ✦ Surrender yourself to the Lord, and wait patiently for him. Do not be preoccupied with an evildoer who succeeds in his way when he carries out his schemes. ✦ You won't fight this battle. Instead, take your position, stand still, and see the victory of the Lord for you. ✦ We can't allow ourselves to get tired of living the right way. Certainly, each of us will receive everlasting life at the proper time, if we don't give up. ✦ See how farmers wait for their precious crops to grow. They wait patiently for fall and spring rains.

*Lamentations 3:26; Psalm 77:9; Psalm 31:22; Luke 18:7–8;
Proverbs 20:22; Psalm 37:7; 2 Chronicles 20:17; Galatians 6:9; James 5:7*

## EVENING READING

Catch the foxes for us, the little foxes that ruin vineyards.
Our vineyards are blooming.

Who can notice every mistake? Forgive my hidden faults. ✦ Make sure that everyone has kindness from God so that bitterness doesn't take root and grow up to cause trouble that corrupts many of you. ✦ You were doing so well. Who stopped you from being influenced by the truth? ✦ God, who began this good work in you, will carry it through to completion on the day of Christ Jesus. ✦ Live as citizens who reflect the Good News about Christ. ✦ In the same way the tongue is a small part of the body, but it can brag about doing important things. A large forest can be set on fire by a little flame. The tongue is that kind of flame. It is a world of evil among the parts of our bodies, and it completely contaminates our bodies. The tongue sets our lives on fire, and is itself set on fire from hell. . . . No one can tame the tongue. It is an uncontrollable evil filled with deadly poison. ✦ Everything you say should be kind and well thought out.

*Song of Songs 2:15; Psalm 19:12; Hebrews 12:15; Galatians 5:7;
Philippians 1:6; Philippians 1:27; James 3:5–6, 8; Colossians 4:6*

## MORNING READING

You won't succeed by might or by power,
but by my Spirit, says the Lord of Armies.

Who has directed the Spirit of the Lord or instructed him as his adviser? ✦ But God chose what the world considers nonsense to put wise people to shame. God chose what the world considers weak to put what is strong to shame. God chose what the world considers ordinary and what it despises—what it considers to be nothing—in order to destroy what it considers to be something. As a result, no one can brag in God's presence. ✦ "The wind blows wherever it pleases. You hear its sound, but you don't know where the wind comes from or where it's going. That's the way it is with everyone born of the Spirit." ✦ These people didn't become God's children in a physical way—from a human impulse or from a husband's desire to have a child. They were born from God. ✦ "My Spirit remains with you. Don't be afraid." ✦ The battle isn't yours. It's God's. ✦ "The Lord can save without sword or spear, because the Lord determines every battle's outcome. He will hand all of you over to us."

*Zechariah 4:6; Isaiah 40:13; 1 Corinthians 1:27–29; John 3:8; John 1:13; Haggai 2:5; 2 Chronicles 20:15; 1 Samuel 17:47*

## EVENING READING

Do as you promised.

Keep your promise to me so that I can fear you. ✦ Then I will have an answer for the one who insults me since I trust your word. ✦ Remember the word you gave me. Through it you gave me hope. ✦ Your laws have become like psalms to me in this place where I am only a foreigner. ✦ The teachings that come from your mouth are worth more to me than thousands in gold or silver. ✦ O Lord, your word is established in heaven forever. Your faithfulness endures throughout every generation. ✦ God . . . wanted to make this perfectly clear to those who would receive his promise, so he took an oath. God did this so that we would be encouraged. God cannot lie when he takes an oath or makes a promise. These two things can never be changed. Those of us who have taken refuge in him hold on to the confidence we have been given. We have this confidence as a sure and strong anchor for our lives. This confidence goes into the holy place behind the curtain where Jesus went before us on our behalf. ✦ He has given us his promises that are of the highest value.

*2 Samuel 7:25; Psalm 119:38; Psalm 119:42; Psalm 119:49; Psalm 119:54; Psalm 119:72; Psalm 119:89–90; Hebrews 6:17–20; 2 Peter 1:4*

## MORNING READING

Blessed is the person who listens to me,
watches at my door day after day, and waits by my doorposts.

As servants depend on their masters, as a maid depends on her mistress, so we depend on the LORD our God until he has pity on us. ✦ For generations to come this will be the daily burnt offering made in the LORD's presence at the entrance to the tent of meeting. There I will meet with you to speak to you. ✦ Wherever I choose to have my name remembered, I will come to you and bless you. ✦ "Where two or three have come together in my name, I am there among them." ✦ "Indeed, the time is coming, and it is now here, when the true worshipers will worship the Father in spirit and truth. The Father is looking for people like that to worship him. God is a spirit. Those who worship him must worship in spirit and truth." ✦ Pray in the Spirit in every situation. Use every kind of prayer and request there is. ✦ Never stop praying.

*Proverbs 8:34; Psalm 123:2; Exodus 29:42; Exodus 20:24;
Matthew 18:20; John 4:23–24; Ephesians 6:18; 1 Thessalonians 5:17*

## EVENING READING

He will be named: Wonderful Counselor.

The Spirit of the LORD will rest on him—the Spirit of wisdom and understanding, the Spirit of advice and power, the Spirit of knowledge and fear of the LORD. He will gladly bear the fear of the LORD. ✦ Does not wisdom call out? Does not understanding raise its voice? . . . "I am calling to all of you, and my appeal is to all people. You gullible people, learn how to be sensible. You fools, get a heart that has understanding. Listen! I am speaking about noble things, and my lips will say what is right. . . . Advice and priceless wisdom are mine. I, Understanding, have strength. ✦ All of this has come from the LORD of Armies. His counsel is wonderful, and his wisdom is great. ✦ If any of you needs wisdom to know what you should do, you should ask God, and he will give it to you. God is generous to everyone and doesn't find fault with them. ✦ Trust the LORD with all your heart, and do not rely on your own understanding. In all your ways acknowledge him, and he will make your paths smooth.

*Isaiah 9:6; Isaiah 11:2–3; Proverbs 8:1, 4–6, 14;
Isaiah 28:29; James 1:5; Proverbs 3:5–6*

## MORNING READING

Always try to do what is good.

God called you to endure suffering because Christ suffered for you. He left you an example so that you could follow in his footsteps. Christ never committed any sin. He never spoke deceitfully. Christ never verbally abused those who verbally abused him. When he suffered, he didn't make any threats but left everything to the one who judges fairly. ✦ Think about Jesus, who endured opposition from sinners, so that you don't become tired and give up. ✦ Since we are surrounded by so many examples of faith, we must get rid of everything that slows us down, especially sin that distracts us. We must run the race that lies ahead of us and never give up. We must focus on Jesus, the source and goal of our faith. He saw the joy ahead of him, so he endured death on the cross and ignored the disgrace it brought him. Then he received the highest position in heaven, the one next to the throne of God. ✦ Finally, brothers and sisters, keep your thoughts on whatever is right or deserves praise: things that are true, honorable, fair, pure, acceptable, or commendable.

*1 Thessalonians 5:15; 1 Peter 2:21–23;*
*Hebrews 12:3; Hebrews 12:1–2; Philippians 4:8*

## EVENING READING

Mighty God.

You are the most handsome of Adam's descendants. Grace is poured on your lips. That is why God has blessed you forever. O warrior, strap your sword to your side with your splendor and majesty. Ride on victoriously in your majesty for the cause of truth, humility, and righteousness. . . . Your throne, O God, is forever and ever. The scepter in your kingdom is a scepter for justice. ✦ Once in a vision you said to your faithful ones: "I set a boy above warriors. I have raised up one chosen from the people." ✦ The man who is my friend, declares the LORD of Armies. ✦ Look! God is my Savior. I am confident and unafraid, because the LORD is my strength and my song. He is my Savior. ✦ But I thank God, who always leads us in victory because of Christ. ✦ God can guard you so that you don't fall and so that you can be full of joy as you stand in his glorious presence without fault. Before time began, now, and for eternity glory, majesty, power, and authority belong to the only God, our Savior, through Jesus Christ our Lord. Amen.

*Isaiah 9:6; Psalm 45:2–4, 6; Psalm 89:19; Zechariah 13:7;*
*Isaiah 12:2; 2 Corinthians 2:14; Jude 24–25*

## MORNING READING

The LORD's ways are right.
Righteous people live by them.
Rebellious people stumble over them.

This honor belongs to those who believe. But to those who don't believe: "[He is] a stone that people trip over, a large rock that people find offensive." ✦ The way of the LORD is a fortress for an innocent person but a ruin to those who are troublemakers. ✦ "Let the person who has ears listen!" ✦ Let those who think they are wise pay attention to these things so that they may understand the LORD's blessings. ✦ "The eye is the lamp of the body. So if your eye is unclouded, your whole body will be full of light." ✦ "Those who want to follow the will of God will know if what I teach is from God or if I teach my own thoughts." ✦ "Those who understand these mysteries will be given more knowledge, and they will excel in understanding them." ✦ "The person who belongs to God understands what God says. You don't understand because you don't belong to God." ✦ "You don't want to come to me to get eternal life." ✦ "My sheep respond to my voice, and I know who they are. They follow me."

*Hosea 14:9; 1 Peter 2:7–8; Proverbs 10:29; Matthew 11:15; Psalm 107:43; Matthew 6:22; John 7:17; Matthew 13:12; John 8:47; John 5:40; John 10:27*

## EVENING READING

Everlasting Father.

Listen, Israel: The LORD is our God. The LORD is the only God. ✦ "The Father and I are one. . . . The Father is in me and that I am in the Father." ✦ "If you knew me, you would also know my Father." ✦ Philip said to Jesus, "Lord, show us the Father, and that will satisfy us." Jesus replied, "I have been with all of you for a long time. Don't you know me yet, Philip? The person who has seen me has seen the Father." ✦ "I am here with the sons and daughters God has given me." ✦ He will see and be satisfied because of his suffering. ✦ "I am the A and the Z," says the Lord God, the one who is, the one who was, and the one who is coming, the Almighty. ✦ "Before Abraham was ever born, I am." ✦ God answered Moses, "I Am Who I Am. This is what you must say to the people of Israel: 'I Am has sent me to you.' " ✦ God said about his Son, "Your throne, O God, is forever and ever." ✦ He existed before everything and holds everything together. ✦ All of God lives in Christ's body.

*Isaiah 9:6; Deuteronomy 6:4; John 10:30, 38; John 8:19; John 14:8–9; Hebrews 2:13; Isaiah 53:11; Revelation 1:8; John 8:58; Exodus 3:14; Hebrews 1:8; Colossians 1:17; Colossians 2:9*

## MORNING READING

You have to suffer different kinds of trouble for a little while now.

Dear friends, don't be surprised by the fiery troubles that are coming in order to test you. Don't feel as though something strange is happening to you, but be happy as you share Christ's sufferings. Then you will also be full of joy when he appears again in his glory. ✦ "My child, pay attention when the Lord disciplines you. Don't give up when he corrects you." . . . We don't enjoy being disciplined. It always seems to cause more pain than joy. But later on, those who learn from that discipline have peace that comes from doing what is right. ✦ We have a chief priest who is able to sympathize with our weaknesses. He was tempted in every way that we are, but he didn't sin. ✦ Because Jesus experienced temptation when he suffered, he is able to help others when they are tempted. ✦ God, who faithfully keeps his promises, will not allow you to be tempted beyond your power to resist.

*1 Peter 1:6; 1 Peter 4:12–13; Hebrews 12:5, 11; Hebrews 4:15; Hebrews 2:18; 1 Corinthians 10:13*

## EVENING READING

Prince of Peace.

He may judge your people with righteousness and your oppressed people with justice. May the mountains bring peace to the people and the hills bring righteousness. . . . May he be like rain that falls on freshly cut grass, like showers that water the land. May righteous people blossom in his day. May there be unlimited peace until the moon no longer shines. ✦ "Glory to God, . . . and on earth peace to those who have his good will!" ✦ "A new day will dawn on us from above because our God is loving and merciful. He will give light to those who live in the dark and in death's shadow. He will guide us into the way of peace." ✦ Peace through Jesus Christ. This Jesus Christ is everyone's Lord. ✦ "I've told you this so that my peace will be with you. In the world you'll have trouble. But cheer up! I have overcome the world." ✦ "I'm leaving you peace. I'm giving you my peace. I don't give you the kind of peace that the world gives." ✦ Then God's peace, which goes beyond anything we can imagine, will guard your thoughts and emotions through Christ Jesus.

*Isaiah 9:6; Psalm 72:2–3, 6–7; Luke 2:14; Luke 1:78–79; Acts 10:36; John 16:33; John 14:27; Philippians 4:7*

## MORNING READING

"Take the finest spices . . .
This will be the holy oil used for anointing."

"It must never be poured on the bodies of other people. Never make any perfumed oil using this formula. It is holy, and you must treat it as holy." ✦ One Spirit. ✦ There are different spiritual gifts, but the same Spirit gives them. ✦ God, your God, has anointed you, rather than your companions, with the oil of joy. ✦ God anointed Jesus from Nazareth with the Holy Spirit and with power. ✦ "God gives [the Son] the Spirit without limit." ✦ Each of us has received one gift after another because of all that the Word is. ✦ The anointing you received from Christ lives in you. . . . Instead, Christ's anointing teaches you about everything. ✦ God establishes us, together with you, in a relationship with Christ. He has also anointed us. In addition, he has put his seal of ownership on us and has given us the Spirit as his guarantee. ✦ But the spiritual nature produces love, joy, peace, patience, kindness, goodness, faithfulness, gentleness, and self-control. There are no laws against things like that.

*Exodus 30:23, 25; Exodus 30:32; Ephesians 4:4;
1 Corinthians 12:4; Psalm 45:7; Acts 10:38; John 3:34;
John 1:16; 1 John 2:27; 2 Corinthians 1:21–22; Galatians 5:22–23*

## EVENING READING

This world in its present form is passing away.

Methuselah lived a total of 969 years; then he died. ✦ Humble believers should be proud because being humble makes them important. Rich believers should be proud because being rich should make them humble. Rich people will wither like flowers. The sun rises with its scorching heat and dries up plants. The flowers drop off, and the beauty is gone. The same thing will happen to rich people. While they are busy, they will die. ✦ You don't know what will happen tomorrow. What is life? You are a mist that is seen for a moment and then disappears. ✦ The world and its evil desires are passing away. But the person who does what God wants lives forever. ✦ "Teach me, O Lord, about the end of my life. Teach me about the number of days I have left so that I may know how temporary my life is." ✦ When people say, "Everything is safe and sound!" destruction will suddenly strike them. It will be as sudden as labor pains come to a pregnant woman. They won't be able to escape. But, brothers and sisters, you don't live in the dark. That day won't take you by surprise as a thief would.

*1 Corinthians 7:31; Genesis 5:27; James 1:9–11; James 4:14;
1 John 2:17; Psalm 39:4; 1 Thessalonians 5:3–4*

## MORNING READING

Christ is your life. When he appears, then you, too, will appear with him in glory.

Jesus said to her, "I am the one who brings people back to life, and I am life itself. Those who believe in me will live even if they die." ✦ God has given us eternal life, and this life is found in his Son. The person who has the Son has this life. The person who doesn't have the Son of God doesn't have this life. ✦ The Lord will come from heaven with a command, with the voice of the archangel, and with the trumpet call of God. First, the dead who believed in Christ will come back to life. Then, together with them, we who are still alive will be taken in the clouds to meet the Lord in the air. In this way we will always be with the Lord. So then, comfort each other with these words! ✦ When Christ appears we will be like him because we will see him as he is. ✦ When the body is planted, it doesn't have any splendor and is weak. When it comes back to life, it has splendor and is strong. ✦ "If I go to prepare a place for you, I will come again. Then I will bring you into my presence so that you will be where I am."

*Colossians 3:4; John 11:25; 1 John 5:11–12; 1 Thessalonians 4:16–18; 1 John 3:2; 1 Corinthians 15:43; John 14:3*

## EVENING READING

Lead me in your truth and teach me.

"When the Spirit of Truth comes, he will guide you into the full truth." ✦ The Holy One has anointed you, so all of you have knowledge. ✦ If people don't speak these words, it is because it doesn't dawn on them. ✦ Every Scripture passage is inspired by God. All of them are useful for teaching, pointing out errors, correcting people, and training them for a life that has God's approval. They equip God's servants so that they are completely prepared to do good things. ✦ The Holy Scriptures . . . have the power to give you wisdom so that you can be saved through faith in Christ Jesus. ✦ "I will instruct you. I will teach you the way that you should go. I will advise you as my eyes watch over you." ✦ "The eye is the lamp of the body. So if your eye is unclouded, your whole body will be full of light." ✦ "Those who want to follow the will of God will know if what I teach is from God or if I teach my own thoughts." ✦ It will be called the Holy Road. Sinners won't travel on it. It will be for those who walk on it.

*Psalm 25:5; John 16:13; 1 John 2:20; Isaiah 8:20; 2 Timothy 3:16–17; 2 Timothy 3:15; Psalm 32:8; Matthew 6:22; John 7:17; Isaiah 35:8*

## MORNING READING

Let them give thanks to the Lord because of his mercy.
He performed his miracles for Adam's descendants.

Taste and see that the Lord is good. Blessed is the person who takes refuge in him. ✦ Your kindness is so great! You reserve it for those who fear you. ✦ I have formed these people for myself. They will praise me. ✦ Because of his love [God] had already decided to adopt us through Jesus Christ. He freely chose to do this so that the kindness he had given us in his dear Son would be praised and given glory . . . that we who had already focused our hope on Christ would praise him and give him glory. ✦ They will be beautiful and lovely. ✦ The Lord is good to everyone and has compassion for everything that he has made. Everything that you have made will give thanks to you, O Lord, and your faithful ones will praise you. Everyone will talk about the glory of your kingdom and will tell the descendants of Adam about your might in order to make known your mighty deeds and the glorious honor of your kingdom.

*Psalm 107:8; Psalm 34:8; Psalm 31:19; Isaiah 43:21; Ephesians 1:5–6, 12; Zechariah 9:17; Psalm 145:9–12*

## EVENING READING

We consider those who endure to be blessed.

We also brag when we are suffering. We know that suffering creates endurance, endurance creates character, and character creates confidence. We're not ashamed to have this confidence, because God's love has been poured into our hearts by the Holy Spirit, who has been given to us. ✦ We don't enjoy being disciplined. It always seems to cause more pain than joy. But later on, those who learn from that discipline have peace that comes from doing what is right. ✦ My brothers and sisters, be very happy when you are tested in different ways. You know that such testing of your faith produces endurance. Endure until your testing is over. Then you will be mature and complete, and you won't need anything. . . . Blessed are those who endure when they are tested. When they pass the test, they will receive the crown of life that God has promised to those who love him. ✦ So I will brag even more about my weaknesses in order that Christ's power will live in me. Therefore, I accept weakness, mistreatment, hardship, persecution, and difficulties suffered for Christ. It's clear that when I'm weak, I'm strong.

*James 5:11; Romans 5:3–5; Hebrews 12:11; James 1:2–4, 12; 2 Corinthians 12:9–10*

## MORNING READING

Since we belong to the day, we must be sober.
We must put on faith and love as a breastplate and
the hope of salvation as a helmet.

Therefore, your minds must be clear and ready for action. Place your confidence completely in what God's kindness will bring you when Jesus Christ appears again. ✦ So then, take your stand! Fasten truth around your waist like a belt. Put on God's approval as your breastplate. . . . In addition to all these, take the Christian faith as your shield. With it you can put out all the flaming arrows of the evil one. Also take salvation as your helmet and the word of God as the sword that the Spirit supplies. ✦ He will swallow up death forever. The Almighty LORD will wipe away tears from every face, and he will remove the disgrace of his people from the whole earth. The LORD has spoken. On that day his people will say, "This is our God; we have waited for him, and now he will save us. This is the LORD. . . . Let us rejoice and be glad because he will save us." ✦ Faith assures us of things we expect and convinces us of the existence of things we cannot see.

*1 Thessalonians 5:8; 1 Peter 1:13;*
*Ephesians 6:14, 16–17; Isaiah 25:8–9; Hebrews 11:1*

## EVENING READING

The Israelites, while camped opposite the Arameans
who filled the country, seemed like two newborn goats.

"This is what the LORD says: Because the Arameans said that the LORD is a god of the hills but not a god of the valleys, I will hand over their entire army to you. Then you will know that I am the LORD." They camped facing one another for seven days, and on the seventh day the battle started. The Israelites killed 100,000 Aramean foot soldiers in one day. ✦ Dear children, you belong to God. So you have won the victory over these people, because the one who is in you is greater than the one who is in the world. ✦ "Don't be afraid, because I am with you. Don't be intimidated; I am your God. I will strengthen you. I will help you. I will support you with my victorious right hand." ✦ "They will fight you, but they will not defeat you. I am with you, and I will rescue you," declares the LORD.

*1 Kings 20:27; 1 Kings 20:28–29; 1 John 4:4; Isaiah 41:10; Jeremiah 1:19*

## MORNING READING

"I set a boy above warriors.
I have raised up one chosen from the people."

I alone am the LORD, and there is no savior except me. ✦ There is one God. There is also one mediator between God and humans—a human, Christ Jesus. ✦ "No one else can save us. Indeed, we can be saved only by the power of the one named Jesus and not by any other person." ✦ Mighty God. ✦ [Christ] emptied himself by taking on the form of a servant, by becoming like other humans, by having a human appearance. He humbled himself by becoming obedient to the point of death, death on a cross. This is why God has given him an exceptional honor—the name honored above all other names. ✦ Jesus was made a little lower than the angels, but we see him crowned with glory and honor because he suffered death. Through God's kindness he died on behalf of everyone. ✦ Since all of these sons and daughters have flesh and blood, Jesus took on flesh and blood to be like them.

*Psalm 89:19; Isaiah 43:11; 1 Timothy 2:5; Acts 4:12; Isaiah 9:6; Philippians 2:7–9; Hebrews 2:9; Hebrews 2:14*

## EVENING READING

"Gather around me, my godly people
who have made a pledge to me through sacrifices."

Christ was sacrificed once to take away the sins of humanity, and after that he will appear a second time. This time he will not deal with sin, but he will save those who eagerly wait for him. ✦ Because Christ offered himself to God, he is able to bring a new promise from God. Through his death he paid the price to set people free . . . so that those who are called can be guaranteed an inheritance that will last forever. ✦ "Father, I want those you have given to me to be with me, to be where I am." ✦ "He will send out his angels, and from every direction under the sky, they will gather those whom God has chosen." ✦ Even if you are scattered to the most distant country in the world, the LORD your God will gather you and bring you back from there. ✦ First, the dead who believed in Christ will come back to life. Then, together with them, we who are still alive will be taken in the clouds to meet the Lord in the air. In this way we will always be with the Lord.

*Psalm 50:5; Hebrews 9:28; Hebrews 9:15; John 17:24; Mark 13:27; Deuteronomy 30:4; 1 Thessalonians 4:16–17*

## Morning Reading

You will want to please him in every way as
you grow in producing every kind of good work
by this knowledge about God.

Brothers and sisters, in view of all we have just shared about God's compassion, I encourage you to offer your bodies as living sacrifices, dedicated to God and pleasing to him. This kind of worship is appropriate for you. Don't become like the people of this world. Instead, change the way you think. Then you will always be able to determine what God really wants—what is good, pleasing, and perfect. ✦ You once offered all the parts of your body as slaves to sexual perversion and disobedience. This led you to live disobedient lives. Now, in the same way, offer all the parts of your body as slaves that do what God approves of. This leads you to live holy lives. ✦ Certainly, it doesn't matter whether a person is circumcised or not. Rather, what matters is being a new creation. Peace and mercy will come to rest on all those who conform to this principle. ✦ "You give glory to my Father when you produce a lot of fruit and therefore show that you are my disciples. . . . I chose you. I have appointed you to go, to produce fruit that will last, and to ask the Father in my name to give you whatever you ask for."

*Colossians 1:10; Romans 12:1–2; Romans 6:19; Galatians 6:15–16; John 15:8, 16*

## Evening Reading

I looked for him but did not find him.

Israel, return to the LORD your God. You have stumbled because of your sins. Return to the LORD, and say these things to him: "Forgive all our sins, and kindly receive us." ✦ When someone is tempted, he shouldn't say that God is tempting him. God can't be tempted by evil, and God doesn't tempt anyone. Everyone is tempted by his own desires as they lure him away and trap him. ✦ My dear brothers and sisters, don't be fooled. Every good present and every perfect gift comes from above, from the Father who made the sun, moon, and stars. The Father doesn't change like the shifting shadows produced by the sun and the moon. ✦ Wait with hope for the LORD. Be strong, and let your heart be courageous. Yes, wait with hope for the LORD. ✦ "It is good to continue to hope and wait silently for the LORD to save us." ✦ "Won't God give his chosen people justice when they cry out to him for help day and night? Is he slow to help them?" ✦ My soul waits calmly for God alone. My salvation comes from him. . . . Wait calmly for God alone, my soul, because my hope comes from him.

*Song of Songs 3:1; Hosea 14:1–2; James 1:13–14; James 1:16–17;
Psalm 27:14; Lamentations 3:26; Luke 18:7; Psalm 62:1, 5*

## MORNING READING

He led them safely.

I walk in the way of righteousness, on the paths of justice. ✦ "I'm going to send a Messenger in front of you to protect you on your trip and bring you to the place I have prepared." ✦ In all their troubles he was troubled, and he was the Messenger who saved them. In his love and compassion he reclaimed them. He always held them and carried them in the past. ✦ It was not with their swords that they took possession of the land. They did not gain victory with their own strength. It was your right hand, your arm, and the light of your presence that did it, because you were pleased with them. ✦ In this way you guided your people to make an honored name for yourself. ✦ O Lord, lead me in your righteousness because of those who spy on me. Make your way in front of me smooth. ✦ Send your light and your truth. Let them guide me. Let them bring me to your holy mountain and to your dwelling place. Then let me go to the altar of God, to God my highest joy, and I will give thanks to you on the lyre, O God, my God.

*Psalm 78:53; Proverbs 8:20; Exodus 23:20; Isaiah 63:9; Psalm 44:3; Isaiah 63:14; Psalm 5:8; Psalm 43:3–4*

## EVENING READING

You have been washed and made holy,
and you have received God's approval.

The blood of his Son Jesus cleanses us from every sin. ✦ He was punished so that we could have peace, and we received healing from his wounds. ✦ Christ loved the church and gave his life for it. He did this to make the church holy by cleansing it, washing it using water along with spoken words. Then he could present it to himself as a glorious church, without any kind of stain or wrinkle—holy and without faults. ✦ "She has been given the privilege of wearing dazzling, pure linen." This fine linen represents the things that God's holy people do that have his approval. ✦ We have been sprinkled with his blood to free us from a guilty conscience, and our bodies have been washed with clean water. ✦ Who will accuse those whom God has chosen? God has approved of them. ✦ Blessed is the person whose disobedience is forgiven and whose sin is pardoned. Blessed is the person whom the Lord no longer accuses of sin and who has no deceitful thoughts.

*1 Corinthians 6:11; 1 John 1:7; Isaiah 53:5; Ephesians 5:25–27; Revelation 19:8; Hebrews 10:22; Romans 8:33; Psalm 32:1–2*

## MORNING READING

To be distressed in a godly way causes people
to change the way they think and act and
leads them to be saved. No one can regret that.

Peter remembered what Jesus had said: "Before a rooster crows, you will say three times that you don't know me." Then Peter went outside and cried bitterly. ✦ God is faithful and reliable. If we confess our sins, he forgives them and cleanses us from everything we've done wrong. ✦ The blood of his Son Jesus cleanses us from every sin. ✦ My sins have caught up with me so that I can no longer see. They outnumber the hairs on my head. I have lost heart. O Lord, please rescue me! Come quickly to help me, O Lord! ✦ Return to your God. Be loyal and fair, and always wait with hope for your God. ✦ The sacrifice pleasing to God is a broken spirit. O God, you do not despise a broken and sorrowful heart. ✦ He is the healer of the brokenhearted. He is the one who bandages their wounds. ✦ You mortals, the Lord has told you what is good. This is what the Lord requires from you: to do what is right, to love mercy, and to live humbly with your God.

*2 Corinthians 7:10; Matthew 26:75; 1 John 1:9; 1 John 1:7; Psalm 40:12–13; Hosea 12:6; Psalm 51:17; Psalm 147:3; Micah 6:8*

## EVENING READING

Ask her how she, her husband, and the boy are doing.
"Everyone's fine," she answered.

We have that same spirit of faith. ✦ As unknown although we are well-known, as dying although, as you see, we go on living. We are punished, but we are not killed. People think we are sad although we're always glad, that we're beggars although we make many people spiritually rich, that we have nothing although we possess everything. ✦ In every way we're troubled, but we aren't crushed by our troubles. We're frustrated, but we don't give up. We're persecuted, but we're not abandoned. We're captured, but we're not killed. We always carry around the death of Jesus in our bodies so that the life of Jesus is also shown in our bodies. . . . That is why we are not discouraged. Though outwardly we are wearing out, inwardly we are renewed day by day. Our suffering is light and temporary and is producing for us an eternal glory that is greater than anything we can imagine. We don't look for things that can be seen but for things that can't be seen. Things that can be seen are only temporary. But things that can't be seen last forever. ✦ I pray that you're doing well in every other way and that you're healthy.

*2 Kings 4:26; 2 Corinthians 4:13; 2 Corinthians 6:9–10; 2 Corinthians 4:8–10, 16–18; 3 John 2*

## Morning Reading

Christ loved the church and gave his life for it.
He did this to make the church holy by cleansing it,
washing it using water along with spoken words.

Live in love as Christ also loved us. He gave his life for us as an offering and sacrifice, a soothing aroma to God. ✦ You have been born again, not from a seed that can be destroyed, but through God's everlasting word that can't be destroyed. ✦ "Use the truth to make them holy. Your words are truth." ✦ "No one can enter the kingdom of God without being born of water and the Spirit." ✦ He saved us, but not because of anything we had done to gain his approval. Instead, because of his mercy he saved us through the washing in which the Holy Spirit gives us new birth and renewal. ✦ Your promise gave me a new life. ✦ The teachings of the Lord are perfect. They renew the soul. The testimony of the Lord is dependable. It makes gullible people wise. The instructions of the Lord are correct. They make the heart rejoice. The command of the Lord is radiant. It makes the eyes shine.

*Ephesians 5:25–26; Ephesians 5:2; 1 Peter 1:23; John 17:17; John 3:5; Titus 3:5; Psalm 119:50; Psalm 19:7–8*

## Evening Reading

Jewish and non-Jewish people can go to the Father in one Spirit.

"I am in them, and you are in me. So they are completely united." ✦ "I will do anything you ask the Father in my name so that the Father will be given glory because of the Son. If you ask me to do something, I will do it. . . . I will ask the Father, and he will give you another helper who will be with you forever. That helper is the Spirit of Truth. The world cannot accept him, because it doesn't see or know him. You know him, because he lives with you and will be in you." ✦ There is one body and one Spirit. In the same way you were called to share one hope. There is one Lord, one faith, one baptism, one God and Father of all, who is over everything, through everything, and in everything. ✦ "When you pray, say this: Father." ✦ Brothers and sisters, because of the blood of Jesus we can now confidently go into the holy place. Jesus has opened a new and living way for us to go through the curtain. . . . Come to him.

*Ephesians 2:18; John 17:23; John 14:13–14, 16–17; Ephesians 4:4–6; Luke 11:2; Hebrews 10:19–20, 22*

## MORNING READING

You are my help and my savior. O my God, do not delay!

A person's steps are directed by the LORD, and the LORD delights in his way. When he falls, he will not be thrown down headfirst because the LORD holds on to his hand. ✦ In the fear of the LORD there is strong confidence, and his children will have a place of refuge. ✦ Why, then, are you afraid of mortals, who must die, of humans, who are like grass? Why have you forgotten the LORD, your Creator? ✦ "I am with you, and I will rescue you." ✦ "Be strong and courageous. Don't tremble! Don't be afraid of them! The LORD your God is the one who is going with you. He won't abandon you or leave you." ✦ But I will sing about your strength. In the morning I will joyfully sing about your mercy. You have been my stronghold and a place of safety in times of trouble. ✦ You are my hiding place. You protect me from trouble. You surround me with joyous songs of salvation.

*Psalm 40:17; Psalm 37:23–24; Proverbs 14:26; Isaiah 51:12–13; Jeremiah 1:8; Deuteronomy 31:6; Psalm 59:16; Psalm 32:7*

## EVENING READING

"How can you live in the jungle along the Jordan River?"

The Jordan overflows all its banks during the harvest season. ✦ The priests who carried the ark of the LORD's promise stood firmly on dry ground in the middle of the Jordan until the whole nation of Israel had crossed the Jordan River on dry ground. ✦ Jesus was made a little lower than the angels, but we see him crowned with glory and honor because he suffered death. Through God's kindness he died on behalf of everyone. ✦ Even though I walk through the dark valley of death, because you are with me, I fear no harm. Your rod and your staff give me courage. ✦ When you go through the sea, I am with you. ✦ "Don't be afraid! I am the first and the last, the living one. I was dead, but now I am alive forever. I have the keys of death and hell."

*Jeremiah 12:5; Joshua 3:15; Joshua 3:17; Hebrews 2:9; Psalm 23:4; Isaiah 43:2; Revelation 1:17–18*

## MORNING READING

God faithfully keeps his promises.
He called you to be partners with his Son Jesus Christ our Lord.

We must continue to hold firmly to our declaration of faith. The one who made the promise is faithful. ✦ As God said, "I will live and walk among them. I will be their God, and they will be my people." ✦ Our relationship is with the Father and with his Son Jesus Christ. ✦ Be happy as you share Christ's sufferings. Then you will also be full of joy when he appears again in his glory. ✦ I also pray that love may be the ground into which you sink your roots and on which you have your foundation. This way, with all of God's people you will be able to understand how wide, long, high, and deep his love is. You will know Christ's love, which goes far beyond any knowledge. I am praying this so that you may be completely filled with God. ✦ God lives in those who declare that Jesus is the Son of God, and they live in God. ✦ Those who obey Christ's commandments live in God, and God lives in them.

*1 Corinthians 1:9; Hebrews 10:23; 2 Corinthians 6:16; 1 John 1:3; 1 Peter 4:13; Ephesians 3:17–19; 1 John 4:15; 1 John 3:24*

## EVENING READING

God has made us what we are.

The king commanded them to quarry large, expensive blocks of stone in order to provide a foundation of cut stone for the temple. ✦ The temple was built with stone blocks that were finished at the quarry. No hammer, chisel, or any other iron tool made a sound at the temple construction site. ✦ You come to him as living stones, a spiritual house that is being built into a holy priesthood. ✦ You are built on the foundation of the apostles and prophets. Christ Jesus himself is the cornerstone. In him all the parts of the building fit together and grow into a holy temple in the Lord. Through him you, also, are being built in the Spirit together with others into a place where God lives. ✦ Once you were not God's people, but now you are. ✦ You are God's building. ✦ Whoever is a believer in Christ is a new creation. The old way of living has disappeared. A new way of living has come into existence. ✦ God has prepared us for this and has given us his Spirit to guarantee it.

*Ephesians 2:10; 1 Kings 5:17; 1 Kings 6:7; 1 Peter 2:5; Ephesians 2:20–22; 1 Peter 2:10; 1 Corinthians 3:9; 2 Corinthians 5:17; 2 Corinthians 5:5*

## MORNING READING

"Use the truth to make them holy. Your words are truth."

"You are already clean because of what I have told you." ✦ Let Christ's word with all its wisdom and richness live in you. ✦ How can a young person keep his life pure? He can do it by holding on to your word. I wholeheartedly searched for you. Do not let me wander away from your commandments. ✦ Wisdom will come into your heart. Knowledge will be pleasant to your soul. Foresight will protect you. Understanding will guard you. ✦ I have followed his footsteps closely. I have stayed on his path and did not turn from it. I have not left his commands behind. I have treasured his words in my heart. ✦ I have more insight than all my teachers, because your written instructions are in my thoughts. ✦ "If you live by what I say, you are truly my disciples. You will know the truth, and the truth will set you free."

*John 17:17; John 15:3; Colossians 3:16; Psalm 119:9–10; Proverbs 2:10–11; Job 23:11–12; Psalm 119:99; John 8:31–32*

## EVENING READING

Citizens together with God's people.

You have come to Mount Zion, to the city of the living God, to the heavenly Jerusalem. You have come to tens of thousands of angels joyfully gathered together and to the assembly of God's firstborn children (whose names are written in heaven). You have come to a judge (the God of all people) and to the spirits of people who have God's approval and have gained eternal life. ✦ All these people died having faith. They didn't receive the things that God had promised them, but they saw these things coming in the distant future and rejoiced. They acknowledged that they were living as strangers with no permanent home on earth. ✦ We, however, are citizens of heaven. We look forward to the Lord Jesus Christ coming from heaven as our Savior. Through his power to bring everything under his authority, he will change our humble bodies and make them like his glorified body. ✦ God has rescued us from the power of darkness and has brought us into the kingdom of his Son, whom he loves. ✦ Since you are foreigners and temporary residents in the world, I'm encouraging you to keep away from the desires of your corrupt nature. These desires constantly attack you.

*Ephesians 2:19; Hebrews 12:22–23; Hebrews 11:13; Philippians 3:20–21; Colossians 1:13; 1 Peter 2:11*

## MORNING READING

How very deep are your thoughts!

We have not stopped praying for you, . . . [asking] God to fill you with the knowledge of his will through every kind of spiritual wisdom and insight. ✦ Then Christ will live in you through faith. I also pray that love may be the ground into which you sink your roots and on which you have your foundation. This way, with all of God's people you will be able to understand how wide, long, high, and deep his love is. You will know Christ's love, which goes far beyond any knowledge. I am praying this so that you may be completely filled with God. ✦ God's riches, wisdom, and knowledge are so deep that it is impossible to explain his decisions or to understand his ways. ✦ "My thoughts are not your thoughts, and my ways are not your ways," declares the Lord. "Just as the heavens are higher than the earth, so my ways are higher than your ways, and my thoughts are higher than your thoughts." ✦ You have done many miraculous things, O Lord my God. You have made many wonderful plans for us. No one compares to you! I will tell others about your miracles, which are more than I can count.

*Psalm 92:5; Colossians 1:9; Ephesians 3:17–19;*
*Romans 11:33; Isaiah 55:8–9; Psalm 40:5*

## EVENING READING

Whatever you plant is what you'll harvest.

Whenever I saw those who plowed wickedness and planted misery, they gathered its harvest. ✦ "The people of Israel plant the wind, but they harvest a storm." ✦ Whoever spreads righteousness earns honest pay. ✦ If you plant in the soil of your corrupt nature, you will harvest destruction. But if you plant in the soil of your spiritual nature, you will harvest everlasting life. We can't allow ourselves to get tired of living the right way. Certainly, each of us will receive everlasting life at the proper time, if we don't give up. Whenever we have the opportunity, we have to do what is good for everyone, especially for the family of believers. ✦ One person spends freely and yet grows richer, while another holds back what he owes and yet grows poorer. A generous person will be made rich, and whoever satisfies others will himself be satisfied. ✦ The farmer who plants a few seeds will have a very small harvest. But the farmer who plants because he has received God's blessings will receive a harvest of God's blessings in return.

*Galatians 6:7; Job 4:8; Hosea 8:7; Proverbs 11:18;*
*Galatians 6:8–10; Proverbs 11:24–25; 2 Corinthians 9:6*

## MORNING READING

He removed it with a fierce blast from the east winds.

"Please let us fall into the Lord's hands because he is very merciful." ✦ "I will correct you with justice. I won't let you go entirely unpunished." ✦ He will not always accuse us of wrong or be angry with us forever. He has not treated us as we deserve for our sins or paid us back for our wrongs. . . . He certainly knows what we are made of. He bears in mind that we are dust. ✦ "I will spare them as a man spares his own son who serves him." ✦ God, who faithfully keeps his promises, will not allow you to be tempted beyond your power to resist. But when you are tempted, he will also give you the ability to endure the temptation as your way of escape. ✦ "Satan has demanded to have you apostles for himself. He wants to separate you from me as a farmer separates wheat from husks. But I have prayed for you, Simon, that your faith will not fail." ✦ You have been a refuge for the poor, a refuge for the needy in their distress, a shelter from the rain, and shade from the heat. (A tyrant's breath is like a rainstorm against a wall.)

*Isaiah 27:8; 2 Samuel 24:14; Jeremiah 30:11; Psalm 103:9–10, 14; Malachi 3:17; 1 Corinthians 10:13; Luke 22:31–32; Isaiah 25:4*

## EVENING READING

I didn't believe the reports until I came and saw it with my own eyes. I wasn't even told half of it.

"The queen from the south will stand up at the time of judgment with you. She will condemn you, because she came from the ends of the earth to hear Solomon's wisdom. But look, someone greater than Solomon is here!" ✦ We saw his glory. It was the glory that the Father shares with his only Son, a glory full of kindness and truth. ✦ I spoke my message with a show of spiritual power so that your faith would not be based on human wisdom but on God's power. ✦ As Scripture says: "No eye has seen, no ear has heard, and no mind has imagined the things that God has prepared for those who love him." God has revealed those things to us by his Spirit. The Spirit searches everything, especially the deep things of God. ✦ Your eyes will see how handsome the king is. ✦ What we will be isn't completely clear yet. We do know that when Christ appears we will be like him because we will see him as he is. ✦ "I will see God in my own flesh." ✦ When I wake up, I will be satisfied with seeing you.

*1 Kings 10:7; Matthew 12:42; John 1:14; 1 Corinthians 2:4–5; 1 Corinthians 2:9–10; Isaiah 33:17; 1 John 3:2; Job 19:26; Psalm 17:15*

## MORNING READING

"You will know them by what they produce."

Dear children, don't let anyone deceive you. Whoever does what God approves of has God's approval as Christ has God's approval. ✦ Do clean and polluted water flow out of the same spring? My brothers and sisters, can a fig tree produce olives? Can a grapevine produce figs? In the same way, a pool of salt water can't produce fresh water. Do any of you have wisdom and insight? Show this by living the right way with the humility that comes from wisdom. ✦ Live decent lives among unbelievers. Then, although they ridicule you as if you were doing wrong while they are watching you do good things, they will praise God on the day he comes to help you. ✦ "Make a tree good, and then its fruit will be good. Or make a tree rotten, and then its fruit will be rotten. A person can recognize a tree by its fruit. . . . Good people do the good things that are in them. But evil people do the evil things that are in them." ✦ What more could have been done for my vineyard than what I have already done for it?

*Matthew 7:20; 1 John 3:7; James 3:11–13;*
*1 Peter 2:12; Matthew 12:33, 35; Isaiah 5:4*

## EVENING READING

"I will honor the place where my feet rest."

This is what the Lord says: Heaven is my throne. The earth is my footstool. ✦ "Does God really live on earth with people? If heaven itself, the highest heaven, cannot hold you, then how can this temple that I have built?" ✦ "This is what the Lord of Armies says: Once again, in a little while, I am going to shake the sky and the earth, the sea and the dry land. I will shake all the nations, and the one whom all the nations desire will come. Then I will fill this house with glory, says the Lord of Armies. . . . This new house will be more glorious than the former, declares the Lord of Armies. And in this place I will give them peace, declares the Lord of Armies." ✦ I saw a new heaven and a new earth, because the first heaven and earth had disappeared, and the sea was gone. . . . I heard a loud voice from the throne say, "God lives with humans! God will make his home with them, and they will be his people. God himself will be with them and be their God."

*Isaiah 60:13; Isaiah 66:1; 2 Chronicles 6:18; Haggai 2:6–7, 9; Revelation 21:1, 3*

## MORNING READING

Although I sit in the dark, the LORD is my light.

When you go through the sea, I am with you. When you go through rivers, they will not sweep you away. When you walk through fire, you will not be burned, and the flames will not harm you. I am the LORD your God, the Holy One of Israel, your Savior. ✦ I will lead the blind on unfamiliar roads. I will lead them on unfamiliar paths. I will turn darkness into light in front of them. I will make rough places smooth. These are the things I will do for them, and I will never abandon them. ✦ Even though I walk through the dark valley of death, because you are with me, I fear no harm. Your rod and your staff give me courage. ✦ Even when I am afraid, I still trust you. I praise the word of God. I trust God. I am not afraid. What can mere flesh and blood do to me? ✦ The LORD is my light and my salvation. Who is there to fear? The LORD is my life's fortress. Who is there to be afraid of?

*Micah 7:8; Isaiah 43:2–3; Isaiah 42:16; Psalm 23:4; Psalm 56:3–4; Psalm 27:1*

## EVENING READING

There is one God.
There is also one mediator between God and humans—
a human, Christ Jesus.

Listen, Israel: The LORD is our God. The LORD is the only God. ✦ A mediator is not used when there is only one person involved, and God has acted on his own. ✦ We have sinned, and so did our ancestors. We have done wrong. We are guilty. When our ancestors were in Egypt, they gave no thought to your miracles. They did not remember your numerous acts of mercy. . . . God said he was going to destroy them, but Moses, his chosen one, stood in his way to prevent him from exterminating them. ✦ Brothers and sisters, you are holy partners in a heavenly calling. So look carefully at Jesus, the apostle and chief priest about whom we make our declaration of faith. Jesus is faithful to God, who appointed him, in the same way that Moses was faithful when he served in God's house. ✦ Jesus . . . brings a better promise from God that is based on better guarantees. . . . [As God said,] "I will forgive their wickedness and I will no longer hold their sins against them."

*1 Timothy 2:5; Deuteronomy 6:4; Galatians 3:20;*
*Psalm 106:6–7, 23; Hebrews 3:1–2; Hebrews 8:6, 12*

## MORNING READING

"I will never turn away anyone who comes to me."

When he cries out to me, I will listen because I am compassionate. ✦ Even when they are in the land of their enemies, I will not reject them or look at them with disgust. I will not reject or cancel my promise to them, because I am the Lord their God. ✦ I will remember the promise that I made with you when you were young, and I will make it a promise that will last forever. ✦ "Come on now, let's discuss this!" says the Lord. "Though your sins are bright red, they will become as white as snow. Though they are dark red, they will become as white as wool." ✦ Let wicked people abandon their ways. Let evil people abandon their thoughts. Let them return to the Lord, and he will show compassion to them. Let them return to our God, because he will freely forgive them. ✦ Then [the thief on the cross] said, "Jesus, remember me when you enter your kingdom." Jesus said to him, "I can guarantee this truth: Today you will be with me in paradise." ✦ He will not break off a damaged cattail. He will not even put out a smoking wick.

*John 6:37; Exodus 22:27; Leviticus 26:44; Ezekiel 16:60; Isaiah 1:18; Isaiah 55:7; Luke 23:42–43; Isaiah 42:3*

## EVENING READING

His Son, whom he loves.

Then a voice from heaven said, "This is my Son, whom I love—my Son with whom I am pleased." ✦ Here is my servant, whom I support. Here is my chosen one, with whom I am pleased. ✦ God's only Son, the one who is closest to the Father's heart. ✦ God has shown us his love by sending his only Son into the world so that we could have life through him. This is love: not that we have loved God, but that he loved us and sent his Son to be the payment for our sins. . . . We have known and believed that God loves us. God is love. Those who live in God's love live in God, and God lives in them. ✦ "I have given them the glory that you gave me. I did this so that they are united in the same way we are. I am in them, and you are in me. So they are completely united. In this way the world knows that you have sent me and that you have loved them in the same way you have loved me." ✦ Consider this: The Father has given us his love. He loves us so much that we are actually called God's dear children.

*Colossians 1:13; Matthew 3:17; Isaiah 42:1; John 1:18; 1 John 4:9–10, 16; John 17:22–23; 1 John 3:1*

## MORNING READING

Pray with the Holy Spirit's help.

"God is a spirit. Those who worship him must worship in spirit and truth." ✦ So Jewish and non-Jewish people can go to the Father in one Spirit. ✦ "Father, if it's possible, let this cup of suffering be taken away from me. But let your will be done rather than mine." ✦ At the same time the Spirit also helps us in our weakness, because we don't know how to pray for what we need. But the Spirit intercedes along with our groans that cannot be expressed in words. The one who searches our hearts knows what the Spirit has in mind. The Spirit intercedes for God's people the way God wants him to. ✦ We are confident that God listens to us if we ask for anything that has his approval. ✦ "When the Spirit of Truth comes, he will guide you into the full truth. He won't speak on his own. He will speak what he hears and will tell you about things to come." ✦ Pray in the Spirit in every situation. Use every kind of prayer and request there is. For the same reason be alert. Use every kind of effort and make every kind of request for all of God's people.

*Jude 20; John 4:24; Ephesians 2:18; Matthew 26:39; Romans 8:26–27; 1 John 5:14; John 16:13; Ephesians 6:18*

## EVENING READING

There is hope for a tree when it is cut down.
It will sprout again. Its shoots will not stop sprouting.

He will not break off a damaged cattail. ✦ He renews my soul. ✦ To be distressed in a godly way causes people to change the way they think and act and leads them to be saved. No one can regret that. But the distress that the world causes brings only death. ✦ We don't enjoy being disciplined. It always seems to cause more pain than joy. But later on, those who learn from that discipline have peace that comes from doing what is right. ✦ Before you made me suffer, I used to wander off, but now I hold on to your word. ✦ "After all that has happened to us because of the evil things we have done and because of our overwhelming guilt, you, our God, have punished us far less than we deserve and have permitted a few of us to survive." ✦ Don't laugh at me, my enemies. Although I've fallen, I will get up. Although I sit in the dark, the LORD is my light. . . . He will bring me into the light, and I will see his victory.

*Job 14:7; Isaiah 42:3; Psalm 23:3; 2 Corinthians 7:10; Hebrews 12:11; Psalm 119:67; Ezra 9:13; Micah 7:8–9*

## MORNING READING

Whoever listens to me will live without worry
and will be free from the dread of disaster.

O Lord, you have been our refuge throughout every generation. ✦ Whoever lives under the shelter of the Most High will remain in the shadow of the Almighty. . . . His truth is your shield and armor. ✦ Your life is hidden with Christ in God. ✦ Whoever touches you touches the apple of his eye. ✦ Don't be afraid! Stand still, and see what the Lord will do to save you today. . . . The Lord is fighting for you! So be still! ✦ God is our refuge and strength, an ever-present help in times of trouble. That is why we are not afraid. ✦ Jesus said, "Calm down! It's me. Don't be afraid!" ✦ "Why are you afraid? Why do you have doubts? Look at my hands and feet, and see that it's really me. Touch me, and see for yourselves. Ghosts don't have flesh and bones, but you can see that I do." ✦ I know whom I trust. I'm convinced that he is able to protect what he had entrusted to me until that day.

*Proverbs 1:33; Psalm 90:1; Psalm 91:1, 4; Colossians 3:3; Zechariah 2:8; Exodus 14:13–14; Psalm 46:1–2; Matthew 14:27; Luke 24:38–39; 2 Timothy 1:12*

## EVENING READING

"My kingdom doesn't belong to this world."

This chief priest made one sacrifice for sins, and this sacrifice lasts forever. Then he received the highest position in heaven. Since that time, he has been waiting for his enemies to be made his footstool. ✦ "From now on you will see the Son of Man in the highest position in heaven. He will be coming on the clouds of heaven." ✦ Christ must rule until God has put every enemy under his control. ✦ Thank God that he gives us the victory through our Lord Jesus Christ. ✦ He worked with that same power in Christ when he brought him back to life and gave him the highest position in heaven. He is far above all rulers, authorities, powers, lords, and all other names that can be named, not only in this present world but also in the world to come. God has put everything under the control of Christ. He has made Christ the head of everything for the good of the church. The church is Christ's body and completes him as he fills everything in every way. ✦ At the right time God will make this known. God is the blessed and only ruler. He is the King of kings and Lord of lords.

*John 18:36; Hebrews 10:12–13; Matthew 26:64; 1 Corinthians 15:25; 1 Corinthians 15:57; Ephesians 1:20–23; 1 Timothy 6:15*

## MORNING READING

"My mother and my brothers are those
who hear and do what God's word says."

Jesus, who makes people holy, and all those who are made holy have the same Father. That is why Jesus isn't ashamed to call them brothers and sisters. He says, "I will tell my people about your name. I will praise you within the congregation." ✦ As far as our relationship to Christ Jesus is concerned, it doesn't matter whether we are circumcised or not. But what matters is a faith that expresses itself through love. ✦ "You are my friends if you obey my commandments." ✦ "How blessed are those who hear and obey God's word." ✦ "Not everyone who says to me, 'Lord, Lord!' will enter the kingdom of heaven, but only the person who does what my Father in heaven wants." ✦ "My food is to do what the one who sent me wants me to do and to finish the work he has given me." ✦ If we say, "We have a relationship with God" and yet live in the dark, we're lying. We aren't being truthful. ✦ Whoever obeys what Christ says is the kind of person in whom God's love is perfected. That's how we know we are in Christ.

*Luke 8:21; Hebrews 2:11–12; Galatians 5:6; John 15:14; Luke 11:28; Matthew 7:21; John 4:34; 1 John 1:6; 1 John 2:5*

## EVENING READING

"What are you doing here, Elijah?"

He knows the road I take. ✦ O LORD, you have examined me, and you know me. You alone know when I sit down and when I get up. You read my thoughts from far away. You watch me when I travel and when I rest. You are familiar with all my ways. ✦ Where can I go to get away from your Spirit? Where can I run to get away from you? . . . If I climb upward on the rays of the morning sun or land on the most distant shore of the sea where the sun sets, even there your hand would guide me and your right hand would hold on to me. ✦ Elijah was human like us. ✦ A person's fear sets a trap for him, but one who trusts the LORD is safe. ✦ When he falls, he will not be thrown down headfirst because the LORD holds on to his hand. ✦ A person's fear sets a trap for him, but one who trusts the LORD is safe. ✦ We can't allow ourselves to get tired of living the right way. Certainly, each of us will receive everlasting life at the proper time, if we don't give up. ✦ "You want to do what's right, but you're weak." ✦ As a father has compassion for his children, so the LORD has compassion for those who fear him.

*I Kings 19:9; Job 23:10; Psalm 139:1–3; Psalm 139:7, 9–10; James 5:17; Proverbs 29:25; Psalm 37:24; Proverbs 24:16; Galatians 6:9; Matthew 26:41; Psalm 103:13*

## MORNING READING

Freed from sin, you were made slaves
who do what God approves of.

"You cannot serve God and wealth." ✦ When you were slaves to sin, you were free from doing what God approves of. What did you gain by doing those things? You're ashamed of what you used to do because it ended in death. Now you have been freed from sin and have become God's slaves. This results in a holy life and, finally, in everlasting life. ✦ Christ is the fulfillment of Moses' Teachings so that everyone who has faith may receive God's approval. ✦ "Those who serve me must follow me. My servants will be with me wherever I will be. If people serve me, the Father will honor them." ✦ "Place my yoke over your shoulders, and learn from me, because I am gentle and humble. Then you will find rest for yourselves because my yoke is easy and my burden is light." ✦ O LORD, our God, you are not the only master to rule us, but we acknowledge only you. ✦ I will eagerly pursue your commandments because you continue to increase my understanding.

*Romans 6:18; Matthew 6:24; Romans 6:20–22; Romans 10:4; John 12:26; Matthew 11:29–30; Isaiah 26:13; Psalm 119:32*

## EVENING READING

Whoever calls on the name of the Lord will be saved.

[Manasseh] did what the LORD considered evil by copying the disgusting things done by the nations. . . . He set up altars dedicated to Baal [and] . . . worshiped and served the entire army of heaven. In the two courtyards of the LORD's temple, he built altars for the entire army of heaven. He burned his son as a sacrifice, consulted fortunetellers, cast evil spells, and appointed royal mediums and psychics. He did many things that made the LORD furious. ✦ When [Manasseh] experienced this distress, he begged the LORD his God to be kind and humbled himself in front of the God of his ancestors. He prayed to the LORD, and the LORD accepted his prayer and listened to his request. ✦ "Come on now, let's discuss this!" says the LORD. "Though your sins are bright red, they will become as white as snow. Though they are dark red, they will become as white as wool." ✦ The Lord . . . is patient for your sake. He doesn't want to destroy anyone but wants all people to have an opportunity to turn to him and change the way they think and act.

*Acts 2:21; 2 Kings 21:2–3, 5–6; 2 Chronicles 33:12–13; Isaiah 1:18; 2 Peter 3:9*

# November 26

## MORNING READING

The Lord is delighted with you.

This is what the Lord says: "Do not be afraid, because I have reclaimed you. I have called you by name; you are mine." ✦ Can a woman forget her nursing child? Will she have no compassion on the child from her womb? Although mothers may forget, I will not forget you. I have engraved you on the palms of my hands. Your walls are always in my presence. ✦ A person's steps are directed by the Lord, and the Lord delights in his way. ✦ [God was] delighted in the human race. ✦ The Lord is pleased with those who fear him, with those who wait with hope for his mercy. ✦ "They will be mine," says the Lord of Armies. "On that day I will make them my special possession. I will spare them as a man spares his own son who serves him." ✦ Once you were separated from God. The evil things you did showed your hostile attitude. But now Christ has brought you back to God by dying in his physical body. He did this so that you could come into God's presence without sin, fault, or blame.

*Isaiah 62:4; Isaiah 43:1; Isaiah 49:15–16; Psalm 37:23; Proverbs 8:31; Psalm 147:11; Malachi 3:17; Colossians 1:21–22*

## EVENING READING

The distress that the world causes brings only death.

When Ahithophel saw that his advice hadn't been followed, he saddled his donkey, left, and went home to his own city. He gave instructions to his family. Then he hanged himself, died, and was buried in his father's tomb. ✦ Who can bear a broken spirit? ✦ Isn't there medicine in Gilead? Aren't there doctors there? Then why hasn't the health of my dear people been restored? ✦ The Lord has anointed me to deliver good news to humble people. He has sent me to heal those who are brokenhearted, . . . to comfort all those who grieve. He has sent me to provide for all those who grieve in Zion, to give them crowns instead of ashes, the oil of joy instead of tears of grief, and clothes of praise instead of a spirit of weakness. ✦ "Come to me, all who are tired from carrying heavy loads, and I will give you rest. Place my yoke over your shoulders, and learn from me, because I am gentle and humble. Then you will find rest for yourselves because my yoke is easy and my burden is light." ✦ Philip told the official the Good News about Jesus. ✦ He is the healer of the brokenhearted. He is the one who bandages their wounds.

*2 Corinthians 7:10; 2 Samuel 17:23; Proverbs 18:14; Jeremiah 8:22; Isaiah 61:1–3; Matthew 11:28–30; Acts 8:35; Psalm 147:3*

## MORNING READING

"I have given them the glory that you gave me."

I saw the Lord sitting on a high and lofty throne. The bottom of his robe filled the temple. Angels were standing above him. . . . They called to each other and said, "Holy, holy, holy is the LORD of Armies! The whole earth is filled with his glory." ✦ Isaiah said this because he had seen Jesus' glory and had spoken about him. ✦ On the throne was a figure that looked like a human. . . . The brightness all around him looked like a rainbow in the clouds. It was like the LORD's glory. ✦ Then Moses said, "Please let me see your glory." . . . [But God said,] "You can't see my face, because no one may see me and live." ✦ No one has ever seen God. God's only Son, the one who is closest to the Father's heart, has made him known. ✦ The same God who said that light should shine out of darkness has given us light. For that reason we bring to light the knowledge about God's glory which shines from Christ's face.

*John 17:22; Isaiah 6:1–3; John 12:41; Ezekiel 1:26, 28; Exodus 33:18, 20; John 1:18; 2 Corinthians 4:6*

## EVENING READING

My son, if sinners lure you, do not go along.

[Eve] took some of the fruit and ate it. She also gave some to her husband, who was with her, and he ate it. ✦ "Didn't Achan, son of Zerah, act faithlessly with the things claimed by the LORD? Didn't the LORD become angry with the whole congregation of Israel? Achan wasn't the only one who died because of his sin." ✦ Never follow a crowd in doing wrong. ✦ "Enter through the narrow gate because the gate and road that lead to destruction are wide. Many enter through the wide gate." ✦ We don't live to honor ourselves. ✦ You were indeed called to be free, brothers and sisters. Don't turn this freedom into an excuse for your corrupt nature to express itself. Rather, serve each other through love. ✦ But be careful that by using your freedom you don't somehow make a believer who is weak in faith fall into sin. ✦ When you sin against other believers in this way and harm their weak consciences, you are sinning against Christ. ✦ We have all strayed like sheep. Each one of us has turned to go his own way, and the LORD has laid all our sins on him.

*Proverbs 1:10; Genesis 3:6; Joshua 22:20; Exodus 23:2; Matthew 7:13; Romans 14:7; Galatians 5:13; 1 Corinthians 8:9; 1 Corinthians 8:12; Isaiah 53:6*

## MORNING READING

A body that doesn't breathe is dead.
In the same way faith that does nothing is dead.

"Not everyone who says to me, 'Lord, Lord!' will enter the kingdom of heaven, but only the person who does what my Father in heaven wants." ✦ Try to live holy lives, because if you don't, you will not see the Lord. ✦ Add integrity to your faith; and to integrity add knowledge; to knowledge add self-control; to self-control add endurance; to endurance add godliness; to godliness add Christian affection; and to Christian affection add love. If you have these qualities and they are increasing, it demonstrates that your knowledge about our Lord Jesus Christ is living and productive. If these qualities aren't present in your life, you're shortsighted and have forgotten that you were cleansed from your past sins. Therefore, brothers and sisters, use more effort to make God's calling and choosing of you secure. If you keep doing this, you will never fall away. ✦ God saved you through faith as an act of kindness. You had nothing to do with it. Being saved is a gift from God. It's not the result of anything you've done, so no one can brag about it.

*James 2:26; Matthew 7:21; Hebrews 12:14; 2 Peter 1:5–10; Ephesians 2:8–9*

## EVENING READING

Since all of these sons and daughters have flesh and blood,
Jesus took on flesh and blood to be like them.
He did this so that . . . he would free those who were slaves
all their lives because they were afraid of dying.

"Death, where is your victory? Death, where is your sting?" . . . Thank God that he gives us the victory through our Lord Jesus Christ. ✦ We are not discouraged. Though outwardly we are wearing out, inwardly we are renewed day by day. ✦ We know that if the life we live here on earth is ever taken down like a tent, we still have a building from God. It is an eternal house in heaven that isn't made by human hands. . . . So we are always confident. We know that as long as we are living in these bodies, we are living away from the Lord. . . . We are confident and prefer to live away from this body and to live with the Lord. ✦ "Don't be troubled. Believe in God, and believe in me. My Father's house has many rooms. If that were not true, would I have told you that I'm going to prepare a place for you? If I go to prepare a place for you, I will come again. Then I will bring you into my presence so that you will be where I am."

*Hebrews 2:14–15; 1 Corinthians 15:55, 57;*
*2 Corinthians 4:16; 2 Corinthians 5:1, 6, 8; John 14:1–3*

## MORNING READING

We will be filled with good food from your house.

I have asked one thing from the LORD. This I will seek: to remain in the LORD's house all the days of my life in order to gaze at the LORD's beauty and to search for an answer in his temple. ✦ "Blessed are those who hunger and thirst for God's approval. They will be satisfied." ✦ "He fed hungry people with good food. He sent rich people away with nothing." ✦ He gave plenty to drink to those who were thirsty. He filled those who were hungry with good food. ✦ "I am the bread of life. Whoever comes to me will never become hungry, and whoever believes in me will never become thirsty." ✦ Your mercy is so precious, O God, that Adam's descendants take refuge in the shadow of your wings. They are refreshed with the rich foods in your house, and you make them drink from the river of your pleasure. Indeed, the fountain of life is with you. In your light we see light.

*Psalm 65:4; Psalm 27:4; Matthew 5:6; Luke 1:53; Psalm 107:9; John 6:35; Psalm 36:7–9*

## EVENING READING

"Now you believe."

My brothers and sisters, what good does it do if someone claims to have faith but doesn't do any good things? Can this kind of faith save him? . . . In the same way, faith by itself is dead if it doesn't cause you to do any good things. ✦ When God tested Abraham, faith led him to offer his son Isaac. Abraham, the one who received the promises from God, was willing to offer his only son as a sacrifice. God had said to him, "Through Isaac your descendants will carry on your name." Abraham believed that God could bring Isaac back from the dead. ✦ Didn't our ancestor Abraham receive God's approval as a result of what he did when he offered his son Isaac as a sacrifice on the altar? . . . You see that a person receives God's approval because of what he does, not only because of what he believes. ✦ The person who continues to study God's perfect teachings that make people free and who remains committed to them will be blessed. People like that don't merely listen and forget; they actually do what God's teachings say. ✦ You will know them by what they produce. "Not everyone who says to me, 'Lord, Lord!' will enter the kingdom of heaven, but only the person who does what my Father in heaven wants." ✦ "If you understand all of this, you are blessed whenever you follow my example."

*John 16:31; James 2:14, 17; Hebrews 11:17–19; James 2:21, 24; James 1:25; Matthew 7:20–21; John 13:17*

## MORNING READING

May the Lord of peace give you his peace
at all times and in every way.
The Lord be with all of you.

Peace to you from the one who is, the one who was, and the one who is coming. ✦ God's peace, which goes beyond anything we can imagine, will guard your thoughts and emotions through Christ Jesus. ✦ Jesus stood among [his disciples]. He said to them, "Peace be with you!" ✦ "I'm leaving you peace. I'm giving you my peace. I don't give you the kind of peace that the world gives. So don't be troubled or cowardly." ✦ "The helper . . . the Spirit of Truth." ✦ The spiritual nature produces love, joy, peace. ✦ The Spirit himself testifies with our spirit that we are God's children. ✦ The LORD answered, "My presence will go with you, and I will give you peace." Then Moses said to him, "If your presence is not going with us, don't make us leave this place. How will anyone ever know you're pleased with your people and me unless you go with us?"

*2 Thessalonians 3:16; Revelation 1:4; Philippians 4:7; Luke 24:36; John 14:27; John 15:26; Galatians 5:22; Romans 8:16; Exodus 33:14–16*

## EVENING READING

We . . . brag when we are suffering.

If Christ is our hope in this life only, we deserve more pity than any other people. ✦ Dear friends, don't be surprised by the fiery troubles that are coming in order to test you. Don't feel as though something strange is happening to you, but be happy as you share Christ's sufferings. Then you will also be full of joy when he appears again in his glory. ✦ People think we are sad although we're always glad. ✦ Always be joyful in the Lord! I'll say it again: Be joyful! ✦ The apostles left the council room. They were happy to have been considered worthy to suffer dishonor for speaking about Jesus. ✦ May God, the source of hope, fill you with joy and peace through your faith in him. ✦ Even if the fig tree does not bloom and the vines have no grapes, even if the olive tree fails to produce and the fields yield no food, even if the sheep pen is empty and the stalls have no cattle—even then, I will be happy with the LORD. I will truly find joy in God, who saves me.

*Romans 5:3; 1 Corinthians 15:19; 1 Peter 4:12–13; 2 Corinthians 6:10; Philippians 4:4; Acts 5:41; Romans 15:13; Habakkuk 3:17–18*

## MORNING READING

Each ruler will be like a shelter from the wind
and a hiding place from the rain.

Since all of these sons and daughters have flesh and blood, Jesus took on flesh and blood to be like them. ✦ "The man who is my friend," declares the LORD of Armies. ✦ "The Father and I are one." ✦ Whoever lives under the shelter of the Most High will remain in the shadow of the Almighty. ✦ [The Lord's glory] will be a shelter from the heat during the day as well as a refuge and hiding place from storms and rain. ✦ The LORD is the shade over your right hand. The sun will not beat down on you during the day, nor will the moon at night. ✦ When I begin to lose heart. Lead me to the rock that is high above me. ✦ You are my hiding place. You protect me from trouble. ✦ You have been a refuge for the poor, a refuge for the needy in their distress, a shelter from the rain, and shade from the heat. (A tyrant's breath is like a rainstorm against a wall.)

*Isaiah 32:2; Hebrews 2:14; Zechariah 13:7; John 10:30; Psalm 91:1; Isaiah 4:6; Psalm 121:5–6; Psalm 61:2; Psalm 32:7; Isaiah 25:4*

## EVENING READING

I will create a new heaven and a new earth.

"The new heaven and earth that I am about to make will continue in my presence," declares the LORD. "So your descendants and your name will also continue in my presence." ✦ But we look forward to what God has promised—a new heaven and a new earth—a place where everything that has God's approval lives. ✦ I saw a new heaven and a new earth, because the first heaven and earth had disappeared, and the sea was gone. Then I saw the holy city, New Jerusalem, coming down from God out of heaven, dressed like a bride ready for her husband. I heard a loud voice from the throne say, "God lives with humans! God will make his home with them, and they will be his people. God himself will be with them and be their God. He will wipe every tear from their eyes. There won't be any more death. There won't be any grief, crying, or pain, because the first things have disappeared." The one sitting on the throne said, "I am making everything new."

*Isaiah 65:17; Isaiah 66:22; 2 Peter 3:13; Revelation 21:1–5*

## MORNING READING

The Holy One has anointed you, so all of you have knowledge.

"You know that God anointed Jesus from Nazareth with the Holy Spirit and with power." ✦ God was pleased to have all of himself live in Christ. ✦ Each of us has received one gift after another because of all that the Word is. ✦ You anoint my head with oil. ✦ The anointing you received from Christ lives in you. You don't need anyone to teach you something else. Instead, Christ's anointing teaches you about everything. His anointing is true and contains no lie. So live in Christ as he taught you to do. ✦ "The helper, the Holy Spirit, whom the Father will send in my name, will teach you everything. He will remind you of everything that I have ever told you." ✦ The Spirit also helps us in our weakness, because we don't know how to pray for what we need. But the Spirit intercedes along with our groans that cannot be expressed in words.

*1 John 2:20; Acts 10:38; Colossians 1:19; John 1:16; Psalm 23:5; 1 John 2:27; John 14:26; Romans 8:26*

## EVENING READING

We have been sprinkled with his blood to free us from a guilty conscience.

The blood of goats and bulls and the ashes of cows sprinkled on unclean people made their bodies holy and clean. The blood of Christ, who had no defect, does even more. Through the eternal Spirit he offered himself to God and cleansed our consciences from the useless things we had done. Now we can serve the living God. ✦ The sprinkled blood that speaks a better message than Abel's. ✦ Through the blood of his Son, we are set free from our sins. God forgives our failures because of his overflowing kindness. ✦ Moses told all the people every commandment. Then he took the blood of calves and goats together with some water, red yarn, and hyssop and sprinkled the scroll and all the people. . . . In the same way, Moses sprinkled blood on the tent and on everything used in worship. As Moses' Teachings tell us, blood was used to cleanse almost everything, because if no blood is shed, no sins can be forgiven.

*Hebrews 10:22; Hebrews 9:13–14; Hebrews 12:24; Ephesians 1:7; Hebrews 9:19, 21–22*

## MORNING READING

"But I would seek God's help and present my case to him."

Is anything too hard for the LORD? ✦ Entrust your ways to the LORD. Trust him, and he will act on your behalf. ✦ Never worry about anything. But in every situation let God know what you need in prayers and requests while giving thanks. ✦ Turn all your anxiety over to God because he cares for you. ✦ Hezekiah took the letter from the messengers, read it, and went to the LORD's temple. He spread it out in front of the LORD and prayed to the LORD. ✦ Before they call, I will answer. While they're still speaking, I will hear. ✦ Prayers offered by those who have God's approval are effective. ✦ I love the LORD because he hears my voice, my pleas for mercy. I will call on him as long as I live because he turns his ear toward me.

*Job 5:8; Genesis 18:14; Psalm 37:5; Philippians 4:6; 1 Peter 5:7; Isaiah 37:14–15; Isaiah 65:24; James 5:16; Psalm 116:1–2*

## EVENING READING

Our bodies have been washed with clean water.

"Make a bronze basin with a bronze stand for washing. Put it between the tent of meeting and the altar, and fill it with water. Aaron and his sons will use it for washing their hands and feet. Before they go into the tent of meeting, they must wash so that they will not die." ✦ Your body is a temple that belongs to the Holy Spirit . . . The Holy Spirit, whom you received from God, lives in you. ✦ If anyone destroys God's temple, God will destroy him because God's temple is holy. You are that holy temple! ✦ "I will see God in my own flesh. I will see him with my own eyes, not with someone else's." ✦ Nothing unclean, no one who does anything detestable, and no liars will ever enter it. ✦ Your eyes are too pure to look at evil. You can't watch wickedness. ✦ Brothers and sisters, in view of all we have just shared about God's compassion, I encourage you to offer your bodies as living sacrifices, dedicated to God and pleasing to him. This kind of worship is appropriate for you.

*Hebrews 10:22; Exodus 30:18–21; 1 Corinthians 6:19; 1 Corinthians 3:17; Job 19:26–27; Revelation 21:27; Habakkuk 1:13; Romans 12:1*

## MORNING READING

"Where can wisdom be found?"

If any of you needs wisdom to know what you should do, you should ask God, and he will give it to you. God is generous to everyone and doesn't find fault with them. When you ask for something, don't have any doubts. A person who has doubts is like a wave that is blown by the wind and tossed by the sea. ✦ Trust the LORD with all your heart, and do not rely on your own understanding. In all your ways acknowledge him, and he will make your paths smooth. ✦ Do not consider yourself wise. Fear the LORD, and turn away from evil. ✦ I, Jeremiah, said, "Almighty LORD, I do not know how to speak. I am only a boy!" But the LORD said to me, "Don't say that you are only a boy. You will go wherever I send you. You will say whatever I command you to say. Don't be afraid of people. I am with you, and I will rescue you," declares the LORD. ✦ "If you ask the Father for anything in my name, he will give it to you. So far you haven't asked for anything in my name. Ask and you will receive so that you can be completely happy." ✦ "Have faith that you will receive whatever you ask for in prayer."

*Job 28:12; James 1:5–6; Proverbs 3:5–6; Proverbs 3:7; Jeremiah 1:6–8; John 16:23–24; Matthew 21:22*

## EVENING READING

"I do not want to live forever."

I said, "If only I had wings like a dove—I would fly away and find rest. . . . I would hurry to find shelter from the raging wind and storm." ✦ In our present tent-like existence we sigh, since we long to put on the house we will have in heaven. . . . While we are in this tent, we sigh. We feel distressed because we don't want to take off the tent, but we do want to put on the eternal house. Then eternal life will put an end to our mortal existence. ✦ I would like to leave this life and be with Christ. That's by far the better choice. ✦ We must run the race that lies ahead of us and never give up. We must focus on Jesus, the source and goal of our faith. He saw the joy ahead of him, so he endured death on the cross and ignored the disgrace it brought him. Then he received the highest position in heaven, the one next to the throne of God. Think about Jesus, who endured opposition from sinners, so that you don't become tired and give up. ✦ So don't be troubled or cowardly.

*Job 7:16; Psalm 55:6, 8; 2 Corinthians 5:2, 4; Philippians 1:23; Hebrews 12:1–3; John 14:27*

## MORNING READING

It was good that I had to suffer in order to learn your laws.

Although Jesus was the Son of God, he learned to be obedient through his sufferings. ✦ If we share in Christ's suffering in order to share his glory, we are heirs together with him. I consider our present sufferings insignificant compared to the glory that will soon be revealed to us. ✦ "He knows the road I take. When he tests me, I'll come out as pure as gold. I have followed his footsteps closely. I have stayed on his path and did not turn from it." ✦ Remember that for 40 years the Lord your God led you on your journey in the desert. He did this in order to humble you and test you. He wanted to know whether or not you would wholeheartedly obey his commands. . . . Learn this lesson by heart: The Lord your God was disciplining you as parents discipline their children. Obey the commands of the Lord your God. Follow his directions, and fear him.

*Psalm 119:71; Hebrews 5:8; Romans 8:17–18; Job 23:10–11; Deuteronomy 8:2, 5–6*

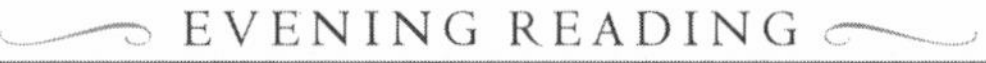

## EVENING READING

"Humans cannot succeed by their own strength."

David told the Philistine, "You come to me with sword and spear and javelin, but I come to you in the name of the Lord of Armies, the God of the army of Israel, whom you have insulted. . . . Then David reached into his bag, took out a stone, hurled it from his sling, and struck the Philistine in the forehead. The stone sank into Goliath's forehead, and he fell to the ground on his face. So using only a sling and a stone, David proved to be stronger than the Philistine. ✦ No king achieves a victory with a large army. No warrior rescues himself by his own great strength. . . . The Lord's eyes are on those who fear him, on those who wait with hope for his mercy. ✦ Riches and honor are in front of you. You rule everything. You hold power and strength in your hands, and you can make anyone great and strong. ✦ I will brag even more about my weaknesses in order that Christ's power will live in me. Therefore, I accept weakness, mistreatment, hardship, persecution, and difficulties suffered for Christ. It's clear that when I'm weak, I'm strong.

*1 Samuel 2:9; 1 Samuel 17:45, 49–50; Psalm 33:16, 18;*
*1 Chronicles 29:12; 2 Corinthians 12:9–10*

## MORNING READING

It is God who produces in you
the desires and actions that please him.

By ourselves we are not qualified in any way to claim that we can do anything. Rather, God makes us qualified. ✦ "People can't receive anything unless it has been given to them from heaven." ✦ "People cannot come to me unless the Father who sent me brings them to me. I will bring these people back to life on the last day." ✦ I will give them the same attitude and the same purpose so that they will fear me as long as they live. ✦ My dear brothers and sisters, don't be fooled. Every good present and every perfect gift comes from above, from the Father who made the sun, moon, and stars. The Father doesn't change like the shifting shadows produced by the sun and the moon. God decided to give us life through the word of truth to make us his most important creatures. ✦ God has made us what we are. He has created us in Christ Jesus to live lives filled with good works that he has prepared for us to do. ✦ O LORD, you will establish peace for us, since you have done everything for us.

*Philippians 2:13; 2 Corinthians 3:5; John 3:27; John 6:44; Jeremiah 32:39; James 1:16–18; Ephesians 2:10; Isaiah 26:12*

## EVENING READING

"You want to do what's right, but you're weak."

Certainly, we wait with hope for you, O LORD, as we follow the path of your guiding principles. We want to remember you and your name. With my soul I long for you at night. Yes, with my spirit I eagerly look for you. ✦ I know that nothing good lives in me; that is, nothing good lives in my corrupt nature. Although I have the desire to do what is right, I don't do it. . . . I take pleasure in God's standards in my inner being. However, I see a different standard at work throughout my body. It is at war with the standards my mind sets and tries to take me captive to sin's standards which still exist throughout my body. ✦ What your corrupt nature wants is contrary to what your spiritual nature wants, and what your spiritual nature wants is contrary to what your corrupt nature wants. They are opposed to each other. As a result, you don't always do what you intend to do. ✦ I can do everything through Christ who strengthens me. ✦ God makes us qualified. ✦ "My kindness is all you need."

*Matthew 26:41; Isaiah 26:8–9; Romans 7:18, 22–23; Galatians 5:17; Philippians 4:13; 2 Corinthians 3:5; 2 Corinthians 12:9*

## MORNING READING

God had Christ, who was sinless,
take our sin so that we might
receive God's approval through him.

The LORD has laid all our sins on him. ✦ Christ carried our sins in his body on the cross so that freed from our sins, we could live a life that has God's approval. His wounds have healed you. ✦ Clearly, through one person's disobedience humanity became sinful, and through one person's obedience humanity will receive God's approval. ✦ When God our Savior made his kindness and love for humanity appear, he saved us, but not because of anything we had done to gain his approval. Instead, because of his mercy he saved us through the washing in which the Holy Spirit gives us new birth and renewal. God poured a generous amount of the Spirit on us through Jesus Christ our Savior. As a result, God in his kindness has given us his approval and we have become heirs who have the confidence that we have everlasting life. ✦ So those who are believers in Christ Jesus can no longer be condemned. ✦ The LORD Our Righteousness.

*2 Corinthians 5:21; Isaiah 53:6; 1 Peter 2:24;*
*Romans 5:19; Titus 3:4–7; Romans 8:1; Jeremiah 23:6*

## EVENING READING

I will be like dew to the people of Israel.

The gentleness and kindness of Christ. ✦ He will not break off a damaged cattail. He will not even put out a smoking wick. ✦ [Jesus read from the book of Isaiah,] "The Spirit of the Lord is with me. He has anointed me to tell the Good News to the poor. He has sent me to announce forgiveness to the prisoners of sin and the restoring of sight to the blind, to forgive those who have been shattered by sin, to announce the year of the Lord's favor." . . . Then he said to them, "This passage came true today when you heard me read it." All the people spoke well of him. They were amazed to hear the gracious words flowing from his lips. ✦ Then the Lord turned and looked directly at Peter. Peter remembered what the Lord had said: "Before a rooster crows today, you will say three times that you don't know me." Then Peter went outside and cried bitterly. ✦ Like a shepherd he takes care of his flock. He gathers the lambs in his arms. He carries them in his arms. He gently helps the sheep and their lambs.

*Hosea 14:5; 2 Corinthians 10:1; Isaiah 42:3;*
*Luke 4:18–19, 21–22; Luke 22:61–62; Isaiah 40:11*

## MORNING READING

Serve each other through love.

Brothers and sisters, if a person gets trapped by wrongdoing, those of you who are spiritual should help that person turn away from doing wrong. Do it in a gentle way. At the same time watch yourself so that you also are not tempted. Help carry each other's burdens. In this way you will follow Christ's teachings. ✦ My brothers and sisters, if one of you wanders from the truth, someone can bring that person back. Realize that whoever brings a sinner back from the error of his ways will save him from death, and many sins will be forgiven. ✦ Love each other with a warm love that comes from the heart. After all, you have purified yourselves by obeying the truth. As a result you have a sincere love for each other. ✦ Pay your debts as they come due. However, one debt you can never finish paying is the debt of love that you owe each other. ✦ Be devoted to each other like a loving family. Excel in showing respect for each other. ✦ All of you must serve each other with humility, because God opposes the arrogant but favors the humble. ✦ So those of us who have a strong faith must be patient with the weaknesses of those whose faith is not so strong. We must not think only of ourselves.

*Galatians 5:13; Galatians 6:1–2; James 5:19–20; 1 Peter 1:22; Romans 13:8; Romans 12:10; 1 Peter 5:5; Romans 15:1*

## EVENING READING

Then the dust of mortals goes back to the ground as it was before.

When the body is planted, it decays. . . . It doesn't have any splendor and is weak. When it comes back to life, it has splendor and is strong. It is planted as a physical body. ✦ The first man was made from the dust of the earth. ✦ "You are dust, and you will return to dust." ✦ "One person dies in his prime and feels altogether happy and contented. . . . Another person, never having tasted happiness, dies with a bitter soul. Together they lie down in the dust, and worms cover them." ✦ My body rests securely. ✦ "Even after my skin has been stripped off my body, I will see God in my own flesh." ✦ The Lord Jesus Christ . . . will change our humble bodies and make them like his glorified body. ✦ "Teach me, O LORD, about the end of my life. Teach me about the number of days I have left so that I may know how temporary my life is." ✦ Teach us to number each of our days so that we may grow in wisdom.

*Ecclesiastes 12:7; 1 Corinthians 15:42–44; 1 Corinthians 15:47; Genesis 3:19; Job 21:23, 25–26; Psalm 16:9; Job 19:26; Philippians 3:20–21; Psalm 39:4; Psalm 90:12*

## MORNING READING

Doing what is right and fair is more
acceptable to the LORD than offering a sacrifice.

You mortals, the LORD has told you what is good. This is what the LORD requires from you: to do what is right, to love mercy, and to live humbly with your God. ✦ "Is the LORD as delighted with burnt offerings and sacrifices as he would be with your obedience? To follow instructions is better than to sacrifice. To obey is better than sacrificing the fat of rams." ✦ "To love him with all your heart, with all your understanding, with all your strength, and to love your neighbor as you love yourself is more important than all the burnt offerings and sacrifices." ✦ Return to your God. Be loyal and fair, and always wait with hope for your God. ✦ Mary sat at the Lord's feet and listened to him talk. ✦ "Mary has made the right choice, and that one thing will not be taken away from her." ✦ It is God who produces in you the desires and actions that please him.

*Proverbs 21:3; Micah 6:8; 1 Samuel 15:22; Mark 12:33; Hosea 12:6; Luke 10:39; Luke 10:42; Philippians 2:13*

## EVENING READING

The breath of life goes back to God who gave it.

Then the LORD God formed the man from the dust of the earth and blew the breath of life into his nostrils. The man became a living being. ✦ "However, there is in humans a Spirit, the breath of the Almighty, that gives them understanding." ✦ "The first man, Adam, became a living being." ✦ Who knows whether a human spirit goes upward? ✦ As long as we are living in these bodies, we are living away from the Lord. . . . We are confident and prefer to live away from this body and to live with the Lord. ✦ To leave this life and be with Christ. That's by far the better choice. ✦ Brothers and sisters, we don't want you to be ignorant about those who have died. We don't want you to grieve like other people who have no hope. We believe that Jesus died and came back to life. We also believe that, through Jesus, God will bring back those who have died. ✦ "I have told you that I'm going to prepare a place for you . . . If I go to prepare a place for you, I will come again. Then I will bring you into my presence so that you will be where I am."

*Ecclesiastes 12:7; Genesis 2:7; Job 32:8; 1 Corinthians 15:45; Ecclesiastes 3:21; 2 Corinthians 5:6, 8; Philippians 1:23; 1 Thessalonians 4:13–14; John 14:2–3*

## MORNING READING

"No one can tear them away from my Father."

I know whom I trust. I'm convinced that he is able to protect what he had entrusted to me until that day. ✦ The Lord will rescue me from all harm and will take me safely to his heavenly kingdom. ✦ The one who loves us gives us an overwhelming victory in all these difficulties. I am convinced that nothing can ever separate us from God's love which Christ Jesus our Lord shows us. We can't be separated by death or life, by angels or rulers, by anything in the present or anything in the future, by forces or powers in the world above or in the world below, or by anything else in creation. ✦ Your life is hidden with Christ in God. ✦ Didn't God choose poor people in the world to become rich in faith and to receive the kingdom that he promised to those who love him? ✦ God our Father loved us and by his kindness gave us everlasting encouragement and good hope. Together with our Lord Jesus Christ, may he encourage and strengthen you to do and say everything that is good.

*John 10:29; 2 Timothy 1:12; 2 Timothy 4:18; Romans 8:37–39; Colossians 3:3; James 2:5; 2 Thessalonians 2:16–17*

## EVENING READING

God's perfect teachings that make people free.

"You will know the truth, and the truth will set you free. . . . I can guarantee this truth: Whoever lives a sinful life is a slave to sin. . . . So if the Son sets you free, you will be absolutely free." ✦ Christ has freed us so that we may enjoy the benefits of freedom. Therefore, be firm in this freedom, and don't become slaves again. . . . You were indeed called to be free, brothers and sisters. Don't turn this freedom into an excuse for your corrupt nature to express itself. Rather, serve each other through love. All of Moses' Teachings are summarized in a single statement, "Love your neighbor as you love yourself." ✦ Freed from sin, you were made slaves who do what God approves of. ✦ A married woman is bound by law to her husband as long as he is alive. But if her husband dies, that marriage law is no longer in effect for her. ✦ The standards of the Spirit, who gives life through Christ Jesus, have set you free from the standards of sin and death. ✦ I will walk around freely because I sought out your guiding principles.

*James 1:25; John 8:32, 34, 36; Galatians 5:1, 13–14; Romans 6:18; Romans 7:2; Romans 8:2; Psalm 119:45*

## MORNING READING

Don't allow anyone to say that what you consider good is evil.

Keep away from every kind of evil. ✦ We intend to do what is right, not only in the sight of the Lord, but also in the sight of people. ✦ God wants you to silence the ignorance of foolish people by doing what is right. ✦ If you suffer, you shouldn't suffer for being a murderer, thief, criminal, or troublemaker. If you suffer for being a Christian, don't feel ashamed, but praise God for being called that name. ✦ You were indeed called to be free, brothers and sisters. Don't turn this freedom into an excuse for your corrupt nature to express itself. Rather, serve each other through love. ✦ But be careful that by using your freedom you don't somehow make a believer who is weak in faith fall into sin. ✦ "It would be best for the person who causes one of them to lose faith to be drowned in the sea with a large stone hung around his neck." ✦ "Whatever you did for one of my brothers or sisters, no matter how unimportant they seemed, you did for me."

*Romans 14:16; 1 Thessalonians 5:22; 2 Corinthians 8:21; 1 Peter 2:15; 1 Peter 4:15–16; Galatians 5:13; 1 Corinthians 8:9; Matthew 18:6; Matthew 25:40*

## EVENING READING

"Wake up, sleeper!
Rise from the dead,
and Christ will shine on you."

It's time for you to wake up. Our salvation is nearer now than when we first became believers. ✦ Therefore, we must not fall asleep like other people, but we must stay awake and be sober. People who sleep, sleep at night; people who get drunk, get drunk at night. Since we belong to the day, we must be sober. We must put on faith and love as a breastplate and the hope of salvation as a helmet. ✦ Arise! Shine! Your light has come, and the glory of the LORD has dawned. Darkness now covers the earth, and thick darkness covers the nations. But the LORD dawns, and his glory appears over you. ✦ Therefore, your minds must be clear and ready for action. Place your confidence completely in what God's kindness will bring you when Jesus Christ appears again. ✦ "Be ready for action, and have your lamps burning. Be like servants waiting to open the door at their master's knock when he returns from a wedding."

*Ephesians 5:14; Romans 13:11; 1 Thessalonians 5:6–8; Isaiah 60:1–2; 1 Peter 1:13; Luke 12:35–36*

## MORNING READING

The LORD, is with you.

"Don't be afraid, because I am with you. Don't be intimidated; I am your God. I will strengthen you. I will help you. I will support you with my victorious right hand." ✦ Strengthen limp hands. Steady weak knees. Tell those who are terrified, "Be brave; don't be afraid. Your God will come with vengeance, with divine revenge. He will come and rescue you." ✦ The LORD your God is with you. He is a hero who saves you. He happily rejoices over you, renews you with his love, and celebrates over you with shouts of joy. ✦ Wait with hope for the LORD. Be strong, and let your heart be courageous. Yes, wait with hope for the LORD. ✦ I heard a loud voice from the throne say, "God lives with humans! God will make his home with them, and they will be his people. God himself will be with them and be their God. He will wipe every tear from their eyes. There won't be any more death. There won't be any grief, crying, or pain, because the first things have disappeared."

*Zephaniah 3:15; Isaiah 41:10; Isaiah 35:3–4; Zephaniah 3:17; Psalm 27:14; Revelation 21:3–4*

## EVENING READING

The LORD said to Moses,
"Why are you crying out to me?
Tell the Israelites to start moving."

"Be strong! Let's prove ourselves strong for our people and for the cities of our God, and the LORD will do what he considers right." ✦ We prayed to our God and set guards to protect us day and night. ✦ "Not everyone who says to me, 'Lord, Lord!' will enter the kingdom of heaven, but only the person who does what my Father in heaven wants." ✦ "Those who want to follow the will of God will know if what I teach is from God or if I teach my own thoughts." ✦ Let's learn about the LORD. Let's get to know the LORD. ✦ "Stay awake, and pray that you won't be tempted." ✦ Be alert. Be firm in the Christian faith. Be courageous and strong. ✦ Don't be lazy in showing your devotion. Use your energy to serve the Lord. ✦ Strengthen limp hands. Steady weak knees. Tell those who are terrified, "Be brave; don't be afraid."

*Exodus 14:15; 1 Chronicles 19:13; Nehemiah 4:9; Matthew 7:21; John 7:17; Hosea 6:3; Matthew 26:41; 1 Corinthians 16:13; Romans 12:11; Isaiah 35:3–4*

## MORNING READING

Find your source of strength in the kindness of Christ Jesus.

We ask him to strengthen you by his glorious might. ✦ You received Christ Jesus the Lord, so continue to live as Christ's people. Sink your roots in him and build on him. Be strengthened by the faith that you were taught, and overflow with thanksgiving. ✦ They will be called Oaks of Righteousness, the Plantings of the Lord, so that he might display his glory. ✦ You are built on the foundation of the apostles and prophets. Christ Jesus himself is the cornerstone. In him all the parts of the building fit together and grow into a holy temple in the Lord. Through him you, also, are being built in the Spirit together with others into a place where God lives. ✦ "I am now entrusting you to God and to his message that tells how kind he is. That message can help you grow and can give you the inheritance that is shared by all of God's holy people." ✦ Jesus Christ will fill your lives with everything that God's approval produces. Your lives will then bring glory and praise to God. ✦ Fight the good fight for the Christian faith. ✦ Don't let your opponents intimidate you in any way.

*2 Timothy 2:1; Colossians 1:11; Colossians 2:6–7; Isaiah 61:3; Ephesians 2:20–22; Acts 20:32; Philippians 1:11; 1 Timothy 6:12; Philippians 1:28*

## EVENING READING

"You reward a person based on what he has done."

After all, no one can lay any other foundation than the one that is already laid, and that foundation is Jesus Christ. . . . If what a person has built survives, he will receive a reward. If his work is burned up, he will suffer the loss. However, he will be saved, though it will be like going through a fire. ✦ All of us must appear in front of Christ's judgment seat. Then all people will receive what they deserve for the good or evil they have done while living in their bodies. ✦ "When you give to the poor, don't let your left hand know what your right hand is doing. Give your contributions privately. Your Father sees what you do in private. He will reward you." ✦ "After a long time the master of those servants returned and settled accounts with them." ✦ By ourselves we are not qualified in any way to claim that we can do anything. Rather, God makes us qualified. ✦ O Lord, you will establish peace for us, since you have done everything for us.

*Psalm 62:12; 1 Corinthians 3:11, 14–15; 2 Corinthians 5:10; Matthew 6:3–4; Matthew 25:19; 2 Corinthians 3:5; Isaiah 26:12*

## MORNING READING

Make his praise glorious.

I have formed these people for myself. They will praise me. ✦ I will cleanse them from all the sins that they have committed against me. I will forgive them for all the sins that they have committed against me and for rebelling against me. Then Jerusalem will be my source of joy, praise, and honor. All the nations on earth will hear about all the blessings that I will give to Jerusalem. ✦ Through Jesus we should always bring God a sacrifice of praise, that is, words that acknowledge him. ✦ I will give thanks to you with all my heart, O Lord my God. I will honor you forever because your mercy toward me is great. You have rescued me from the depths of hell. ✦ "Who is like you, . . . O LORD? . . . You are glorious because of your holiness and awe-inspiring because of your splendor. You perform miracles. ✦ I want to praise the name of God with a song. I want to praise its greatness with a song of thanksgiving. ✦ [They were] singing the song of God's servant Moses and the song of the lamb. They sang, "The things you do are spectacular and amazing, Lord God Almighty."

*Psalm 66:2; Isaiah 43:21; Jeremiah 33:8–9; Hebrews 13:15; Psalm 86:12–13; Exodus 15:11; Psalm 69:30; Revelation 15:3*

## EVENING READING

Because of our nature
we deserved God's anger just like everyone else.

Indeed, we, too, were once stupid, disobedient, and misled. We were slaves to many kinds of lusts and pleasures. We were mean and jealous. We were hated, and we hated each other. ✦ "Don't be surprised when I tell you that all of you must be born from above." ✦ Job answered the LORD, "I'm so insignificant. How can I answer you? I will put my hand over my mouth." ✦ The LORD asked Satan, "Have you thought about my servant Job? No one in the world is like him! He is a man of integrity: He is decent, he fears God, and he stays away from evil." ✦ Indeed, I [David] was born guilty. I was a sinner when my mother conceived me. ✦ "God spoke favorably about David. He said, 'I have found that David, son of Jesse, is a man after my own heart. He will do everything I want him to do.' " ✦ In the past I [Paul] cursed him, persecuted him, and acted arrogantly toward him. However, I was treated with mercy.

*Ephesians 2:3; Titus 3:3; John 3:7; Job 40:3–4; Job 1:8; Psalm 51:5; Acts 13:22; 1 Timothy 1:13*

## MORNING READING

Help carry each other's burdens.
In this way you will follow Christ's teachings.

Don't be concerned only about your own interests, but also be concerned about the interests of others. Have the same attitude that Christ Jesus had. . . . He emptied himself by taking on the form of a servant. ✦ "The Son of Man . . . didn't come so that others could serve him. He came to serve and to give his life as a ransom for many people." ✦ He died for all people so that those who live should no longer live for themselves but for the man who died and was brought back to life for them. ✦ When Jesus saw her crying, and the Jews who were crying with her, he was deeply moved and troubled. ✦ Jesus cried. ✦ Be happy with those who are happy. Be sad with those who are sad. ✦ Everyone must live in harmony, be sympathetic, love each other, have compassion, and be humble. Don't pay people back with evil for the evil they do to you, or ridicule those who ridicule you. Instead, bless them, because you were called to inherit a blessing.

*Galatians 6:2; Philippians 2:4–5, 7; Mark 10:45; 2 Corinthians 5:15; John 11:33; John 11:35; Romans 12:15; 1 Peter 3:8–9*

## EVENING READING

"Son, go to work in the vineyard today."

You are no longer slaves but God's children. Since you are God's children, God has also made you heirs. ✦ So consider yourselves dead to sin's power but living for God in the power Christ Jesus gives you. Therefore, never let sin rule your physical body so that you obey its desires. Never offer any part of your body to sin's power. No part of your body should ever be used to do any ungodly thing. Instead, offer yourselves to God as people who have come back from death and are now alive. Offer all the parts of your body to God. ✦ Because you are children who obey God, don't live the kind of lives you once lived. Once you lived to satisfy your desires because you didn't know any better. But because the God who called you is holy you must be holy in every aspect of your life. Scripture says, "Be holy, because I am holy." ✦ Set apart for the master's use, prepared to do good things. ✦ So, then, brothers and sisters, don't let anyone move you off the foundation of your faith. Always excel in the work you do for the Lord. You know that the hard work you do for the Lord is not pointless.

*Matthew 21:28; Galatians 4:7; Romans 6:11–13; 1 Peter 1:14–16; 2 Timothy 2:21; 1 Corinthians 15:58*

## MORNING READING

Jesus loved his own who were in the world,
and he loved them to the end.

"I pray for them. I'm not praying for the world but for those you gave me, because they are yours. Everything I have is yours, and everything you have is mine. I have been given glory by the people you have given me. . . . I'm not asking you to take them out of the world but to protect them from the evil one. They don't belong to the world any more than I belong to the world." ✦ "I have loved you the same way the Father has loved me. So live in my love." ✦ "The greatest love you can show is to give your life for your friends. You are my friends if you obey my commandments." ✦ "I'm giving you a new commandment: Love each other in the same way that I have loved you." ✦ God, who began this good work in you, will carry it through to completion on the day of Christ Jesus. ✦ Christ loved the church and gave his life for it. He did this to make the church holy by cleansing it, washing it using water along with spoken words.

*John 13:1; John 17:9–10, 15–16; John 15:9; John 15:13–14; John 13:34; Philippians 1:6; Ephesians 5:25–26*

## EVENING READING

The deep things of God.

"I don't call you servants anymore, because a servant doesn't know what his master is doing. But I've called you friends because I've made known to you everything that I've heard from my Father." ✦ "Knowledge about the mysteries of the kingdom of heaven has been given to you." ✦ Now, we didn't receive the spirit that belongs to the world. Instead, we received the Spirit who comes from God so that we could know the things which God has freely given us. ✦ This is the reason I kneel in the presence of the Father from whom all the family in heaven and on earth receives its name. I'm asking God to give you a gift from the wealth of his glory. I pray that he would give you inner strength and power through his Spirit. Then Christ will live in you through faith. I also pray that love may be the ground into which you sink your roots and on which you have your foundation. This way, with all of God's people you will be able to understand how wide, long, high, and deep his love is. You will know Christ's love, which goes far beyond any knowledge. I am praying this so that you may be completely filled with God.

*1 Corinthians 2:10; John 15:15; Matthew 13:11; 1 Corinthians 2:12; Ephesians 3:14–19*

## MORNING READING

Give us life again, and we will call on you.

"Life is spiritual." ✦ At the same time the Spirit also helps us in our weakness, because we don't know how to pray for what we need. But the Spirit intercedes along with our groans that cannot be expressed in words. The one who searches our hearts knows what the Spirit has in mind. The Spirit intercedes for God's people the way God wants him to. ✦ Use every kind of prayer and request there is. For the same reason be alert. ✦ I will never forget your guiding principles, because you gave me a new life through them. ✦ "The words that I have spoken to you are spiritual. They are life." ✦ What was written brings death, but the Spirit brings life. ✦ "If you live in me and what I say lives in you, then ask for anything you want, and it will be yours." ✦ We are confident that God listens to us if we ask for anything that has his approval. ✦ No one can say, "Jesus is Lord," except by the Holy Spirit.

*Psalm 80:18; John 6:63; Romans 8:26–27; Ephesians 6:18; Psalm 119:93; John 6:63; 2 Corinthians 3:6; John 15:7; 1 John 5:14; 1 Corinthians 12:3*

## EVENING READING

Have nothing to do with the useless works
that darkness produces.
Instead, expose them for what they are.

Don't let anyone deceive you. Associating with bad people will ruin decent people. ✦ Don't you know that a little yeast spreads through the whole batch of dough? Remove the old yeast of sin. . . . In my letter to you I told you not to associate with people who continue to commit sexual sins. I didn't tell you that you could not have any contact with unbelievers who commit sexual sins, are greedy, are dishonest, or worship false gods. If that were the case, you would have to leave this world. Now, what I meant was that you should not associate with people who call themselves brothers or sisters in the Christian faith but live in sexual sin, are greedy, worship false gods, use abusive language, get drunk, or are dishonest. Don't eat with such people. ✦ Then you will be blameless and innocent. You will be God's children without any faults among people who are crooked and corrupt. You will shine like stars among them in the world. ✦ In a large house there are not only objects made of gold and silver, but also those made of wood and clay. Some objects are honored when they are used; others aren't.

*Ephesians 5:11; 1 Corinthians 15:33;
1 Corinthians 5:6–7, 9–11; Philippians 2:15; 2 Timothy 2:20*

## MORNING READING

So we can go confidently to the throne of God's kindness
to receive mercy and find kindness,
which will help us at the right time.

Never worry about anything. But in every situation let God know what you need in prayers and requests while giving thanks. Then God's peace, which goes beyond anything we can imagine, will guard your thoughts and emotions through Christ Jesus. ✦ You haven't received the spirit of slaves that leads you into fear again. Instead, you have received the spirit of God's adopted children by which we call out, "Abba! Father!" ✦ I didn't say to Jacob's descendants, "Search for me in vain!" ✦ Brothers and sisters, because of the blood of Jesus we can now confidently go into the holy place. Jesus has opened a new and living way for us to go through the curtain. (The curtain is his own body.) We have a superior priest in charge of God's house. We have been sprinkled with his blood to free us from a guilty conscience, and our bodies have been washed with clean water. So we must continue to come to him with a sincere heart and strong faith. ✦ So we can confidently say, "The Lord is my helper. I will not be afraid. What can mortals do to me?"

*Hebrews 4:16; Philippians 4:6–7; Romans 8:15;
Isaiah 45:19; Hebrews 10:19–22; Hebrews 13:6*

## EVENING READING

"You will know the truth, and the truth will set you free."

Wherever the Lord's Spirit is, there is freedom. ✦ The standards of the Spirit, who gives life through Christ Jesus, have set you free from the standards of sin and death. ✦ "If the Son sets you free, you will be absolutely free." ✦ Brothers and sisters, we are not children of a slave woman but of the free woman. ✦ Yet, we know that people don't receive God's approval because of their own efforts to live according to a set of standards, but only by believing in Jesus Christ. So we also believed in Jesus Christ in order to receive God's approval by faith in Christ and not because of our own efforts. People won't receive God's approval because of their own efforts to live according to a set of standards. ✦ The person who continues to study God's perfect teachings that make people free and who remains committed to them will be blessed. ✦ Christ has freed us so that we may enjoy the benefits of freedom. Therefore, be firm in this freedom, and don't become slaves again.

*John 8:32; 2 Corinthians 3:17; Romans 8:2; John 8:36;
Galatians 4:31; Galatians 2:16; James 1:25; Galatians 5:1*

## MORNING READING

Light will shine in the dark for a decent person.

Who among you fears the LORD and obeys his servant? Let those who walk in darkness and have no light trust the name of the LORD and depend upon their God. ✦ When he falls, he will not be thrown down headfirst because the LORD holds on to his hand. ✦ The command is a lamp, the teachings are a light. ✦ Don't laugh at me, my enemies. Although I've fallen, I will get up. Although I sit in the dark, the LORD is my light. I have sinned against the LORD. So I will endure his fury until he takes up my cause and wins my case. He will bring me into the light, and I will see his victory. ✦ "The eye is the lamp of the body. So if your eye is unclouded, your whole body will be full of light. But if your eye is evil, your whole body will be full of darkness. If the light in you is darkness, how dark it will be!"

*Psalm 112:4; Isaiah 50:10; Psalm 37:24;*
*Proverbs 6:23; Micah 7:8–9; Matthew 6:22–23*

## EVENING READING

Like a shepherd he takes care of his flock.
He gathers the lambs in his arms.
He carries them in his arms.
He gently helps the sheep and their lambs.

Jesus . . . said, "I feel sorry for the people. They have been with me three days now and have nothing to eat. I don't want to send them away hungry, or they may become exhausted on their way home." ✦ We have a chief priest who is able to sympathize with our weaknesses. ✦ Some people brought little children to Jesus. . . . Jesus put his arms around the children and blessed them by placing his hands on them. ✦ I have wandered away like a lost lamb. Search for me. ✦ "The Son of Man has come to seek and to save people who are lost." ✦ You were like lost sheep. Now you have come back to the shepherd and bishop of your lives. ✦ "Don't be afraid, little flock. Your Father is pleased to give you the kingdom." ✦ I will take care of my sheep and lead them to rest, declares the Almighty LORD.

*Isaiah 40:11; Matthew 15:32; Hebrews 4:15; Mark 10:13, 16;*
*Psalm 119:176; Luke 19:10; 1 Peter 2:25; Luke 12:32; Ezekiel 34:15*

## MORNING READING

Before the creation of the world, he chose us through Christ.

To be holy and perfect in his presence. ✦ In the beginning he chose you to be saved through a life of spiritual devotion and faith in the truth. With this in mind he called you . . . so that you would obtain the glory of our Lord Jesus Christ. ✦ This is true because he already knew his people and had already appointed them to have the same form as the image of his Son. Therefore, his Son is the firstborn among many children. He also called those whom he had already appointed. He approved of those whom he had called, and he gave glory to those whom he had approved of. ✦ God the Father knew you long ago and chose you to live holy lives with the Spirit's help so that you are obedient to Jesus Christ and are sprinkled with his blood. ✦ I will give you a new heart and put a new spirit in you. I will remove your stubborn hearts and give you obedient hearts. ✦ God didn't call us to be sexually immoral but to be holy.

*Ephesians 1:4; Ephesians 1:4; 2 Thessalonians 2:13–14; Romans 8:29–30; 1 Peter 1:2; Ezekiel 36:26; 1 Thessalonians 4:7*

## EVENING READING

"Could this happen even if the LORD
poured rain through windows in the sky?"

"Have faith in God!" ✦ No one can please God without faith. ✦ "Everything is possible for God." ✦ Am I too weak to reclaim you? Don't I have the power to rescue you? ✦ "My thoughts are not your thoughts, and my ways are not your ways," declares the LORD. "Just as the heavens are higher than the earth, so my ways are higher than your ways, and my thoughts are higher than your thoughts." ✦ "Test me in this way," says the LORD of Armies. "See if I won't open the windows of heaven for you and flood you with blessings." ✦ The LORD is not too weak to save or his ear too deaf to hear. ✦ "LORD, there is no one except you who can help those who are not strong." ✦ We would stop trusting ourselves and learn to trust God, who brings the dead back to life.

*2 Kings 7:2; Mark 11:22; Hebrews 11:6; Matthew 19:26; Isaiah 50:2; Isaiah 55:8–9; Malachi 3:10; Isaiah 59:1; 2 Chronicles 14:11; 2 Corinthians 1:9*

# December 21

## MORNING READING

Your days of sadness will be over.

"In the world you'll have trouble." ✦ We know that all creation has been groaning with the pains of childbirth up to the present time. However, not only creation groans. We, who have the Spirit as the first of God's gifts, also groan inwardly. We groan as we eagerly wait for our adoption, the freeing of our bodies from sin. ✦ While we are in this tent, we sigh. We feel distressed because we don't want to take off the tent, but we do want to put on the eternal house. Then eternal life will put an end to our mortal existence. ✦ "These are the people who are coming out of the terrible suffering. They have washed their robes and made them white in the blood of the lamb. That is why they are in front of the throne of God. They serve him day and night in his temple. The one who sits on the throne will spread his tent over them. They will never be hungry or thirsty again. Neither the sun nor any burning heat will ever overcome them. The lamb in the center near the throne will be their shepherd. He will lead them to springs filled with the water of life, and God will wipe every tear from their eyes."

*Isaiah 60:20; John 16:33; Romans 8:22–23; 2 Corinthians 5:4; Revelation 7:14–17*

## EVENING READING

"Teacher, don't you care that we're going to die?"

The LORD is good to everyone and has compassion for everything that he has made. ✦ "Everything that lives and moves will be your food. I gave you green plants as food; I now give you everything else." ✦ "As long as the earth exists, planting and harvesting, cold and heat, summer and winter, day and night will never stop." ✦ The LORD is good. He is a fortress in the day of trouble. He knows those who seek shelter in him. ✦ God heard the boy [Ishmael] crying, and the Messenger of God called to Hagar from heaven. "What's the matter, Hagar?" he asked her. "Don't be afraid! God has heard the boy crying from the bushes. . . . God opened her eyes. Then she saw a well. She filled the container with water and gave the boy a drink. ✦ "Don't ever worry and say, 'What are we going to eat?' or 'What are we going to drink?'. . . Your heavenly Father certainly knows you need all of them." ✦ They should place their confidence in God who richly provides us with everything to enjoy.

*Mark 4:38; Psalm 145:9; Genesis 9:3; Genesis 8:22; Nahum 1:7; Genesis 21:17, 19; Matthew 6:31–32; 1 Timothy 6:17*

## MORNING READING

Your faith is active.

"God wants to do something for you so that you believe in the one whom he has sent." ✦ Faith by itself is dead if it doesn't cause you to do any good things. ✦ A faith that expresses itself through love. ✦ If you plant in the soil of your corrupt nature, you will harvest destruction. But if you plant in the soil of your spiritual nature, you will harvest everlasting life. ✦ God has made us what we are. He has created us in Christ Jesus to live lives filled with good works that he has prepared for us to do. ✦ He gave himself for us to set us free from every sin and to cleanse us so that we can be his special people who are enthusiastic about doing good things. ✦ We always have to thank God for you, brothers and sisters. It's right to do this because your faith is showing remarkable growth and your love for each other is increasing. . . . We always pray that our God will make you worthy of his call. We also pray that through his power he will help you accomplish every good desire and help you do everything your faith produces. ✦ It is God who produces in you the desires and actions that please him.

*1 Thessalonians 1:3; John 6:29; James 2:17; Galatians 5:6; Galatians 6:8; Ephesians 2:10; Titus 2:14; 2 Thessalonians 1:3, 11; Philippians 2:13*

## EVENING READING

"What's happened to his promise to return?"

Enoch, from the seventh generation after Adam, prophesied about them. He said, "The Lord has come with countless thousands of his holy angels. He has come to judge all these people." ✦ Look! He is coming in the clouds. Every eye will see him, even those who pierced him. Every tribe on earth will mourn because of him. ✦ The Lord will come from heaven with a command, with the voice of the archangel, and with the trumpet call of God. First, the dead who believed in Christ will come back to life. Then, together with them, we who are still alive will be taken in the clouds to meet the Lord in the air. In this way we will always be with the Lord. ✦ After all, God's saving kindness has appeared for the benefit of all people. It trains us to avoid ungodly lives filled with worldly desires so that we can live self-controlled, moral, and godly lives in this present world. At the same time we can expect what we hope for—the appearance of the glory of our great God and Savior, Jesus Christ.

*2 Peter 3:4; Jude 14–15; Revelation 1:7; 1 Thessalonians 4:16–17; Titus 2:11–13*

## MORNING READING

Let them come to me for protection.
Let them make peace with me.

I know the plans that I have for you, declares the LORD. They are plans for peace and not disaster, plans to give you a future filled with hope. ✦ "There is no peace for the wicked," says the LORD. ✦ Through Christ Jesus you, who were once far away, have been brought near by the blood of Christ. So he is our peace. ✦ God was pleased to have all of himself live in Christ. God was also pleased to bring everything on earth and in heaven back to himself through Christ. He did this by making peace through Christ's blood sacrificed on the cross. ✦ God showed that Christ is the throne of mercy where God's approval is given through faith in Christ's blood. In his patience God waited to deal with sins committed in the past. . . . This shows that he is a God of justice, a God who approves of people who believe in Jesus. ✦ If we confess our sins, he forgives them and cleanses us from everything we've done wrong. ✦ Trust the LORD always, because the LORD, the LORD alone, is an everlasting rock.

*Isaiah 27:5; Jeremiah 29:11; Isaiah 48:22; Ephesians 2:13–14; Colossians 1:19–20; Romans 3:24–26; 1 John 1:9; Isaiah 26:4*

## EVENING READING

God has given us eternal life, and this life is found in his Son.

"The Father is the source of life, and he has enabled the Son to be the source of life too." ✦ "In the same way that the Father brings back the dead and gives them life, the Son gives life to anyone he chooses." ✦ "I am the one who brings people back to life, and I am life itself. Those who believe in me will live even if they die. Everyone who lives and believes in me will never die." ✦ "I am the good shepherd. The good shepherd gives his life for the sheep. . . . I give my life in order to take it back again. No one takes my life from me. I give my life of my own free will. I have the authority to give my life, and I have the authority to take my life back again." ✦ "No one goes to the Father except through me." ✦ The person who has the Son has this life. The person who doesn't have the Son of God doesn't have this life. ✦ You have died, and your life is hidden with Christ in God. Christ is your life. When he appears, then you, too, will appear with him in glory.

*1 John 5:11; John 5:26; John 5:21; John 11:25–26; John 10:11, 17–18; John 14:6; 1 John 5:12; Colossians 3:3–4*

## MORNING READING

If you live by your corrupt nature,
you are going to die.
But if you use your spiritual nature to put to
death the evil activities of the body, you will live.

Now, the effects of the corrupt nature are obvious: illicit sex, perversion, promiscuity, . . . and similar things. I've told you in the past and I'm telling you again that people who do these kinds of things will not inherit the kingdom of God. But the spiritual nature produces love, joy, peace, patience, kindness, goodness, faithfulness, gentleness, and self-control. There are no laws against things like that. Those who belong to Christ Jesus have crucified their corrupt nature along with its passions and desires. If we live by our spiritual nature, then our lives need to conform to our spiritual nature. ✦ God's saving kindness has appeared for the benefit of all people. It trains us to avoid ungodly lives filled with worldly desires so that we can live self-controlled, moral, and godly lives in this present world. At the same time we can expect what we hope for—the appearance of the glory of our great God and Savior, Jesus Christ. He gave himself for us to set us free from every sin and to cleanse us so that we can be his special people who are enthusiastic about doing good things.

*Romans 8:13; Galatians 5:19, 21–25; Titus 2:11–14*

## EVENING READING

The Philistine officers asked,
"What are these Hebrews doing here?"

If you are insulted because of the name of Christ, you are blessed because the Spirit of glory—the Spirit of God—is resting on you. If you suffer, you shouldn't suffer for being a murderer, thief, criminal, or troublemaker. ✦ Don't allow anyone to say that what you consider good is evil. ✦ Live decent lives among unbelievers. ✦ Stop forming inappropriate relationships with unbelievers. Can right and wrong be partners? Can light have anything in common with darkness? . . . We are the temple of the living God. . . . The Lord says, "Get away from unbelievers. Separate yourselves from them. Have nothing to do with anything unclean." ✦ You are chosen people, a royal priesthood, a holy nation, people who belong to God. You were chosen to tell about the excellent qualities of God, who called you out of darkness into his marvelous light.

*1 Samuel 29:3; 1 Peter 4:14–15; Romans 14:16;
1 Peter 2:12; 2 Corinthians 6:14, 16–17; 1 Peter 2:9*

## MORNING READING

God our Savior made his kindness and love for humanity appear.

"I love you with an everlasting love." ✦ God has shown us his love by sending his only Son into the world so that we could have life through him. This is love: not that we have loved God, but that he loved us and sent his Son to be the payment for our sins. ✦ When the right time came, God sent his Son into the world. A woman gave birth to him, and he came under the control of God's laws. God sent him to pay for the freedom of those who were controlled by these laws so that we would be adopted as his children. ✦ The Word became human and lived among us. We saw his glory. It was the glory that the Father shares with his only Son, a glory full of kindness and truth. ✦ The mystery that gives us our reverence for God is acknowledged to be great: He appeared in his human nature. ✦ Since all of these sons and daughters have flesh and blood, Jesus took on flesh and blood to be like them. He did this so that by dying he would destroy the one who had power over death (that is, the devil).

*Titus 3:4; Jeremiah 31:3; 1 John 4:9–10;*
*Galatians 4:4–5; John 1:14; 1 Timothy 3:16; Hebrews 2:14*

## EVENING READING

I thank God for his gift that words cannot describe.

Shout happily to the LORD, all the earth. Serve the LORD cheerfully. Come into his presence with a joyful song. Enter his gates with a song of thanksgiving. Come into his courtyards with a song of praise. Give thanks to him; praise his name. ✦ A child will be born for us. A son will be given to us. The government will rest on his shoulders. He will be named: Wonderful Counselor, Mighty God, Everlasting Father, Prince of Peace. ✦ God didn't spare his own Son but handed him over to death for all of us. ✦ "He had one more person to send. That person was his son, whom he loved. Finally, he sent his son to them." ✦ Let them give thanks to the LORD because of his mercy. He performed his miracles for Adam's descendants. ✦ Praise the LORD, my soul! Praise his holy name, all that is within me. ✦ "My soul praises the Lord's greatness! My spirit finds its joy in God, my Savior."

*2 Corinthians 9:15; Psalm 100:1–2, 4; Isaiah 9:6; Romans 8:32;*
*Mark 12:6; Psalm 107:21; Psalm 103:1; Luke 1:46–47*

## MORNING READING

Don't let anyone move you off the foundation of your faith.
Always excel in the work you do for the Lord.

You know that the hard work you do for the Lord is not pointless. ✦ You received Christ Jesus the Lord, so continue to live as Christ's people. Sink your roots in him and build on him. Be strengthened by the faith that you were taught, and overflow with thanksgiving. ✦ "The person who endures to the end will be saved." ✦ "The seeds that were planted on good ground are people who also hear the word. But they keep it in their good and honest hearts and produce what is good despite what life may bring." ✦ You are firmly established in the Christian faith. ✦ "We must do what the one who sent me wants us to do while it is day. The night when no one can do anything is coming." ✦ If you plant in the soil of your corrupt nature, you will harvest destruction. But if you plant in the soil of your spiritual nature, you will harvest everlasting life. We can't allow ourselves to get tired of living the right way. Certainly, each of us will receive everlasting life at the proper time, if we don't give up. Whenever we have the opportunity, we have to do what is good for everyone, especially for the family of believers.

*1 Corinthians 15:58; 1 Corinthians 15:58; Colossians 2:6–7;
Matthew 24:13; Luke 8:15; 2 Corinthians 1:24; John 9:4; Galatians 6:8–10*

## EVENING READING

He is always able to save those who come to God through him.

"I am the way, the truth, and the life. No one goes to the Father except through me." ✦ "No one else can save us. Indeed, we can be saved only by the power of the one named Jesus and not by any other person." ✦ "My sheep respond to my voice, and I know who they are. They follow me, and I give them eternal life. They will never be lost, and no one will tear them away from me." ✦ I'm convinced that God, who began this good work in you, will carry it through to completion on the day of Christ Jesus. ✦ Is anything too hard for the LORD? ✦ God can guard you so that you don't fall and so that you can be full of joy as you stand in his glorious presence without fault. Before time began, now, and for eternity glory, majesty, power, and authority belong to the only God, our Savior, through Jesus Christ our Lord. Amen.

*Hebrews 7:25; John 14:6; Acts 4:12; John 10:27–28;
Philippians 1:6; Genesis 18:14; Jude 24–25*

## MORNING READING

We don't look for things that can be seen
but for things that can't be seen.
Things that can be seen are only temporary.
But things that can't be seen last forever.

We don't have a permanent city here. ✦ You have a better and more permanent possession. ✦ "Don't be afraid, little flock. Your Father is pleased to give you the kingdom." ✦ You have to suffer different kinds of trouble for a little while now. ✦ There the wicked stop their raging. There the weary are able to rest. ✦ While we are in this tent, we sigh. We feel distressed. ✦ "He will wipe every tear from their eyes. There won't be any more death. There won't be any grief, crying, or pain, because the first things have disappeared." ✦ I consider our present sufferings insignificant compared to the glory that will soon be revealed to us. ✦ Our suffering is light and temporary and is producing for us an eternal glory that is greater than anything we can imagine.

*2 Corinthians 4:18; Hebrews 13:14; Hebrews 10:34; Luke 12:32; 1 Peter 1:6; Job 3:17; 2 Corinthians 5:4; Revelation 21:4; Romans 8:18; 2 Corinthians 4:17*

## EVENING READING

He is our peace.

God was using Christ to restore his relationship with humanity. He didn't hold people's faults against them. . . . God had Christ, who was sinless, take our sin so that we might receive God's approval through him. ✦ God was also pleased to bring everything on earth and in heaven back to himself through Christ. He did this by making peace through Christ's blood sacrificed on the cross. Once you were separated from God. The evil things you did showed your hostile attitude. But now Christ has brought you back to God by dying in his physical body. He did this so that you could come into God's presence without sin, fault, or blame. ✦ He did this by erasing the charges that were brought against us by the written laws God had established. He took the charges away by nailing them to the cross. ✦ He brought an end to the commandments and demands found in Moses' Teachings so that he could take Jewish and non-Jewish people and create one new humanity in himself. So he made peace. ✦ "I'm leaving you peace. I'm giving you my peace. I don't give you the kind of peace that the world gives. So don't be troubled or cowardly."

*Ephesians 2:14; 2 Corinthians 5:19, 21; Colossians 1:20–22; Colossians 2:14; Ephesians 2:15; John 14:27*

## MORNING READING

"Your sins are forgiven."

"I will forgive their wickedness and I will no longer hold their sins against them." ✦ "Who besides God can forgive sins?" ✦ I alone am the one who is going to wipe away your rebellious actions for my own sake. I will not remember your sins anymore. ✦ Blessed is the person whose disobedience is forgiven and whose sin is pardoned. Blessed is the person whom the Lord no longer accuses of sin. ✦ Who is a God like you? You forgive sin. ✦ God has forgiven you through Christ. ✦ The blood of his Son Jesus cleanses us from every sin. If we say, "We aren't sinful" we are deceiving ourselves, and the truth is not in us. God is faithful and reliable. If we confess our sins, he forgives them and cleanses us from everything we've done wrong. ✦ As far as the east is from the west—that is how far he has removed our rebellious acts from himself. ✦ Certainly, sin shouldn't have power over you because you're not controlled by laws, but by God's favor. ✦ Freed from sin, you were made slaves who do what God approves of.

*Mark 2:5; Jeremiah 31:34; Mark 2:7; Isaiah 43:25; Psalm 32:1–2; Micah 7:18; Ephesians 4:32; 1 John 1:7–9; Psalm 103:12; Romans 6:14; Romans 6:18*

## EVENING READING

"We would like to meet Jesus."

Certainly, we wait with hope for you, O Lord, as we follow the path of your guiding principles. We want to remember you and your name. ✦ The Lord is near to everyone who prays to him, to every faithful person who prays to him. ✦ "Where two or three have come together in my name, I am there among them." ✦ "I will not leave you all alone. I will come back to you." ✦ "Remember that I am always with you until the end of time." ✦ We must run the race that lies ahead of us and never give up. We must focus on Jesus, the source and goal of our faith. ✦ Now we see a blurred image in a mirror. Then we will see very clearly. ✦ I would like to leave this life and be with Christ. That's by far the better choice. ✦ Dear friends, now we are God's children. What we will be isn't completely clear yet. We do know that when Christ appears we will be like him because we will see him as he is. So all people who have this confidence in Christ keep themselves pure, as Christ is pure.

*John 12:21; Isaiah 26:8; Psalm 145:18; Matthew 18:20; John 14:18; Matthew 28:20; Hebrews 12:1–2; 1 Corinthians 13:12; Philippians 1:23; 1 John 3:2–3*

## MORNING READING

Understand what the Lord wants.

It is God's will that you keep away from sexual sin as a mark of your devotion to him. ✦ "Be in harmony and at peace with God. In this way you will have prosperity." ✦ "This is eternal life: to know you, the only true God, and Jesus Christ, whom you sent." ✦ We know that the Son of God has come and has given us understanding so that we know the real God. We are in the one who is real, his Son Jesus Christ. This Jesus Christ is the real God and eternal life. ✦ We have not stopped praying for you. . . . We ask God to fill you with the knowledge of his will through every kind of spiritual wisdom and insight. ✦ I pray that the glorious Father, the God of our Lord Jesus Christ, would give you a spirit of wisdom and revelation as you come to know Christ better. Then you will have deeper insight. You will know the confidence that he calls you to have and the glorious wealth that God's people will inherit. You will also know the unlimited greatness of his power as it works with might and strength for us, the believers.

*Ephesians 5:17; 1 Thessalonians 4:3; Job 22:21; John 17:3; 1 John 5:20; Colossians 1:9; Ephesians 1:17–19*

## EVENING READING

Come close to God, and he will come close to you.

Enoch walked with God. ✦ Do two people ever walk together without meeting first? ✦ Being united with God is my highest good. ✦ "The LORD is with you when you are with him. If you will dedicate your lives to serving him, he will accept you. But if you abandon him, he will abandon you." . . . But when they were in trouble, they turned to the LORD God of Israel. When they searched for him, he let them find him. ✦ I know the plans that I have for you, declares the LORD. They are plans for peace and not disaster, plans to give you a future filled with hope. Then you will call to me. You will come and pray to me, and I will hear you. When you look for me, you will find me. When you wholeheartedly seek me. ✦ We can now confidently go into the holy place. Jesus has opened a new and living way for us to go through the curtain. . . . We have a superior priest in charge of God's house. . . . So we must continue to come to him with a sincere heart and strong faith.

*James 4:8; Genesis 5:24; Amos 3:3; Psalm 73:28; 2 Chronicles 15:2, 4; Jeremiah 29:11–13; Hebrews 10:19–22*

## MORNING READING

So that no one can accuse you of anything
on the day of our Lord Jesus Christ.

Once you were separated from God. The evil things you did showed your hostile attitude. But now Christ has brought you back to God by dying in his physical body. He did this so that you could come into God's presence without sin, fault, or blame. This is on the condition that you continue in faith without being moved from the solid foundation of the hope that the Good News contains. ✦ Then you will be blameless and innocent. You will be God's children without any faults among people who are crooked and corrupt. You will shine like stars among them in the world. ✦ Therefore, dear friends, with this to look forward to, make every effort to have him find you at peace, without spiritual stains or blemishes. ✦ Determine what is best and be pure and blameless until the day of Christ. ✦ God can guard you so that you don't fall and so that you can be full of joy as you stand in his glorious presence without fault. Before time began, now, and for eternity glory, majesty, power, and authority belong to the only God, our Savior, through Jesus Christ our Lord.

*1 Corinthians 1:8; Colossians 1:21–23; Philippians 2:15;
2 Peter 3:14; Philippians 1:10; Jude 24–25*

## EVENING READING

He safeguards the steps of his faithful ones.

If we say, "We have a relationship with God" and yet live in the dark, we're lying. We aren't being truthful. But if we live in the light in the same way that God is in the light, we have a relationship with each other. And the blood of his Son Jesus cleanses us from every sin. ✦ "People who have washed are completely clean. They need to have only their feet washed. All of you, except for one, are clean." ✦ I have taught you the way of wisdom. I have guided you along decent paths. When you walk, your stride will not be hampered. Even if you run, you will not stumble. . . . Do not stray onto the path of wicked people. Do not walk in the way of evil people. Avoid it. Do not walk near it. Turn away from it, and keep on walking. . . . Let your eyes look straight ahead and your sight be focused in front of you. Carefully walk a straight path, and all your ways will be secure. Do not lean to the right or to the left. Walk away from evil. ✦ The Lord will rescue me from all harm and will take me safely to his heavenly kingdom. Glory belongs to him forever! Amen.

*1 Samuel 2:9; 1 John 1:6–7; John 13:10;
Proverbs 4:11–12, 14–15; 25–27; 2 Timothy 4:18*

# December 31

## MORNING READING

The LORD your God carried you, as parents carry their children.
He carried you wherever you went until you came to this place.

"I carried you on eagles' wings and brought you to my mountain." ✦ In his love and compassion he reclaimed them. He always held them and carried them in the past. ✦ Like an eagle that stirs up its nest, hovers over its young, spreads its wings to catch them, and carries them on its feathers, so the LORD alone led his people. ✦ Even when you're old, I'll take care of you. Even when your hair turns gray, I'll support you. I made you and will continue to care for you. I'll support you and save you. ✦ "This God is our God forever and ever. He will lead us beyond death." ✦ Turn your burdens over to the LORD, and he will take care of you. He will never let the righteous person stumble. ✦ "Stop worrying about what you will eat, drink, or wear. . . . Your heavenly Father certainly knows you need all of them." ✦ "Until now the LORD has helped us."

*Deuteronomy 1:31; Exodus 19:4; Isaiah 63:9; Deuteronomy 32:11–12; Isaiah 46:4; Psalm 48:14; Psalm 55:22; Matthew 6:25, 32; 1 Samuel 7:12*

## EVENING READING

"There is a lot of land left to be conquered."

It's not that I've already reached the goal or have already completed the course. But I run to win that which Jesus Christ has already won for me. ✦ "That is why you must be perfect." ✦ Because of this, make every effort to add integrity to your faith; and to integrity add knowledge; to knowledge add self-control; to self-control add endurance; to endurance add godliness; to godliness add Christian affection; and to Christian affection add love. ✦ I pray that your love will keep on growing because of your knowledge and insight. ✦ As Scripture says: "No eye has seen, no ear has heard, and no mind has imagined the things that God has prepared for those who love him." God has revealed those things to us by his Spirit. ✦ Therefore, a time of rest and worship exists for God's people. ✦ Your eyes will see how handsome the king is. You will see a land that stretches into the distance.

*Joshua 13:1; Philippians 3:12; Matthew 5:48; 2 Peter 1:5–7; Philippians 1:9; 1 Corinthians 2:9–10; Hebrews 4:9; Isaiah 33:17*

# Daily Reading Plan

This reading plan takes you through every chapter in the Bible during one year.

| | | | | | |
|---|---|---|---|---|---|
| **Jan. 1** | ☐ | Genesis 1:1–3:24 | **Jan. 24** | ☐ | Leviticus 8:1–10:20 |
| **Jan. 2** | ☐ | Genesis 4:1–5:32 | **Jan. 25** | ☐ | Leviticus 11:1–17:16 |
| **Jan. 3** | ☐ | Genesis 6:1–8:22 | **Jan. 26** | ☐ | Leviticus 18:1–22:33 |
| **Jan. 4** | ☐ | Genesis 9:1–11:32 | **Jan. 27** | ☐ | Leviticus 23:1–25:55 |
| **Jan. 5** | ☐ | Genesis 12:1–14:24 | **Jan. 28** | ☐ | Leviticus 26:1–27:34 |
| **Jan. 6** | ☐ | Genesis 15:1–17:27 | **Jan. 29** | ☐ | Numbers 1:1–4:49 |
| **Jan. 7** | ☐ | Genesis 18:1–20:18 | **Jan. 30** | ☐ | Numbers 5:1–10:10 |
| **Jan. 8** | ☐ | Genesis 21:1–23:20 | **Jan. 31** | ☐ | Numbers 10:11–14:45 |
| **Jan. 9** | ☐ | Genesis 24:1–28:9 | **Feb. 1** | ☐ | Numbers 15:1–21:35 |
| **Jan. 10** | ☐ | Genesis 28:10–30:43 | **Feb. 2** | ☐ | Numbers 22:1–25:18 |
| **Jan. 11** | ☐ | Genesis 31:1–36:43 | **Feb. 3** | ☐ | Numbers 26:1–31:54 |
| **Jan. 12** | ☐ | Genesis 37:1–41:57 | **Feb. 4** | ☐ | Numbers 32:1–34:29 |
| **Jan. 13** | ☐ | Genesis 42:1–45:28 | **Feb. 5** | ☐ | Numbers 35:1–36:13 |
| **Jan. 14** | ☐ | Genesis 46:1–50:26 | **Feb. 6** | ☐ | Deuteronomy 1:1–5:33 |
| **Jan. 15** | ☐ | Exodus 1:1–4:31 | **Feb. 7** | ☐ | Deuteronomy 6:1–11:32 |
| **Jan. 16** | ☐ | Exodus 5:1–7:13 | **Feb. 8** | ☐ | Deuteronomy 12:1–16:17 |
| **Jan. 17** | ☐ | Exodus 7:14–12:30 | **Feb. 9** | ☐ | Deuteronomy 16:18–20:20 |
| **Jan. 18** | ☐ | Exodus 12:31–18:27 | **Feb. 10** | ☐ | Deuteronomy 21:1–26:19 |
| **Jan. 19** | ☐ | Exodus 19:1–24:18 | **Feb. 11** | ☐ | Deuteronomy 27:1–30:20 |
| **Jan. 20** | ☐ | Exodus 25:1–31:18 | **Feb. 12** | ☐ | Deuteronomy 31:1–34:12 |
| **Jan. 21** | ☐ | Exodus 32:1–34:35 | **Feb. 13** | ☐ | Joshua 1:1–5:12 |
| **Jan. 22** | ☐ | Exodus 35:1–40:38 | **Feb. 14** | ☐ | Joshua 5:13–8:35 |
| **Jan. 23** | ☐ | Leviticus 1:1–7:38 | **Feb. 15** | ☐ | Joshua 9:1–12:24 |

| | | |
|---|---|---|
| **Feb. 16** | ☐ | Joshua 13:1–19:51 |
| **Feb. 17** | ☐ | Joshua 20:1–24:33 |
| **Feb. 18** | ☐ | Judges 1:1–3:6 |
| **Feb. 19** | ☐ | Judges 3:7–8:35 |
| **Feb. 20** | ☐ | Judges 9:1–12:15 |
| **Feb. 21** | ☐ | Judges 13:1–16:31 |
| **Feb. 22** | ☐ | Judges 17:1–21:25 |
| **Feb. 23** | ☐ | Ruth 1:1–4:22 |
| **Feb. 24** | ☐ | 1 Samuel 1:1–3:21 |
| **Feb. 25** | ☐ | 1 Samuel 4:1–7:17 |
| **Feb. 26** | ☐ | 1 Samuel 8:1–12:25 |
| **Feb. 27** | ☐ | 1 Samuel 13:1–15:35 |
| **Feb. 28** | ☐ | 1 Samuel 16:1–17:58 |
| **Mar. 1** | ☐ | 1 Samuel 18:1–20:42 |
| **Mar. 2** | ☐ | 1 Samuel 21:1–26:25 |
| **Mar. 3** | ☐ | 1 Samuel 27:1–31:13 |
| **Mar. 4** | ☐ | 2 Samuel 1:1–4:12 |
| **Mar. 5** | ☐ | 2 Samuel 5:1–7:29 |
| **Mar. 6** | ☐ | 2 Samuel 8:1–10:19 |
| **Mar. 7** | ☐ | 2 Samuel 11:1–12:31 |
| **Mar. 8** | ☐ | 2 Samuel 13:1–14:33 |
| **Mar. 9** | ☐ | 2 Samuel 15:1–20:26 |
| **Mar. 10** | ☐ | 2 Samuel 21:1–24:25 |
| **Mar. 11** | ☐ | 1 Kings 1:1–4:34 |
| **Mar. 12** | ☐ | 1 Kings 5:1–8:66 |
| **Mar. 13** | ☐ | 1 Kings 9:1–11:43 |
| **Mar. 14** | ☐ | 1 Kings 12:1–16:34 |
| **Mar. 15** | ☐ | 1 Kings 17:1–19:21 |
| **Mar. 16** | ☐ | 1 Kings 20:1–22:53 |
| **Mar. 17** | ☐ | 2 Kings 1:1–8:15 |
| **Mar. 18** | ☐ | 2 Kings 8:16–10:36 |
| **Mar. 19** | ☐ | 2 Kings 11:1–13:25 |
| **Mar. 20** | ☐ | 2 Kings 14:1–17:41 |
| **Mar. 21** | ☐ | 2 Kings 18:1–21:26 |
| **Mar. 22** | ☐ | 2 Kings 22:1–25:30 |
| **Mar. 23** | ☐ | 1 Chronicles 1:1–9:44 |
| **Mar. 24** | ☐ | 1 Chronicles 10:1–12:40 |
| **Mar. 25** | ☐ | 1 Chronicles 13:1–17:27 |
| **Mar. 26** | ☐ | 1 Chronicles 18:1–22:1 |
| **Mar. 27** | ☐ | 1 Chronicles 22:2–27:34 |
| **Mar. 28** | ☐ | 1 Chronicles 28:1–29:30 |
| **Mar. 29** | ☐ | 2 Chronicles 1:1–5:1 |
| **Mar. 30** | ☐ | 2 Chronicles 5:2–9:31 |
| **Mar. 31** | ☐ | 2 Chronicles 10:1–14:1 |
| **Apr. 1** | ☐ | 2 Chronicles 14:2–16:14 |
| **Apr. 2** | ☐ | 2 Chronicles 17:1–20:37 |
| **Apr. 3** | ☐ | 2 Chronicles 21:1–24:27 |
| **Apr. 4** | ☐ | 2 Chronicles 25:1–28:27 |
| **Apr. 5** | ☐ | 2 Chronicles 29:1–32:33 |
| **Apr. 6** | ☐ | 2 Chronicles 33:1–35:27 |
| **Apr. 7** | ☐ | 2 Chronicles 36:1–23 |
| **Apr. 8** | ☐ | Ezra 1:1–2:70 |
| **Apr. 9** | ☐ | Ezra 3:1–6:22 |
| **Apr. 10** | ☐ | Ezra 7:1–8:36 |
| **Apr. 11** | ☐ | Ezra 9:1–10:44 |
| **Apr. 12** | ☐ | Nehemiah 1:1–2:10 |
| **Apr. 13** | ☐ | Nehemiah 2:11–3:32 |
| **Apr. 14** | ☐ | Nehemiah 4:1–7:73 |
| **Apr. 15** | ☐ | Nehemiah 8:1–10:39 |
| **Apr. 16** | ☐ | Nehemiah 11:1–13:31 |
| **Apr. 17** | ☐ | Esther 1:1–2:23 |
| **Apr. 18** | ☐ | Esther 3:1–4:17 |
| **Apr. 19** | ☐ | Esther 5:1–10:3 |
| **Apr. 20** | ☐ | Job 1:1–2:13 |
| **Apr. 21** | ☐ | Job 3:1–14:22 |
| **Apr. 22** | ☐ | Job 15:1–21:34 |
| **Apr. 23** | ☐ | Job 22:1–31:40 |
| **Apr. 24** | ☐ | Job 32:1–37:24 |
| **Apr. 25** | ☐ | Job 38:1–41:34 |
| **Apr. 26** | ☐ | Job 42:1–17 |
| **Apr. 27** | ☐ | Psalms 1:1–4:8 |
| **Apr. 28** | ☐ | Psalms 5:1–8:9 |
| **Apr. 29** | ☐ | Psalms 9:1–12:8 |
| **Apr. 30** | ☐ | Psalms 13:1–16:11 |
| **May 1** | ☐ | Psalms 17:1–20:9 |
| **May 2** | ☐ | Psalms 21:1–24:10 |
| **May 3** | ☐ | Psalms 25:1–28:9 |
| **May 4** | ☐ | Psalms 29:1–32:11 |
| **May 5** | ☐ | Psalms 33:1–36:12 |
| **May 6** | ☐ | Psalms 37:1–41:13 |

| | | |
|---|---|---|
| **May 7** | ☐ | Psalms 42:1–45:17 |
| **May 8** | ☐ | Psalms 46:1–49:20 |
| **May 9** | ☐ | Psalms 50:1–53:6 |
| **May 10** | ☐ | Psalms 54:1–56:13 |
| **May 11** | ☐ | Psalms 57:1–59:17 |
| **May 12** | ☐ | Psalms 60:1–62:12 |
| **May 13** | ☐ | Psalms 63:1–65:13 |
| **May 14** | ☐ | Psalms 66:1–68:35 |
| **May 15** | ☐ | Psalms 69:1–72:20 |
| **May 16** | ☐ | Psalms 73:1–75:10 |
| **May 17** | ☐ | Psalms 76:1–78:72 |
| **May 18** | ☐ | Psalms 79:1–81:16 |
| **May 19** | ☐ | Psalms 82:1–84:12 |
| **May 20** | ☐ | Psalms 85:1–89:52 |
| **May 21** | ☐ | Psalms 90:1–92:15 |
| **May 22** | ☐ | Psalms 93:1–95:11 |
| **May 23** | ☐ | Psalms 96:1–98:9 |
| **May 24** | ☐ | Psalms 99:1–101:8 |
| **May 25** | ☐ | Psalms 102:1–104:35 |
| **May 26** | ☐ | Psalms 105:1–106:48 |
| **May 27** | ☐ | Psalms 107:1–109:31 |
| **May 28** | ☐ | Psalms 110:1–112:10 |
| **May 29** | ☐ | Psalms 113:1–115:18 |
| **May 30** | ☐ | Psalms 116:1–118:29 |
| **May 31** | ☐ | Psalm 119:1–176 |
| **June 1** | ☐ | Psalms 120:1–124:8 |
| **June 2** | ☐ | Psalms 125:1–129:8 |
| **June 3** | ☐ | Psalms 130:1–134:3 |
| **June 4** | ☐ | Psalms 135:1–137:9 |
| **June 5** | ☐ | Psalms 138:1–140:13 |
| **June 6** | ☐ | Psalms 141:1–144:15 |
| **June 7** | ☐ | Psalms 145:1–150:6 |
| **June 8** | ☐ | Proverbs 1:1–33 |
| **June 9** | ☐ | Proverbs 2:1–22 |
| **June 10** | ☐ | Proverbs 3:1–35 |
| **June 11** | ☐ | Proverbs 4:1–27 |
| **June 12** | ☐ | Proverbs 5:1–23 |
| **June 13** | ☐ | Proverbs 6:1–35 |
| **June 14** | ☐ | Proverbs 7:1–27 |
| **June 15** | ☐ | Proverbs 8:1–36 |
| **June 16** | ☐ | Proverbs 9:1–18 |
| **June 17** | ☐ | Proverbs 10:1–32 |
| **June 18** | ☐ | Proverbs 11:1–31 |
| **June 19** | ☐ | Proverbs 12:1–28 |
| **June 20** | ☐ | Proverbs 13:1–25 |
| **June 21** | ☐ | Proverbs 14:1–35 |
| **June 22** | ☐ | Proverbs 15:1–33 |
| **June 23** | ☐ | Proverbs 16:1–33 |
| **June 24** | ☐ | Proverbs 17:1–28 |
| **June 25** | ☐ | Proverbs 18:1–24 |
| **June 26** | ☐ | Proverbs 19:1–29 |
| **June 27** | ☐ | Proverbs 20:1–30 |
| **June 28** | ☐ | Proverbs 21:1–31 |
| **June 29** | ☐ | Proverbs 22:1–29 |
| **June 30** | ☐ | Proverbs 23:1–35 |
| **July 1** | ☐ | Proverbs 24:1–34 |
| **July 2** | ☐ | Proverbs 25:1–28 |
| **July 3** | ☐ | Proverbs 26:1–28 |
| **July 4** | ☐ | Proverbs 27:1–27 |
| **July 5** | ☐ | Proverbs 28:1–28 |
| **July 6** | ☐ | Proverbs 29:1–27 |
| **July 7** | ☐ | Proverbs 30:1–33 |
| **July 8** | ☐ | Proverbs 31:1–31 |
| **July 9** | ☐ | Ecclesiastes 1:1–2:26 |
| **July 10** | ☐ | Ecclesiastes 3:1–5:20 |
| **July 11** | ☐ | Ecclesiastes 6:1–8:17 |
| **July 12** | ☐ | Ecclesiastes 9:1–12:14 |
| **July 13** | ☐ | Song of Songs 1:1–8:14 |
| **July 14** | ☐ | Isaiah 1:1–6:13 |
| **July 15** | ☐ | Isaiah 7:1–12:6 |
| **July 16** | ☐ | Isaiah 13:1–18:7 |
| **July 17** | ☐ | Isaiah 19:1–23:18 |
| **July 18** | ☐ | Isaiah 24:1–27:13 |
| **July 19** | ☐ | Isaiah 28:1–31:9 |
| **July 20** | ☐ | Isaiah 32:1–35:10 |
| **July 21** | ☐ | Isaiah 36:1–39:8 |
| **July 22** | ☐ | Isaiah 40:1–48:22 |
| **July 23** | ☐ | Isaiah 49:1–52:12 |
| **July 24** | ☐ | Isaiah 52:13–55:13 |
| **July 25** | ☐ | Isaiah 56:1–59:21 |

| | | |
|---|---|---|
| **July 26** | ☐ | Isaiah 60:1–66:24 |
| **July 27** | ☐ | Jeremiah 1:1–6:30 |
| **July 28** | ☐ | Jeremiah 7:1–10:25 |
| **July 29** | ☐ | Jeremiah 11:1–15:21 |
| **July 30** | ☐ | Jeremiah 16:1–20:18 |
| **July 31** | ☐ | Jeremiah 21:1–24:10 |
| **Aug. 1** | ☐ | Jeremiah 25:1–29:32 |
| **Aug. 2** | ☐ | Jeremiah 30:1–33:26 |
| **Aug. 3** | ☐ | Jeremiah 34:1–38:28 |
| **Aug. 4** | ☐ | Jeremiah 39:1–45:5 |
| **Aug. 5** | ☐ | Jeremiah 46:1–52:34 |
| **Aug. 6** | ☐ | Lamentations 1:1–5:22 |
| **Aug. 7** | ☐ | Ezekiel 1:1–3:27 |
| **Aug. 8** | ☐ | Ezekiel 4:1–11:25 |
| **Aug. 9** | ☐ | Ezekiel 12:1–17:24 |
| **Aug. 10** | ☐ | Ezekiel 18:1–24:27 |
| **Aug. 11** | ☐ | Ezekiel 25:1–32:32 |
| **Aug. 12** | ☐ | Ezekiel 33:1–39:29 |
| **Aug. 13** | ☐ | Ezekiel 40:1–48:35 |
| **Aug. 14** | ☐ | Daniel 1:1–3:30 |
| **Aug. 15** | ☐ | Daniel 4:1–6:28 |
| **Aug. 16** | ☐ | Daniel 7:1–12:13 |
| **Aug. 17** | ☐ | Hosea 1:1–3:5 |
| **Aug. 18** | ☐ | Hosea 4:1–5:15 |
| **Aug. 19** | ☐ | Hosea 6:1–10:10 |
| **Aug. 20** | ☐ | Hosea 10:11–14:9 |
| **Aug. 21** | ☐ | Joel 1:1–2:27 |
| **Aug. 22** | ☐ | Joel 2:28–3:21 |
| **Aug. 23** | ☐ | Amos 1:1–2:16 |
| **Aug. 24** | ☐ | Amos 3:1–6:14 |
| **Aug. 25** | ☐ | Amos 7:1–9:15 |
| **Aug. 26** | ☐ | Obadiah 1:1–21 |
| **Aug. 27** | ☐ | Jonah 1:1–2:10 |
| **Aug. 28** | ☐ | Jonah 3:1–4:11 |
| **Aug. 29** | ☐ | Micah 1:1–3:12 |
| **Aug. 30** | ☐ | Micah 4:1–5:15 |
| **Aug. 31** | ☐ | Micah 6:1–7:20 |
| **Sept. 1** | ☐ | Nahum 1:1–3:19 |
| **Sept. 2** | ☐ | Habakkuk 1:1–3:19 |
| **Sept. 3** | ☐ | Zephaniah 1:1–3:20 |
| **Sept. 4** | ☐ | Haggai 1:1–2:23 |
| **Sept. 5** | ☐ | Zechariah 1:1–8:23 |
| **Sept. 6** | ☐ | Zechariah 9:1–14:21 |
| **Sept. 7** | ☐ | Malachi 1:1–4:6 |
| **Sept. 8** | ☐ | Matthew 1:1–4:25 |
| **Sept. 9** | ☐ | Matthew 5:1–48 |
| **Sept. 10** | ☐ | Matthew 6:1–34 |
| **Sept. 11** | ☐ | Matthew 7:1–29 |
| **Sept. 12** | ☐ | Matthew 8:1–10:42 |
| **Sept. 13** | ☐ | Matthew 11:1–13:53 |
| **Sept. 14** | ☐ | Matthew 13:54–15:39 |
| **Sept. 15** | ☐ | Matthew 16:1–18:35 |
| **Sept. 16** | ☐ | Matthew 19:1–20:34 |
| **Sept. 17** | ☐ | Matthew 21:1–23:39 |
| **Sept. 18** | ☐ | Matthew 24:1–25:46 |
| **Sept. 19** | ☐ | Matthew 26:1–28:20 |
| **Sept. 20** | ☐ | Mark 1:1–3:35 |
| **Sept. 21** | ☐ | Mark 4:1–7:23 |
| **Sept. 22** | ☐ | Mark 7:24–9:1 |
| **Sept. 23** | ☐ | Mark 9:2–10:52 |
| **Sept. 24** | ☐ | Mark 11:1–12:44 |
| **Sept. 25** | ☐ | Mark 13:1–37 |
| **Sept. 26** | ☐ | Mark 14:1–16:20 |
| **Sept. 27** | ☐ | Luke 1:1–4:13 |
| **Sept. 28** | ☐ | Luke 4:14–6:49 |
| **Sept. 29** | ☐ | Luke 7:1–9:50 |
| **Sept. 30** | ☐ | Luke 9:51–10:42 |
| **Oct. 1** | ☐ | Luke 11:1–54 |
| **Oct. 2** | ☐ | Luke 12:1–59 |
| **Oct. 3** | ☐ | Luke 13:1–14:35 |
| **Oct. 4** | ☐ | Luke 15:1–16:31 |
| **Oct. 5** | ☐ | Luke 17:1–19:27 |
| **Oct. 6** | ☐ | Luke 19:28–21:38 |
| **Oct. 7** | ☐ | Luke 22:1–71 |
| **Oct. 8** | ☐ | Luke 23:1–56 |
| **Oct. 9** | ☐ | Luke 24:1–53 |
| **Oct. 10** | ☐ | John 1:1–2:12 |
| **Oct. 11** | ☐ | John 2:13–3:36 |
| **Oct. 12** | ☐ | John 4:1–42 |
| **Oct. 13** | ☐ | John 4:43–6:71 |

**Oct. 14** ☐ John 7:1–10:42
**Oct. 15** ☐ John 11:1–12:50
**Oct. 16** ☐ John 13:1–14:31
**Oct. 17** ☐ John 15:1–17:26
**Oct. 18** ☐ John 18:1–19:42
**Oct. 19** ☐ John 20:1–21:25
**Oct. 20** ☐ Acts 1:1–4:37
**Oct. 21** ☐ Acts 5:1–8:3
**Oct. 22** ☐ Acts 8:4–12:24
**Oct. 23** ☐ Acts 12:25–15:35
**Oct. 24** ☐ Acts 15:36–18:14
**Oct. 25** ☐ Acts 18:15–21:14
**Oct. 26** ☐ Acts 21:15–28:30
**Oct. 27** ☐ Romans 1:1–3:20
**Oct. 28** ☐ Romans 3:21–5:21
**Oct. 29** ☐ Romans 6:1–8:39
**Oct. 30** ☐ Romans 9:1–11:36
**Oct. 31** ☐ Romans 12:1–16:27
**Nov. 1** ☐ 1 Corinthians 1:1– 4:21
**Nov. 2** ☐ 1 Corinthians 5:1–6:20
**Nov. 3** ☐ 1 Corinthians 7:1–40
**Nov. 4** ☐ 1 Corinthians 8:1–11:1
**Nov. 5** ☐ 1 Corinthians 11:2–14:40
**Nov. 6** ☐ 1 Corinthians 15:1–16:24
**Nov. 7** ☐ 2 Corinthians 1:1–2:11
**Nov. 8** ☐ 2 Corinthians 2:12–7:16
**Nov. 9** ☐ 2 Corinthians 8:1–9:15
**Nov. 10** ☐ 2 Corinthians 10:1–13:14
**Nov. 11** ☐ Galatians 1:1–2:21
**Nov. 12** ☐ Galatians 3:1–4:31
**Nov. 13** ☐ Galatians 5:1–6:18
**Nov. 14** ☐ Ephesians 1:1–3:21
**Nov. 15** ☐ Ephesians 4:1–6:24
**Nov. 16** ☐ Philippians 1:1–30
**Nov. 17** ☐ Philippians 2:1–30
**Nov. 18** ☐ Philippians 3:1–21
**Nov. 19** ☐ Philippians 4:1–23
**Nov. 20** ☐ Colossians 1:1–2:23
**Nov. 21** ☐ Colossians 3:1–4:18
**Nov. 22** ☐ 1 Thessalonians 1:1–3:13
**Nov. 23** ☐ 1 Thessalonians 4:1–5:28
**Nov. 24** ☐ 2 Thessalonians 1:1–2:17
**Nov. 25** ☐ 2 Thessalonians 3:1–18
**Nov. 26** ☐ 1 Timothy 1:1–17
**Nov. 27** ☐ 1 Timothy 1:18–3:16
**Nov. 28** ☐ 1 Timothy 4:1–6:21
**Nov. 29** ☐ 2 Timothy 1:1–2:26
**Nov. 30** ☐ 2 Timothy 3:1–4:22
**Dec. 1** ☐ Titus 1:1–16
**Dec. 2** ☐ Titus 2:1–15
**Dec. 3** ☐ Titus 3:1–15
**Dec. 4** ☐ Philemon 1:1–25
**Dec. 5** ☐ Hebrews 1:1–2:18
**Dec. 6** ☐ Hebrews 3:1–4:13
**Dec. 7** ☐ Hebrews 4:14–7:28
**Dec. 8** ☐ Hebrews 8:1–10:23
**Dec. 9** ☐ Hebrews 10:24–13:25
**Dec. 10** ☐ James 1:1–27
**Dec. 11** ☐ James 2:1–3:12
**Dec. 12** ☐ James 3:13–5:20
**Dec. 13** ☐ 1 Peter 1:1–2:12
**Dec. 14** ☐ 1 Peter 2:13–4:19
**Dec. 15** ☐ 1 Peter 5:1–14
**Dec. 16** ☐ 2 Peter 1:1–21
**Dec. 17** ☐ 2 Peter 2:1–22
**Dec. 18** ☐ 2 Peter 3:1–18
**Dec. 19** ☐ 1 John 1:1–2:27
**Dec. 20** ☐ 1 John 2:28–4:21
**Dec. 21** ☐ 1 John 5:1–21
**Dec. 22** ☐ 2 John 1:1–3 John 1:15
**Dec. 23** ☐ Jude 1:1–25
**Dec. 24** ☐ Revelation 1:1–3:22
**Dec. 25** ☐ Revelation 4:1–5:14
**Dec. 26** ☐ Revelation 6:1–8:6
**Dec. 27** ☐ Revelation 8:7–11:19
**Dec. 28** ☐ Revelation 12:1–14:20
**Dec. 29** ☐ Revelation 15:1–16:21
**Dec. 30** ☐ Revelation 17:1–20:15
**Dec. 31** ☐ Revelation 21:1–22:21

# Fast Track Reading Plan

This reading plan gives you an overview of the Bible in 100 readings.

- ☐ Genesis 1:1–2:3
- ☐ Genesis 3:1–3:24
- ☐ Genesis 6:9–7:24
- ☐ Genesis 8:1–9:17
- ☐ Genesis 17:1–22
- ☐ Genesis 22:1–14
- ☐ Genesis 25:19–34
- ☐ Genesis 27:1–46
- ☐ Genesis 37:1–36
- ☐ Genesis 41:1–57
- ☐ Genesis 45:1–28
- ☐ Exodus 1:8–2:10
- ☐ Exodus 3:1–4:17
- ☐ Exodus 5:1–6:1
- ☐ Exodus 12:1–36
- ☐ Exodus 13:17–14:31
- ☐ Exodus 16:1–36
- ☐ Exodus 20:1–21
- ☐ Numbers 13:1–33
- ☐ Joshua 2:1–24
- ☐ Joshua 6:1–27
- ☐ Judges 16:4–31
- ☐ 1 Samuel 1:1–28
- ☐ 1 Samuel 3:1–21
- ☐ 1 Samuel 10:1–27
- ☐ 1 Samuel 16:1–13
- ☐ 1 Samuel 17:1–58
- ☐ 1 Samuel 24:1–22
- ☐ 2 Samuel 11:1–27
- ☐ 2 Samuel 12:1–25
- ☐ 1 Kings 3:4–28
- ☐ 1 Kings 18:16–46
- ☐ 2 Kings 2:1–18
- ☐ 2 Kings 4:8–37
- ☐ 2 Kings 22:1–23:30
- ☐ 2 Chronicles 36:1–23
- ☐ Esther 2:1–23
- ☐ Esther 6:1–7:10
- ☐ Job 1:1–22
- ☐ Job 42:1–17
- ☐ Psalm 23:1–6
- ☐ Psalm 51:1–19

- ☐ Psalm 99–100
- ☐ Psalm 121
- ☐ Psalm 145:1–21
- ☐ Proverbs 5:1–23
- ☐ Ecclesiastes 11:9–12:14
- ☐ Isaiah 53:1–12
- ☐ Daniel 1:1–21
- ☐ Daniel 3:1–30
- ☐ Daniel 6:1–28
- ☐ Jonah 1:1–2:10
- ☐ Jonah 3:1–4:11
- ☐ Matthew 1:18–2:23
- ☐ Matthew 5:1–16
- ☐ Matthew 6:1–7:12
- ☐ Matthew 14:13–36
- ☐ Matthew 21:1–17
- ☐ Matthew 26:57–75
- ☐ Matthew 27:15–56
- ☐ Matthew 27:57–66
- ☐ Matthew 28:1–20
- ☐ Luke 1:26–56
- ☐ Luke 2:1–20
- ☐ Luke 10:25–42
- ☐ Luke 14:24–35
- ☐ Luke 15:1–32
- ☐ Luke 22:1–20
- ☐ Luke 24:13–35
- ☐ Luke 24:36–53
- ☐ John 1:1–18
- ☐ John 3:1–21
- ☐ John 4:1–42
- ☐ John 8:1–11
- ☐ John 11:1–44
- ☐ John 14:1–31
- ☐ John 18:1–27
- ☐ Acts 2:1–47
- ☐ Acts 8:26–40
- ☐ Acts 9:1–31
- ☐ Acts 11:1–18
- ☐ Acts 16:11–40
- ☐ Romans 3:1–31
- ☐ Romans 5:1–11
- ☐ Romans 8:1–39
- ☐ Romans 12:1–21
- ☐ 1 Corinthians 13:1–13
- ☐ 1 Corinthians 15:1–34
- ☐ Ephesians 2:1–22
- ☐ Ephesians 6:10–20
- ☐ Philippians 3:1–4:9
- ☐ Colossians 3:1–4:1
- ☐ 1 Thessalonians 4:1–18
- ☐ Hebrews 11:1–40
- ☐ James 1:2–27
- ☐ James 3:1–18
- ☐ 1 Peter 1:3–25
- ☐ 1 John 1:1–2:11
- ☐ Revelation 21:1–22:5
- ☐ Revelation 22:6–21